Brazos Theological Commentary on the Bible

ACTS

JAROSLAV PELIKAN

Brazos **Press**

Grand Rapids, Michigan

Published by Brazos Press
a division of Baker Publishing Group
P.O. Box 6287, Grand Rapids, MI 49516-6287
www.brazospress.com

Printed in the United States of America

Library of Congress Cataloging-in-Publication Data
Pelikan, Jaroslav Jan, 1923–
    Acts / Jaroslav Pelikan.
        p.   cm. (Brazos theological commentary on the Bible)
    Includes bibliographical references (p.) and index.
    ISBN 1-58743-094-0 (cloth)
        1. Bible. N.T. Acts—Commentaries. I. Title. II. Series.
BS2625.53.P38 2005
226.6'077—dc22   2005050090

To my liturgical family at Saint Vladimir's

And they continued stedfastly
in the apostles' doctrine
and fellowship,
and in breaking of bread,
and in prayers.
—Acts 2:42 AV

CONTENTS

Series Preface   11
Preface   17
Abbreviations   19
Introduction: From Apostolic Church to Church Catholic   23

Acts 1   *37*

1:2–3   "As the Lord Jesus Christ Himself Instructed Us": The Gospel of the Forty Days

1:11   "He Went Up, He Is Coming Again": Ascension and Second Coming

1:14   Mary the Theotokos

Acts 2   *48*

2:1   "And in the Holy Spirit": The Fullness of the Church

2:31   "Rose Up on the Third Day": The Centrality of the Resurrection of Christ

2:42   "*One*, Holy, Catholic, and Apostolic Church": Marks of Continuity

Acts 3   *62*

3:18   *Crucifixus pro nobis*: Reconciliation and Atonement

3:21   Universal Restoration/ Salvation Only by the Name of Christ

3:25   "The Purpose of Calling Israel": The Abiding Covenant

Acts 4   *72*

4:20   "This Is the Catholic Faith": The Confessional Imperative

4:24–30   Orthodoxy as Correct Worship and Correct Doctrine

4:32   "One, *Holy*, Catholic, and Apostolic Church": Transvaluation of All Values

Acts 5   *82*

5:3–4   "The Holy Spirit, the Lord": The Deity of the Holy Spirit

5:29a   "One, Holy, Catholic, and *Apostolic* Church": The Twelve and the Primacy of Peter

5:29b   "One Lord": The Sovereignty That Trumps Any Human Authority

Acts 6   *91*

6:2–4   "Faith and Order"

6:6   The Laying-on of Hands
6:8   Miracles as "Signs"

Acts 7   *100*
7:22   "What Has Athens to Do with
          Jerusalem?"
7:47–48   The Paradox of Sacred Space
          and Sacred Time
7:59–60   *The Imitation of Christ*

Acts 8   *109*
8:25   ˙The Communication of
          Divine Revelation
8:30–31   "In Accordance with the
          Scriptures"
8:37   Credo: "The Rule of Faith"

Acts 9   *120*
9:1–4   *A Grammar of Assent*
9:4–5   The Church as "the Body of
          Christ"
9:15   Paul the "Chosen Instrument"

Acts 10   *128*
10:15   The "Yoke" of the Mosaic Law
10:34–35 The Unity and Equality of All
          Humanity before God
10:38   *De servo arbitrio*: Sin Defined
          as Captivity to the Devil

Acts 11   *137*
11:23   *Grace Abounding*
11:26   The Given Name of Christ's
          Disciples
11:29   Mutual Support among the
          Members of Christ's Family

Acts 12   *144*
12:7   "Both Seen and Unseen": The
          Angels as "Ministering Spirits"
12:13–16 A Humor That Is Not
          "Unseemly"
12:21–23 Sin Defined as "Refusing to
          Let God Be God"

Acts 13   *153*
13:8–11   *Christus Victor*
13:38–39 The Language of Justification
13:48   Foreknowledge/Election/
          Predestination

Acts 14   *162*
14:11–15 "And Became Incarnate":
          Incarnation and *Theosis*
14:15–17 "The Love Which Moves the
          Sun and the Other Stars"
14:22   *The Cost of Discipleship*

Acts 15   *170*
15:2   Controversy and Polemics
15:8–9   The Historical "Economies" of
          the Living God
15:28   Authority *at* Church Councils
          and the Authority *of* Church
          Councils

Acts 16   *179*
16:4a   Canon Law—Its Legitimacy
          and Its Limits
16:4b   Apostolic Tradition and
          Apostolic Dogma
16:9   Visions and Private Revelations

Acts 17   *189*
17:18   Christian Theology in
          Encounter with Greco-Roman
          Philosophy
17:23   Apophatic Theology:
          Negation as the Affirmation of
          Metaphysical Transcendence
17:24–29 "One God the Father, All-
          Powerful Maker"

Acts 18   *199*
18:15   Theological "Bickering about
          Words and Names"
18:24–26a "Accuracy" in the Confession
          of Christian Doctrine
18:24–26b The Ministry of Women

Acts 19 *207*

19:2–3   The Abiding Theological
            Significance of Saint John the
            Forerunner
19:26   Images of the Divine?
19:28   "We Believe in One God":
            Monotheism in Conflict with
            Polytheism and Idolatry

Acts 20 *216*

20:7   The Breaking of Bread
20:28a   The Theological Import of
            Textual Variants
20:28b   "One Christ, One Son, One
            Lord"

Acts 21 *224*

21:9–10   "Who Spoke [and Speaks]
            through the Prophets"
21:13–14   *Religious Affections*
21:37   "Debtor to Greek": Language
            and Languages

Acts 22 *234*

22:6   "The Uncreated Light" as a
            Divine Energy
22:16   "We Acknowledge One
            Baptism for the Forgiving of
            Sins"
22:27   "One, Holy, *Catholic*, and
            Apostolic Church": "Every
            Native Land a Foreign Land"

Acts 23 *245*

23:1   The Testimony of a "Good
            Conscience"
23:8   "We Look Forward to a
            Resurrection of the Dead and
            Life in the Age to Come"

23:25   Epistles—Jewish, Roman, and
            Christian

Acts 24 *254*

24:1–2   The Christian Appropriation
            of Classical Rhetoric
24:24–25a   "*We* Believe": *Fides quae
            creditur*
24:25b   Ascetic Discipline and Self-
            Denial

Acts 25 *263*

25:8   The Law of Reason, the Law of
            Nations, the Law of God
25:11   "Under Pontius Pilate": "The
            Powers That Be"
25:16   "Due Process"

Acts 26 *270*

26:18   "*I* Believe": *Fides qua creditur*
26:20   "The Forgiving of Sins": The
            Component "Parts of Penance"
26:26   Public Evidence for a Mystery?

Acts 27 *279*

27:1   "The Predicament of the
            Christian Historian"
27:3   *De amicitia*: The Divine Gift
            of Friendship
27:24   "Sail with Those Who Sail"

Acts 28 *290*

28:14   Launched into World History
28:23   "His Kingdom Will Have No
            End"
28:31   "Freedom from External
            Coercion"

Bibliography   *298*
Subject Index   *305*
Scripture Index   *314*

SERIES PREFACE

Near the beginning of his treatise against Gnostic interpretations of the Bible, *Against the Heresies*, Irenaeus observes that Scripture is like a great mosaic depicting a handsome king. It is as if we were owners of a villa in Gaul who had ordered a mosaic from Rome. It arrives, and the beautifully colored tiles need to be taken out of their packaging and put into proper order according to the plan of the artist. The difficulty, of course, is that Scripture provides us with the individual pieces, but the order and sequence of various elements are not obvious. The Bible does not come with instructions that would allow interpreters to simply place verses, episodes, images, and parables in order as a worker might follow a schematic drawing in assembling the pieces to depict the handsome king. The mosaic must be puzzled out. This is precisely the work of scriptural interpretation.

Origen has his own image to express the difficulty of working out the proper approach to reading the Bible. When preparing to offer a commentary on the Psalms he tells of a tradition handed down to him by his Hebrew teacher:

> The Hebrew said that the whole divinely inspired Scripture may be likened, because of its obscurity, to many locked rooms in our house. By each room is placed a key, but not the one that corresponds to it, so that the keys are scattered about beside the rooms, none of them matching the room by which it is placed. It is a difficult task to find the keys and match them to the rooms that they can open. We therefore know the Scriptures that are obscure only by taking the points of departure for understanding them from another place because they have their interpretive principle scattered among them.[1]

As is the case for Irenaeus, scriptural interpretation is not purely local. The key in Genesis may best fit the door of Isaiah, which in turn opens up the

---

1. Fragment from the preface to *Commentary on Psalms 1–25*, preserved in the *Philokalia* (trans. Joseph W. Trigg; London: Routledge, 1998), 70–71.

meaning of Matthew. The mosaic must be put together with an eye toward the overall plan.

Irenaeus, Origen, and the great cloud of premodern biblical interpreters assumed that puzzling out the mosaic of Scripture must be a communal project. The Bible is vast, heterogeneous, full of confusing passages and obscure words, and difficult to understand. Only a fool would imagine that he or she could work out solutions alone. The way forward must rely upon a tradition of reading that Irenaeus reports has been passed on as the rule or canon of truth that functions as a confession of faith. "Anyone," he says, "who keeps unchangeable in himself the rule of truth received through baptism will recognize the names and sayings and parables of the scriptures."[2] Modern scholars debate the content of the rule on which Irenaeus relies and commends, not the least because the terms and formulations Irenaeus himself uses shift and slide. Nonetheless, Irenaeus assumes that there is a body of apostolic doctrine sustained by a tradition of teaching in the church. This doctrine provides the clarifying principles that guide exegetical judgment toward a coherent overall reading of Scripture as a unified witness. Doctrine, then, is the schematic drawing that will allow the reader to organize the vast heterogeneity of the words, images, and stories of the Bible into a readable, coherent whole. It is the rule that guides us toward the proper matching of keys to doors.

If self-consciousness about the role of history in shaping human consciousness makes modern historical-critical study critical, then what makes modern study of the Bible modern is the consensus that classical Christian doctrine distorts interpretive understanding. Benjamin Jowett, the influential nineteenth-century English classical scholar, is representative. In his programmatic essay "On the Interpretation of Scripture," he exhorts the biblical reader to disengage from doctrine and break its hold over the interpretive imagination. "The simple words of that book," writes Jowett of the modern reader, "he tries to preserve absolutely pure from the refinements or distinctions of later times." The modern interpreter wishes to "clear away the remains of dogmas, systems, controversies, which are encrusted upon" the words of Scripture. The disciplines of close philological analysis "would enable us to separate the elements of doctrine and tradition with which the meaning of Scripture is encumbered in our own day."[3] The lens of understanding must be wiped clear of the hazy and distorting film of doctrine.

Postmodernity, in turn, has encouraged us to criticize the critics. Jowett imagined that when he wiped away doctrine he would encounter the biblical text in its purity and uncover what he called "the original spirit and intention of the authors."[4] We are not now so sanguine, and the postmodern mind thinks interpretive frameworks inevitable. Nonetheless, we tend to remain modern

---

2. *Against the Heretics* 9.4.
3. Benjamin Jowett, "On the Interpretation of Scripture," in *Essays and Reviews* (London: Parker, 1860), 338–39.
4. Ibid., 340.

in at least one sense. We read Athanasius and think him stage-managing the diversity of Scripture to support his positions against the Arians. We read Bernard of Clairvaux and assume that his monastic ideals structure his reading of the Song of Songs. In the wake of the Reformation, we can see how the doctrinal divisions of the time shaped biblical interpretation. Luther famously described the Epistle of James as a "strawy letter," for, as he said, "it has nothing of the nature of the Gospel about it."[5] In these and many other instances, often written in the heat of ecclesiastical controversy or out of the passion of ascetic commitment, we tend to think Jowett correct: doctrine is a distorting film on the lens of understanding.

However, is what we commonly think actually the case? Are readers naturally perceptive? Do we have an unblemished, reliable aptitude for the divine? Have we no need for disciplines of vision? Do our attention and judgment need to be trained, especially as we seek to read Scripture as the living word of God? According to Augustine, we all struggle to journey toward God, who is our rest and peace. Yet our vision is darkened and the fetters of worldly habit corrupt our judgment. We need training and instruction in order to cleanse our minds so that we might find our way toward God.[6] To this end, "the whole temporal dispensation was made by divine Providence for our salvation."[7] The covenant with Israel, the coming of Christ, the gathering of the nations into the church—all these things are gathered up into the rule of faith, and they guide the vision and form of the soul toward the end of fellowship with God. In Augustine's view, the reading of Scripture both contributes to and benefits from this divine pedagogy. With countless variations in both exegetical conclusions and theological frameworks, the same pedagogy of a doctrinally ruled reading of Scripture characterizes the broad sweep of the Christian tradition from Gregory the Great through Bernard and Bonaventure, continuing across Reformation differences in both John Calvin and Cornelius Lapide, Patrick Henry and Bishop Bossuet, and on to more recent figures such as Karl Barth and Hans Urs von Balthasar.

Is doctrine, then, not a moldering scrim of antique prejudice obscuring the Bible, but instead a clarifying agent, an enduring tradition of theological judgments that amplifies the living voice of Scripture? And what of the scholarly dispassion advocated by Jowett? Is a noncommitted reading, an interpretation unprejudiced, the way toward objectivity, or does it simply invite the languid intellectual apathy that stands aside to make room for the false truism and easy answers of the age?

This series of biblical commentaries was born out of the conviction that dogma clarifies rather than obscures. Brazos Theological Commentary on the Bible advances upon the assumption that the Nicene tradition, in all its diversity

5. *Luther's Works*, vol. 35 (ed. E. Theodore Bachmann; Philadelphia: Fortress, 1959), 362.
6. *On Christian Doctrine* 1.10.
7. *On Christian Doctrine* 1.35.

and controversy, provides the proper basis for the interpretation of the Bible as Christian Scripture. God the Father Almighty, who sends his only begotten Son to die for us and for our salvation and who raises the crucified Son in the power of the Holy Spirit so that the baptized may be joined in one body—faith in *this* God with *this* vocation of love for the world is the lens through to view the heterogeneity and particularity of the biblical texts. Doctrine, then, is not a moldering scrim of antique prejudice obscuring the meaning of the Bible. It is a crucial aspect of the divine pedagogy, a clarifying agent for our minds fogged by self-deceptions, a challenge to our languid intellectual apathy that will too often rest in false truisms and the easy spiritual nostrums of the present age rather than search more deeply and widely for the dispersed keys to the many doors of Scripture.

For this reason, the commentators in this series have not been chosen because of their historical or philological expertise. In the main, they are not biblical scholars in the conventional, modern sense of the term. Instead, the commentators were chosen because of their knowledge of and expertise in using the Christian doctrinal tradition. They are qualified by virtue of the doctrinal formation of their mental habits, for it is the conceit of this series of biblical commentaries that theological training in the Nicene tradition prepares one for biblical interpretation, and thus it is to theologians and not biblical scholars that we have turned. "War is too important," it has been said, "to leave to the generals."

We do hope, however, that readers do not draw the wrong impression. The Nicene tradition does not provide a set formula for the solution of exegetical problems. The great tradition of Christian doctrine was not transcribed, bound in folio, and issued in an official, critical edition. We have the Niceno-Constantinopolitan Creed, used for centuries in many traditions of Christian worship. We have ancient baptismal affirmations of faith. The Chalcedonian definition and the creeds and canons of other church councils have their places in official church documents. Yet the rule of faith cannot be limited to a specific set of words, sentences, and creeds. It is instead a pervasive habit of thought, the animating culture of the church in its intellectual aspect. As Augustine observed, commenting on Jer. 31:33, "The creed is learned by listening; it is written, not on stone tablets nor on any material, but on the heart."[8] This is why Irenaeus is able to appeal to the rule of faith more than a century before the first ecumenical council, and this is why we need not itemize the contents of the Nicene tradition in order to appeal to its potency and role in the work of interpretation.

Because doctrine is intrinsically fluid on the margins and most powerful as a habit of mind rather than a list of propositions, this commentary series cannot settle difficult questions of method and content at the outset. The editors of the series impose no particular method of doctrinal interpretation.

8. *Sermon* 212.2.

We cannot say in advance how doctrine helps the Christian reader assemble the mosaic of Scripture. We have no clear answer to the question of whether exegesis guided by doctrine is antithetical to or compatible with the now-old modern methods of historical-critical inquiry. Truth—historical, mathematical, or doctrinal—knows no contradiction. But method is a discipline of vision and judgment, and we cannot know in advance what aspects of historical-critical inquiry are functions of modernism that shape the soul to be at odds with Christian discipline. Still further, the editors do not hold the commentators to any particular hermeneutical theory that specifies how to define the plain sense of Scripture—or the role this plain sense should play in interpretation. Here the commentary series is tentative and exploratory.

Can we proceed in any other way? European and North American intellectual culture has been de-Christianized. The effect has not been a cessation of Christian activity. Theological work continues. Sermons are preached. Biblical scholars turn out monographs. Church leaders have meetings. But each dimension of a formerly unified Christian practice now tends to function independently. It is as if a weakened army had been fragmented, and various corps had retreated to isolated fortresses in order to survive. Theology has lost its competence in exegesis. Scripture scholars function with minimal theological training. Each decade finds new theories of preaching to cover the nakedness of seminary training that provides theology without exegesis and exegesis without theology.

Not the least of the causes of the fragmentation of Christian intellectual practice has been the divisions of the church. Since the Reformation, the role of the rule of faith in interpretation has been obscured by polemics and counterpolemics about *sola scriptura* and the necessity of a magisterial teaching authority. The Brazos Theological Commentary on the Bible series is deliberately ecumenical in scope, because the editors are convinced that early church fathers were correct: church doctrine does not compete with Scripture in a limited economy of epistemic authority. We wish to encourage unashamedly dogmatic interpretation of Scripture, confident that the concrete consequences of such a reading will cast far more light on the great divisive questions of the Reformation than either reengaging in old theological polemics or chasing the fantasy of a pure exegesis that will somehow adjudicate between competing theological positions. You shall know the truth of doctrine by its interpretive fruits, and therefore in hopes of contributing to the unity of the church, we have deliberately chosen a wide range of theologians whose commitment to doctrine will allow readers to see real interpretive consequences rather than the shadow boxing of theological concepts.

Brazos Theological Commentary on the Bible has no dog in the current translation fights, and we endorse a textual ecumenism that parallels our diversity of ecclesial backgrounds. We do not impose the thankfully modest inclusive-language agenda of the New Revised Standard Version, nor do we insist upon the glories of the Authorized Version, nor do we require our commentators to create a new translation. In our communal worship, in our private devotions, in our theological scholarship, we use a range of scriptural translations. Precisely as Scripture—a living, functioning text in the present life of faith—the Bible is not semantically fixed. Only a modernist, literalist hermeneutic could imagine that this modest fluidity is a liability. Philological precision and stability is a consequence of, not a basis for, exegesis. Judgments about the meaning of a text fix its literal sense, not the other way around. As a result, readers should expect an eclectic use of biblical translations, both across the different volumes of the series and within individual commentaries.

We cannot speak for contemporary biblical scholars, but as theologians we know that we have long been trained to defend our fortresses of theological concepts and formulations. And we have forgotten the skills of interpretation. Like stroke victims, we must rehabilitate our exegetical imaginations, and there are likely to be different strategies of recovery. Readers should expect this reconstructive—not reactionary—series to provide them with experiments in postcritical doctrinal interpretation, not commentaries written according to the settled principles of a well-functioning tradition. Some commentators will follow classical typological and allegorical readings from the premodern tradition; others will draw on contemporary historical study. Some will comment verse by verse; others will highlight passages, even single words that trigger theological analysis of Scripture. No reading strategies are proscribed, no interpretive methods foresworn. The central premise in this commentary series is that doctrine provides structure and cogency to scriptural interpretation. We trust in this premise with the hope that the Nicene tradition can guide us, however imperfectly, diversely, and haltingly, toward a reading of Scripture in which the right keys open the right doors.

R. R. Reno

PREFACE

In 1905, exactly a hundred years ago, Adolf von Harnack urged upon his pupil and colleague, Karl Holl, his "fundamental conviction that those church historians whose concentration is, as ours is, on *early* church history must always be ready, when the situation requires it, to take on the exposition of a book of the New Testament."[1] He lived up to that rule himself when he published his book on Acts in 1908, which soon thereafter was translated into English.[2] I have always believed in that rule, too. But I have never been able to live up to it myself until now, when I am also doing so with a commentary on Acts, as part of this series of theological commentaries on the Bible. Examining the first account of the first generations does seem a fitting way to follow up on over a half century of studying the history of the church and the development of its doctrine from those first generations and into all subsequent periods.

In many ways I am at heart a philologist, and, coming from a polyglot home, I have since childhood taken special delight in the permutations of grammar and etymology, especially then also in Greek and Latin. But whenever I have been asked whether I am a classicist, I have usually replied that I am interested in Greek and Latin only after they became world languages, for by training and scholarly experience I am a historian of Christian doctrine. As a rule, I have not so much investigated what the Bible *meant* as what it *has been taken to mean*. But the invitation, in my eightieth year, to join other scholars outside the biblical field in this theological commentary project was irresistible.

Even more than usual, therefore, I owe special thanks for the scholarly guidance of colleagues who concentrate on this material, and in particular to Luke Timothy Johnson not only for his own superb commentary of 1992, but for his criticisms and suggestions, which have improved my manuscript at many places. R. R. Reno invited me to undertake the project and encouraged me at

---

1. Zahn-Harnack 1951, 279 (emphasis original).
2. Harnack 1909.

every stage, and Michael Root gave the entire work a careful and very helpful reading. Rebecca Cooper and her colleagues at Brazos Press coped with the difficult editorial and technical problems of the manuscript. Above all, David Aiken, my copyeditor, has, with care and sensitivity, saved me from several howlers, whether trivial or embarrassing. At least as much as it does otherwise (and probably even more), the customary disclaimer applies, that I myself am responsible for whatever mistakes still remain.

The dedication is a welcome opportunity to acknowledge a still deeper debt, which is at once scholarly and yet personal.

ABBREVIATIONS

Bible Versions

AV	Authorized (King James) Version
LXX	Septuagint (see Rahlfs 1979)
NEB	New English Bible
NJB	New Jerusalem Bible
NRSV	New Revised Standard Version
REB	Revised English Bible
RSV	Revised Standard Version
TPR	*textus a patribus receptus* (see Boismard 2000)
Vulgate	Vulgate (see *Nova vulgata* 1986)

Bible Books

Acts	Acts		Eccl.	Ecclesiastes
Add. Esth.	Additions to Esther		Eph.	Ephesians
Amos	Amos		1 Esd.	1 Esdras
Bar.	Baruch		2 Esd.	2 Esdras
Bel	Bel and the Dragon		Esth.	Esther
1 Chr.	1 Chronicles		Exod.	Exodus
2 Chr.	2 Chronicles		Ezek.	Ezekiel
Col.	Colossians		Ezra	Ezra
1 Cor.	1 Corinthians		Gal.	Galatians
2 Cor.	2 Corinthians		Gen.	Genesis
Dan.	Daniel		Hab.	Habakkuk
Deut.	Deuteronomy		Hag.	Haggai
			Heb.	Hebrews
			Hos.	Hosea
			Isa.	Isaiah
			Jas.	James
			Jdt.	Judith
			Jer.	Jeremiah
			Job	Job
			Joel	Joel
			John	John
			1 John	1 John
			2 John	2 John
			3 John	3 John
			Jonah	Jonah
			Josh.	Joshua
			Jude	Jude
			Judg.	Judges
			1 Kgs.	1 Kings
			2 Kgs.	2 Kings
			Lam.	Lamentations

Let. Jer.	Letter of Jeremiah	Prov.	Proverbs
Lev.	Leviticus	Ps.	Psalms
Luke	Luke	Ps. 151	Psalm 151
1 Macc.	1 Maccabees	Rev.	Revelation
2 Macc.	2 Maccabees	Rom.	Romans
3 Macc.	3 Maccabees	Ruth	Ruth
4 Macc.	4 Maccabees	1 Sam.	1 Samuel
Mal.	Malachi	2 Sam.	2 Samuel
Mark	Mark	Sg. Three	Song of the Three Children
Matt.	Matthew	Sir.	Sirach
Mic.	Micah	Song	Song of Songs
Nah.	Nahum	Sus.	Susanna
Neh.	Nehemiah	1 Thess.	1 Thessalonians
Num.	Numbers	2 Thess.	2 Thessalonians
Obad.	Obadiah	1 Tim.	1 Timothy
1 Pet.	1 Peter	2 Tim.	2 Timothy
2 Pet.	2 Peter	Titus	Titus
Phil.	Philippians	Tob.	Tobit
Phlm.	Philemon	Wis.	Wisdom of Solomon
Pr. Azar.	Prayer of Azariah	Zech.	Zechariah
Pr. Man.	Prayer of Manasseh	Zeph.	Zephaniah

Bibliographic

ABD   *The Anchor Bible Dictionary* (ed. David Noel Freedman et al.; 6 vols.; New York: Doubleday, 1992)

ACW   Ancient Christian Writers (ed. Johannes Quasten et al.; 58 vols. to date; Westminster, Md.: Newman, 1946–)

ANF   *The Ante-Nicene Fathers* (10 vols.; repr. Grand Rapids: Eerdmans, 1957)

BAGD   Walter Bauer, *A Greek-English Lexicon of the New Testament and Other Early Christian Literature* (2nd ed. rev. by F. Wilbur Gingrich and Frederick W. Danker, based on previous English edition by William F. Arndt and F. Wilbur Gingrich; Chicago: University of Chicago Press, 1979)

BDAG   Walter Bauer, *A Greek-English Lexicon of the New Testament and Other Early Christian Literature* (3rd ed. rev. by Frederick W. Danker, based on previous English editions by William F. Arndt, F. Wilbur Gingrich, and Frederick W. Danker; Chicago: University of Chicago Press, 2000)

BDF   Friedrich Blass and Albert Debrunner, *A Greek Grammar of the New Testament and Other Early Christian Literature* (ed./trans. Robert W. Funk; Chicago: University of Chicago Press, 1961)

CCF   *Creeds and Confessions of Faith in the Christian Tradition* (ed. Jaroslav Pelikan and Valerie Hotchkiss; 3 vols.; New Haven: Yale University Press, 2003)

Chr. Trad.   Jaroslav Pelikan, *The Christian Tradition: A History of the Development of Doctrine* (5 vols.; Chicago: University of Chicago Press, 1971–89)

DTC   *Dictionnaire de théologie catholique* (ed. Alfred Vacant, Émile Mangenot, and Émile Amann; 15 vols.; Paris: Letouzey & Ané, 1903–50), with *Tables générales* (ed. B. Lott and A. Michel; 3 vols.; Paris: Letouzey & Ané, 1951–72)

LCL	Loeb Classical Library (Cambridge: Harvard University Press)
LTK	*Lexikon für Theologie und Kirche* (ed. Josef Höfer and Karl Rahner; 2nd ed.; 10 vols. and index; Freiburg im Breisgau: Herder, 1957–67)
NA[27]	*Novum Testamentum Graece* (ed. Erwin Nestle, Kurt Aland, et al.; 27th ed.; Stuttgart: Deutsche Bibelgesellschaft, 1999)
NPNF[1]	*A Select Library of the Nicene and Post-Nicene Fathers of the Christian Church*, first series (14 vols.; repr. Grand Rapids: Eerdmans, 1956)
NPNF[2]	*A Select Library of the Nicene and Post-Nicene Fathers of the Christian Church*, second series (14 vols.; repr. Grand Rapids: Eerdmans, 1956)
OCD	*Oxford Classical Dictionary* (ed. Simon Hornblower and Antony Spawforth; 3rd ed.; Oxford: Oxford University Press, 1996)
ODCC	*The Oxford Dictionary of the Christian Church* (ed. F. L. Cross and E. A. Livingstone; 3rd ed.; Oxford: Oxford University Press, 1997)
OED	*The Oxford English Dictionary* (ed. J. A. Simpson and E. S. C. Weiner; 20 vols.; Oxford: Clarendon, 1989)
PG	Patrologia graeca (ed. Jacques Paul Migne; 162 vols.; Paris: Lutetiae Parisiorum, 1857–66)
PGL	*A Patristic Greek Lexicon* (ed. Geoffrey W. H. Lampe; Oxford: Clarendon, 1961)
PL	Patrologia latina (ed. Jacques Paul Migne; 221 vols.; Paris: Lutetiae Parisiorum, 1844–64)
RE	*Realencyklopädie für protestantische Theologie und Kirche* (ed. Johann Jakob Herzog and Albert Hauck; 3rd ed.; 21 vols. and index; Leipzig: Hinrichs, 1896–1909)
SVS	Popular Patristic Series: translations of the church fathers in an unnumbered series edited by John Behr and published by Saint Vladimir's Theological Seminary Press (Crestwood, N.Y.)

INTRODUCTION

From Apostolic Church to Church Catholic

"Moses . . . was a powerful speaker and a man of action" (7:22 NEB) is the characterization of the Jewish lawgiver Moses by the Christian deacon and protomartyr Stephen here in the Acts of the Apostles (a title that is apparently not original), echoing Philo and Josephus (→7:22),[1] as part of his capsule history of the people of Israel since the days of "our father Abraham" (7:2). It also echoes Homer's characterization of Achilles as "both a speaker of words and a doer of deed" (μύθων τε ῥητῆρ . . . πρηκτῆρά τε ἔργων).[2] It could be applied to the entire narrative of the book of Acts itself.

Acts is a book of frenetic action amid a constantly shifting scene: conspiracy and intrigue and ambush, hostile confrontations and fierce conflicts sometimes to the death, rioting lynch mobs and personal violence (→28:31), "journeyings often" (2 Cor. 11:26 AV) and incessant travel on an Odysseus-like scale all over the Mediterranean world (→27:24), complete with shipwreck and venomous serpents, "chains and imprisonment" (Heb. 11:36), followed in at least two instances by a successful jailbreak, though only with the aid of celestial mechanics (5:17–20; 12:6–11; 16:26–28), famine and earthquake, crime and punishment (as well as a great deal of punishment, sometimes even capital punishment, without any real crime ever having been committed).

Gerhard A. Krodel quotes the eloquent description of the book by Edgar Johnson Goodspeed:

> Where, within eighty pages, will be found such a varied series of exciting events—
> trials, riots, persecutions, escapes, martyrdoms, voyages, shipwrecks, rescues—set
> in that amazing panorama of the ancient world—Jerusalem, Antioch, Philippi,

---

1. An arrow (→) indicates a cross-reference to a *locus communis*; see pp. 29–30 below.
2. Homer, *Iliad* 9.443 (LCL 170:415).

> Corinth, Athens, Ephesus, Rome? And with such scenery and settings—temples, courts, prisons, deserts, ships, barracks, theaters? Has any opera such variety? A bewildering range of scenes and actions (and of speeches) passes before the eye of the historian. And in all of them he sees the providential hand that has made and guided this great movement for the salvation of mankind.[3]

The author of this endorsement, E. J. Goodspeed, had studied the Acts of the Apostles carefully, not simply to interpret it but to translate it for *The New Testament: An American Translation*, which came out in 1923. This is, in many ways, the ultimate test for any interpreter, because the translator is not permitted to omit a phrase or a verse; a commentator, on the other hand, including the present one, is often obliged by the economies of space to do just that, as is explained later in this introduction.

Acts has more touches of humor (→12:13–16) than all other books of the New Testament combined. The dizzying catalog of place-names entitled "The Peregrinations [περίοδοι] of the Apostle Paul," which was compiled by Archbishop Theophylact of Bulgaria a thousand years ago as part of his commentary on the Acts of the Apostles,[4] explains why, also today, the book of Acts cannot be understood without constant recourse to a Bible dictionary and a historical atlas. A special problem with using any atlas to study the book of Acts is the need for an identification of the cities and territories of Asia Minor also according to their modern Turkish place-names, by which, for example, "Iconium" (Ἰκόνιον) of 13:51 and elsewhere became "Konya."[5] Taken simply as a tale of adventure, it is by far the most action-packed book in the New Testament, and chapter 27 would deserve an honored place in any anthology of sailing literature, invoking as it does mariners' jargon, some of which goes back at least as far as the Homeric epics (→27:24).

But leaving it at that would even be worse than calling *The Tempest* or *Moby Dick* a sea story and saying no more about it. "Man of action" in Stephen's one-sentence portrait of Moses is coupled with "powerful speaker"—although, according to the book of Exodus of which he is traditionally regarded as the writer, Moses himself tried to evade the Lord's summons by describing himself as "slow of speech and of tongue" (Exod. 4:10), which he negated repeatedly, above all in the long and rhetorically powerful (→24:1–2) series of discourses that are put into his mouth to form the book of Deuteronomy. Thus Moses was not only a man of action but a man of words and a man of ideas. He was depicted by Josephus and Philo, and then by Saint Gregory of Nyssa in his *Life of Moses*, as a practitioner of what the Greeks called "the active life" as a statesman and field general, but no less as an adept of what the Greeks called "the contemplative life."[6] He was said to have been "instructed in all

3. Quoted in Krodel 1986, 13.
4. Theophylact, Exposition of the Acts of the Apostles preface (PG 125:488–89).
5. W. Ward Gasque in *ABD* 3:357–58.
6. O. Schmucki in *LTK* 10:815–17.

the wisdom of the Egyptians" and in all secular learning (→7:22), and God was revealed to him by the voice from the burning bush—in a metaphysical formula that was seen at one and the same time to bring together and yet to challenge the entire history of Greek ontological speculation—as "The one who is" (ὁ ὤν) (Exod. 3:14 LXX). So also the book of Acts belongs to the normative canon of Christian Scripture not only as a database of information about "the mission and expansion of Christianity,"[7] which it supremely and indispensably is, but as an authoritative statement of the church's rule of faith (→8:37) and as a confession of its doctrine. That makes it, as Saint Augustine reminded his readers,

> the only book that has been reckoned worthy of acceptance in the Church as a history of the Acts of the Apostles; while all these other writers who attempted, although deficient in the trustworthiness which was the first requisite, to compose an account of the doings and sayings of the apostles, have met with rejection. And, further, Mark and Luke certainly wrote at a time when it was quite possible to put them to the test not only by the Church of Christ, but also by the apostles themselves who were still alive in the flesh.[8]

Along with the geography and prosopography of the narratives, therefore, the reader needs to be attentive to the theology of the book of Acts[9]—which is the primary concentration of the present commentary.

Commentary has been, moreover, the primary means of theological reflection in both the Jewish and the Christian tradition. Far more than the philosophical speculation (→17:18) or even the doctrinal controversy and polemics (→15:2) that have together tended to dominate modern textbooks and courses in historical theology, the question and the counterquestion formulated in the book of Acts—"Do you understand what you are reading?" and "How can I understand, unless someone instructs me?" (8:30–31 TPR)—have been the garden in which theologies have grown. The case for this primacy of commentary is formulated persuasively by Leon Wieseltier:

> One of the many mistakes that post-modernism has visited upon American life is the idea that commentary is in some way a benighted activity, a secondary or tertiary activity rather than a primary one. Anyone who knows the history of commentary knows that it was for many centuries, and in some ways still is—at least in the books that will really matter—one of the great intellectual opportunities for originality, indeed radicalism, of thought. Certainly the great works of Jewish philosophy are almost all of them works of scriptural commentary, from Philo through the medieval tradition, most notably through Maimonides and his *The Guide of the Perplexed* (which is the greatest single book ever written by a Jew), through Hermann Cohen. The majesty, the depth, the diversity

---

7. Harnack 1961, 80.
8. Augustine, *Harmony of the Gospels* 4.8.9 (*NPNF*[1] 6:231).
9. Jervell 1996; J. Bellamy in *DTC* 1:349–52; L. Venard in *DTC* 9:984–1000.

of this tradition strongly suggests that it is almost incumbent upon a serious philosophical mind to engage in the work of commentary.[10]

As these words are eminently true of the book of Genesis and the Jewish tradition of commentary on it, about which they were written, so they apply also to the book of Acts and to the Christian tradition of commentary on it.

Such a concentration of the theology of Acts entails, for this commentator at any rate, continuing reference to the tradition of the church as it has been prayed and sung in its liturgy, confessed in its creeds and confessions of faith, defended by its seven ecumenical councils, and articulated by its "cloud of witnesses" (Heb. 12:1): not what Acts or its putative sources[11] may have "originally meant," but what it has been taken to mean by the church as part of the total canon of Scripture and as an inseparable and normative constituent element of the tradition. That enterprise is rendered more difficult by the position that the book of Acts occupies (or rather, the position that it does *not* occupy) in the official and liturgical life of the church. Even in the postils expounding the assigned pericopes for the church year,[12] Acts does not figure prominently, with only the following portions designated as epistle lessons in the calendar of the Western church for Sundays and chief holidays:

1:1–11	Feast of the Ascension
2:1–13	Feast of Pentecost
6:8–14 and 7:54–59	Feast of Saint Stephen
9:1–22	Feast of the Conversion of Saint Paul
10:34–43	Easter Monday
13:26–39	Easter Tuesday

Hence this commentary will repeatedly have to draw on the use of Acts in the broader corpus of patristic literature and thought, Eastern as well as Western. (Whenever possible, patristic and other citations will refer to existing translations in English, on the assumption that such references will enable any interested reader to find the passage also in an edition of the original, whereas a reference to the original would not be as easily and universally helpful in the other direction.)

Particularly valuable, therefore, are the four commentaries on the book of Acts, two Eastern and two Western, that definitely date from the first half of the history of the church. Apparently these are the only four about which it is possible to speak with considerable certainty, because the commentary on Acts by "Heraclitus in the reign of Commodus and Severus" reported by Jerome,[13] to cite one instance, has been lost, and the provenance of the

10. Leon Wieseltier in Kass et al. 2004, 7–8.
11. Dupont 1964 provides a critical examination of the historical-critical literature on this question.
12. Walter Caspari in *RE* 15:131–59.
13. Jerome, *Lives of Illustrious Men* 46 (*NPNF*[2] 3:372).

commentary erroneously attributed in the Patrologia graeca to the tenth-cen-
tury bishop "Oecumenius" of Trikka seems impossible to identify with any
precision.[14] Four commentaries is certainly a very small number, especially
in comparison with all the patristic commentaries on one or another of the
Gospels or on the Pauline Epistles.[15] By far the most important of these four,
which is described by Johannes Quasten as "the only complete commentary
on Acts that has survived from the first ten centuries,"[16] is the exposition by
Saint John Chrysostom; this commentary consists of the fifty-five homilies
delivered by him as archbishop of Constantinople in 400, and it occupies
an entire volume of Patrologia graeca.[17] The next two commentators wrote
in Latin: Cassiodorus[18] and the Venerable Bede, with both an *Exposition*
and *Retractations*.[19] Coming just after the end of the first millennium was
the commentary by Archbishop Theophylact of Bulgaria, who was heavily
dependent on Chrysostom, as he himself gratefully acknowledges throughout.[20] In fact, all three of these latter expositions incorporate quotations from
various earlier interpreters, which nowadays is usually thought to demonstrate
their "lack of independence" or of creativity and originality, and therefore
to count against their value,[21] but which actually adds to their value for our
purposes here.

Unavoidably, therefore, the exegesis being offered in the present commentary
must be acknowledged to be, in one sense, highly anachronistic, above all, for
example, for not invoking an argument from silence to conclude that there
could not already have been, even in oral form, a "rule of faith" with which
the later baptismal, catechetical, and conciliar creeds of the early centuries of
the church stand in recognizable continuity, as they themselves consistently
claimed to be doing (→8:37; 20:7). Already in the formulation that is probably
the earliest of all explicit postbiblical references to the Acts of the Apostles,
the words of Saint Irenaeus from the second century, who is also the author
who "provides the most ancient explicit attribution of the Third Gospel to
Saint Luke,"[22] the book of Acts was linked directly and inseparably with the
authority of the rule of faith: "It may be, indeed," wrote Irenaeus, "that it was
with this view that God set forth very many Gospel truths, through Luke's
instrumentality, which all should esteem it necessary to use, in order that all
persons, *following his subsequent testimony, which treats upon the acts and the
doctrine of the apostles, and holding the unadulterated rule of truth*, may be

14. PG 118:43–119; Beck 1959, 418.
15. K. H. Schelkle in *LTK* 3:1278–80 (with bibliography).
16. Quasten et al. 1951–86, 3:440.
17. PG 60; *NPNF*[1] 11:1–328.
18. PL 70:1381–1406.
19. PL 92:937–1032.
20. PG 125:483–1132.
21. Manitius 1911–31, 1:50 (Cassiodorus), 87 (Bede); Beck 1959, 650 (Theophylact).
22. L. Venard in *DTC* 9:971.

saved."[23] Coming from the ancient Christian writer who documented more fully than any of his contemporaries or near-contemporaries the emergence of bishop, creed, and canon as the multiple and yet single criterion (→2:42) for the tradition of the apostolic continuity,[24] Irenaeus's formulation located the study and exposition of the book of Acts in that historical and theological context.

At a time when it may sometimes seem as though any hypothesis about the New Testament, no matter how extravagant it might be, is able to claim its Warholian fifteen minutes of fame, this commentary, then, is based on what may turn out to be the most radical presupposition of all: that the church really did get it right in its liturgies, creeds, and councils—yes, and even in its dogmas. Therefore, as the title of this introduction indicates, this commentary presupposes that in the transition from "apostolic church" to "church catholic" the church somehow continued to be "apostolic," as well as both "one" and "holy" and therefore that this Nicene-Chalcedonian faith may legitimately provide an a posteriori organizing principle for the exegetical task, perhaps above all and in a special way for the Acts of the Apostles.

This transition of the early church was dramatically analyzed in another (and, by comparison, far less momentous) revolutionary transition, which took place from the first edition to the second edition of Albrecht Ritschl's *Rise of the Old Catholic Church* (*Die Entstehung der altkatholischen Kirche*). In its first edition in 1850, Ritschl's account accepted the brilliant Hegelian hypothesis of "the Tübingen school," especially of its coryphaeus and founder Ferdinand Christian Baur: that early Catholicism as we know it from Irenaeus and other second-century sources arose as a "synthesis" out of the "antithesis" of Paul, the apostle to the Gentiles, to the original "thesis" of Jewish Christianity represented by Peter; that this tension, which was so vividly described in the first two chapters of Paul's Epistle to the Galatians, was largely suppressed and glossed over in the official version of "the apostolic council" as carried by the fifteenth chapter of the book of Acts (→15:28; →16:4b); and therefore that the canonical Acts of the Apostles, which presented itself as a contemporary or near-contemporary account (→27:1), could not have come from any period earlier than the middle of the second century, roughly the time of Irenaeus.[25] The radical implications of this hypothesis set the terms for much of the scholarly interpretation of Acts at the middle of the nineteenth century, above all at the Protestant theological faculties of German universities, which dominated the theological scholarship of the time. But in the second edition of his book, published in 1857, Ritschl backed off from the extremes of Baur's hypothesis to a more positive assessment of the historiography of the book of Acts.[26] In that revisionist understanding

23. Irenaeus, *Against Heresies* 3.15.1 (*ANF* 1:439) (emphasis added).
24. *Chr. Trad.* 1:108–20.
25. Hodgson 1966, 205–6.
26. Hefner 1966, 12–44.

both of Acts and of its author, he was followed by one of the most influential of all modern interpreters of Acts—and of the literature and doctrine of early Christianity in its entirety—Adolf von Harnack.[27]

It is, however, an ecumenical consensus, now at any rate,[28] that theology must be firmly grounded in philology, which implies for the Acts of the Apostles the obligation of a close and careful *explication de texte* on the basis of the Greek original. This theological commentary, accordingly, would have been impossible without the painstaking philological work of the New Testament scholars whose books on the Acts of the Apostles are listed in the bibliography and are being gratefully cited throughout (and have repeatedly been used even for passages where they are not explicitly cited). Among these late-twentieth-century commentaries, three have been especially helpful: those by Charles Kingsley Barrett (1994–98), Hans Conzelmann (1987), and Luke Timothy Johnson (1992).

Because this commentary is intended to be primarily theological rather than philological, the discussion of an individual theological issue or *locus communis*, which is printed in bold type, has been concentrated at one or another particular passage of the book of Acts where that issue and doctrine are prominent, with consideration of other passages in Acts related to this discussion; and the headings of these discussions often include quotations from or references to the tradition of creeds, councils, and liturgies, as well as to the biblical text. For example, there are numerous references to the angels scattered throughout most of Acts, all the way from 1:10 to 23:8, so that discussing the doctrine in full at each location would have been cumbersome and repetitive, while discussing the peculiar angelology of any single passage in isolation from the doctrine as a whole would have been fragmentary and disconnected. Bringing together in its heading a quotation from the Niceno-Constantinopolitan Creed (art. 1) and one from the Epistle to the Hebrews (1:14), the consideration of the doctrine of angels, therefore, is concentrated at 12:7: "'Both Seen and Unseen': The Angels as 'Ministering Spirits,'" with a cross-reference to this *locus communis* (identified by → and chapter + verse) at the other passages about angels. Obviously, such a discussion could in many instances have been attached to any of several passages in Acts, and its assignment to one location rather than another is admittedly somewhat arbitrary; but this arrangement made it possible to distribute the *loci communes* evenly across the entire book. To the possible disappointment of the reader looking up an individual passage, not every single verse received its own comment; if it had, the work would, as for example Barrett 1994–98 did, easily have grown into two stout volumes. But most of the theologically significant verses have

27. Harnack 1907; Harnack 1909.
28. Dei verbum: Decree of the Second Vatican Council on Divine Revelation (*CCF* 3:650–62).

received attention, on their own or as part of one or more *loci communes* (a full list of *loci communes* is given in the table of contents).

The most celebrated application of the classical and Renaissance concept of τόποι or *loci communes* to biblical exegesis was the work of the young Philip Melanchthon, whose book under that title, published in 1521, was prepared in connection with his lectures on the Epistle to the Romans and was intended to serve not as a systematic theology, much less as a replacement for the *Summa theologica* of Saint Thomas Aquinas, but as a handbook and guide for the study of the Scripture. But because of the structure of the theological and rhetorical argument in Romans,[29] these *loci communes* easily evolved into the logical sequence of topics for a book of dogmatics, beginning from the relation between reason and revelation and going on through the Trinity to the incarnation to the atonement to justification to church and sacraments to ethics (initially seen as an integral part of dogmatics) to eschatology; and *Loci theologici* became a standard title for sixteenth-century and seventeenth-century Protestant dogmaticians, both Lutheran and Reformed, and even for some Roman Catholic theologians.[30] The sequence of theological topics here in the Acts of the Apostles, which is a historical narrative rather than an argumentative brief, is far less systematic than it is in the Epistle to the Romans and may often seem downright higgledy-piggledy. But by the time these eighty-four *loci communes* (three per chapter) have all had their say, most of the content of Christian theology has come in for attention—though not in the order to which students of systematic theology may be accustomed or which logic may seem to require. In addition, there are several, perhaps somewhat idiosyncratic, *loci* on topics not ordinarily to be found in the conventional exposition of Christian theology, such as humor (→12:13–16), religious affections (→21:13–14), due process of law (→25:16), friendship as a divine gift (→27:3), and sailing as a Christian theological metaphor (→27:24).

In keeping with its distinctive mission and in accordance with the prescription for the entire series of which it is a part, this commentary on the Acts of the Apostles is, as the editors' instructions put it, "based upon the final form of the text, taken in its canonical context." Therefore the writer of Acts—and of the Gospel to whose narrative Acts attaches itself as a continuation (1:1–2)—will throughout be referred to simply as "Saint Luke." The traditional view of his authorship is widely dispersed throughout ancient Christian writers.[31] It was summarized by Saint Jerome:

> Luke, a physician of Antioch, as his writings indicate, was not unskilled in the Greek language. An adherent of the apostle Paul, and companion of all his journeying, he wrote a *Gospel,* concerning which the same Paul says, "We send

29. Donfried 1974; Wuellner 1976.
30. Johannes Kunze in *RE* 11:570–72; A. Lang in *LTK* 6:1110–12.
31. Loisy 1920, 6–17.

with him a brother whose praise in the gospel is among all the churches" [2 Cor. 8:18] and to the Colossians "Luke the beloved physician salutes you" [Col. 4:14] and to Timothy "Luke only is with me" [2 Tim. 4:11]. He also wrote another excellent volume to which he prefixed the title *Acts of the Apostles*, a history which extends to the second year of Paul's sojourn at Rome, that is to the fourth year of Nero, from which we learn that the book was composed in that same city.[32]

Use of that nomenclature here does imply that the author of the Third Gospel (Luke 1:1–4) was also the author of Acts (1:1), as the opening verses of the two books and the common address to Theophilus also indicate. Cross-references to the four Gospels here will, therefore, in the first instance cite the Gospel of Luke if possible, and the other three Gospels as appropriate.

But this does not, or at any rate need not, imply an answer, one way or the other, to the mooted historical-critical question of the traditional identification of the author with Paul's companion: "Luke the beloved physician" (Col. 4:14).[33] Harnack, whom "no one could accuse . . . of any prejudice whatsoever in favor of either orthodox theology or traditional views in the realm of biblical criticism"[34]—or, for that matter, in the realm of ecclesiastical dogma—nevertheless affirms the traditional identification in his *Luke the Physician*, arguing at least partly on the basis of the medical vocabulary in the Gospel and in Acts, in which he found evidence of the professional knowledge and training of a physician.[35] And the traditional identification—"the author of the two-volume work is probably Luke the physician (Col. 4:14)"[36]—persists in the scholarly literature. But Henry J. Cadbury, in a dissertation published as *The Style and Literary Method of Luke*,[37] "virtually demolished the contention that St Luke's writing betrayed any specifically medical knowledge or interests"[38] beyond what Aristophanes or Lucian or any other well-educated person could be assumed to possess at the time, thereby giving rise to the almost irresistible bon mot that "Doctor Cadbury acquired his doctor title by depriving Saint Luke of his."

According to a considerably later tradition, Luke, who is commemorated in both the Eastern and Western liturgical calendars on October 18, was not only a physician and the patron saint of physicians, but one of the first Christian iconographers and the patron saint of iconographers.[39] This identification was an application of the widely held belief that "above all Mary, mother of Jesus, may be regarded as the principal source, more or less indirect, for the account of the infancy of the Savior"[40] that is found in the first two chapters

32. Jerome, *Lives of Illustrious Men* 7 (*NPNF*² 3:363).
33. Haenchen 1971, 3–14 pulls together most of the available material.
34. Gasque 1975, 146.
35. Harnack 1907.
36. Hengel 1979, 66.
37. Cadbury 1920.
38. *ODCC* 259.
39. Onasch and Schnieper 1997, 187, 235.
40. L. Venard in *DTC* 9:981.

of the Gospel of Luke (→1:14). Since an icon was said to be not drawn but written (hence the term icono*graphy*), Byzantine writers, notably Andrew of Crete in the eighth century, and then writers in the West, worked out what Ernst von Dobschütz calls "a parallelism between his activity as an evangelist and as a painter," so that Luke's literary portrait of the Virgin Mary and his iconographic portrait of the Theotokos were seen as not very far apart.[41] But by extension, it seems even more appropriate to claim him also as patron saint of church historians, because he had decided, as he explains in the prologue to his Gospel, "having followed all things closely for some time past, to write an orderly account" (Luke 1:3), which is an apt thumbnail description of the two things that historians of the church still do as scholars—to research "closely" and on that basis to write up the results of their research in more or less "orderly" fashion. He did this, moreover, not only in the Gospel according to Saint Luke, about which he first wrote these words, but in the Acts of the Apostles, as a second part of his two-volume work or "diptych."[42]

The assignment to base all the commentaries in the series Brazos Theological Commentary on the Bible "upon the final form of the text, taken in its canonical context," becomes unusually complicated in the case of the book of Acts—more complicated, in fact, than in the case of any other book of either the Old or the New Testament.[43] In the manuscripts and early versions, Acts presents itself to us not only with the usual collection of more or less significant textual variants (→20:28a), but with something that amounts to two distinct texts, which may in fact be two separate *editions*, even, according to a few scholars such as Friedrich Blass and Theodor Zahn, two successive editions that were both prepared by the author himself (though there is less than total agreement about which edition came first).[44] One of these—which is a major component, among others, of the Greek text underlying several of the most important translations of Acts, including the Syriac, the Old Latin, Luther's German Bible, and the Authorized ("King James") Version of the English Bible—is represented in Codex Bezae Cantabrigiensis, so named because it once belonged to Calvin's colleague Theodore Beza, who gave it to the University of Cambridge; in the textual apparatus of critical editions of the Greek New Testament, Codex Bezae is identified by the siglum D. As Philip Carrington says of this recension of Acts:

> It is not merely a question of accidental variation, or of occasional correction by a well-meaning scribe, or of a little addition or alteration; it is a question of a process of revision and re-writing not very long after its composition; and in

41. Dobschütz 1899, 2:275–76; most of the early sources are compiled and critically examined in 2:267–80.
42. Marguerat 1999, 91–92; Tarazi 2001, 19.
43. Trocmé 1957, 21–27; Bruce 1990; Strange 1992.
44. Nock 1972, 2:826–27.

the case of Acts it has been done very thoroughly. . . . It is impossible to resist the impression that this reviser knew what he was doing.[45]

It has acquired the (quite misleading) designation "Western Text," which, after several attempts to tinker with the nomenclature in various ways, is a title that has probably outlived its usefulness.[46] During the second half of the twentieth century the effort to compare the Western Text of Acts with the rest of the manuscript tradition, both philologically and theologically, evoked a substantial scholarly literature,[47] as a result of which the geographical label "Western" is recognized as having been quite inaccurate.[48] Such comparison suggested, for example, a significant distinctiveness in its treatment of the doctrine of the Holy Spirit.[49] Among the other issues in the debate is its allegedly antifeminist (→18:24–26b) prejudice.[50]

In place of the tag Western Text, however, it could, with much greater justification, be labeled *textus a patribus receptus* ("text accepted by church fathers"), and it will be so designated here (with the abbreviation TPR), because, as a leading investigator of it says:

> It is of great importance also that *most of the earliest Church Fathers* who quote the NT reflect the "Western" text substantially, such as Marcion, Tatian (= Diatessaron), Irenaeus, Tertullian, and Cyprian. Ephraem of Syria (4th century) is a notable witness for Acts. . . .
>
> "Western" readings can be identified in some abundance in early Church Fathers like Marcion, Justin Martyr, Tatian, Irenaeus, and Cyprian in the 2d century, and like Clement of Alexandria, Hippolytus, and even Origen in the 3d century.[51]

And, he could have added, Hilary and Augustine in the fourth and fifth centuries. The title "Textus Receptus" is sometimes restricted to the influential edition of the Greek New Testament published by Robert Estienne ("Stephanus") in 1550.[52] But it can be in fact a much broader term, being used to identify not only that edition but any established text of the New Testament, whether Greek or Latin, as well as the text of Old Testament, whether Hebrew or Greek.[53] *Textus a patribus receptus*, therefore, seems to be an appropriate way

---

45. Carrington 1957, 1:288.
46. Eldon Jay Epp in *ABD* 6:909–12.
47. The scholarly literature and the state of the question have been carefully summarized by Epp 1966, 172–85, and for the two decades after that, by Aland 1986; see also the earlier work of Klijn 1949.
48. Hanson 1965–66.
49. Black 1981.
50. Witherington 1984.
51. Eldon Jay Epp in *ABD* 6:909–10 (emphasis added).
52. Pelikan, Hotchkiss, and Price 1996, 16–17, 102–3.
53. E. J. Revell in *ABD* 6:435.

of designating a special version of the text of the book of Acts that enjoyed such wide circulation and acceptance among ancient Christian writers as well as among later translators and exegetes.

Much of this TPR is documented throughout the books of the New Testament in the apparatus of NA[27], especially in its citations of Codex D, although without many of the patristic citations. But it has now been carefully reconstituted as a complete edition of the Greek text of Acts unto itself, with the Alexandrian Text in parallel columns, by Dominican New Testament scholar Marie-Émile Boismard of the École Biblique.[54] His edition provides thorough documentation not only from Codex D and other Greek manuscripts, but from patristic sources, both Greek and Latin, as well as from the early Latin, Syriac, Coptic, and Ethiopic versions, on the basis of a rich collection of manuscripts preserved in many places (including the Ethiopian manuscripts of the Monastic Microfilm Library at Saint John's Abbey in Collegeville, Minnesota); for this documentation Boismard was often obliged to engage in the admittedly tricky enterprise of "retrotranslation" into Greek. Absent the wide-ranging linguistic and scholarly competence that would have been needed to criticize and revise them in detail, Boismard's reconstructions are followed here as they stand. For the purposes of this theological commentary on Acts, then, the prescription of being based on "the final form of the text, in its canonical context," seems to mean usually privileging the variant readings of this TPR where they are not altogether trivial or theologically insignificant. That is not tantamount to claiming it as *the* final form of the text, but certainly to accepting it as *one* final form—also because of its creedal passages (→8:37) and its version of the Golden Rule (15:29), neither of which can be found in other manuscript families. Therefore the English translation of Acts will usually—though not always (→18:24–26b)—be based whenever possible on the TPR (i.e., Boismard 2000), with the RSV serving as the default translation and not specifically identified where the TPR does not present any significant variants. Where there are such variants, they are translated and incorporated into the RSV quotation but under the siglum TPR, so as not to appear to be attributing the variant reading to the RSV; in some cases where the AV reflects the TPR, this translation is used and identified as such (e.g., 8:37 TPR AV).

By a similar methodological logic, quotations from the Old Testament are based on the Septuagint, which must be regarded as Saint Luke's Bible, and will usually be translated from it (i.e., from Rahlfs 1979) and identified accordingly (to avoid confusion, I use standard English verse numbers for the Old Testament—rather than the numbering systems peculiar to the Hebrew Bible, Septuagint, or Vulgate). For example: when, near the beginning of his Gospel (Luke 3:4–6), Luke recounts the inaugural message of Jesus as proclaimed in the synagogue at Nazareth, he has Jesus read from the fortieth chapter of Isaiah (Isa. 40:3–5). In first-century Nazareth such a reading would certainly have

---

54. Boismard 2000.

been delivered in Hebrew, probably followed by a targum in Aramaic. But the block quotation in Luke is taken directly from the Septuagint, as though it had been read out in Greek. The same is true of the myriad quotations from the Psalms, Isaiah, and the other prophets that appear throughout both the Gospel of Luke and the book of Acts; significant parts of Acts may without exaggeration be called a catena of such quotations with specifically Christian explanations (→8:30–31). There appears to be no convincing reason to believe that the author of the Acts of the Apostles knew any Hebrew, much less, as Clement of Alexandria is said by Eusebius to have suggested, that he "carefully translated" the Epistle to the Hebrews into Greek (which would have been a formidable literary and linguistic assignment, assuming of course that Hebrews was originally composed in Hebrew or Aramaic in the first place).[55] Rather, it may be concluded that he "knew Greek better than he did Hebrew," as the Venerable Bede rather gently put it.[56] The three references in Acts (21:40; 22:2; 26:14) to someone, Paul in the first two and Jesus in the third, speaking τῇ Ἑβραΐδι διαλέκτῳ mean "Aramaic" and not Hebrew, as does the reference in the Gospel of John to the three languages of the inscription on the cross of Jesus: Ἑβραϊστί, Ῥωμαϊστί, Ἑλληνιστί (John 19:20). Nor, for that matter, is there incontrovertible evidence (though there may be some indication) that the writer of Acts was acquainted with any other Greek translation from the Hebrew than the Septuagint, much less that he himself could have made such a translation or even corrected the Septuagint on his own. From this it seems to follow that here, in interpreting his book, translations into English from the Septuagint rather than from the "original" Hebrew are in order.

---

55. Eusebius, *Church History* 6.14.2 (*NPNF*[2] 1:261), citing Clement of Alexandria's *Hypotyposes,* which is now lost but was still known to Photius in the ninth century (Quasten et al. 1951–86, 2:16–17).

56. Bede, *Exposition of the Acts of the Apostles* dedicatory epistle (PL 92:938).

ACTS 1

1:1 AV The former treatise have I made, O Theophilus, of all that Jesus began both to do and to teach.

The opening verse is clearly intended to be both an introduction to the present book and a cross-reference to the introduction of the Gospel of Luke (Luke 1:1). Chrysostom explains the cross-reference: "The Gospels . . . are a history of what Christ did and said; but the Acts, of what that 'other Comforter' [John 14:16 AV] said and did."[1] For Luke the author, whether of his Gospel or of the book of Acts, as well as for the authors of the other three Gospels, the acts of Jesus and the teachings of Jesus were inseparable, which may be suggested here grammatically by the use of τε/καί ("both/and") rather than simple καί; it is so construed in the AV's "*both* to do *and* to teach." Yet in the Epistles of Paul, where the message of "Christ crucified" (1 Cor. 1:23) is so central (Gal. 6:14), there is a remarkable selectivity about the "doing"—and very little of the "teaching." The only things Jesus "did" to receive mention from Saint Paul anywhere were the events of Holy Week, his passion and resurrection; there are no infancy narratives, no travels through Judea and Galilee, no miracles, no controversies with his opponents. And the one and only thing Jesus "said" to be quoted verbatim anywhere in the Epistles of Paul—apart from the somewhat oblique reference in 1 Cor. 7:10–12 to what he did *not* say—also comes from Holy Week, the words of institution of the Eucharist (1 Cor. 11:23–27); there are no parables, no Sermon on the Mount, not even the Lord's Prayer, although here in Acts Paul does quote "the words of the Lord, for he himself said, 'The one who gives is blessed rather than the one who receives [μακάριος ὁ διδὼν μᾶλλον ἢ ὁ λαμβάνων]'" (20:35 TPR). The classic creeds (→8:37) followed Paul in making Jesus the teacher and the doer of deeds secondary to Jesus the incarnate, crucified, and risen Lord. They moved directly from confessing

1. Chrysostom, *Homilies on Acts* 1 (*NPNF*[1] 11:7).

that he "became incarnate from the Holy Spirit and the Virgin Mary, became human," to declaring that he "was crucified on our behalf under Pontius Pilate,"[2] bypassing most of the content of all four Gospels. Nevertheless, the periodic effort, especially in the history of modern theology, to redress this balance by concentrating the significance of Jesus Christ almost exclusively on his teachings can easily, and even fatally, sever the unity in this phrase "both to do and to teach"—and sever both of these from the suffering of Christ.

"As the Lord Jesus Christ Himself Instructed Us": The Gospel of the Forty Days

1:2–3 TPR He chose the apostles through the Holy Spirit and commanded the preaching of the gospel, . . . for forty days appearing to them and teaching the doctrines about the kingdom of God [διδάσκων τὰ περὶ τῆς βασιλείας τοῦ θεοῦ].

In concluding its statement of faith, which was to set the norm for the church's doctrine of the person of Christ for the subsequent millennium and a half, until long after the Protestant Reformation, the Council of Chalcedon in 451 put forth the apparently presumptuous claim that everything it was confessing—including the affirmation that the two natures of Christ "undergo no confusion, no change, no division, no separation [ἀσυγχύτως, ἀτρέπτως, ἀδιαιρέτως, ἀχωρίστως]"—was "[1] just as the prophets taught from the beginning about him, and [2] as the Lord Jesus Christ himself instructed us, and [3] as the creed of the fathers handed down to us."[3] Ultimately, these three authorities were in fact a single authority: the Holy Scriptures as Christ had interpreted and fulfilled them according to the tradition (→16:4b). "As the Lord Jesus Christ himself instructed us," therefore, did not refer only to the four Gospels, but also to this "gospel of the forty days" of "teaching the doctrines about the kingdom of God," just as there was believed to be an oral Torah given to Moses on Mount Sinai alongside the written Torah.[4] As Paul Nadim Tarazi says:

> The authoritative character of Jesus' teaching is emphasized not only by calling it a "commandment" (*enteilamenos*) but also by immediately thereafter mentioning the "40 days" between the resurrection and ascension. The combination of these two terms could not help but call to the hearer's mind the giving of the Torah during the journey in the wilderness after the Exodus, when Moses spent 40 days receiving God's commandments.[5]

2. Niceno-Constantinopolitan Creed 3–4 (*CCF* 1:163).
3. Definition of Faith of the Council of Chalcedon 18, 25–27 (*CCF* 1:181).
4. Jacob Neusner in Neusner et al. 1999, 3:1447–58.
5. Tarazi 2001, 187.

This "teaching of the gospel for forty days" (*evangelium quadraginta dierum*), which some of the Gnostics seem to have expanded to a period of eighteen months,[6] is a continuation of the instruction given by the risen Lord to his disciples. Earlier, at the conclusion of his Gospel, Luke described this instruction as having begun with the disciples at Emmaus, when, "beginning with Moses and all the prophets, [the risen but as yet unrecognized Christ] interpreted to them in all the scriptures the things concerning himself" (Luke 24:27). Its authority was then invoked by the tradition as an explanation of the puzzling differences that are so obvious between the teachings of Jesus about the kingdom of God before the resurrection, as these are presented in the four Gospels, and the structure of the church's kerygma so soon after the resurrection and ascension. The Gospels do not claim to be exhaustive, explaining quite to the contrary that "Jesus did many other signs in the presence of the disciples, which are not written in this book" (John 20:30); and here in Acts (20:35 TPR), for example, Luke includes an important and oft-quoted saying of Jesus, whether from before the resurrection or from the "gospel of the forty days" after the resurrection, that does not appear in his Gospel or in any of the other three canonical Gospels, but is one of the agrapha:[7] "The one who gives is blessed rather than the one who receives."

Paul's account in 1 Corinthians of the several "appearings" of Christ after the resurrection ("for forty days appearing to them and teaching the doctrines about the kingdom of God"), including the appearance to himself "as to one untimely born" (ὡσπερεὶ τῷ ἐκτρώματι) (1 Cor. 15:5–8)—an appearance that is narrated in greater detail three times in the book of Acts (→9:1–4), and with words spoken by Christ—makes no reference to any formal "teaching." But it is to this gospel of the forty days that the fragmentary concluding sections of the Gospels, together with this (also fragmentary) introductory section of Acts—taken all together, a body of text that is considerably shorter than the Sermon on the Mount (Matt. 5–7)—trace many of the component elements of what was to become the central teaching, worship, and structure of the church. Thus despite some earlier anticipations in the Gospels (Matt. 24:14; 26:13), it is to this period of Christ's association with his disciples and to "the sacred and imperishable proclamation of eternal salvation" (Mark 16:9 variant) that the vision of a message for "all nations" (Matt. 28:19; Luke 24:47), indeed for "the whole creation" (Mark 16:15), was attributed; on the basis of this, as the rest of the book of Acts is to narrate, Peter and the twelve, and then Paul and Barnabas, would bring the message from Jerusalem to Athens (→17:18) and to Rome (→28:14). During these final encounters, their confession of Jesus Christ moved from Peter's dramatic earlier recognition of him as "the Christ, the Son of the living God" (Matt. 16:16) to the formula by which Thomas, in Augustine's words, "saw and touched the man, and acknowledged the God

6. Irenaeus, *Against Heresies* 1.3.2 (*ANF* 1:319).
7. Émile Mangenot in *DTC* 1:625–27.

whom he neither saw nor touched,"[8] thus, as orthodoxy read the words, confessing him as identical with the God of Abraham, Isaac, and Jacob, as "my Lord and my God" (ὁ κύριός μου καὶ ὁ θεός μου) (John 20:28). From this time, rather than from that covered by the main body of the Gospels, the disciples' learning "the name of the Father and of the Son and of the Holy Spirit" (Matt. 28:19) can be dated, and therefore the skeletal outline of the creed, oral at first and later (much later) written down (→8:37). The Gospels ascribe to these manifestations the imperative to baptize (Matt. 28:19; Mark 16:16), which is, far more than the breaking of bread in the Eucharist (→20:7), the sacramental foundation of the church in the theology of Acts (→22:16), as well as in the Niceno-Constantinopolitan Creed.[9] The earlier promise and charge to Peter, which was framed in the future tense "I will build [οἰκοδομήσω] my church" and "I will give [δώσω] you the keys" (Matt. 16:18–19) and then was extended to all the disciples with verbs also in the future tense (Matt. 18:18), could now be spoken in the present tense: "As the Father has sent me, even so I send [πέμπω] you. . . . If you forgive the sins of any, they are forgiven [ἀφέωνται]" (John 20:21, 23). And it was in this instruction from the risen Lord that the normative method for understanding and interpreting "*all* the scriptures" was grounded (Luke 24:27), on the basis of which the church of the centuries to follow was to build the massive structure of its central theological activity, which was at its core not the construction of speculative systems but the exegesis of Scripture (→8:30–31).

As Reinhold Seeberg says of these several component elements, "these are not Old Testament or Jewish ideas; rather, they are thoughts and provocations that the disciples were convinced they had received from the Risen One."[10] The narrative of Acts, indeed the history of the early church in the following centuries, can be read as the process of making explicit what was implicit in this "gospel of the forty days," of giving ritual form and eventually written form to a tradition, attributed to none less than the risen Lord himself, that was oral in its origins and in its transmission. This certainly did not happen at once; the report in this chapter of the last exchange of question and answer between Christ and his disciples (1:6–8 TPR)—"Is it at this time that you will bring about the restoration, and when will the kingdom of Israel be?" and the answer, "No one can know the time or the seasons," the kingdom of God being the very topic that is used here in 1:3 as a summary of his instruction (→28:23)—stands as a refutation of any such simplistic notion. But it is to this dominical corpus of remembered insights and entrusted beliefs, identified specifically with the precious interval between the resurrection and the ascension, that the church would ever recur. In the second century, Irenaeus, urging that "we must keep the rule [κανών] of faith unswervingly," summoned

8. Augustine, *Tractates on the Gospel of John* 121.5 (*NPNF*[1] 7:438).
9. Niceno-Constantinopolitan Creed 10 (*CCF* 1:163).
10. Seeberg 1953, 1:75–79.

his reader back to these very components of the faith.[11] In the third century, Cyprian of Carthage strung together in his *Testimonies* hundreds of passages that he explained in accordance with the rule of faith, as the risen Christ had commanded.[12] And in the fourth century, Athanasius employed this normative hermeneutic to expound key passages of Scripture in defending the Nicene faith against Arianism.[13]

1:4–5 TPR Which, he said, you heard from my mouth.

Within the narrower context of Luke-Acts, "the promise of the Father which you heard from my mouth" here refers explicitly to passages such as Luke 12:12, "the Holy Spirit will teach you," and it anticipates the account of Pentecost in the following chapter (→2:1). But within the broader context of the four Gospels as an entirety, it may be taken as a reference to the closing discourses "from the mouth" of Jesus, which are set down most fully not in any of the Synoptics, but in the Gospel of John (John 14:26; 15:26; 16:13–15). The command "not to depart from Jerusalem" sets up the chiaroscuro of a narrative that in succeeding chapters would cover the vast territory of Asia Minor and the Mediterranean world and would find its intellectual and philosophical climax in Athens (→17:18) and then its political and historical climax in Rome (→28:14).

1:6–8 TPR "Lord, is it at this time that you will bring about the restoration [ἀποκατασταθήσῃ], and when will the kingdom of Israel be?" . . . "No one can know the time or the seasons. . . . And you will be witnesses to me."

The verb attributed to the disciples here, "to bring about the restoration" (ἀποκαθίστημι), is connected to the noun "universal restoration" (ἀποκατάστασις πάντων) (3:21 NJB) and may be an anticipation of its use later (→3:21). "Witnesses" here is used in the dual sense of "eyewitnesses" and "witness-bearers" (→2:31).

1:10 Like the "two men . . . in dazzling apparel" in Luke's telling of the Easter story (Luke 24:4), these were not "men" at all, but angels (→12:7).

"He Went Up, He Is Coming Again": Ascension and Second Coming

1:11 This Jesus, who was taken up from you into heaven, will come in the same way as you saw him go into heaven.

11. Irenaeus, *On the Apostolic Preaching* 3–6 (SVS 41–44).
12. Cyprian, *Testimonies* (*ANF* 5:507–57).
13. Athanasius, *Discourses against the Arians* 1–3 (*NPNF²* 4:303–432).

In the Epistles of Saint Paul, when they are compared with the Gospels, the resurrection of Christ and the ascension of Christ sometimes seem to be conflated.[14] For example, in the formula "therefore God has highly exalted him" (Phil. 2:9), which may have come from an earlier hymn or creed, it is not clear which of the two is meant or whether both are meant or even whether there is any distinction between them at all. His great chapter (1 Cor. 15) on the resurrection of Christ (→2:31) and on the general resurrection of the dead (→23:8) not only argues for the resurrection on a variety of grounds, including scriptural exegesis (1 Cor. 15:54–55), early Christian baptismal practice (1 Cor. 15:29), and analogies from nature (1 Cor. 15:37–42), but chronicles the appearances of the resurrected Christ, whether this chronicling is intended as historical evidence or not (→26:26): "He appeared to Cephas, then to the twelve. Then he appeared to more than five hundred brethren at one time, most of whom are still alive, though some have fallen asleep. Then he appeared to James, then to all the apostles. Last of all, as to one untimely born, he appeared also to me" (1 Cor. 15:5–8). But this catalog does not make any distinction of kind, only a distinction of time, between all those appearances before the ascension and the one to Paul on the road to Damascus (→9:1–4), which came after the ascension, followed as this appearance was also by other appearances of the risen Christ throughout the narrative of Acts (→16:9). By contrast, the chronological sequence of Luke's "unsentimental, almost uncannily austere"[15] narrative, like the chronological sequence of the eventual creeds (→8:37), clearly distinguishes between them. The ascension of Christ also appears at the close of Luke's Gospel (Luke 24:50–51), but in much briefer form and without the accompanying promise of the second coming.

With this equation between the Christ who came and the Christ who is to come, Christianity becomes once more—after a brief interval of "realization" during which it could be said that "the kingdom of God has come [ἔφθασεν]" (Luke 11:20) and that it is present "in the midst of you" (ἐντὸς ὑμῶν) (Luke 17:21)—a religion of waiting:[16] "In the Resurrection they saw the end, but not the beginning, and in the Ascension they saw the beginning, but not the end."[17] Thus the Niceno-Constantinopolitan Creed concludes its recital of what he was and did with the affirmation: "He is coming again with glory to judge the living and the dead; his kingdom will have be no end."[18] This perspective necessitated, already in the New Testament and then in the early centuries of the church, distinguishing among the messianic promises of the prophets (→8:30–31) between those that had come true in the historical birth, life, death, and resurrection of Jesus and those that would come true only at his "second"

14. See the overall discussions in Davies 1958 and Lohfink 1971.
15. Haenchen 1971, 151.
16. Erich Grässer in Kremer 1979, 99–127.
17. Chrysostom, *Homilies on Acts* 2 (*NPNF*[1] 11:13).
18. Niceno-Constantinopolitan Creed 7 (*CCF* 1:163).

coming.[19] Most of the time, the language of the prophets speaks of "the day of his coming" (ἡμέρα εἰσόδου αὐτοῦ) (Mal. 3:2 LXX) in the singular, as though there were only one coming. This has compelled the exegetes of the church to distinguish between the "first coming," in which the prophecy of Isaiah about the suffering servant (Isa. 53) had already been fulfilled (→8:30–31), and the "second coming," prior to which the prophecy of Isaiah about the wolf and the lamb feeding together (Isa. 65:25) would not be fulfilled, and to assign the various prophecies to one or the other of these.

By now, the period between the beginnings of the messianic hope in the people of Israel and the (first) coming of Christ, when his followers felt able to say that the time of waiting had ended, has shrunk to one-half or even one-third of the period since that first coming. Therefore the Christian church has been waiting for the Messiah much longer than Israel had been waiting for the Messiah when it was told, "Today this scripture has been fulfilled in your hearing" (Luke 4:21). The history of the church suggests that Christians are not very good at such waiting, as they have oscillated between an occasional eschatological fervor that stands on tiptoe and asks eagerly (and repeatedly), "Lord, is it at this time that you will bring about the restoration, and when will the kingdom of Israel be?" (1:6 TPR), and their more customary torpor, which has needed to be reminded yet again "that the end of the world comes suddenly," as Cyprian put it on the basis of this passage from Acts.[20] The relation between 1 Thessalonians (4:15–5:4) and 2 Thessalonians (2:1–12), and between the interpretations of each, documents this oscillation.

Therefore Christians need to be reminded that though the usual contrast may be accurate up to a point, it is not adequate to contrast Jewish and Christian belief as the difference between expectation and realization: both of them celebrate the memory and the present reality of "the Lord God of Israel, for he has visited and redeemed his people" (Luke 1:68) in the exodus and in the incarnation; and both of them still await the coming of the Messiah.

1:13 Although the sequence of the names of the apostles in the TPR is the same as the one reflected in the RSV and other versions, some other manuscripts read not "John and James and Andrew," but "James and John and Andrew," acknowledging the special standing of James, as this would make itself evident at the apostolic council in Jerusalem (15:13–21). Some manuscripts even read: "Andrew and James and John," reflecting the unique position of Andrew as "the first-called" (πρωτόκλητος),[21] which, because Andrew was remembered as the missionary to the Black Sea region and therefore eventually as the apostle to Constantinople, was to take on church-political significance, conferring on Constantinople its own "primacy" alongside Old Rome.[22] What the lists of

19. *Chr. Trad.* 1:123–32.
20. Cyprian, *Testimonies* 3.89 (*ANF* 5:553).
21. Sophocles 1870, 958.
22. Dvornik 1958.

the names of the apostles in Acts all have in common—and what they share with all the other rosters of disciples and apostles throughout the New Testament—is that the name Peter always appears first (→5:29a).

Mary the Theotokos

1:14 Together with the women and Mary the mother of Jesus.

The RSV rendering of σύν in 1:14 as "together with," rather than simply "with," as in the AV, serves to emphasize association rather than mere accompaniment, and therefore the solidarity of the disciples then, and of the church ever since, with Mary the mother of Jesus, as well as the unique and special place of the one who on the basis of Luke's Gospel has been saluted as "blessed . . . among women" (Luke 1:42) in the Christian community from the very beginning. While the Apostle Paul does not mention the virginal conception of Christ and refers to Mary the Theotokos only indirectly (Gal. 4:4) and never by name, much less by that later title (→19:26), Luke invokes her name more often, and allots more space to her story, than the other evangelists, including John, into whose care she was entrusted by Christ on the cross (John 19:26–27), or all the other New Testament writers combined. On the basis of his repeated statements that "Mary kept all these things, pondering them in her heart" (Luke 2:19, 51), it is taken to be evident, to "anyone who accepts the total historicity of this account," that "above all Mary, mother of Jesus, may be regarded as the principal source, more or less indirect, for the account of the infancy of the Savior" in his first two chapters,[23] or even that Luke based those chapters and his word portrait of the Blessed Virgin Mary on personal interviews with her. His identification of his historical source in the tradition "delivered to us by those who from the beginning [ἀπ᾿ ἀρχῆς] were eyewitnesses and ministers of the word" (Luke 1:2) would then be above all a reference to her. Specifically, she was the single eyewitness "from the [*very*] beginning" and the preeminent human actor for his narratives of the annunciation, nativity, and infancy, with their translationlike Greek (especially in the Magnificat) and their many unique and intimate details, which would have been known to her but to no one else (Luke 1–2). It was a recognition of this privileged position when, in the iconographic tradition, Luke was eventually portrayed (often also in icons) as having written the original icon of her, drawn from life.[24] Again in this verse, he singles out only her name, along with those of the (eleven) apostles and "*the* women" (the Greek article being distinctive of the TPR, although the RSV does employ it in English), as those who "with one accord devoted themselves to prayer" (→4:24–30).

23. L. Venard in *DTC* 9:981.
24. Onasch and Schnieper 1997, 187, 235.

As part of the typological interpretation of the Old Testament (→8:30–31), there developed a parallelism between the First and the Second Eve, corresponding to the parallelism in the Pauline Epistles between the First and the Second Adam (Rom. 5:12–15; 1 Cor. 15:21–22):[25] Eve sinned by voluntarily disobeying the word of God (Gen. 3:1–6); Mary believed and obeyed it by her voluntary declaration, "Let it be to me according to your word" (Luke 1:38). By the time this parallelism between Eve and Mary became explicit and was written down, which happened sometime in the second century,[26] it was not being proposed as a novelty or argued as a point of controversy, but appears to be taken for granted as a topic with which readers could be expected to be already familiar. Similarly, the earliest written references to the title "Mother of God" (θεοτόκος) for her are ambiguous, being identified by the lexicon as "interpolated" or "if authentic."[27] But the use of this term by Alexander of Alexandria, who died only three years after the Council of Nicea, was almost matter-of-fact;[28] and not long afterward, the emperor Julian "the Apostate" criticized his onetime fellow believers for constantly invoking the title "Theotokos."[29] That was why the Council of Ephesus in 431 felt entitled to claim, perhaps somewhat surprisingly, that in promulgating it, it was doing so "not by way of addition but in the manner of a full statement [οὐκ ἐν προσθήκης μέρει, ἀλλ' ἐν πληροφορίας εἴδει], even as we have received and possess it from of old from the Holy Scriptures and from the tradition of the holy fathers."[30] "In the icons of the Ascension," therefore, "the Mother of God occupies a very special position. Placed directly below the ascending Savior, she is as it were the axis of the whole composition." Thus "the principal place in them is given to a group consisting of the Mother of God, angels and apostles, whereas the principal figure, the ascending Savior Himself, is almost always much smaller than the other persons depicted and is as it were secondary in relation to them."[31]

The reference here to the "brothers" of Jesus has also been seen to call for some explanation, because it seems to contradict the references to Mary as ever virgin (ἀειπάρθενος, *semper virgo*), which are early though not primitive (at any rate in the written sources as these have come down to us).[32] The most detailed patristic explanation of the title "brothers," which was shared and even quoted by Luther, comes from Saint Jerome. As the translator of the Bible into Latin and as probably the greatest biblical scholar in the ancient church after Origen,

25. Daniélou 1960, 40–41.
26. Irenaeus, *On the Apostolic Preaching* 33 (SVS 61); *Against Heresies* 5.19.1 (*ANF* 1:547).
27. *PGL* 639.
28. Alexander of Alexandria, *Epistle to Alexander of Constantinople* 12 (PG 18:569).
29. Julian, *Against the Galileans* 262 (LCL 157:399).
30. Formula of Union of the Council of Ephesus (*CCF* 1:169).
31. Ouspensky and Lossky 1999, 194–95.
32. Among the earliest, Athanasius, *Discourses against the Arians* 2.70 (*NPNF*[2] 4:386 and note).

Jerome certainly knew this and the other New Testament passages referring to "brothers of Jesus" at least as well as the gainsayers of his time (and of our time); but he argued against Helvidius that "in Holy Scripture there are four kinds of brethren—by nature, race, kindred, love," so that passages such as this did not necessarily contradict the perpetual virginity of Mary.[33]

1:15 TPR Peter stood up in the midst of the disciples.

Although the TPR version of several crucial passages does present interesting variations, the primacy of Peter in these early chapters is evident (→5:29a), raising more questions than it answers about the primitive structure of "faith and order" in the church (→6:2–4).

1:16–20 The scripture had to be fulfilled.

This is the first of many references throughout Acts to the "fulfillment," and therefore to the normative interpretation, of this or that Old Testament Scripture (→8:30–31). The difference between the remorse of Judas and the repentance of Peter, together with the recurring use of phraseology such as "this scripture *had to* [δεῖ] be fulfilled" (1:16 TPR) gave rise, in Augustine and Calvin and in many lesser theological minds, to deeply troubling reflection about the relation between divine foreknowledge and human free will (→13:48): Could it be, in the inscrutable mystery of the ways of God (Rom. 11:33), that Judas Iscariot had been divinely predestined both to his shocking act of betrayal and to his own terrible end?

1:21–22 In his Gospel (Luke 6:13), Luke recorded how Jesus "called his disciples, and chose from them twelve, whom he named apostles," and their names are recorded. From 1:15, which in the TPR reads "among the *disciples*" rather than "among the brethren," and then from this sentence and from the usage here in Acts (→6:2–4), it is clear that the company of those with the title "disciples," which could also "increas[e] in number" (6:1) and could include relative neophytes (19:1–7) as well as woman disciples (→18:24–26b), was much more inclusive than the twelve "apostles." With the apostasy of Judas, the integrity of the twelve had to be restored, perhaps because of the typology of the twelve tribes of Israel (Luke 22:28–30). These verses list, in almost technical language, the credentials that a candidate had to possess to be added to the other apostles, beginning with being "a male" (ἀνήρ) (→18:24–26b); and Matthias possessed the credentials. But did Paul qualify as an apostle on this basis? On some later lists and in some later depictions of the twelve, the two groups of six are headed by Peter and by Paul, with no mention of Matthias.[34] Paul's claim to be "an apostle" because he had "seen Jesus our Lord"

33. Jerome, *Against Helvidius* 16–18 (*NPNF*[2] 6:341–43).
34. Onasch and Schnieper 1997, 188–89.

(1 Cor. 9:1) on the Damascus road (→9:1–4; →16:9), even though he had not "known Christ after the flesh" (2 Cor. 5:16 AV), did make him "a witness with us to his resurrection" in a special way, which was shared by Stephen, though only in the hour of his death (7:56). But "witness to his resurrection" here as elsewhere seems to refer primarily to those in any generation who bear witness to it—"witnesses *to me*" (μοι μάρτυρες), the TPR has at 1:8, not μου μάρτυρες ("my witnesses")—rather than only to those of the first generation who had witnessed it (→2:31).

1:23–24 TPR And he put forward two . . . and he prayed and said.

This is one of the many striking textual variants included in the TPR of Acts: καὶ ἔστησεν (rather than ἔστησαν, "they put forward") δύο and καὶ προσευξάμενος εἶπεν (rather than προσευξάμενοι εἶπαν, "they prayed and said"). This use of the singular would locate in only one of the apostles, presumably in Peter who had been speaking (1:15), the authority for nominating the candidates to fill the office vacated by Judas and for praying on behalf of all, although both textual traditions attribute the casting of lots to all the apostles—the TPR reads ἔδωκαν κλήρους αὐτῶν rather than αὐτοῖς—and the ultimate decision remains exclusively a divine one in either textual tradition, through the casting of lots, which was seen not as a matter of "dumb luck" (τύχη) but as a revelation of the will of God.[35]

1:24 With its reminiscences of passages such as "O Lord, thou hast proved me and known me" (κύριε, ἐδοκίμασάς με καὶ ἔγνως με) (Ps. 139:1 LXX), the uniquely Christian adjective "knower of hearts" (καρδιογνώστης) identifies one of the distinctive attributes of "the living God" (→15:8–9), who has "set . . . our secret sins in the light of thy countenance" (Ps. 90:8).

1:25 NEB Which Judas abandoned to go where he belonged.

This could mean simply "where he deserved to go" or, more ominously, "where he was intended to go" (→13:48).

1:26 TPR And he was numbered among the twelve apostles.

With δώδεκα rather than the ἕνδεκα of the manuscript tradition underlying the RSV, the TPR is employing "the twelve" as a technical title (→5:29a). Augustine (in Latin) uses, and seems to reflect, a compromise reading between the two: "as the twelfth, together with the eleven apostles" (*cum undecim apostolis duodecimus*).[36]

35. Beardslee 1960–61.
36. Boismard 2000, 59.

ACTS 2

"And in the Holy Spirit": The Fullness of the Church

2:1 AV When the day of Pentecost was fully come.

The affirmative articles of the Nicene Creed of 325 conclude with the words "and in the Holy Spirit," with no further explanation.[1] But it was the expansion of these words about the doctrine of the Holy Spirit in the closing articles of the Niceno-Constantinopolitan Creed of 381 that made the latter creed a full-blown confession of the Trinity in a way that the creed of 325 had not been, which is why "the expounding of the dogma of the Trinity is the fundamental theological theme of the festival of Pentecost."[2] But the Niceno-Constantinopolitan Creed did not content itself with repeating the method it had employed in its articles about the second hypostasis of the Trinity—"begotten from the Father before all the ages, light from light, true God from true God, begotten not made, consubstantial [ὁμοούσιος] with the Father"—by explaining why a confession of faith in the third hypostasis was legitimate because the Spirit was "proceeding forth from the Father, co-worshiped and co-glorified with Father and Son" (→4:24–30).[3] Instead, the subject of these closing articles was the fullness of the church as "one, holy, catholic, and apostolic," as this was constituted by baptism and as it was sustained by the hope of eternal life.[4]

Therefore the AV's translation "when the day of Pentecost was fully come" here, like the Vulgate's *cum compleretur*, is an attempt to convey an emphasis on the "fullness" (πλήρωμα) of the Holy Spirit, which seems to be suggested by the Greek ἐν τῷ συμπληροῦσθαι, but which does not come through as explicitly

1. Nicene Creed 8 (*CCF* 1:159).
2. Ouspensky and Lossky 1999, 200.
3. Niceno-Constantinopolitan Creed 8 (*CCF* 1:163).
4. Niceno-Constantinopolitan Creed 2, 9–12 (*CCF* 1:163).

in the more prosaic "had come" of RSV and NRSV or even the "came round" of NJB. There are at least two significant parallels to this locution elsewhere in the New Testament: the "hinge passage" of transition to the passion story in Luke's Gospel, "When the days for his being lifted up had been fulfilled [ἐν τῷ συμπληροῦσθαι τὰς ἡμέρας τῆς ἀναλήμψεως αὐτοῦ], he set his face to go to Jerusalem" (Luke 9:51); and the words of Paul, "When the fulness of the time was come [ὅτε δὲ ἦλθεν τὸ πλήρωμα τοῦ χρόνου], God sent forth his Son" (Gal. 4:4 AV). As is evident in both of these passages, the first on the passion and the second on the incarnation, the emphasis on the time having "fully come" is "not understood in a strictly chronological sense, but in the setting of the history of salvation."[5] The coming of the Holy Spirit on the disciples at Pentecost fulfilled "the promise of the Father, which, he said, you heard from my mouth" (1:4 TPR), which, as Luke had written earlier (Luke 12:2) and as the Gospel of John described at considerably greater length (John 14:16–17; 15:26–27; 16:7–15), had been given by Jesus during the days of his earthly ministry.

This theological theme of the connection between the Holy Spirit and "fullness" runs through the entire narrative of Acts.[6] Here in the Pentecost event, "they were all filled with the Holy Spirit" (2:4); and here in the Pentecost sermon of Peter (2:28), the promise of the Psalm (Ps. 16:11 LXX), "thou wilt fill me with joy with thy countenance," is said to have been uniquely carried out in Jesus Christ. As he was defending the message before the high priest, "Peter [was] filled with the Holy Spirit" (4:8), and the company of believers "were all filled with the Holy Spirit and spoke the word of God with boldness to anyone who was willing to believe" (4:31 TPR). In a dramatic contrast between the two diametrically opposite ways of "being filled," with Ananias it was "Satan [who] has filled your heart to lie to the Holy Spirit" (5:3). The requirement stipulated for the new deacons who were to be appointed was that they be "full of the Spirit and of wisdom" (6:3); and one of them was "Stephen, a man full of faith and of the Holy Spirit" (6:5), who was "full of grace and power" (6:8) and who at his protomartyr's death, "full of the Holy Spirit, gazed into heaven and saw the glory of God, and Jesus standing at the right hand of God" (7:55). Barnabas, too, "was a good man, full of the Holy Spirit and of faith" (11:24). After his conversion, Saul was assured by Ananias that he would "regain [his] sight and be filled with the Holy Spirit" (9:17), and so "Saul, who is also called Paul, [was] filled with the Holy Spirit" when he denounced the sorcerer as "you son of the devil, you enemy of all righteousness, full of all deceit and villainy" (13:9–10). Not only Paul, but all "the disciples were filled with joy and with the Holy Spirit" (13:52).

Although, as the defenders of orthodoxy had to acknowledge,[7] there were not early liturgical prayers addressed to the Holy Spirit (→5:3–4) as there were to

5. Grässer 1957, 208.
6. David Peterson in Winter and Clarke 1993–94, 1:83–104.
7. Gregory of Nazianzus, *Orations* 31.12 (SVS 125–26).

the Son of God (7:59), so that they could not use such prayers as proof texts for the deity of the Spirit (→4:24–30)—the great exception being the Gloria Patri, with variants in the prepositions that became themselves the occasion of controversy[8]—the definitive formulation of the dogma of the Holy Trinity by the First Council of Constantinople in 381 eventually gave rise to such prayers to the Holy Spirit. Before the formal opening of the Liturgy of Saint John Chrysostom the priest prays to the "Heavenly King, the Comforter, the Spirit of truth, who art everywhere and fillest all things"; and in the Latin West, probably in the ninth century, there arose this prayer for the fullness that the Holy Spirit grants:

Veni, Creator Spiritus,	Come, Holy Ghost, Creator blest,
mentes tuorum visita,	Vouchsafe within our souls to rest.
imple superna gratia,	Come with thy power and heavenly aid,
quae tu creasti, pectora.	And *fill* the hearts which thou hast made.[9]

It is sung not only at Pentecost, but for ordinations and for the opening of synods and church councils[10]—and any church council that sings it at its opening must be prepared to deal with the possible consequences! It is also the text for the first movement of Gustav Mahler's *Eighth Symphony*.

The sneer "they are filled with new wine" (2:13) and Peter's dismissive and even humorous (→12:13–16) response to this canard, "These men are not drunk, as you suppose, it being only the third hour of the day" (2:15 TPR), do call to mind the contrast drawn by Paul between the right and the wrong way of being filled: "Do not get drunk with wine, for that is debauchery; but be filled with the Spirit, addressing one another in psalms and hymns and spiritual songs, singing and making melody to the Lord with all your heart" (Eph. 5:18–19). It is right to want to be "filled" with something, and the drunkard quite properly recognizes that human nature stands in need of some power that will take it out of itself (as alcohol and drugs do). But this need also includes the requirement that such fullness will in the process not corrupt and destroy it (as alcohol also does), but fulfill it by loosening the tongue and making it sing—but "to the Lord." As Cyril of Jerusalem paraphrased Peter's words here, "They are drunken, with a sober drunkenness, deadly to sin and life-giving to the heart, a drunkenness contrary to that of the body; for this last causes forgetfulness even of what was known, but that bestows the knowledge even of what was not known."[11] This paradox was to become a theme especially in the literature of Christian mysticism in both East and West.[12]

The concept of the fullness of the Holy Spirit also becomes evident in the account (19:2–6 TPR) of those "disciples" in Ephesus whom Paul asked, "Did

8. Basil of Caesarea, *On the Holy Spirit* 1.3 (SVS 17–18).
9. Raby 1959, 116.
10. Julian 1957, 1206–11.
11. Cyril of Jerusalem, *Catechetical Lectures* 17.19 (*NPNF*[2] 7:128).
12. On "sober drunkenness," see Lewy 1929.

you receive the Holy Spirit when you believed?" and who replied, "No, we have never even heard that some have received the Holy Spirit" (or even, as in the AV and RSV, "No, we have never even heard that there is a Holy Spirit"). When they received Christian baptism "in the name of the Lord Jesus for the forgiveness of sins" (→22:16) in place of the baptism of John (→19:2–3), and when Paul laid his hand on them (→6:6), "the Holy Spirit fell on them, and they spoke in tongues and interpreted them themselves and prophesied" (19:6 TPR). Although they are specifically identified as already being "disciples" (μαθηταί) (19:1) in spite of their inadequacy, they achieved the fullness of that discipleship only when they received baptism and the Holy Spirit.

The primacy of the free divine initiative in the "coming" of the Holy Spirit is dramatically heightened in those several passages of the book of Acts where the Holy Spirit is described as not only "coming upon" persons, but as "falling" upon them. In the passage just quoted (19:6), the TPR has "the Holy Spirit fell [ἐπέπεσεν] on them" rather than "the Holy Spirit came to [ἦλθε] them," which other manuscripts have; and at the conclusion of the account of the baptism of the Ethiopian eunuch it has the report that "when they came up out of the water, the Holy Spirit fell upon the eunuch" (8:39 TPR). But all the textual traditions, not only the TPR, read that way at several other places: "While Peter was still saying this, the Holy Spirit fell on [ἐπέπεσεν] all who heard the word" (10:44); again, in the words of Peter: "As I began to speak, the Holy Spirit fell on them just as on us at the beginning" (11:15); earlier, too: "the Holy Spirit . . . had not yet fallen on any of them" (8:15–16). The words of Peter, "just as on us at the beginning," suggest that the freedom of the Holy Spirit to "blow where it wills" (John 3:8) is often implied even in places where the verb πίπτειν ("to fall") is not being employed, as particularly here in the account of Pentecost. Above all, that implication is at work in the standard transitive verb for the "coming" of the Holy Spirit, which is "to send" (πέμπειν): especially in the Gospel of John, where it is the usual technical term for the coming of the Son of God as sent by his Father, it is also employed for the coming of the Holy Spirit (John 14:26; 15:26; 16:7).[13] In the light of subsequent controversy[14] it bears explaining, on the basis of the distinction between "theology" and "economy" (→15:8–9), that this "sending" of the Holy Spirit by the Father *and the Son* was described as "economic," that is, within the dispensation of human history, by contrast with the eternal "proceeding" (ἐκπορεύεσθαι) within the Godhead, which was "from the Father" and not from the Son (John 15:26).[15] The range of that freedom of the Spirit is also the theological presupposition for the varieties of how Christians have experienced conversion, whether they were instantaneously "born anew" (John 3:3) or "were persuaded" (ἐπείσθησαν)

13. BDAG 794.
14. *Chr. Trad.* 2:183–98.
15. Niceno-Constantinopolitan Creed 8 (*CCF* 1:162–63); Niceno-Constantinopolitan Creed: Occidental Recension 8 (*CCF* 1:672).

(17:4) gradually, sometimes almost imperceptibly, through the preaching and teaching of the word of God (→9:1–4).

The varieties in the manifestation of the Spirit would include the special inspiration of the apostles. "Peter, filled with the Holy Spirit, said to them" (4:8): when combined with the apostolic claim to be speaking "in words not taught by human wisdom but taught by the Spirit" (1 Cor. 2:13) and with the apostolic extension of this authority from "word of mouth" to "letter" (2 Thess. 2:15), this inspiring action of the Holy Spirit was eventually taken to include the New Testament in the attribute "inspired by God" (θεόπνευστος) (2 Tim. 3:16) that had originally been predicated only of the Old Testament (→8:25). Also included as a manifestation of the Spirit was the gift of tongues here at Pentecost. From the experience of the church at Corinth it is evident that ecstatic speech under the extraordinary working of the Holy Spirit was one of the special "spiritual gifts" (πνευματικά) (1 Cor. 12:1), sometimes—especially after the New Testament—called χαρίσματα,[16] that continued to appear, if sporadically, also after Pentecost, including "gifts of healing," "the working of miracles" (→6:8), "various kinds of tongues," and "the interpretation of tongues" (1 Cor. 12:4–11). In the modern era, the presence or absence of these spiritual gifts has not only become an issue in the rise of Pentecostalism as a radical form of "dynamic" Protestantism in opposition to the supposedly "static" elements of the Catholic tradition, but in the "charismatic renewal movement" that has been taking place within the Roman Catholic, Anglican, and other traditional churches.[17]

The catholicity of the church (→22:27) here is defined as linguistic and geographic, "run[ning] from east to west,"[18] rather than ethnic. It is anticipated in the variety of territories that are represented (though only, it seems, by "Jews, devout men from every nation under heaven . . . both Jews and proselytes" (2:5, 10), not by pagan Gentiles from those nations) and into which the message would eventually penetrate, beginning already in the later chapters of Acts. But among the creedal marks of the church as "one, holy, catholic, and apostolic,"[19] the emphasis in the Pentecost miracle is on the unity of the church even more than on its catholicity, because Pentecost represents the undoing of the Tower of Babel, where the human race, which until then "was one lip, and there was one language to all," had been punished for its pride by God, who "confused the language of all the earth . . . that they may not understand each the voice of his neighbor" (Gen. 11:1–9 LXX). Language, especially the eloquent and persuasive language that is the object of rhetorical study, is a prominent feature of the narrative here in Acts (→24:1–2); but so are languages in their infinite variety (→21:37), which are the object of linguistic study. The text speaks

16. BDAG 837, 1081; *PGL* 1104–5, 1518–19.
17. *ODCC* 1253–54, 321.
18. Chrysostom, *Homilies on Acts* 4 (*NPNF*[1] 11:26).
19. Niceno-Constantinopolitan Creed 9 (*CCF* 1:163).

expressly of "other tongues" (ἑτέραις γλώσσαις) (2:4), apparently meaning the languages spoken by the Parthian Jews, Arabian Jews, and all the others. But at 2:8 the word is "*we hear*, each of us" (ἀκούομεν ἕκαστος), which suggests the appearance here not of a polyglot congregation but of the phenomenon of glossalalia familiar from the experience of the Christian community in Corinth (1 Cor. 14). Did the apostles actually speak—or did those present only hear—all of these other languages?[20]

This catalog of nations is by no means exhaustive, for as Pope John Paul II said in his Pentecost homily at Gniezno, on 3 June 1979, upon his first visit to his Polish homeland after his election, describing the mission of Cyril and Methodius, "equals to the apostles,"[21] to Greater Moravia in the ninth century:

> After so many centuries the Jerusalem upper room was again opened up and amazement fell no longer on the peoples of Mesopotamia and Judea, Egypt and Asia, and visitors from Rome, but also on the Slav peoples and the other peoples living in this part of Europe, as they heard the apostles of Jesus Christ speaking in their tongue and telling in their language "the mighty works of God." . . . These languages cannot fail to be heard especially by the first Slav Pope in the history of the Church. Perhaps that is why Christ has chosen him, perhaps that is why the Holy Spirit has led him—in order that he might introduce into the communion of the Church the understanding of the words and of the languages that still sound strange to the ear accustomed to the Romance, Germanic, English and Celtic tongues.[22]

2:14 Ordinarily "the twelve" (οἱ δώδεκα) is the technical term for the disciples throughout the New Testament (e.g., Luke 8:1); but it was reduced to "eleven" in these early chapters of Acts, or even to "ten" here in the TPR of this verse, either to take account of the apostasy of Judas (1:26) or—though this is considerably less likely, except perhaps in a passage like this one—to single out the primacy of Peter (→5:29a).

2:15 Peter's observation that it was too early in the day for these men to be drunk does carry at least a touch of humor (→12:13–16).

2:22–23 (→6:8; →26:26). Except perhaps for the words in the first chapter about Judas "go[ing] where he belonged" (1:25 NEB), this is the first reference in Acts to the mysterious—and ultimately unfathomable—relation between the accountability of human free will and the omniscient "foreknowledge" (πρόγνωσις) of God, which does not observe human action as though God were a neutral and helpless spectator, but has what is termed here a "definite

20. Bede, *Exposition of the Acts of the Apostles* 2 (PL 92:947).
21. Sophocles 1870, 603.
22. Pope John Paul II in Levi 1982, 1:3–4.

plan" (ὡρισμένη βουλή) for it. Here this term applies directly to the death of Christ (→13:48), but as the central event of the total "economy" or plan of salvation (→15:8–9). This reference to Pontius Pilate and the Roman authorities as "lawless men," whose "hands" were the most directly responsible for the unjust killing of the innocent Jesus, must be seen in the total context of how the book of Acts depicts the Roman Empire, its emperor and entire power structure (→25:11), as well as of how it deals with Roman law (→25:8), and, on the other hand, in the light of how it speaks about the Jewish adversaries of Jesus (→3:25) and about the "law" in Judaism (→10:15).

"Rose Up on the Third Day": The Centrality of the Resurrection of Christ

2:31 He foresaw and spoke of the resurrection of the Christ.

Luke the historian and theologian (→27:1) is able to move from his Gospel to the book of Acts smoothly and seamlessly. The only overlap between the two accounts is his telling of the ascension, first in the final chapter of the Gospel (Luke 24:50–53) and then somewhat more extensively in the opening chapter of Acts (1:1–11). But the numerous other cross-references between the two, many of them obvious but some of them more subtle (→7:59–60), help to assure the literary unity and the theological coherence of the two-volume work seen as a single composition, indeed, as a "diptych";[23] they are also the reason that parallel passages to the book of Acts from the Gospels in this commentary are, if possible, being drawn from Luke.

But the literary unity and the theological coherence of Luke-Acts are carried preeminently by the resonances of the Easter narrative from the final chapter of the Gospel (Luke 24) throughout the chapters of the Acts, as "with great power the apostles gave their testimony to the resurrection of the Lord Jesus" (4:33), over and over and to a great variety of audiences. The bemused account that Festus the governor gave "about one Jesus, who was dead, but whom Paul asserted to be alive" had, as he himself admitted, left him "at a loss" (25:19–20). In his Pentecost homily in this chapter (2:14–36) Saint Peter rang the changes of the confession that was to be finalized in the formula of the Niceno-Constantinopolitan Creed: "And rose up on the third day."[24]

"How to speak about the resurrection of Christ?"[25] The resurrection of Christ was the supreme manifestation of the divine dialectic that had been typologically foreshadowed in the recognition scene between the patriarch Joseph and his brothers: "You took counsel against me for evil, but God took

23. Marguerat 1999, 91–92; Tarazi 2001, 19.
24. Niceno-Constantinopolitan Creed 5 (*CCF* 1:163).
25. Nikanor 1905, 1:30, 59.

counsel on my behalf for good" (Gen. 50:20 LXX); that declaration "but God took counsel" (ὁ δὲ θεὸς ἐβουλεύσατο) is suggested also in the phrase of this chapter, "the definite plan and foreknowledge of God" (τῇ ὡρισμένῃ βουλῇ καὶ προγνώσει τοῦ θεοῦ) (2:23), and in Paul's boast to the Ephesian elders of having "declar[ed] . . . the whole counsel of God [πᾶσαν τὴν βουλὴν τοῦ θεοῦ]" (20:27). Therefore the confession that "God raised him up" (2:24) is part of a sentence the other clause of which refers to how "you crucified and killed" him "by the hands of lawless men" (2:23). And so it is with most of the references in Acts to the resurrection of Christ. In the next chapter Saint Peter declares at Solomon's Portico: You "killed the Author of life, whom God raised from the dead" (3:15). In the chapter after that he announces "the name of Jesus Christ of Nazareth, whom you crucified, whom God raised from the dead" (4:10). In the chapter after that he confesses: "The God of our fathers raised Jesus whom you killed by hanging him on a tree" (5:30). And so the refrain of the dialectic of crucifixion and resurrection continues (10:39–40; 13:28–30).

Quoting (2:27) the words of Ps. 16:10 LXX, "For thou wilt not abandon my soul to Hades, or let thy Holy One see corruption," Peter affirms the resurrection of Christ as the vindication of the power of the living God (→15:8–9), as the Epistle to the Hebrews says, "that through death he might destroy him who has the power of death, that is, the devil, and deliver all those who through fear of death were subject to lifelong bondage" (Heb. 2:14–15). In the crucifixion and resurrection of Christ, his conflict with the powers of sin, death, and the devil (→13:8–11), as seen already in the temptation at the inauguration of his ministry (Luke 4:1–13) and in his authority over the demons, reaches its climax when "God raised him up, having loosed the pangs of death, because it was not possible for him to be held by it" (2:24). In the twentieth century, the Masai Creed picks up this apostolic witness with its dramatic confession: "He lay buried in the grave, but the hyenas did not touch him, and on the third day, he rose from the grave."[26]

The crucifixion and resurrection supremely documented the fulfillment of prophecy. It was the prophecy of the crucifixion in Isaiah's account of the suffering servant (Isa. 53:7–8) that the Ethiopian was reading aloud when "Philip opened his mouth, and beginning with this scripture he told him the good news of Jesus" (8:35). Peter's Pentecost message was a catena of the familiar passages from the prophets and the Psalms in which David "foresaw [προϊδών] and spoke of the resurrection of the Christ" (2:31). As if in anticipation of the Ethiopian's question to Philip concerning Isaiah, "About whom, pray, does the prophet say this, about himself or about some one else?" (8:34), Peter combined a close reading of David's psalm (Ps. 16:8–11) with the public evidence (→26:26) of a Jewish pilgrimage site, to argue that in this affirmation of the power of life over death David could not have been speaking about himself, because "he both died and was buried, and his tomb is with us to this day,"

26. Masai Creed 2 (*CCF* 3:569).

but could only have been speaking about "one of his descendants" (2:29–30), namely, Jesus of Nazareth.

When Peter went on to say, "This Jesus God raised up, and of that we all are witnesses [μάρτυρες]" (2:32), it does not seem to be straining the language unduly to take him to be using the word "witness"[27] in both of its meanings in the modern English usage of the word: as "eyewitness" (αὐτόπτης) (Luke 1:2), meaning someone who saw the risen Christ; and as one who bears witness and gives testimony about the risen Christ, being a "witness to me" (μοι μάρτυς) (1:8 TPR). The most comprehensive catalog of "witnesses" to the resurrection in the former sense is from Saint Paul: "That he was buried, that he was raised on the third day in accordance with the scriptures, and that he appeared to Cephas, then to the twelve. Then he appeared to more than five hundred brethren at one time. . . . Then he appeared to James, then to all the apostles. Last of all, as to one untimely born, he appeared also to me" (1 Cor. 15:4–8). That accumulating of eyewitnesses in Saint Paul's First Epistle to the Corinthians does appear to be laying claim to evidentiary force (→26:26), as does his arguing to the Athenians that "of this he has given assurance to all men [πίστιν παρασχών πᾶσιν] by raising him from the dead" (17:31), the Greek term πίστις apparently being used here in the sense of "proof" as it usually is in Aristotle's *Rhetoric*,[28] rather than in the sense of "faith" as it usually is in the New Testament.[29] But in another sermon Peter downplays any such claim to evidentiary force with the important qualifier: "God raised him on the third day and made him to be manifest; *not to all the people but to us* who were chosen by God as witnesses, who ate and drank with him after he rose from the dead" (10:40–41); as Origen had to acknowledge in response to the pagan critic Celsus,[30] the only ones who ever saw the risen Christ were already converts or (in the case of Paul who was "one born out of due time [ἔκτρωμα]"; 1 Cor. 15:8 AV) were about to be converted. The importance of what we have called the second sense of the English word "witness," which is what "martyr" (μάρτυς) means, is underlined in the report that "with great power the apostles gave their testimony [ἀπεδίδουν τὸ μαρτύριον] to the resurrection of the Lord Jesus" (4:33), which the church has continued to do in its worship, preaching, and confession of faith long after the last "witness" in the first sense of the English word had died.

Both in the dissertation on the resurrection in 1 Cor. 15 and here in Acts, the theological connection between the resurrection of Christ and the general resurrection (→23:8) appears to be somewhat problematic. On the one hand, the burden of the apostolic proclamation is "Jesus in the resurrection of the dead" (4:2 TPR), making the general resurrection causally dependent on the resurrection of Jesus; but on the other hand, the question of Paul to Agrippa,

27. On its use in early Christianity, see Origen, *Commentary on John* 28 (*ANF* 10:343).
28. Grimaldi 1980, 19–21.
29. BDAG 818–20.
30. Origen, *Contra Celsum* 2.63 (Chadwick 1953, 114).

"Why is it thought incredible by any of you that God raises the dead?" (26:8), appears to posit the general resurrection as an article of Jewish (or at any rate Pharisaic) doctrine (23:8; 24:15), even independently of the resurrection of Christ. In 1 Corinthians Paul does seem to be taking the latter tack when he argues: "If there is no resurrection of the dead, then Christ has not been raised" (1 Cor. 15:13).

2:36 The initial impression upon reading the word "made" (ἐποίησεν) might seem to be that Jesus had been neither "Lord" (κύριος) nor "Christ" (χριστός) and Messiah until the resurrection, as some early heretics were charged with teaching; but this passage needs to be considered in the light of the entire confession of the early church (→1:11; →8:37; →15:8–9; →24:24–25a).

2:37 This is only one among many references throughout the book of Acts to the power of the spoken word that could "cut to the heart" and effect contrition (→26:20). This spoken word of the gospel was a means of grace by which the power of the Holy Spirit was conveyed and conferred (→8:25). It was thus also an instrument by which, sometimes dramatically and sometimes more gradually, conversion took place (→9:1–4). But Peter's speech here—and, more generally, the place of speeches and sermons in the narrative of Acts—must also be seen in the light of the Christian adaptation of classical rhetoric, which was also designed to cut to the human heart (→24:1–2).

2:38 Repent, and be baptized every one of you in the name of Jesus Christ for the forgiveness of your sins; and you shall receive the gift of the Holy Spirit.

A capsule summary itemizes all the constituent elements of the early Christian doctrine of baptism (→22:16).

2:41 This is one of several statistical passages about church growth, but it also raises, at least by implication, the problem of continuity as the "apostolic" church was becoming "catholic."

"One, Holy, Catholic, and Apostolic Church": Marks of Continuity

2:42 TPR And they were persisting in the doctrine of the apostles and in fellowship, in the breaking of bread and in prayer.

While it is, strictly speaking, accurate to observe with Jacob Jervell that in Acts "Luke does not speak of the Christians primarily as 'church,' but as a people,"[31] so that he can have James say that "God first visited the Gentiles, to

31. Jervell 1996, 34; see also Esler 1987.

take out of them *a people* for his name" (15:14) where one might have expected
church, it does not do violence to the text of Acts to make "the church" a major
doctrinal theme running through the entire book (→2:1; →2:42; →4:32; →5:29a;
→9:4–5; →15:28; →22:27).

Among the four identifying marks of the church as listed in the catalog of
the Niceno-Constantinopolitan Creed, "one, holy, catholic, and apostolic,"[32]
unity comes first. In the formula of Saint Cyprian of Carthage, which he took
to be based on the "common mind [that] prevailed once, in the time of the
Apostles," as this "common mind" was documented in the opening chapters of
Acts, "God is one, and Christ is one, and His Church is one; one is the faith,
and one the people cemented together by harmony into the strong unity of
a body."[33]

This verse is, in the first instance, intended as a *de*scriptive statement, in
keeping with the historiographical design of the entire narrative, written for the
situation of the Christian community some decades later. It explains both "the
internal state and the external position of the church of Christ":[34] that although
even after the resurrection and "the gospel of the forty days" (→1:2–3) there
were still large gaps in theological perception (→18:24–26a) among those who
adhered to "the Way" (→11:26), the ascension of Christ had not left his followers
"desolate" (ὀρφανούς) (John 14:18); but by the gift of the Holy Spirit "they were
persisting" and maintaining a continuity with him and with his apostles in this
communion of saints. But theologically, it is also *pre*scriptive, as an itemized list
of the criteria by which the church in any age would both preserve and manifest
its continuity with the apostles.

Such a continuity with the apostles was both necessary and potentially controversial. When it is said that these first-generation believers "were persisting"
(ἦσαν . . . προσκαρτεροῦντες), such a periphrastic use of the participle with a
verb that even by itself can be taken to mean to "continue" or "persevere"[35]
refers to what Luke Timothy Johnson calls "continuing and consistent patterns
of behavior."[36] Continuity is also the theme of the visit of Barnabas to Antioch,
as Luke reports: "He exhorted them all to remain faithful to the Lord with
steadfast purpose [τῇ προθέσει τῆς καρδίας προσμένειν τῷ κυρίῳ]" (11:23). Challenges to this apostolic continuity came from opposite directions: from those
who insisted on a continuity in the observance of the law of Moses about diet
and circumcision (→10:15) and a few decades later from Marcion of Pontus,
who accused the church of wrongly maintaining an excessive continuity with
Judaism and thus of having disrupted apostolic continuity with Paul, the only

32. Niceno-Constantinopolitan Creed 9 (*CCF* 1:163).
33. Cyprian, *Unity of the Catholic Church* 23–25 (ACW 25:65–66).
34. Bogolepov 1900, 405–8.
35. BDAG 881.
36. Johnson 1992, 58.

genuine apostle.[37] As described here by Luke, the continuity with the apostles was preserved in these four areas:

1. *Apostolic "doctrine"* (διδαχή). Central to this "doctrine of the apostles," whether or not it was already embodied in a more or less stabilized oral creed (→8:37), was, as this chapter had made clear earlier (→2:31), the witness to the resurrection of Christ, together with the confession (→4:20): "I believe that Jesus Christ is the Son of God" (8:37 TPR AV). Not only from the ambiguous language of the apostles' witness in this chapter (2:36) and elsewhere, but from the candid admission in a later chapter that someone who was "well versed in the scriptures" and had been "instructed in the way of the Lord" nevertheless needed to have a sister (Priscilla) and a brother (Aquila) "expound to him the way of God more accurately" (→18:24–26a), it is evident that, during the three centuries between this time and the Councils of Nicea (325) and Constantinople (381), the confession of this apostolic doctrine would require further clarification, though without changing in its substance. This paradoxical phenomenon has been called, since John Henry Newman's *Essay* of 1845, "the development of Christian doctrine." A major historical force in bringing it about was theological controversy (→15:2), together with the deeper study of the Scriptures (→8:30–31).

2. *Apostolic "fellowship"* (κοινωνία). In Chrysostom's reminder, based on this passage, "the fellowship was not only in prayers, nor in doctrine alone, but also in social relations [πολιτεία]."[38] With a great variety of other meanings,[39] κοινωνία in the New Testament also referred to ἡ κοινωνία τῆς διακονίας (2 Cor. 8:4), a sharing in and an adherence to the apostolic ministry through the laying-on of hands (→6:2–4; →6:6). It is above all in the Pastoral Epistles, 1–2 Timothy and Titus, that this component of apostolic continuity is articulated: a gradually emerging distinction between "the office of bishop" (1 Tim. 3:1) and that of "deacons" (1 Tim. 3:8), an emphasis on "the gift . . . which was given you by prophetic utterance when the council of elders laid their hands upon you" (1 Tim. 4:14), and the imperative of guarding the "deposit" of faith (1 Tim. 6:20 Vulgate). At least partly because this view of the apostolic ministry seems so advanced by comparison with the usage here in Acts and in the other Pauline Epistles, many (but by no means all) modern New Testament critics question whether Paul was really, as the texts claimed (1 Tim. 1:1; 2 Tim. 1:1; Titus 1:1), the author of the Pastoral Epistles.

3. *Apostolic "breaking of bread" and the other sacraments.* The New Testament does not present us with a total sacramental system, which, in fact,

37. *Chr. Trad.* 1:71–81.
38. Chrysostom, *Homilies on Acts* 7 (*NPNF*[1] 11:45).
39. BDAG 552–53.

took many centuries until it developed in the medieval Scholasticism of the Western church.[40] What it does describe are individual actions that were eventually defined as a *sacramentum* or μυστήριον—in a technical sense that these terms do not possess in New Testament usage, not even in the passages that were later applied to the seven sacraments (1 Cor. 4:1; Eph. 5:32). But the Acts of the Apostles does single out baptism (→22:16) and the Eucharist (→20:7), which between them would also define the terms to which other actions had to conform to be identified as "sacraments," above all dominical institution (whether such an act of instituting by Christ was explicitly cited in the Gospels or authenticated by tradition).

4. *Apostolic "prayer" and worship* (→4:24–30). If the definite article here, τῇ προσευχῇ ("the prayer") in the TPR or ταῖς προσευχαῖς ("the prayers") in NA[27], is not "generic" but "individual,"[41] which may be more likely with the plural than with the singular, it does appear to suggest the presence, already at this early stage, of more or less fixed texts and liturgical forms: the Lord's Prayer in a special category, although the variations in its text both within the New Testament (Matt. 6:9–13; Luke 11:2–4) and in the next generations, together with the textually dubious (→20:28a) closing doxology, must fundamentally qualify any claims that the prayers were unchangeable; the eucharistic prayer or prayers, as documented in the *Didache*;[42] and such a prayer as the one quoted in a later chapter of Acts (→4:24–30), which at least may be said to follow a standard outline or template, if not a standard text. At the same time, descriptions of prayers and services in Acts provided a historian of the church such as Socrates Scholasticus with evidence that in the area of liturgical observance "many differences existed even in the apostolic age of the church."[43]

The interrelation between these four criteria, and particularly between the first two (defined in modern ecumenical usage as "faith and order"; →6:2–4), would dominate all subsequent efforts to understand the unity of the church and the divisions within Christendom, as well as the efforts to obey the imperative of Christ's prayer "that they may all be one" (John 17:21).

2:43 As Christ had promised it would be, his power to perform "wonders and signs" was communicated to the disciples (→6:8).

40. *Chr. Trad.* 3:184–214.
41. BDF §252.
42. *Didache* 9 (ACW 6:20).
43. Socrates Scholasticus, *Ecclesiastical History* 5.22 (*NPNF*[2] 2:133).

2:44–45 The fundamental question to be asked about the primitive "communism" of the early church was not only whether it was universal, but above all whether it was compulsory (→4:32; →11:29).

2:46–47 (→3:25; →20:7). There is no gainsaying the repeated emphasis of Acts on the "number" of "those who were being saved," and even upon what appear to be precise statistics (with due allowance for the possible workings of number mysticism); but the "catholicity" of the church is not made dependent on the statistics.

ACTS 3

3:1 Even after the crucifixion, resurrection, ascension, and Pentecost, the disciples of Jesus continued to be observant Jews (→3:25).[1] They went on with prayer at the appointed times (→4:24–30) and at the appointed places (→7:47–48) as these had been prescribed by Jewish law. Still to come was the revelation that the ceremonial laws of Moses were no longer binding on Gentiles who came to the Christian gospel directly rather than through conversion as Jewish proselytes (→10:15), an issue that went on being divisive (→15:2), until it was adjudicated by the apostolic council at Jerusalem and its "decrees" (δόγματα) (→16:4b). Even in those very decrees, moreover, as the range of the variations in the transmitted texts demonstrates (→20:28a), it remained less than clear which laws were permanent and which had been intended only for Jewish believers in Christ.

3:6 In their combination of poverty (Luke 9:58) and generosity, the disciples were imitating the example of their Master (→7:59–60), in whose name they performed this miracle. The pettifoggery of some commentators on this passage, who point out, on the basis of 4:35, that Peter and the other disciples actually did have silver and gold and that "distribution was made to each as any had need," should be evaluated in the light of the larger context of early Christian attitudes toward economic and social questions (→4:32).

3:8–12 It was characteristic of biblical miracles, including such miracles of healing as this, that those through whom the miracles were performed did not attribute them to their own "power or piety," but to the power of God, so that it was more precise and complete to say that "*God did extraordinary miracles by the hands of Paul*" (19:11), which set such "miracles as signs" (→6:8) apart

1. Origen, *Contra Celsum* 2.1 (Chadwick 1953, 66–67).

from the prodigies that had previously been executed by those sorcerers and magicians who, in response to Paul's (or God's!) miracles, "brought their books together and burned them in the sight of all" (19:19).

3:16 The "faith" that is a constant theme of Acts was, as this passage insisted again, not some generalized feeling, but a specific faith "in" the name and revelation of Christ (→24:24–25a; →26:18): "his name, by faith in his name."

3:17 As he does elsewhere in Acts (→7:59–60), Luke harks back to his "first book" and to "all that Jesus began to do and teach" (1:1) as he has recorded it there. In this case as in many others, these actions and teachings are unique to his Gospel: "And Jesus said, 'Father, forgive them; for they know not what they do'" (Luke 23:34). Although the text of this saying in the Gospel of Luke, which is usually counted, also in homiletical and musical treatments, as the first among "the seven last words of Christ from the cross," does not have universal attestation in the manuscripts of the Gospels (→20:28a), the text of 3:17 here, backed as it is by the evidence of all the textual witnesses, may even be taken to provide some secondary corroboration for the reading in Luke 23:34.

Crucifixus pro nobis: Reconciliation and Atonement

3:18 TPR God foretold by the mouth of all the prophets that his Christ should suffer, and he has fulfilled it.

In the language of Christian theology, the prepositions can sometimes be just as important as the propositions, even though church fathers such as Saint Basil of Caesarea could blame the attention to prepositions on the influence of pagan philosophy.[2] Although the Apostles' Creed contents itself with the historical statement *passus sub pontio pilato* ("suffered under Pontius Pilate"),[3] the Niceno-Constantinopolitan Creed has him σταυρωθέντα ὑπὲρ ἡμῶν ἐπὶ Ποντίου Πιλάτου, *crucifixus etiam pro nobis sub Pontio Pilato* ("crucified on our behalf under Pontius Pilate"), identifying the purpose of the history.[4] There is both philological and theological justification for more than one rendering of these Greek and Latin prepositions ὑπέρ and *pro*: "on our behalf" is perhaps the least specific, "for our sakes" more pointed, and "in our stead" probably the most specific.[5] In its account of the meeting of the Apostle Philip with him (8:26–40), Acts has the Ethiopian eunuch reading (from the Septuagint, and apparently aloud) the fifty-third chapter of the prophet Isaiah, which has provided, since the New Testament itself, the most explicit exegetical support

2. Basil of Caesarea, *On the Holy Spirit* 2–4 (SVS 18–22).
3. Apostles' Creed 4 (*CCF* 1:669).
4. Niceno-Constantinopolitan Creed 4 (*CCF* 1:162–63).
5. BDAG 1030–31.

for taking ὑπέρ in "crucified on our behalf" to mean "crucified in our stead": οὗτος τὰς ἁμαρτίας ἡμῶν φέρει καὶ περὶ ἡμῶν ὀδυνᾶται ("this one bears our sins and is made powerless in our stead") (Isa. 53:4 LXX).

Thus the most crucial—and the most difficult—point of theological controversy in the entire apostolic definition of the normative interpretation of Holy Scripture (→8:30–31) was this attempt of Christian exegesis to make three basic points simultaneously: (1) to equate the Messiah of biblical prophecy with the suffering servant, the παῖς μου (Isa. 52:13 LXX) of biblical prophecy; (2) to proclaim him as the resurrected Lord (→2:31); and (3) to identify both the suffering servant and the resurrected Lord with the historical figure of Jesus of Nazareth as "the crucified Messiah," because the fact "that the title Messiah was inextricably bound up with the name of Jesus can only be explained by presupposing that Jesus was actually crucified as the Messiah."[6] Therefore the question of the Ethiopian eunuch to the Apostle Philip, "About whom, pray, does the prophet say this, about himself or about some one else?" (8:34), referring to the prophecy of Isaiah, is not a matter of "mere" interpretation—if any interpretation of Scripture might be called "mere"—but involves the central affirmation of redemption in the Christian message.

The possible answers to the question "about whom, pray, does the prophet say this?" when he speaks this way about the suffering παῖς of God, might include the following: the person of the prophet himself, as apparently the Ethiopian initially surmised; some other individual contemporary to the prophecy; the people of Israel as a whole, often described, in the Septuagint of Isaiah (Isa. 41:8 LXX) but also in the authorship of Luke (Luke 1:54), as the παῖς of God; some future figure in the history of Israel, yet to be identified (but not, in the usual Jewish exegesis of Isa. 53, taken to be the Messiah). But Philip's reply, "beginning with this scripture," was to tell "him the good news of Jesus" (8:35), not only because "this scripture" of Isaiah was the passage over which the Ethiopian happened to be puzzling as he was reading in his chariot, but because it was the key to the Ethiopian's question about the identity of the suffering παῖς of God. Luke thus attaches his exegesis of the prophets throughout Acts to "the gospel of the forty days" (→1:2–3), as he himself had quoted the words of the risen Christ on the road to Emmaus in the final chapter of his Gospel: "And he said to them, 'O foolish men, and slow of heart to believe all that the prophets have spoken! Was it not necessary [ἔδει] that the Christ should suffer these things and enter into his glory?' And beginning with Moses and all the prophets, he interpreted to them in all the scriptures the things concerning himself" (Luke 24:25–27). That becomes the burden of Peter's message to his Jewish audience, that "God foretold it by the mouth of all the prophets that his Christ should suffer, and he has fulfilled it" (3:18 TPR).

Saint Paul, too, although he learned this not on the road to Emmaus but on the road to Damascus and in his subsequent instruction (→9:1–4), makes

6. Dahl 1974, 24.

it the burden of his message. In the Jewish synagogue at Thessalonica he, "as was his custom, . . . argued with them from the scriptures, explaining and proving [διανοίγων καὶ παρατιθέμενος]" the very same three basic points: "[1] that it was necessary [ἔδει] for the Christ to suffer and [2] to rise from the dead, and saying, [3] 'This Jesus, whom I proclaim to you, is the Christ'" (17:2–4). In the following chapter he went on doing so in the synagogue at Corinth, taking time between synagogues to "explain and prove" his case (with results that were at best indifferent) to a philosophical audience at Athens (→17:18), not "from the scriptures" of the Septuagint this time, but from a Greek poet and from the puzzling inscription "To an unknown god" (→17:23). But in the Corinthian synagogue he "was occupied with preaching, testifying to the Jews that the Christ was Jesus" (18:5). And in Achaia the Alexandrian convert from Judaism, Apollos, who was "an eloquent man, well versed in the scriptures" and who taught on the basis of what he had already learned about the Way (18:24–25), used that eloquence and that biblical knowledge in "showing by the scriptures that the Christ was Jesus" (18:28).

The three basic points are comprehensively summarized again in Paul's message to King Agrippa: "To this day I have had the help that comes from God, and so I stand here testifying both to small and great, saying nothing but what the prophets said would come to pass; for it is written in Moses: that the Christ must suffer, and that, by being the first to rise from the dead, he would proclaim light both to the people and to the Gentiles" (26:22–23 TPR). In a real sense, therefore, the apostles throughout the Acts of the Apostles are engaged in providing a comprehensive answer to the Ethiopian's question: "About whom, pray, does the prophet say this, about himself or about some one else?" (8:34). Because it was by no means obvious from the text itself that the passages promising a Messiah, beginning with the protevangel of Gen. 3:15, and the passages predicting the suffering servant, notably Isa. 53 (→8:30–31), referred to one and the same person, it was repeatedly necessary for the apostolic kerygma to affirm this identification and to argue for it from the Scriptures (17:2–3): "For it is written in Moses" (26:22 TPR).

By defining sin as the violation of the *rectitudo* and honor of God (→12:21–23), Saint Anselm of Canterbury in *Cur deus homo* (*Why God Became Man*) interpreted *crucifixus etiam pro nobis* as explicitly a reference to the "satisfaction"—the third of the three component parts of penance, after contrition and confession (→26:20)—which was rendered to God by a being who, being truly human, could effectually act for (= in the stead of) fallen human beings, but who, being at the same time fully divine, could apply that "satisfaction" to the entire human race, rather than merely to himself. But in the other major historic set of images for the atonement, sin is seen as captivity to the oppression of the devil (→10:38), and therefore σταυροθέντα ὑπὲρ ἡμῶν ἐπὶ Ποντίου Πιλάτου, *crucifixus etiam pro nobis sub Pontio Pilato* ("crucified on our behalf under Pontius Pilate") refers to the victory over demonic powers accomplished by the crucifixion and the resurrection of *Christus Victor*, which are seen together as a single saving action (→13:8–11).

3:19 Repentance (μετανοήσατε) and conversion (ἐπιστρέψατε) are described here as inseparable, because sorrow for sin by itself was necessary but not sufficient, and conversion had to be grounded in a penitential acknowledgment that, in the words that Luke had put in the mouth of the prodigal son: *pater, peccavi* (Luke 15:21 Vulgate). This mutual and inseparable relation between repentance and conversion, repeated repentance and repeated conversion, was to be the foundation for the church's sacrament of penance (→26:20).

Universal Restoration/Salvation Only by the Name of Christ

3:21; 4:12 NJB Whom heaven must keep till the universal restoration comes which God proclaimed, speaking through his holy prophets. . . . Only in him is there salvation; for of all the names in the world given to men, this is the only one by which we can be saved.

Separated by less than twenty verses and standing on the same page of the Bible in many editions (including the NJB, which is quoted here), these two passages—this promise of an ἀποκατάστασις πάντων ("universal restoration"), Latinized and later Anglicized as "apocatastasis,"[7] which is then followed by this unambiguously exclusivistic statement—have from earliest times been a challenge to Christian exegetes. The most famous effort to respond to the challenge came from Origen of Alexandria in the third century, who took the words of Paul, "When everything has been subjected to him, then the Son himself will be subjected to the One who has subjected everything to him, so that God may be all in all" (1 Cor. 15:28 NJB), to mean that after undergoing purification the entire fallen creation, including even the demons, would be restored through Christ.[8] For his speculative teachings (though not specifically including this one) Origenism was condemned by the Second Council of Constantinople in 553.[9] A century after Origen, however, this teaching was taken up by Saint Gregory of Nyssa, most fully in his dialogue *On the Soul and the Resurrection*, in which the principal speaker is his remarkable older sister, Saint Macrina, whom he called there his "sister and teacher" (ἀδελφὴ καὶ διδάσκαλος); both Gregory and Macrina are saints of the church both in the Orthodox East and in the Catholic West. Their dialogue concludes with the hope of a universal restoration in Christ by which, "when such things are cleansed and purified away by the treatment through fire, each of the better qualities will come in their place: incorruptibility, life, honor, grace, glory,

7. *OED* 1:550.
8. Origen, *On First Principles* 1.6 (*ANF* 4:260–62); Méhat 1956.
9. Second Council of Constantinople: Exposition of Faith (*CCF* 1:219).

power, and whatever else of this kind we recognize in God Himself and in His image, which is our human nature,"[10] "so that God may be all in all" (1 Cor. 15:28 NJB). The challenge was succinctly formulated in the words of the title of a lecture by Bishop Kallistos Ware, "Dare We Hope for the Salvation of All? Origen, St. Gregory of Nyssa, and St. Isaac the Syrian."[11]

Textual criticism (→20:28a) really does not help very much in dealing with the conflict between these two passages of Acts. For although it is the case that the opening clause of the second, "only in him is there salvation," is missing in the TPR and some other Greek manuscripts, nevertheless the rest of the sentence ends up saying the same thing in negative language. Likewise, the words of Jesus, "He that believeth and is baptized shall be saved; but he that believeth not shall be damned" (Mark 16:16 AV), are part of the long ending of Mark's Gospel, which is enclosed in brackets in critical editions of the Greek New Testament (e.g., NA[27]) and is identified as textually "doubtful" by modern English versions such as the NRSV; but the words of Jesus elsewhere about "eternal fire" (Matt. 18:8) have the universal attestation of all the manuscripts and all the editions. Biblical support for even considering the possibility of a yes answer to Bishop Kallistos's question has come chiefly from the prophecy that at "the end," after "all [enemies have been put] under [Christ's] feet," including death as "the last enemy," then God will be "all in all" (πάντα ἐν πᾶσιν) (1 Cor. 15:24–28 AV); and from the unqualified declaration of the universal salvific will of God, by which "God our Savior . . . desires *all men* to be saved and to come to the knowledge of the truth" (1 Tim. 2:3–4), which is what all believers pray for when they say, as Jesus commanded:

Thy kingdom come,
thy will be done,
on earth as it is in heaven. (Matt. 6:10)

But the will of God is not always done on earth, as every sinner has to learn anew every day.

The resources provided by the book of Acts for resolving the dilemma are considerably more sparse than rational speculation would desire. In the grim summary of the betrayal of Jesus by Judas Iscariot (1:16–20), there is no indication whatever that Peter and "the brethren" prayed that forgiveness, much less salvation, would come to Judas. The same is true of the dishonesty of Ananias and Sapphira, whose punishment is swift and sure, indeed immediate, without any mention even of an opportunity for repentance, much less a hope for eventual salvation (5:1–11). When Herod allowed himself to become the object of an idolatrous worship that said "the sounds of a god, and not of man!" the punishment was no less swift, coming, the text says, "immediately"

10. Gregory of Nyssa, *On the Soul and the Resurrection* 10 (SVS 121).
11. Ware 2002, 193–215.

(παραχρῆμα) (12:21–23). The language of the book of Acts about the devil
(→10:38) consistently employs the modality—and the finality—of either/or,
with no third possibility and no modification of the antithesis.

Yet this text does speak about nothing less than "universal restoration."
Moreover, it comes after the earlier question of the disciples to the risen Christ
just before his ascension: "Is it at this time that you will bring about the restoration [ἀποκατασθήση]?" (1:6 TPR), which, in the context, seems to refer
primarily, if not exclusively, to the restoration of the kingdom to Israel; making
it ἀποκατάστασις πάντων here seems to go beyond that question by broaden-
ing the hope to include *all* Jews and *all* Gentiles, even all of the cosmos. In
its treatment of the past both of Jews and of Gentiles, moreover, the book of
Acts is surprisingly conciliatory. To the Jews, after attacking them because "you
denied the Holy and Righteous One, and asked for a murderer to be granted
to you, and killed the Author of life," Peter immediately adds: "You acted in
ignorance, as did also your rulers" (3:14–17). To the Gentiles Paul describes
a divine economy (→15:8–9) by which "in past generations he allowed all the
nations to walk in their own ways" (14:16), "times of ignorance [which] God
overlooked" (17:30). Toward both Jews and Gentiles, then, the God whose
workings are described in Acts is a God of "kindness and forbearance and
patience" (Rom. 2:4). All of this put together still leaves more questions than
answers, confirming the nineteenth-century maxim: "Anyone who does not
believe in the universal restoration is an ox, but anyone who teaches it is an
ass"[12]—to which must be added the astute qualifying observation that both
"the ox and the ass were already at the stable in Bethlehem before the wise
men had found their way to it."[13]

3:22–23 The prophecy given by Moses in Deut. 18, which in its original context sounds like a prediction that the leadership of Israel after Moses would be
assumed by Joshua (whose name was Ἰησοῦς in some places of the Septuagint,
as well as once here in Acts [7:45]), became here a promise of the coming of
Jesus (Ἰησοῦς) (→8:30–31), including the imperative to "listen to him," as
this was reinforced by the voice of God himself at the transfiguration of Jesus
(Luke 9:35).

"The Purpose of Calling Israel": The Abiding Covenant

3:25 The covenant which God gave to your fathers.

In the summary that Origen gives of an early version of the rule of faith
(→8:37), God "sent the Lord Jesus Christ, first for the purpose of calling Israel."[14]

12. Quoted in Pelikan 1988, 5.
13. Quoted in Ware 2002, 214 n. 42.
14. Origen, *On First Principles* 1.4 (*CCF* 1:63); see Sanders 1987.

The emphasis here in Peter's address to Jews on the "covenant" (διαθήκη) of God with the people of Israel as represented by their father Abraham, which Stephen in another address to Jews calls "the covenant of circumcision" (διαθήκη περιτομῆς) (7:8), and the use of the same Greek term διαθήκη in the words of institution of the Eucharist in the first two of our Gospels (Matt. 26:28; Mark 14:24), which appears as "the *new* covenant" (ἡ καινὴ διαθήκη) both in Luke (Luke 22:20) and in Paul (1 Cor. 11:25), referring to the covenant with the church, make it obligatory to consider the relation—not only chronological, but above all theological—between the two covenants. In his explanation of the covenant with Abraham, Stephen carefully stipulates that of "this land in which you are now living . . . he gave him no inheritance in it, not even a foot's length, but promised to give it to him in possession and to his posterity after him, though he had no child" (7:4–5), thus disaggregating "holy people" and "holy land" (→7:47–48). (The translation of διαθήκη into Latin as *testamentum* and into English as *testament* eventually led, first in Latin and then in many Western languages, including English, to the designations "Old Testament" and "New Testament" for the two volumes of the Christian Bible.)

As part of his emphasis on how the disciples of Jesus follow and imitate him (→7:59–60), even to the point of sharing the attacks and slanders against him, Luke has Jesus accused in the Gospel of "perverting our nation" (Luke 23:2), and then he has his disciple, the deacon Stephen, accused of the same crime here: "They set up false witnesses who said, 'This man never ceases to speak words against this temple and the law; for we have heard him say that this Jesus of Nazareth is destroying this temple, and changing the custom which Moses delivered to us'" (6:13–14 TPR).

Therefore the book of Acts, which puts its narrative of the early church into the context of world history (→28:14), is nevertheless (or rather, therefore) at pains to point out over and over that the disciples and apostles of Jesus continued to be observant Jews. At the beginning of his Gospel, Luke has Simeon hail

> thy salvation,
> which thou hast prepared in the presence of *all peoples*,
> a light for revelation to the Gentiles,
> and for glory to thy people Israel. (Luke 2:31–32)

Simon thus confirms and even amplifies the glory of Israel even as he brings revelation to the Gentiles. The Pentecost event, even with its far-reaching implications for "every nation under heaven" (→2:1), took place on a Jewish holiday and was something that happened to Jews (2:5, 10, 22, 29, 36). "Day by day," as Acts describes the early believers (2:46), they were "attending the temple together." After being condemned by the Jewish council, they were "every day in the temple" (5:42). And the Paul of Acts,[15] speaking in Greek,

---

15. Brawley 1987, 68–83.

could say to a Gentile, "I am a Jew" (ἐγὼ ἄνθρωπος μέν εἰμι Ἰουδαῖος) (21:39), and then immediately after that, speaking in Aramaic, could say also to a Jewish audience, "I am a Jew" (22:3). According to the variant reading (→20:28a) in the TPR, he asserted, "I must by all means keep this feast that cometh in Jerusalem" (δεῖ με πάντως τὴν ἑορτὴν τὴν ἐρχομένην ποιῆσαι εἰς Ἰεροσόλυμα) (18:21 TPR AV); and according to all the manuscripts he was able to declare that he still "came to bring to my nation alms and offerings" (24:17), and that "though I had done nothing against the people or the customs of our fathers, yet I was delivered prisoner from Jerusalem into the hands of the Romans" (28:17). Such observance of "the customs of our fathers," made evident for example in Paul's circumcising of Timothy even though only his mother was Jewish (16:1–3), was to be understood in the light of an eventual stratification of the commandments in the law of Moses (→10:15), at any rate for Gentile converts to the gospel (15:6–21). The continuing Christian observance of the Jewish Sabbath on Saturday (13:14, 44; 16:13; 18:4), though it was for the purpose of evangelizing Jews, must be seen in the light of the Christian observance of Sunday, "the first day of the week" (20:7; cf. 1 Cor. 16:2), as the time (→7:47–48) when the community "met to break bread" (→20:7). But the continuity of the church with the covenant of the people of Israel was expressed not only in its praxis, but in its teaching. "But this I admit to you," Paul said, "that according to the Way, which they call a sect [αἵρεσις], I worship the God of our fathers, believing everything laid down by the law or written in the prophets" (24:14): "the Way" did not cancel "the faith of our fathers," but confirmed it. For the book of Acts, as for the New Testament overall, "Scripture" (γραφή), whether in the singular or the plural, meant what later Christians were to label "the Old Testament," properly understood in the light of the relation between prophecy and fulfillment (→8:30–31). Jews who became Christian continued to look to the exodus from Egypt as the defining event of their early history (7:34–36), and Moses continued to be seen as a prophet of the one true God, who was "the God of Abraham and of Isaac and of Jacob" (7:32). It was this one true God, as Peter says earlier in this chapter, "the God of our fathers," who has "glorified his servant Jesus" (3:13).

But Peter continues: Jesus, "whom you delivered up and denied in the presence of Pilate, when he had decided to release him. But you denied the Holy and Righteous One, and asked for a murderer to be granted to you, and killed the Author of life, whom God raised from the dead" (3:13–15). Yet he adds almost immediately, and while still calling them ἀδελφοί: "And now, brethren, I know that you acted in ignorance, as did also your rulers" (3:17), once again imitating Christ (→7:59–60) in his prayer on the cross (Luke 23:34). It is consistent with this dual emphasis when Luke not only describes the persecution of the Christian believers by Jews (21:37–39; 23:12–14), but, conversely, describes as well the persecution of Christian believers by pagans precisely on the grounds that "these men *are Jews* and they are disturbing our city. They advocate customs which it is not lawful for us Romans to accept or practice"

(16:20–21; cf. 19:34). It was such continuing solidarity with Judaism that enabled Paul to say of his arrest: "It is because of the hope of Israel that I am bound with this chain" (28:20).[16] Paul's full-length exposition of this "hope of Israel" is worked out in the central chapters of his Epistle to the Romans (Rom. 9–11).

16. Rakocy 2000, 154–58.

ACTS 4

4:2 TPR Proclaiming Jesus in the resurrection of the dead.

Once again, the followers of Jesus were seen as taking sides between the two Jewish parties, the Pharisees and the Sadducees, and as being closer to the former than the two parties were to each other on the doctrine of the general resurrection (→23:8), even though both Jewish parties were in agreement, against the disciples, in rejecting the evidentiary claim (→26:26) that Jesus had been raised from the dead (→2:31).

4:3–4 The almost dialectical juxtaposition of "they arrested them" and "many of those who heard the word believed" was repeated in one account after another of the encounter of the gospel with its gainsayers, not only, as here, with Jewish gainsayers, but also with Greeks, of whom "some mocked" and others "joined him" (17:32–34).

4:5–7 The mention of the names of Annas and Caiaphas connects this account of the clash of the disciples with the Jewish religious authorities to the account of their Lord's clash with Annas and Caiaphas (John 18:13–14), as part of the larger pattern by which the disciples would learn to imitate Christ in death as in life (→7:59–60).

4:10 Together with "the Way," the "name" of Christ, crucified and risen, was a Christian mark of identity (→2:31; →11:26).

4:12 NJB Only in him is there salvation; for of all the names in the world given to men, this is the only one by which we can be saved.

This sweepingly exclusivistic claim must be read in some sort of tension and harmony with the universalism of other statements (→3:21) and with the attitudes expressed throughout Acts toward the history of human aspirations before the coming of Christ (→15:8–9).

4:13 TPR Hearing the boldness of Peter and John.

As if in anticipation of Stephen's upcoming portrait of the Egyptian education and worldly learning of Moses (→7:22), 4:13 seems to have made a special point of portraying Peter and John as "uneducated, common men," but also of celebrating their imitation of their Master under persecution (→7:59–60).

4:16 TPR It is very evident to all who dwell in Jerusalem that a remarkable sign has been performed by them, and we cannot deny it.

"Sign" was the theologically more precise way of speaking about a "miracle" (→6:8). The admission that "we cannot deny it" opens up the question of the verifiability of such an act (→26:26).

"This Is the Catholic Faith": The Confessional Imperative

4:20 TPR We cannot commit apostasy [ἀρνεῖσθαι] from what we have seen and heard.

The TPR here employs the term ἀρνεῖσθαι: "deny, repudiate, disown . . . usu[ally] of apostasy fr[om] the Christian faith,"[1] where the texts on which the AV and RSV are based have the less specific μὴ λαλεῖν: "We cannot but speak of what we have seen and heard." With the danger of such apostasy in view, the Western, Latin creed that was fathered on Saint Athanasius opens with the confessional imperative, "Whoever desires to be saved must above all things hold the catholic faith," and it reaffirms that confessional imperative in its conclusion, "This is the catholic faith. Unless one believes it faithfully and steadfastly, one will not be able to be saved."[2] The events of divine revelation and the faith that they evoke carry with them an inner obligation and an urgent need, which is altogether different from any kind of "external coercion" (→28:31), to "speak of what we have seen and heard" and to confess the faith (→24:24–25a) as a *fides quae creditur,* "the faith which was once for all [ἅπαξ] delivered to the saints" (Jude 3). That obligation to confess the faith, which entails "declaring . . . the whole counsel of God" (20:27) but is concentrated with unique force on the resurrection of Christ (→2:31), is the source of the urgency and of the "boldness" (παρρησία) that mark the life and the witness of the church as they are described here in these opening chapters of Acts. Peter feels empowered to

1. BADG 107; *PGL* 227.
2. Athanasian Creed 1, 42 (*CCF* 1:676).

speak "confidently" (μετὰ παρρησίας) when, in addressing a Jewish audience, he contrasts "the patriarch David," who is dead and gone, with the living Christ whom God has raised from the dead (2:29). It is especially here in Acts 4 that this confessional παρρησία can be seen at work. The apostles pray to God to "grant to thy servants to speak thy word with all boldness" (4:29). The immediate divine answer to that prayer is that "they were all filled with the Holy Spirit and spoke the word of God with boldness to everyone who wanted to believe" (4:31 TPR). Therefore when the Jewish authorities "saw the boldness of Peter and John, and perceived that they were uneducated, common men, they wondered; and they recognized that they had been with Jesus" (4:13), this "recognizing" apparently being the result of their boldness, which enables them to make confession of their faith, even as laymen without the benefit of a formal theological and rabbinic education. "Even in death," as Chrysostom says, their theme remains constant, "Confession and Preaching."[3]

In the second and longer part of the book of Acts, the confessional imperative "we cannot commit apostasy from what we have seen and heard" pervades the ministry of the Apostle Paul, who would make believing and confessing coordinate by writing to the church in Rome, in a passage that has become the standard proof text for the confessional imperative:[4] "If you *confess* with your lips that Jesus is Lord and believe in your heart that God raised him from the dead, you will be saved. For man believes with his heart and so is justified, and he *confesses* with his lips and so is saved" (Rom. 10:9–10). Employing later in Acts some phraseology that is identical to that of the apostles here, he describes Ananias as having told him at his conversion, "You will be a witness for him to all men of *what you have seen and heard*" (22:15). And he carries out that confessional witness—which, it must be said, is obscured and weakened when, as in the RSV and again in the NRSV, the technical New Testament and patristic term ὁμολογεῖν[5] is translated as "I admit" rather than as "I confess," as it is in the AV and in the Vulgate *confiteor*—by asserting in almost creedal form: "This I confess unto thee, that after the way which they call heresy, so worship I the God of my fathers, believing all things which are written in the law and in the prophets: and have hope toward God, which they themselves also allow, that there shall be a resurrection of the dead, both of the just and unjust" (24:14–15 AV).

Eventually the content of "what we have seen and heard" has come to include not only the events outlined in the early kerygma and creed, but the entire subsequent history of the church (→27:1), now that, as Saint Gregory of Nazianzus the Theologian put it, "the Spirit resides amongst us, giving us a clearer manifestation of himself than before."[6] The apostolic generation could

---

3. Chrysostom, *Homilies on Acts* 18 (*NPNF*[1] 11:113).
4. Pelikan 2003, 35–63.
5. BDAG 708–9; *PGL* 957–58.
6. Gregory of Nazianzus, *Orations* 31.26 (SVS 137).

speak about "that which was from the beginning, which we have heard, which we have seen with our eyes, which we have looked upon and touched with our hands" (1 John 1:1). But for most generations in the history of the church, "what we have heard" has predominated over "what we have seen," because, even then but also now, "faith comes from what is heard, and what is heard comes by the preaching of Christ" (Rom. 10:17). Therefore it was very much of a quantitative increase, but not in essence a qualitative alteration, when, with the ever-sharpening demand for doctrinal precision (→18:24–26a) and even for terminological accuracy, this "confession," beginning as it did with faith in the "one God" of Israel and concluding with the hope of "the resurrection of the dead and the life of the age to come," became the trinitarian confession of the Niceno-Constantinopolitan Creed, and then on that basis went on to become the hundreds and hundreds of creeds, confessions, and rules of faith that the church has been producing down to the present day, as these have been collected in Philip Schaff's *Creeds of Christendom* and now in *Creeds and Confessions of Faith in the Christian Tradition* (→8:37; →24:24–25a).

Orthodoxy as Correct Worship and Correct Doctrine

4:24–30 NEB Sovereign Lord, maker of heaven and earth and sea and of everything in them, . . . mark their threats, and enable thy servants to speak thy word with all boldness. Stretch out thy hand to heal and cause signs and wonders to be done through the name of thy holy servant Jesus.

Although it is unavoidable, as well as correct, to emphasize the role of the sermons and speeches in this earliest example of Christian historiography, with their parallels not only to the speeches of Moses, above all in the book of Deuteronomy, but to the speeches in the Greek and Roman historiography of Thucydides and Livy,[7] and in that connection to examine the Christian appropriation and adaptation of the insights and techniques of classical rhetoric (→24:1–2), that emphasis on the sermons should not be permitted to obscure the position that is occupied by prayer and worship throughout the narrative of Acts, which is at least as important, if not more important in some respects.[8] When the Niceno-Constantinopolitan Creed confesses the deity of the Holy Spirit (→5:3–4), it does so by going beyond the lapidary formula of the Nicene Creed, "And in the Holy Spirit,"[9] to affirm that the Holy Spirit is "co-worshiped and co-glorified with [or even: together with] Father and Son" (σὺν πατρὶ καὶ υἱῷ συμπροσκυνούμενον καὶ συνδοξαζόμενον),[10] a joint worship that would be idolatrous unless the Holy Spirit were God in the same sense and on the

---

7. Dibelius 1949.
8. Bachmann 1980, 332–69.
9. Nicene Creed 8 (*CCF* 1:159).
10. Niceno-Constantinopolitan Creed 8 (*CCF* 1:162–63).

same level as the Father and the Son in the oneness of the Godhead. On this doctrine as on all the others in Acts, moreover, the worship came earlier than the theology.[11] In Acts, Luke describes the early Christians, both individually and collectively, as people of prayer, "declaring both by the urgency and by the agreement of their praying," in the words of Saint Cyprian's explanation of these chapters in Acts, that God "only admits into the divine and eternal home those among whom prayer is unanimous";[12] or, in Bede's formula, "whoever wishes to receive his promised gifts, must steadfastly continue in prayers motivated by brotherly love."[13] In his Gospel, similarly, Luke had repeatedly described their Lord at prayer.[14]

As it is one of the few vernacular languages (→21:37) with its own vocable for "gospel" (→8:25),[15] so also theological English has, in the word "worship,"[16] a native term for various Greek verbs such as λατρεύειν (7:7, 42; 24:14; 26:7; 27:23), λειτουργεῖν (13:2), προσκυνεῖν (7:43; 8:27; 10:25; 24:11), and σέβεσθαι (13:43, 50; 16:14; 17:4, 17; 18:7, 13; 19:27). In Acts "worship" is not always addressed to the one true God, but is sometimes idolatrous (→10:38); and these Greeks verbs, preeminently standing for true worship, can be used also to describe idolatry, whether genuine or alleged (7:42–43; 18:13). The contrast between right worship and wrong worship comes out the most dramatically in the account of King Herod, who "put on his royal robes, took his seat upon the throne, and made an oration to them. And . . . the people shouted, 'The sounds of a god, and not of a man!' Immediately an angel of the Lord smote him, because he did not give God the glory; and coming down from the throne, he was eaten alive by worms and died" (12:21–23 TPR). From the Greek word in the formula "did not give God the glory" (οὐκ ἔδωκεν τὴν δόξαν τῷ θεῷ) there came the standard term for "correct worship," ὀρθοδοξία, so that the Feast of Orthodoxy was prescribed by the Byzantine Church in 843 to commemorate the restoration of correct worship with the return of the icons after the iconoclastic controversy (→19:26).[17] But "correct worship" and "correct doctrine" are two sides of the same coin, and "orthodoxy" ultimately refers to both.

Together with the apostolic doctrine, the apostolic fellowship or community, and the apostolic practice of breaking of bread in the Eucharist, therefore, "the prayer" (TPR) or "the prayers" (RSV) are described as that to which the early believers "devoted themselves" (→2:42)—"continued stedfastly in" (AV) or even "persevered in."[18] The believers are described as doing so, moreover, "together with . . . Mary the mother of Jesus" (1:14), as most Christians have been doing

11. Norden 1913, 250–63.
12. Cyprian, *On the Lord's Prayer* 8 (*ANF* 5:449).
13. Bede, *Exposition of the Acts of the Apostles* 1 (PL 92:943).
14. Johnson 1992, 300.
15. *OED* 6:697–98.
16. *OED* 20:575–77.
17. *ODCC* 1199.
18. Johnson 1992, 58.

ever since (→1:14). The Greek plural ταῖς προσευχαῖς with definite article, "the prayers," would seem to suggest habitual or designated prayers, perhaps even, at least inchoately, fixed formulas of prayer. By contrast with Matthew, who incorporates the Lord's Prayer into the Sermon on the Mount (Matt. 6:9–13), Luke makes it a response to the disciples' request, "Lord, teach us to pray, as John taught his disciples," and has Jesus preface it with the instruction "when [or even 'whenever': ὅταν] you pray, say" (Luke 11:1–2);[19] but he does not repeat it in his second volume here, as he might conceivably have been expected to. Nevertheless, in the light of the later prayer echoing the second petition of the Lord's Prayer, "the will of the Lord be done" (21:14),[20] it seems at least possible that the term "*the* prayers" refers to the Lord's Prayer and possibly to other formulas such as the primitive eucharistic prayer reproduced in the *Didache*, which is coupled with the admonition to pray the Our Father three times a day.[21] The reference in Acts to Paul and Silas "praying and singing hymns to God" (προσευχόμενοι ὕμνουν τὸν θεόν) (16:25), which is amplified in Colossians to "psalms and hymns and spiritual songs" (Col. 3:16), is likewise an indication of prepared rather than merely spontaneous prayers and songs.[22] These included (but were not restricted to) those in the book of Psalms, which the New Testament writers, including Luke here in Acts, quote constantly as applying to Christ and to the church (→8:30–31).

It is in order to "devote [them]selves to prayer and to the ministry of the word" (6:4) that the apostles authorize the appointment of deacons. The habit of prayer is evident also in Peter's observance of the noon hour (which was to become Sext, the "Little Hour" in the Western monastic breviary) as a stated time (→7:47–48) to offer prayers (10:9). To the early disciples as observant Jews (→3:25), the temple at Jerusalem goes on being a special venue for prayer (3:1; 22:17), but not to the exclusion of other designated "place[s] of prayer" (16:16). The practice of prayer is sometimes combined with the ascetic practice of fasting (→24:25b), as in the appointment of presbyters "in every church" (14:23) or in the command from the Holy Spirit to appoint Barnabas and Saul, which took place "while they were worshiping the Lord and fasting" (13:2–4). Above all, it is evident from Luke's description of a liturgical event in which he himself was a participant (→27:1), "on the first day of the week [ἐν δὲ τῇ μιᾷ τῶν σαββάτων], when we were gathered together to break bread" (20:7), that he is using the identical words, "on the first day of the week" (τῇ δὲ μιᾷ τῶν σαββάτων), that in his Gospel he had employed for Sunday, as the day of the resurrection of Christ (Luke 24:1).

In addition to such more or less stated occasions for prayer, it also comes in response to particular needs or special occasions. The vacancy in the apostolic

19. Origen, *Prayer* 18.2–3 (ACW 19:65–66).
20. See also *Martyrdom of Polycarp* 7 (*ANF* 1:40).
21. *Didache* 8–9 (ACW 6:19–20).
22. Nikanor 1905, 1:97.

college of the twelve (→5:29a), brought about by the betrayal and suicide of Judas Iscariot, requires the remaining apostles to function as a search committee of the whole and to pray, "Lord, who knowest the hearts of all men, show which one of these two thou hast chosen to take the place in this ministry and apostleship from which Judas turned aside" (1:24–25). At the arrest of Peter, "earnest prayer [προσευχὴ . . . ἐκτενῶς, which was virtually a technical term for prayer in the Septuagint][23] for him was made to God by the church" (12:5); and this continued (12:12). After their own arrest, "Paul and Silas were praying and singing hymns to God, and the prisoners were listening to them" (16:25). The travels of Paul called for prayer at various junctures. After his deeply felt (→21:13–14) farewell and *apologia pro vita sua* to the presbyters of Ephesus, "he knelt down and prayed with them all" (20:36). After a week with the believers at Tyre and before embarking on the voyage, "they all, with wives and children, brought us on our way till we were outside the city; and kneeling down on the beach we prayed and bade one another farewell" (21:5–6). Adrift at sea by night, "they let down four anchors from the stern, and prayed for day to come" (27:29).

This prayer here at 4:24–30, in which it is "possible for us to recognize the early rooting in liturgy of the designation of Jesus as the Servant of God"[24] and which does sound like a liturgical prayer rather than a spontaneous expression, is a model of the elements that are usually identified as components of authentic Christian prayer.[25] It begins with the acknowledgment of God as "sovereign Lord, maker of heaven and earth and sea and of everything in them" (→17:24–29). It continues by quoting the word of God in the second psalm and finding its fulfillment in the events of the death of Jesus. Then it beseeches God for his intervention, which will "enable thy servants to speak thy word with all boldness." And, in accordance with Christ's promise (John 15:16), it closes with the stock formula that is still being employed today in the collects of the church: "Through the name of thy holy servant Jesus" (4:24, 30 NEB). It is entirely consonant with the liturgical character of these verses that the most powerful commentary ever written on the verses of the second psalm that are being quoted in this prayer is the bass solo in George Frideric Handel's oratorio *Messiah*.

4:31 TPR They were all filled with the Holy Spirit and spoke the word of God with boldness to everyone who wanted to believe.

The "filling with the Holy Spirit," therefore, was not confined to the single event of Pentecost (→2:1). "The word of God" could also be called "the word of the Lord [Jesus]" or simply "the gospel" (→8:25).

23. BDAG 310.
24. Hahn 1969, 377.
25. *ODCC* 375–76.

"One, *Holy*, Catholic, and Apostolic Church": Transvaluation of All Values

4:32 TPR The company of those who believed were of one soul and heart, and there was no discrimination among them at all.

Any reader of the New Testament will see in 4:32 a contrast, whether intentional or not, with the most detailed description we have of a dysfunctional Christian congregation, the one at Corinth (1 Cor. 1:10–17), and therefore a concrete definition of holiness in action. Among the four attributes of the church listed in the Niceno-Constantinopolitan Creed—"one, holy, catholic, and apostolic"[26]—the attribute of holiness holds a special place, which is why the Western Apostles' Creed singles it out, together with catholicity, omitting the other two and confessing simply: "the holy catholic church."[27] When at Thessalonica some ruffians formed a mob, shouting, "These men who have turned the world upside down have come here also" (17:5–6), this was not only yet another instance of mob violence and external coercion in matters of faith (→28:31) as well as of the charge of sedition, which Acts is intent on refuting (→25:11), but an unintended recognition of the historical process by which the coming of the gospel and the founding of "the holy catholic church" brought with it the transvaluation of all values—that is, at any rate, how the situation looks from the hindsight of twenty centuries.

The affirmation of a divine sovereignty that trumps "any human authority" (→5:29b) would seem to make every sin ultimately a sin of idolatry (→12:21–23), and conversely to transvalue all values, whether moral or political, economic or social. At the beginning of its narrative, the second chapter of Acts appears to be identifying not a general trend or a statement of average but a total and comprehensive phenomenon by its repetition of the word "all" in both the masculine plural and the neuter plural: "All [πάντες] who believed were together and had all things [ἅπαντα] in common" (2:44). The chapter goes on to describe the steps by which this commonality was achieved: "And they sold their possessions and goods and distributed them to all, as any had need" (2:45).[28] And therefore in the following chapter Peter responded to the importuning of a lame beggar: "I have no silver and gold, but I give you what I have; in the name of Jesus Christ of Nazareth, walk" (3:6). Toward the end of the narrative, Paul felt entitled to "boast," but not "beyond limit" (2 Cor. 10:13) about his ministry: "I coveted no one's silver or gold or apparel. You yourselves know that these hands ministered to my necessities, and to those who were with me. In all things I have shown you that by so toiling one must help the weak, remembering the words of the Lord Jesus, how he said, 'The one who gives is blessed rather than the one who receives [μακάριος ὁ διδῶν μᾶλλον

26. Niceno-Constantinopolitan Creed 9 (*CCF* 1:163).
27. Apostles' Creed 9 (*CCF* 1:669).
28. Haenchen 1971, 230–35.

ἢ ὁ λαμβάνων]'" (20:33–35 TPR). At the very end of the narrative, moreover, there is the observation that in Rome Paul "lived . . . two whole years at his own expense" (28:30). And here in this tragic story of greed and hypocrisy, both Ananias and his wife Sapphira were struck dead for their violations. It should not be surprising, therefore, that the critics of acquisitiveness and the advocates of socialism and communism have repeatedly pointed to the example of this primitive "utopian" communism, for which something resembling the traditional rule "from each according to his ability, to each according to his need" seems to have been the slogan.

Nevertheless, "when we turn to the picture of the leaders and missionaries in the Acts of the Apostles, the evidence concerning possessions is . . . diverse."[29] Except for occasional "communistic" experiments throughout Christian history—and the "angelic life" of poverty, chastity, and obedience in monastic communities (→24:25b)—the utopian idealism of this picture in Acts is marred by the complaint of the "Hellenists" (apparently Jewish Christians who spoke Greek) against the "Hebrews" (presumably Jewish Christians who spoke Aramaic) "because their widows were neglected in the daily distribution" (6:1); as Luke Timothy Johnson observes, citing 1 Tim. 5:3–16, "every welfare system has difficulties balancing need and resources."[30] The questions of Peter to Ananias here (5:4), "While it remained unsold, did it not remain your own? And after it was sold, was it not at your disposal?"—which Chrysostom paraphrases, "Was there any obligation and force? Do we constrain you against your will?"[31]— would appear, moreover, to prove that the "communism" of the primitive Christians coexisted with some sort of acknowledgment of the right of private property and that the community of goods described here and earlier (2:44–47) is to be seen as voluntary rather than compulsory, just as the violation of it is an expression of the free and responsible human will, not an action over which the sinner has no control. Therefore the root sin in this tragedy of Ananias and Sapphira was deception and hypocrisy rather than possession of property as such. Further qualification of the thesis of the transvaluation of all economic and social values comes from the account of the goldsmiths in Ephesus (19:23–41), who were condemned for their aiding and abetting of idolatry rather than for their entrepreneurship as such, as well as from the story (16:16–19), which the author of Acts seems to have witnessed for himself (→27:1), of the "slave girl who had a spirit of divination and brought her owners much gain by soothsaying." In dealing with her case, the apostles did not mount an attack on slavery, but on sorcery and superstition. Together with the Epistle to Philemon, this is evidence of a willingness to go along even with the institution of slavery, a willingness that would continue through many centuries of Christian history, until the transvaluation finally

29. Johnson 1981, 24.
30. Johnson 1992, 106.
31. Chrysostom, *Homilies on Acts* 12 (*NPNF*¹ 11:76).

reached it, too. So also the seemingly callous statement of Jesus, "The poor you always have with you, but you do not always have me" (John 12:8), stands both as an admonition about the priority of the claim that Christ lays upon his disciples and as a poignant reminder: "When was there ever a shortage of the poor in the church?" Saint Augustine could ask on the basis of these words of Jesus.[32]

The homily of Clement of Alexandria, *Who Is the Rich Man That Shall Be Saved?* (which was written in Greek though it is usually cited by its Latin title, *Quis dives salvetur?*) is, according to Ernst Troeltsch, among patristic writings "the only work which deals with the problem [of possessions] directly."[33] Addressing explicitly the Gospel account of the rich young ruler, including the severe statement of Jesus, "It is easier for a camel to go through the eye of a needle than for a rich man to enter the kingdom of God," together with the disciples' astonished question in response, "Who then can be saved?" (Matt. 19:24–25), Clement's treatise implicitly considered this precedent in the apostolic church.[34] Taking as his model the entrepreneurship of the innkeeper in Jesus' parable of the Good Samaritan as recorded by Luke (Luke 10:30–37), Clement asked, "If no one had anything, what room would be left among men for giving?" and "Why should wealth have ever sprung from the earth at all, if it is the author and patron of death?"[35]

4:33 The resurrection of Christ is the only point of the Christian creed to be singled out here specifically, because it was the burden of the apostolic message, here and throughout the book of Acts (→2:31; →8:37).

4:34–37 With a tragic sense and a highly dramatic awareness, this thumbnail sketch of how the believers dealt with their real estate holdings and with other worldly goods was evidently intended to provide a preface and a contrast to the history of Ananias and Sapphira coming up in chapter 5.

32. Augustine, *Tractates on the Gospel of John* 50.12 (*NPNF*[1] 7:282) (translation revised).
33. Troeltsch 1960, 184.
34. Clement of Alexandria, *Who Is the Rich Man That Shall Be Saved?* (*ANF* 2:591–604).
35. Clement of Alexandria, *Who Is the Rich Man That Shall Be Saved?* 13, 26 (*ANF* 2:594, 598).

ACTS 5

"The Holy Spirit, the Lord": The Deity of the Holy Spirit

5:3–4 Why has Satan filled your heart to lie to the Holy Spirit? . . . You have not lied to men but to God.

With a parallel phraseology in the Gospel of John (John 13:27), Luke has described in his Gospel (Luke 22:3) how "Satan entered into Judas called Iscariot" (→10:38; →13:8–11). Thereby he defines the sin of Ananias and Sapphira as one of not giving the glory to God (→12:21–23)—and therefore of not acknowledging, in the later formula of the creed, "the Holy Spirit [as] the Lord." In the original Greek of this passage from the Niceno-Constantinopolitan Creed of 381, τὸ πνεῦμα τὸ ἅγιον, τὸ κύριον,[1] both ἅγιον and κύριον are adjectives, so that the English translations should read, to be altogether precise, "the Spirit, the holy one, the lordly one." But in the Latin text of the decree of the council, and then in the Latin text of the authoritative Western Recension of the creed (and therefore in the English translations of the Latin), τὸ κύριον is translated as a noun (as though it had read τὸν κύριον instead): *Spiritum Sanctum Dominum* ("the Holy Spirit, the Lord)";[2] that makes it a precise (and probably intentional) counterpart to the earlier confession of this creed: *Et in unum Dominum Jesum Christum* ("and in one Lord, Jesus Christ)",[3] where the Greek εἰς ἕνα κύριον actually is a noun.[4] Whatever may or may not be the validity of other Western changes to the text of the Niceno-Constantinopolitan Creed—especially the addition of "and from the Son" (*Filioque*) to the clause of this article on the proceeding of the Holy Spirit[5]—this one clearly does carry

---

1. Niceno-Constantinopolitan Creed 8 (*CCF* 1:162).
2. Niceno-Constantinopolitan Creed: Western Recension 8 (*CCF* 1:672).
3. Niceno-Constantinopolitan Creed: Western Recension 2 (*CCF* 1:672).
4. Niceno-Constantinopolitan Creed 2 (*CCF* 1:162).
5. Niceno-Constantinopolitan Creed: Western Recension 2 (*CCF* 1:672).

ACTS

5:3-4

out the original intent of the council, which was to affirm that the Holy Spirit is God, a hypostasis of the Holy Trinity that is no less divine than the Father or the Son. This it did in response to the awkward situation pointed out by its critics, that both the biblical and the liturgical evidence in support of such an affirmation appeared to be weaker in the case of the Holy Spirit than it was in the case of the Son of God.

As "the greatest Greek orator since Demosthenes,"[6] Saint Gregory of Nazianzus often had the ability to formulate his opponents' arguments more effectively than they themselves had done: "But who worshiped the Spirit? Is there any ancient or modern example? Who prays to the Spirit? Where is the scriptural authority for worshiping or praying to him, from where did you get the idea?"[7] When the Apostle Paul, in the course of catechizing "some disciples" (τινας μαθητάς) at Ephesus, received the amazing response, "No, we have never even heard that there is a Holy Spirit" (19:2), that was symptomatic of a situation that was to continue for centuries. Even after the Council of Nicea in 325 (which had been content to formulate "and [we believe] in the Holy Spirit," with no further elaboration), as Gregory of Nazianzus ruefully acknowledged, "to be only slightly in error [about the deity of the Holy Spirit] was to be orthodox."[8] The struggle to clarify the doctrine of the deity of the Holy Spirit in the following decades, leading up to the First Council of Constantinople in 381 (which codified the doctrine of the Holy Spirit as coequally God in the Niceno-Constantinopolitan Creed) was, as even its defenders had to admit, inhibited by "the silence of Scripture" and the silence of the liturgy. The most important answer both to the exegetical question and to the liturgical one was the baptismal formula (Matt. 28:19), especially as this was expounded, together with the Gloria Patri, by Saint Basil of Caesarea in the most influential of the patristic treatises on the doctrine of the Holy Spirit:[9] baptism "into the name [εἰς τὸ ὄνομα] of Father, Son, and Holy Spirit" did not lump together a creature (the Holy Spirit) with the Creator (the Father and the Son), but affirmed the one divine essence or οὐσία by the singular "the name" (τὸ ὄνομα), and the three divine persons or ὑποστάσεις by putting Father, Son, and Holy Spirit on the same level.

But by a curious twist not without parallel in the history of Christian doctrine—for example, the use of infant baptism (→22:16) by Saint Augustine and others, beginning with Saint Cyprian,[10] to corroborate the doctrine of original sin, thus in effect making the malady suit the remedy[11]—the combination, in consecutive verses of this tragic story, of the apostolic question, "Why has

6. Kennedy 1994, 261.
7. Gregory of Nazianzus, *Orations* 31.12 (SVS 125).
8. Gregory of Nazianzus, *Orations* 21.33 (*NPNF*[2] 7:279).
9. Basil of Caesarea, *On the Holy Spirit* 12.28 (SVS 48–50).
10. Cyprian, *Epistles* 58.5 (*ANF* 5:354).
11. Augustine, *On Forgiveness of Sins, and Baptism* 1.30.58 (*NPNF*[1] 5:37–38); *On Original Sin* 2.16.17 (*NPNF*[1] 5:243).

Satan filled your heart to *lie to the Holy Spirit*?" and of the apostolic assertion, "You have not *lied* to men but *to God*," served as one of the most explicit scriptural proof texts for this doctrine.[12] Saint Basil argued: "This shows that to sin against the Holy Spirit is to sin against God. Understand from this that in every question, the Holy Spirit is indivisibly united with the Father and the Son."[13] Or, in the rhetorical question of Saint Basil's associate, Saint Gregory of Nazianzus the Theologian, "Men . . . who so frighteningly placarded the guilty Ananias and Sapphira, when they lied to the Spirit, as 'liars to God not to man'—are those men, in your opinion, preaching that the Holy Spirit is God or that he is something else?"[14] In a similar exegetical twist, the scornful question of Jesus' detractors, "Who can forgive sins but God alone?" (Mark 2:7), became for Saint Ambrose a syllogism in support of his deity: only God can forgive sins (as you have rightly declared); Jesus Christ has forgiven sins (and backed it up by a miracle of healing, which you have seen with your own eyes); therefore he is God.[15]

The obliqueness of this exegetical argument is further documentation of the status of the dogma (→16:4b) of the Holy Trinity as a doctrine that is not stated in its entirety in any one passage of Scripture, not even in the baptismal formula (Matt. 28:19) and certainly not in the textually unsupportable (→20:28a) *comma johanneum* (1 John 5:7), but that is indispensable to a faithful and theologically "accurate" exegesis (→18:24–26a) of every passage of Scripture and is therefore foundational for its normative interpretation (→8:30–31). Whatever may have been the creedal form or forms in use during the first century (→8:37), the doctrine of the Trinity eventually came to be seen as the only way to speak about Jesus Christ as the church had always been doing and to affirm the deity of the Holy Spirit, without sacrificing the biblical monotheism (→19:28) that was confessed, also by Christ himself (Mark 12:29), in the words of the Shema (Deut. 6:4): "Hear, O Israel: The LORD our God is one LORD."

There are passages in Acts, including perhaps the question Paul asked at Ephesus, "Did you receive the Holy Spirit when you believed?" (19:2), where "the Holy Spirit" seems to mean primarily not the person or hypostasis of the Holy Spirit in the Trinity, but "the gift of the Holy Spirit," which "fell" (19:6 TPR) upon believers at baptism but also on other occasions (→2:1), what Joseph Fitzmyer calls "the nonpersonified activity of the Spirit."[16] That is the logic underlying the apostle's explanation of "the spiritual gifts" (τὰ πνευματικά) (1 Cor. 12:1) in relation to "the same Spirit" (τὸ . . . αὐτὸ πνεῦμα) (1 Cor. 12:4): the sometimes bewildering diversity of these gifts, as it seems

12. Bede, *Exposition of the Acts of the Apostles* 5 (PL 92:955).
13. Basil of Caesarea, *On the Holy Spirit* 16.37 (SVS 61).
14. Gregory of Nazianzus, *Orations* 31.30 (SVS 141).
15. Ambrose of Milan, *On the Christian Faith* 2.12.116 (*NPNF*[2] 10:238–39).
16. Joseph Fitzmyer in Verheyden 1999, 179.

to have manifested itself at Corinth (and as it has manifested itself repeatedly through the centuries), was not to be explained by polytheistically ascribing each one to a separate deity or "spirit," but "all these are inspired by one and the same Spirit, who apportions to each one individually as he wills" (1 Cor. 12:11). In a curious way, that lends added force to this argument for the deity of the Holy Spirit on the basis of the apostle's words about lying not to mere human beings but to God, and therefore to the Latin creedal formula *Spiritum Sanctum Dominum.*

5:4–11 In describing Paul's involvement in the justice system of the Roman Empire (→25:8) and his appeal from local authorities to the central authority of the tribunal of Caesar (→25:11), the book of Acts puts great emphasis on the constitutional principle—constitutional in the Roman sense as well as in the American sense—of "due process of law" (→25:16). But at any rate as it is described in these verses, the theocratic Petrine justice system in these two trials does seem to have been largely unencumbered by such a principle, casting the divinely inspired apostle in the role of judge and jury—and God the Holy Spirit in the role of executioner. By contrast with the deliberations of the apostolic council to be described later (→15:28), therefore, this peremptory trial procedure was, it seems safe to conclude, not intended, even for the more extreme advocates of papal authority, to serve as a "biblical model" of "decision-making in the church"[17] for later generations. At least it can be said to have fulfilled, in a grim way, another traditional constitutional principle: "Justice delayed is justice denied."

5:12 The term "sign" (σημεῖον), used here, is fundamental to the biblical understanding of miracles (→6:8), which were not an end in themselves, but were seen as pointing beyond themselves to the power and the mercy of God, whom the most complete and accurate (→18:24–26a) references to such actions therefore described, as this verse does, as having performed the miracles "through" human agency (19:11).

5:18–19 Unjust imprisonment followed by angelic intervention (→12:7) was a persistent pattern. It was to be repeated, though with much more narrative detail, in Peter's arrest by orders of King Herod (12:1–11) and then in the arrest of Paul and Silas, which climaxed in a liberating earthquake (16:19–40). But because it was the divine plan for Paul to be brought to Rome and (though after the narrative in Acts) to be executed there (20:24), his appeal to the tribunal of Caesar (25:11) was to be allowed to work its way through the Roman legal procedure (→25:16) without the interference of angels or miracles.

17. Johnson 1983.

5:26 But without violence.

Although this stipulation is not quite unique in the chapters of the book of Acts, there was enough violence and coercion of all kinds to make this refusal to resort to brute force a noteworthy exception (→28:31).

5:28 We strictly charged you not to teach in this name, yet here you have filled Jerusalem with your teaching and you intend to bring this man's blood upon us.

The exchange between Pilate and the people, "I am innocent of *this man's blood*" and "*his blood* be on us and on our children!" (Matt. 27:24–25), which has played such a terrifying role in the history of Christian anti-Semitism as supposedly the self-imposed curse on the Jewish people for being the killers of Christ, does not appear in Luke's Gospel. But it—or, at any rate, this way of speaking, going back to the Old Testament formula "to lay their blood upon [τὸ αἷμα αὐτῶν ἐπιθεῖναι] their brother Abimelech, who slew them, and upon the men of Sicima, because they strengthened his hands to slay his brethren" (Judg. 9:24 LXX)—does seem to be at work here, as it is later in the words of Paul to the Ephesian elders asseverating his innocence (20:26).

"One, Holy, Catholic, and *Apostolic* Church": The Twelve and the Primacy of Peter

5:29a TPR But Peter, answering, said to him.

In the TPR it is Peter alone who speaks here, without reference to "the apostles" as in the Greek text underlying the RSV, just as the TPR earlier says that "he [Peter] put forward two [candidates as successors of Judas] . . . and he [Peter] prayed and said" (1:23–24 TPR). Even if the correct reading of this text is the RSV's "Peter and the apostles," moreover, it does not say "Peter and the *other* apostles." Nor is it plausible, as it might be in the case of the formula of the angel to the myrrh-bearing women at the resurrection, "Tell his disciples *and Peter*" (Mark 16:7), to explain such a distinction between "Peter" and "the apostles" on the ground that Peter was being set apart from the body of the disciples because of his having denied Christ, for by this time he had been restored to his position, with a threefold commission from Christ to match his threefold denial of Christ (John 21:15–19). Rather, this text makes it obligatory to come to terms with the primacy of the Apostle Peter in the college of the apostles, and ultimately with the more comprehensive problem of authority, which can be encapsulated in the formula "the twelve/the seven [→6:6]/Paul [→9:15]."[18]

18. Bihler 1963, 209–16.

Central to the history of the postresurrection church from the very beginning has been the issue of apostolic authority.[19] After the rosters of the twelve
apostles in each of the three Synoptic Gospels (Matt. 10:2–4; Mark 3:16–19;
Luke 6:14–16)—there is, for some reason, no such roster in the Gospel of
John—Acts 1:13 is the first in which only eleven names are listed, with the
deletion of the name of the one whom Luke already in his first catalog of
apostles, the one in his Gospel, had identified proleptically as "Judas Iscariot,
who became a traitor" (Luke 6:16); the name Judas had come last not only in
the Gospel of Luke, but in all three of those lists. Within all three, moreover,
the order varies in other ways as well, and even more so in some manuscripts
(1:13)—except for the one striking fact, which it is extremely difficult to explain as an accident, that the name Peter always comes first, as it still does in
Acts. The Gospel of Matthew, which contains the promise, "You are Peter, and
on this rock I will build my church, and the powers of death shall not prevail
against it" (Matt. 16:18), also stipulates, "The names of the twelve apostles
are these: *first, Simon, who is called Peter*"; the word "first" in this passage is
an adjective, πρῶτος, not an adverb (Matt. 10:2), which would seem to give
it more significance than merely that of a sequence in an itemized list. The
Gospel of Luke, which does not contain that promise to Peter, does contain
the promise, which is also emblazoned on the wall of Saint Peter's Basilica in
Rome and which has in some respects been no less important in the history
of Petrine and papal primacy because of the magisterial role it assigns to Peter
in relation to the body of the apostles (and therefore, presumably, also in relation to the body of the church for all time): "I have prayed for you that your
faith may not fail; and you, when once you have been converted, strengthen
your brothers [*et tu, aliquando conversus, confirma fratres tuos*]" (Luke 22:32
Vulgate). In 1 Corinthians, Paul's roster of those who have been what Luke in
his Gospel characterizes as "eyewitnesses" "from the beginning" (οἱ ἀπ᾽ ἀρχῆς
αὐτόπται) (1:2), specifically of the resurrection of Christ (→2:31), begins with
"he appeared to Cephas, then to the twelve" (1 Cor. 15:5), and later adds "to
James, then to all the apostles" (1 Cor. 15:7). Once again—and, it would seem,
not only for the reason of simple chronology, since the first appearance was
not to any of these male disciples at all but to "Mary Magdalene and Joanna
and Mary the mother of James and the other women with them," who then
(→18:24–26b) told it to "the apostles" (Luke 24:10)—Peter's name came first,
and once again he was being distinguished from the twelve (or the eleven) while
still also remaining one of them.

In the beginning chapter of the book of Acts—after Christ himself (1:4, 7–8),
the errant disciples as a group (1:6), and the angels (1:10–11)—the first to speak
officially, according to all the manuscripts, is "Peter, [who] stood up among the
brethren (the company of persons was in all about a hundred twenty)" (1:15).
Moreover, if we are to follow the singular verb in a textual variant (→20:28a)

19. Kirsopp Lake in Foakes Jackson and Lake 1979, 5:37–59; Jervell 1972, 75–112.

contained in the TPR of 1:23 but not in other manuscripts, "and he put forward" (καὶ ἔστησεν), the nomination of "Joseph called Barsabbas, who was surnamed Justus, and Matthias" came from Peter alone, not from the college of apostles as a group. Again in the second chapter it was "Peter, standing with the ten apostles" (2:14 TPR), who acted as spokesman for the twelve and for the church as a whole. Later, when the time came for a decision on a question threatening the unity of the church, "the apostles and the elders were gathered together to consider this matter. After there had been much debate, Peter rose and said to them" (15:6–7). Nevertheless, the authoritative appeal there was definitely not directed to Peter individually but to this council of the apostles and the elders (→15:28), for whom, it should also be noted, it was the Apostle James, not the Apostle Peter, who functioned as the spokesman, "standing up and saying: 'Brethren, listen to *me*. . . . *My* judgment is that . . .'" (15:13, 19 TPR). As Chrysostom felt obliged to explain, "Peter does everything with the common consent; nothing imperiously."[20] And it was the council of apostles and elders as a whole, rather than Peter or James or any other individual apostle, that laid claim to the right to invoke this momentous formula of decisive authority and divine inspiration, which later statements of faith were to appropriate:[21] "It has seemed good to the Holy Spirit and to us" (→15:28).

"One Lord": The Sovereignty That Trumps Any Human Authority

5:29b We must obey God rather than men.

The unambiguous monotheism of the Christian confession, even and especially of the confession of the "one God" and "one Lord" in the trinitarian formulary of the Niceno-Constantinopolitan Creed,[22] carried with it this affirmation and obligation, "We must obey God rather than men," which, as it stands, has been the unanimous teaching of both the Old and the New Testament, as well as of the subsequent history of the church since the earliest centuries:[23] Moses before Pharaoh, Elijah before Ahab and Jezebel, John the Baptist before Herod, Paul before the Sanhedrin and before Festus—and Ambrose before Theodosius, Theodore of Studios before Constantine VI, Luther before Charles V at the Diet of Worms, and Martin Luther King before the power structure of White America—all were expressing this obligation to appeal from the abuse of political power by human authorities to the ultimate sovereignty of God. The law of nations was not permitted to contravene the law of God (→25:8). Sometimes with greater, sometimes with lesser, effect, this imperative has acted as a restraint on the recurring tendency of institutional

20. Chrysostom, *Homilies on Acts* 3 (*NPNF*[1] 11:18).
21. Pelikan 2003, 100.
22. Niceno-Constantinopolitan Creed 1–2 (*CCF* 1:163).
23. Dionysius of Alexandria, *Epistles* 10.4 (*ANF* 6:105).

Christendom to use passages such as Rom. 13 to strike a Faustian bargain with
the political powers that be (→25:11). But in the face of twentieth-century totalitarianism these words have come to occupy a special place. The Indonesian
Batak Confession of 1951 cited Rom. 13 in support of its teaching that "the
government which has authority comes from God," but then it immediately
went on to add: "Nevertheless one should also remember what is written in
Acts 5.29: 'We ought to obey God rather than man.'"[24] And in the spirit of this
formula from the book of Acts, the heroic reaffirmation of the Christian faith
against Nazi neopaganism, the Barmen Declaration of the German Evangeli-
cal Church of 1934, which was to become one of the authoritative sources for
the Batak Confession, had responded to the threat of National Socialism by
confessing: "We reject the false doctrine, as though the state, over and beyond
its special commission, should and could become the single and totalitarian
order of human life, thus fulfilling the church's vocation as well."[25]

But in the confessions coming out of the Protestant Reformation, this
absolute priority of "God rather than man" took on a new meaning and an
added force, when the exclusionary term "any human authority" was taken
to refer not only to civil government but also to the authority of the ecclesiastical hierarchy. Thus the Heidelberg Catechism was speaking for most of
these confessions when it invoked this passage to declare: "I should rather
turn my back on all creatures than do the least thing against his will."[26] In
its final article, "The Power of Bishops," the Augsburg Confession quoted
this formula of Acts verbatim to affirm that if bishops "cannot be persuaded
to mitigate or abrogate regulations which are not to be observed without
sin, we are bound to follow the apostolic rule which commands us to obey
God rather than men."[27] This was in opposition not only to the medieval
Roman Catholic doctrine enunciated in Unam Sanctam of 1302, that in its
superiority to political rulers church authority, "although given to a man and
exercised by a man, is not human, but rather divine, given at God's mouth
to Peter,"[28] but to the more universally Catholic and Orthodox doctrine of
authority, as this was formulated, for example, by Dositheus and the Eastern
Orthodox Synod of Jerusalem in 1672, that "for the catholic church, as never
having spoken or speaking from herself but from the Spirit of God . . . it is
impossible to err in any way, or to deceive at all or be deceived; but like the
Divine Scripture, she is infallible and has perpetual authority."[29] Therefore
the subordination of all human authority in this passage was not to be taken
to apply to Holy Church as administered by human beings any more than

24. Batak Confession of Faith 12 (*CCF* 3:553).
25. Barmen Declaration 5 (*CCF* 3:508).
26. Heidelberg Catechism 94 (*CCF* 2:449).
27. Augsburg Confession 28.75 (*CCF* 2:116).
28. Unam Sanctam (*CCF* 1:746–47).
29. Confession of Dositheus 2 (*CCF* 1:616).

it did to Holy Scripture as written by human beings, but only to "purely human" authorities.[30]

5:31 TPR Him God exalted with his glory as Leader and Savior.

The "christological titles of majesty"[31] "Leader" (ἀρχηγός) and "Savior" (σωτήρ) were employed here are part of the vocabulary of Acts and of other books of the New Testament, by which, like the church in every century since, it sought, drawing on the Greek of the Septuagint as well as on other sources, to put into words and formulas the faith of the church concerning Christ and his relation to God the Father (→8:37). Here Jesus was said to be exalted with the glory of God by the conferral of the title of ἀρχηγός, which had been used by the book of Isaiah to show that "Jerusalem is in ruins and Judah has fallen," because there was no one who could claim to be an authentic ἀρχηγός (Isa. 3:6–8 LXX); and of the title of σωτήρ, as in the Septuagint prayer to God: "Blessed art thou, the Savior of Israel" (εὐλογητὸς εἶ, ὁ σωτὴρ Ἰσραηλ) (1 Macc. 4:30 LXX).

5:33 Violence and "rage" by its enemies persisted as reactions to the gospel (→14:22; →21:13–14; →28:31).

5:38–39 TPR If this authority comes from human will, its power will fail.

The deliberations of this "council" or Sanhedrin were a foil to the subsequent "council" of the apostles (→15:28). But this statement of Gamaliel, whom Paul in a later chapter (22:3) was to identify as having been his mentor in rabbinic study, continued to be quoted by Christian writers as "the very wise saying of Gamaliel, recorded in the Acts of the Apostles,"[32] because it constituted an appeal to the workings of the divine economy in human history as a form of revelation (→15:8–9).

5:41 Rejoicing that they were counted worthy to suffer dishonor for the name.

The theme of martyrdom and the cost of discipleship would have its most climactic expression in the account of the death of Stephen (7:58–8:3), but this "worth[iness] to suffer dishonor" (and worse) runs through the entire narrative. Both "the name" and "the Way" in this passage are technical terms of self-identification for those who eventually came to be called "Christians" (→11:26).

5:42 The temple in Jerusalem was still the place to which the disciples went to teach and preach that Jesus was the Messiah (→3:25).

---

30. Nikanor 1905, 1:116.
31. Hahn 1969.
32. Origen, *Contra Celsum* 1.57 (Chadwick 1953, 52–53).

ACTS 6

"Faith and Order"

6:2–4 And the twelve summoned the body of the disciples and said, "It is not right that we should give up preaching the word of God to serve tables. Therefore, brethren, pick out from among you seven men of good repute, full of the Spirit and of wisdom, whom we may appoint to this duty. But we will devote ourselves to prayer and to the ministry of the word."

The selection of these seven deacons, with the allocation to them of certain duties that had previously fallen to the apostles themselves, has long been interpreted as the institution of the traditional threefold ministry of bishop, presbyter, and deacon,[1] with, at least eventually, various related gradations of these offices such as archbishop, protopresbyter, subdeacon, and the like. In the debates that have been carried on over faith *and* order since the Reformation of the sixteenth century and in the ecumenical effort since the nineteenth century to address and resolve those debates, many of the major denominational divisions especially within Anglo-Saxon Protestantism—as the labels "Episcopalian," "Presbyterian," and "Congregationalist" attest—have defined themselves primarily on the basis of questions of ministry and polity rather than on the basis of issues of doctrine and confession as such. Or, to be more precise, as Wilhelm Niesel puts it, not only doctrine but "church order, too, bears a confessional character" there as well as throughout the Reformed tradition.[2] As a consequence, the technical terms for ministry especially in the book of Acts and in the Pastoral Epistles have been an object of painstaking scrutiny, if not of anything approaching theological consensus. Even the question of how

---

1. Irenaeus, *Against Heresies* 3.23.10; 4.26.2 (*ANF* 1:434, 497); Eusebius, *Church History* 2.1.1 (*NPNF*² 1:103–4).
2. Niesel 1938, v.

to translate these terms, above all here in the book of Acts, has proven to be a daunting theological and scholarly challenge, as the variations among the English translations of the Acts of the Apostles document. Paul's farewell to the leaders of the church of Ephesus, which is even as literature one of the most moving scenes in the book (→21:13–14), is an apt illustration of the ambiguity: in introducing the farewell address, the writer of Acts calls these leaders τοὺς πρεσβυτέρους τῆς ἐκκλησίας (20:17), but a few verses later Paul in his address to them says that the Holy Spirit had made these same men ἐπισκόπους over the church (20:28). In such a passage at any rate, it does seem, as even Roman Catholic scholarship must acknowledge, that "this terminology appears to fluctuate a bit,"[3] and that the title πρεσβύτερος and the title ἐπίσκοπος refer to the same person at the same time, so that it would be anachronistic to read the later distinction back into this text. Although the Greek titles πρεσβύτερος and ἐπίσκοπος are historically the etymological origin of the English titles "presbyter/priest" and "bishop," the AV, RSV, and NRSV all translate them in Acts 20 with "elder" and "overseer," respectively. Both "bishop" (ἐπίσκοπος) (20:28) and "presbyter" (πρεσβύτερος) (11:30; 14:23; 15:2, 4, 6, 22, 23; 16:4; 21:18) appear in the book of Acts several times as titles for incumbents of a ministerial office; διάκονος ("deacon"), however, does not, although διακονία ("ministry") does, but it is applied, not to a third rank of "diaconate" alongside episcopacy and prebyterate, but to the life and ministry of the Apostle Paul (20:24; 21:19).

Also beyond these titles, the nomenclature for ministerial office (or offices) in the book of Acts is far from clear—or consistent. Thus the title "prophet" (προφήτης) applies chiefly to the Hebrew prophets and to their books, but also to a continuing office in the Christian church (→21:9–10). Beyond "the twelve," which is itself a technical title (→5:29a), "disciple" (μαθητής) expands its meaning as its numbers expand, to include a wider circle of later followers of Jesus, whether or not this usage implies any church office rather than simply a religious status as a synonym for "Christian," which became in fact a synonym for it (→11:26). Thus in the present passage "the twelve" are clearly distinguished from "the body of the disciples," and a few verses later "the number of the disciples" is said to have "multiplied greatly" (6:7). At least sometimes (9:1–2), "disciples" includes women (→18:24–26b); and there is even a special term, μαθήτρια in Greek and *discipula* in Latin (which occurs only once in the New Testament), for a women disciple, Tabitha (9:36). In one place (1:15), where most manuscripts and versions have "Peter stood up among the brethren [ἀδελφῶν]," the TPR has "disciples" (μαθητῶν).

More crucial for the problem of faith and order is the title "apostle." The preface to Acts makes a point of stipulating that it is referring to "the apostles whom he [Jesus] had chosen [οὓς ἐξελέξατο]" already before the resurrection (1:2), and Luke identifies "the twelve" by the title "apostles" (Luke 9:1, 10, 12).

3. J. Bellamy in *DTC* 1:350.

In his epistles Paul presented his credentials (→9:15) by identifying himself as one who has been "called to be an apostle, set apart for the gospel of God" (Rom. 1:1) and, when this came under attack, by making clear that it meant "an apostle—not from men nor through man, but through Jesus Christ and God the Father" (Gal. 1:1), unworthy though he personally was of this title because of his having "persecuted the church of God" (1 Cor. 15:8–9). Here in Acts, though the narrative account of his being "called and set apart" appears three times (→9:1–4), it was the title "disciple" of which the other disciples initially deemed him to be unworthy (9:26); but there does not appear to be any explicit event or rite of initiation assigning to him the title "apostle." Indeed, in the wording of the description of the events leading up to the apostolic council in Jerusalem (→15:28), "Paul and Barnabas and some of the others were appointed to go up to Jerusalem to the apostles and elders [πρὸς τοὺς ἀποστόλους καὶ πρεσβυτέρους] about this question" (15:2), as well as in the wording of the four subsequent appearances of this designation "apostles and elders" later in the same chapter (15:4, 6, 22, 23), there would seem to be some sort of distinction being made not only between "apostles" (ἀπόστολοι) and "elders" (πρεσβύτεροι), but between both of these categories and Paul (as well as Barnabas).

The legitimate, indeed obligatory, striving for "accuracy" (ἀκρίβεια) and precision (→18:24–26a) in the defining not only of "faith" but also of "order" cannot be used (though it sometimes seems to be used) to justify an effort to impose a greater precision on the biblical text than its own language warrants. As the Lima Text, one of the most careful and thoughtful of modern ecumenical confessions, makes clear, "the New Testament does not describe a single pattern of ministry which might serve as a blueprint or continuing norm for all future ministry in the church. . . . [Only] during the second and third centuries, a threefold pattern of bishop, presbyter, and deacon became established as the pattern of ordained ministry throughout the church."[4] The question of the permanent normative authority of that pattern of ordained ministry for the church of subsequent centuries, therefore, cannot be decided by the authority of "Scripture alone," but depends on the authority that one accords to apostolic tradition in relation to the authority of apostolic Scripture (→16:4b).

6:5 It has been noted that "these Greek names show that the majority were chosen from among the Hellenists."[5] Stephen is listed among them as "only" a deacon, who is charged with "serving tables" so that the apostles can "devote [them]selves to prayer and to the ministry of the word." But in the following chapter (7:1–53) he proceeds to deliver one of the most rhetorically powerful (→24:1–2) and scripturally learned (→8:30–31) exercises of "the ministry of the word" in the whole of Acts, and well beyond.

4. Lima Text: Baptism, Eucharist, Ministry 3.19 (*CCF* 3:832).
5. Lopuchin 1895, 608.

The Laying-on of Hands

6:6 These [seven candidates for the diaconate] they set before the apostles, and they prayed and laid their hands upon them.

Taken for granted here rather than explained, 6:6 is the first of several references in the book of Acts to a ritual laying-on of hands,[6] which is designated by the technical term χειροτονεῖν (14:23); the grammatical antecedent of "*they laid their hands*" in this verse, Bede explains, is not those who "set them before the apostles," but "the apostles."[7] Without imposing arbitrary distinctions, it is possible, also with the aid of parallels in the Old Testament and in the Gospels, to distinguish several distinct functions and meanings of the ritual of χειροτονία in the book of Acts:

1. In imitation of Christ (→7:59–60), to whom the ruler of the synagogue came with the petition, "My daughter has just died; but come and lay your hand on her, and she will live" (Matt. 9:18), and in fulfillment of his promise that his disciples "will lay their hands on the sick, and they will recover" (Mark 16:18), the act of a disciple in laying hands on someone could confer the gift of miraculous healing (→6:8). As was announced to Saul/Paul (9:12) in an extraordinary vision (→16:9) at the very beginning of his apostolic ministry, the sudden blindness that came upon him when he was overpowered by the uncreated light (→22:6) on the road to Damascus was healed when Ananias, "laying his hands on him . . . said, 'Brother Saul, the Lord Jesus who appeared to you on the road by which you came, has sent me that you may regain your sight and be filled with the Holy Spirit.' And immediately something like scales fell from his eyes and he regained his sight. Then he rose and was baptized" (9:17–18). Near the end of Paul's apostolic ministry, as he was sailing (→27:24) toward Rome, he did the same for the father of Publius, the "chief man" of Malta, when he "visited him and prayed, and putting his hands on him healed him" (28:8).
2. But it is evident from the first of these two accounts of healing involving Paul that the laying-on of hands often included much more than miraculous healing: ". . . that you may regain your sight *and be filled with the Holy Spirit*. . . . Then he rose and was baptized" (9:17–18 TPR). And so, when Peter and John "came down [to Samaria] and prayed for them that they might receive the Holy Spirit," this prayer was answered through the laying-on of hands: "Then they laid their hands on them and they received the Holy Spirit" (8:15–17). In Ephesus, similarly, "when Paul had laid his hands upon [some who were already 'disciples'], the Holy Spirit

6. J. Coppens in Kremer 1979, 405–38.
7. Bede, *Retractations on the Acts of the Apostles* 6 (PL 92:1012).

came on them; and they spoke with tongues and prophesied" (19:6). In both of these instances, moreover, the laying-on of hands was closely tied to the administration of baptism (→22:16).

3. Laying-on of hands was also tied to another of the "sacraments" (if it is not anachronistic to use that language): Ananias's administration of the rite of laying-on of hands upon Saul may also suggest that this was the means of his being ordained to the ministry of the church (→9:15), because it is in this same context that "the Lord said to [Ananias], 'Go, for he is a chosen instrument [σκεῦος ἐκλογῆς] of mine to carry my name before the Gentiles and kings and the sons of Israel'" (9:15). The connection with ordination clearly seems to be the implication of the laying-on of hands in the present passage, as "the apostles . . . prayed and laid their hands upon them," ordaining them as deacons (→6:2–4), including Stephen. On the other hand, it does not appear to be the rite of ordination when the Holy Spirit says to the church at Antioch, "'Set apart for me [ἀφορίσατε . . . μοι] Barnabas and Paul for the work to which I have called them.' Then after fasting and praying they laid their hands on them and sent them off" (13:2–3 TPR). Their actual ordination would seem to have preceded this, for Barnabas was already listed, and even listed first, among the "prophets and teachers" (προφῆται καὶ διδάσκαλοι) at Antioch (13:1), and Paul was already carrying on his apostolic ministry and "increas[ing] all the more in strength" (9:22).

Anyone coming to the reading of Acts from a knowledge of the Septuagint would recognize in this rite a continuation of the ordination of the Levites, in which "the sons of Israel shall lay their hands [ἐπιθήσουσιν . . . τὰς χεῖρας αὐτῶν] upon the Levites" (Num. 8:10 LXX), and in particular of the ordination of Joshua to stand in unbroken continuity (→2:42) with the ministry of Moses: "And Joshua the son of Naue was filled with the spirit of knowledge, for Moses had laid his hands upon him [ἐπέθηκεν γὰρ Μωυσῆς τὰς χεῖρας αὐτοῦ ἐπ᾽ αὐτόν]" (Deut. 34:9 LXX). This Old Testament precedent and the usage here in Acts, in turn, supply the context for the references in the Pastoral Epistles to the laying-on of hands, also in association with a ritual act of ordination to the ministry of the church: "Do not neglect the gift you have, which was given you by prophetic utterance when the council of elders laid their hands upon you [μετὰ ἐπιθέσεως τῶν χειρῶν τοῦ πρεσβυτερίου]" (1 Tim. 4:14); "hence I remind you to rekindle the gift of God that is within you through the laying on of my hands" (2 Tim. 1:6). In Chrysostom's summary, "This is the meaning of χειροτονία (i.e., 'putting forth the hand') or ordination: the hand of the man is laid upon (the person), but the whole work is of God, and it is His hand which toucheth the head of the one ordained, if he be duly ordained."[8]

8. Chrysostom, *Homilies on Acts* 14 (*NPNF*[1] 11:90).

On the darker side, watching the power of the Spirit being conferred by the disciples through this rite was also the provocation for Simon Magus, the sorcerer (→10:38; →19:28), to try to buy it for himself, "saying, 'Give me also this power, that any one on whom I lay my hands may receive the Holy Spirit,'" and for Peter's devastating response to Simon's request: "Your silver perish with you, because you thought you could obtain the gift of God with money!" (8:19–20). Therefore it is specifically as the purchasing of ecclesiastical ordination for money that "simony" is defined.[9]

6:7 TPR And a great many in the temple were obedient to the faith.

If, instead of the TPR, we read "and a great many of the priests were obedient to the faith" (RSV), this would be a rare case of a laudatory reference to "a great many of the priests," for in the writings of Luke, as in the other books of the New Testament, Jewish "priests" and "chief priests" receive a bad press, as the parable of the Good Samaritan illustrates (Luke 10:31). In the New Testament neither the disciples/apostles nor their successors, whether bishops or presbyters, are adorned with the title "priest" (ἱερεύς), which in its Christian sense is either reserved for Christ, especially throughout the Epistle to the Hebrews, or is shared by all believers (1 Pet. 2:9; Rev. 1:6; 5:10). Just to complicate the nomenclature of the doctrine of the ministry still further, the English title "priest," which regularly translates ἱερεύς and *sacerdos*, is itself the abbreviated corruption of the New Testament title πρεσβύτερος.[10]

Miracles as "Signs"

6:8 TPR Stephen, full of grace and power, did great wonders and signs among the people in the name of Jesus Christ.

A special form of the imitation of Christ (→7:59–60) in the Acts of the Apostles is the fulfillment in the apostles and their ministry of the extraordinary promise of Christ to his disciples, which is recorded not in the Gospel of Luke, but in the closing discourses of the Gospel of John: "He who believes in me will also do the works that I do; and *greater works than these will he do* [καὶ μείζονα τούτων ποιήσει], because I go to the Father" (John 14:12), thus promising explicitly that, although "a disciple is not above his teacher" (Luke 6:40), the disciple would surpass his teacher in performing what this verse calls "great wonders and signs." Repeatedly, therefore, in the midst of a narrative like the sailing stories of Acts (→27:24), large portions of which can sound almost naturalistic, there come such accounts of miraculous deeds by

9. A. Bride in *DTC* 14:2141–60.
10. *OED* 12:464.

the apostles (27:23–26). It likewise needs to be pointed out in this context that all of the acts of healing in this book—whether or not, as tradition has maintained, it was written by "Luke the beloved physician" (Col. 4:14), who would presumably have been interested (and trained) in the practice of Hellenistic naturalistic medicine[11]—were miraculous, even, for example, when it was from snakebite, with the characteristic symptoms described in some clinical detail (28:3–6). These miraculous powers, moreover, were not only borne by particular persons, but even by inanimate physical objects, the "handkerchiefs or aprons" that had touched Paul's skin (19:12) or even the nonmaterial shadow of Peter (5:15).[12]

It is necessary to read the miracle accounts of the Gospels and the Acts in the context of the understandings of miracle and natural law in late antiquity and at the same time to recognize their special function in the New Testament narratives. Nearly contemporary sources such as the *Life of Apollonius of Tyana* show that these miracle accounts in the Gospels and the book of Acts were by no means unique and that there was a widespread belief in the power of the divine—and of those human beings with special powers conferred by the divine—to break out of the confines not only of time and space, but of ordinary and natural causality.[13]

The primary interest here in Acts, nevertheless, was not in these "extraordinary miracles" (δυνάμεις . . . τυχούσας) (19:11) as spectacles, but in the sovereignty of God the Creator over his creation (→17:24–29) and over its laws, not only at the beginning of time but throughout and to the very end (→28:23). In the first century no less than in the twenty-first, announcing that sovereignty of God over the laws of nature, above all its implications for the lordship of the Creator even over the power of death (→2:31), was the best way to evoke "mockery" (17:32), also from a philosophically minded audience of those who "spent their time in nothing except telling or hearing something new" (17:21): apparently this celebrated eagerness for τι καινότερον did have its limits. The natural curiosity of author or reader about the minutiae of such healing miracles is curbed by the consistent reminder of divine agency that "*God* did extraordinary miracles by the hands of Paul" (19:11), which was therefore being implied even when (as here) it was said that "*Stephen* . . . did great wonders and signs," to which the TPR adds the stipulation: "in the name of Jesus Christ." Even Jesus himself, whom Peter called "the Author of life" (3:15), was, in Peter's message, "a man attested to you by God with mighty works and wonders and signs *which God did through him* in your midst" (2:22). It was not the apostles themselves, then, but the Lord "who bore witness to the word of his grace, granting signs and wonders to be done by their hands [διὰ τῶν χειρῶν αὐτῶν]" (14:3), this prepositional phrase in Greek being a "Hebraistic circumlocution"

11. See pp. 30–31 above.
12. Haenchen 1971, 242–46; Marguerat 1999, 175–204.
13. Grant 1952.

to indicate instrumentality or agency.[14] When Barnabas and Paul recounted their experiences to "all the assembly" of the apostolic council at Jerusalem, they "related what signs and wonders *God had done through them* among the Gentiles" (15:12).

"Stephen . . . did great wonders and signs [τέρατα καὶ σημεῖα μεγάλα]." In many ways the key to terms used in connection with miracles—δύναμις, θάμβος, θαῦμα, σημεῖον, τέρας, φανερόν—in the vocabulary of Acts, and in the vocabulary of the New Testament generally, is σημεῖον,[15] which explicitly points beyond the deed, howsoever spectacular it might be, to that *signatum* for which the deed served as *signum*. A miracle was not a stained-glass window to be looked *at*, but a transparent window to be looked *through*. Therefore σημεῖον often appears in combination with one of these other terms and as a clarification of it, as in "mighty works and wonders and signs" (δυνάμεσι καὶ τέρασι καὶ σημείοις) (2:22), "wonders and signs" (τέρατα καὶ σημεῖα) (here and in 2:43; 7:36), and "signs and wonders" (σημεῖα καὶ τέρατα) (4:30; 5:12; 15:12).

The sign-character of miracles was underscored by their relation to the word of God. In his epistles, Saint Paul drew the sharpest possible contrast between those who "demand signs" (σημεῖα αἰτοῦσιν) or who "seek wisdom" (σοφίαν ζητοῦσιν), be they Jews or Greeks, and the word of God proclaiming "Christ crucified" (1 Cor. 1:22–25). In Luke's Gospel, Christ crucified and risen was himself the "sign," as Simeon predicted in the temple (Luke 2:34–35) and as Christ himself confirmed (Luke 11:29–32). And here in the Acts of the Apostles, Christ "grant[ed] signs and wonders to be done by [the] hands of" Paul and Barnabas as a means of bearing "witness to the word of his grace" (14:3).

The ambiguity of miracles as signs became evident from the reaction of unbelievers to them. Their exasperation was palpable: "What shall we do with these men? For it is very evident [φανερότερον] to all who dwell in Jerusalem that a remarkable sign [γνωστὸν σημεῖον] has been performed by them, and we cannot deny it" (4:16 TPR). But sometimes their response entailed a total misunderstanding of the sign, as when at Lystra the miracles performed by Paul and Barnabas made the natives believe that they were Olympian deities and try to make sacrifices to them (14:8–18), or when at Philippi the rescue of Paul and Silas from prison by the miracle of an earthquake made their jailer contemplate suicide—but then become a believer in the one true God (16:25–34). This ambiguity of miracles as signs for those outside the faith was closely related to the issue of public verifiability, both the verifiability of the miracles themselves and their use to establish the credibility of the gospel message (→26:26).

14. BDF §217.
15. BDAG 920–21.

6:11–14 These trumped-up charges are, it would seem intentionally, reminiscent of the charges against Jesus at his trial (→3:25; →7:47–48; →7:59–60; →16:4a).

6:15 And gazing at him, all who sat in the council saw that his face was like the face of an angel.

Together with other items in the narrative from this chapter onward, this striking detail, and the language in which it is described sounds like something that might have come from the recollections of the Apostle Paul, who, as one of the "eyewitnesses" (αὐτόπται) (Luke 1:2) of these events, would have provided the same kind of information for the book of Acts that various "eyewitnesses and ministers of the word," perhaps including the Blessed Virgin Mary, had supplied to Saint Luke as he was "investigating everything carefully from the very first" (Luke 1:2–3 NRSV) for his Gospel (→27:1). If it did come from Paul formerly Saul, such a haunting memory of the innocent face of Stephen the dying protomartyr, which is described in a later chapter as having remained vivid in the mind of one who many years later was still rehearsing his role in this event—"when the blood of Stephen thy witness was shed, I also was standing by and approving, and keeping the garments of those who killed him" (22:20)—must be seen as part of what, with apologies or at any rate with appropriate caution, we may call the "psychological profile" of his conversion (→9:1–4). It also provides a sidelight on the question of images in the worship of the church, and even of Hellenistic Judaism (→19:26), for how could they know what "the face of an angel" looked like unless there were a representation of it somewhere (→12:7)?

ACTS 7

7:2–3 Because "Abram believed God, and it was accounted to him for righteousness" (ἐπίστευσεν Ἀβραμ τῷ θεῷ, καὶ ἐλογίσθη αὐτῷ εἰς δικαιοσύνην) (Gen. 15:6 LXX), Abraham became for Christians a paradigm both of faith (→26:18) and of righteousness/justification (→13:38–39) and of the two in combination. The two actions above all by which he manifested that faith were (1) his obedience to God to the point of being willing to offer up Isaac, the son of promise, commemorated in Judaism as the Akedah, "the binding of Isaac,"[1] and interpreted typologically by Christianity as a foreshadowing of the God who "did not spare his own Son but gave him up for us all" (Rom. 8:32); and (2) his readiness "by faith" to obey "when he was called to go out to a place which he was to receive as an inheritance . . . not knowing where he was to go" (Heb. 11:8), which Stephen was celebrating here.

7:4–5 God removed him from there into this land in which you are now living; yet he gave him no inheritance in it, not even a foot's length, but promised to give it to him in possession and to his posterity after him, though he had no child.

In Christian eschatology the promise of the Holy Land to Abraham, guaranteeing it to his posterity, together with other references to sacred space (→7:47–48), has usually been spiritualized into the promised land of life eternal (→23:8), often without consideration of the status of God's abiding covenant with the people of Israel (→3:25) and of the permanent validity of the promise in the context of the historical "economies" or dispensations of God also within this world (→15:8–9).

1. Steven T. Katz in Neusner et al. 1999, 1:406–7.

7:8 The covenant with Abraham was seen as belonging to the longer history of divine covenants (→3:25).

7:9–16 The history of the patriarch Joseph, above all the comprehensive theological meaning of his declaration, "You took counsel against me for evil, but God took counsel on my behalf for good" (Gen. 50:20 LXX), was a key to the workings of God in human history, as these had climaxed in the resurrection of Christ (→2:31).

7:20 The somewhat surprising adjective "beautiful" (ἀστεῖος) applied to Moses is a quotation from the Septuagint (Exod. 2:2 LXX), where the AV and the RSV, on the basis of the Hebrew of the book of Exodus, have only the rather colorless adjective "goodly."

"What Has Athens to Do with Jerusalem?"

7:22 And Moses was instructed in all the wisdom of the Egyptians, and he was mighty in his words and deeds.

This challenging question of the connection between Athens and Jerusalem was formulated by Tertullian, citing the authority of "the porch of Solomon" from Acts (3:11) as a polar opposite to the "porch" (στοά) from which Stoicism took its name: "What indeed has Athens to do with Jerusalem? What concord is there between the Academy and the Church?"[2] According to a widespread patristic consensus, the answer was given by this description of Moses: Athens has considerably more to do with Jerusalem than Tertullian had supposed, for "Wisdom" (σοφία) and "justice/righteousness" (δικαιοσύνη) (→13:38–39) are, together with "law" (νόμος) (→25:8), among the most important elements common to the vocabulary of classical Greek philosophy and Christian Greek theology (→17:18) as well as to the vocabulary of Jewish Scripture as available through the Septuagint. In that portion of Jewish Scripture known significantly as wisdom literature, consisting (in the Septuagint) of Proverbs, Ecclesiastes, Job, Wisdom of Solomon, and Ecclesiasticus (Wisdom of Jesus Ben Sirach), wisdom (or, with its name capitalized in its personified form, Wisdom, Sophia) had taken on an increasingly ontological status, until, in the eighth chapter of Proverbs, so beloved of the fourth-century Greek church fathers as an anticipation of the prologue to the Gospel of John,[3] Wisdom-Sophia could speak of having existed "before time [πρὸ τοῦ αἰῶνος], before he made the earth" and of having been right next to God at the creation (Prov. 8:22–31 LXX).

2. Tertullian, *On Prescription against Heretics* 7 (*ANF* 3:246).
3. Athanasius, *Discourses against the Arians* 2.18–67 (*NPNF*² 4:357–85).

But the wisdom literature was also one of the most fertile points of contact between biblical revelation and the traditions of the ancient Near East and Egypt. It was through that prism that the Judaism of Alexandria in Egypt came to view Moses. *The Life of Moses* by Philo of Alexandria, which was adapted and expanded into a Christian biography by Saint Gregory of Nyssa, explained how in the Egyptian court "learned Egyptians . . . instructed him in the philosophy conveyed in symbols. . . . He had Greeks to teach him the rest of the regular school course, and the inhabitants of the neighbouring countries for Assyrian letters and the Chaldean science of the heavenly bodies."[4] Quoting Philo and other sources, Clement of Alexandria described Moses as "the first wise man, and the first that imparted grammar to the Jews, that the Phoenicians received it from the Jews, and the Greeks from the Phoenicians."[5] As these examples of Philo, Clement, and Saint Gregory of Nyssa themselves showed, Moses became for Christians as well as for Jews a model of the believer in the one true God who was at the same time receptive to all the authentic wisdom of natural reason as having come ultimately from the same one true God. "'The wisdom of the Egyptians' is the principal image for the knowledge of various natural subjects," as Metropolitan Nikanor explains.[6]

The uniquely privileged position of Moses as the recipient of the luminous revelation of the name of God, which was not a name but a declaration of God as Being (→17:23), "I am the one who is" (ἐγὼ εἰμι ὁ ὤν) (Exod. 3:14 LXX), and as the giver of the law (→10:15) did not, by some divine sort of frontal lobotomy, eliminate or negate any authentic "wisdom" in which he had been reared as the putative son of Pharaoh's daughter. Therefore, as Origen put it, "in the Acts of the Apostles Stephen testified to Moses' scholarship, no doubt basing his statement on ancient documents which have not come to the notice of the multitude."[7] Saint Augustine quoted this verse as the biblical support for his argument that

> if those who are called philosophers, and especially the Platonists, have said aught that is true and in harmony with our faith, we are not only not to shrink from it, but to claim it for our own use. . . . All branches of heathen learning have not only false and superstitious fancies and heavy burdens of unnecessary toil, which every one of us, when going out under the leadership of Christ from the fellowship of the heathen, ought to abhor and avoid; but they contain also liberal instruction which is better adapted to the use of the truth, and some excellent precepts of morality; and some truths in regard even to the worship of the One God are found among them.[8]

4. Philo of Alexandria, *Life of Moses* 1.23–24 (LCL 289:287–89).
5. Clement of Alexandria, *Stromata* 1.23 (*ANF* 2:335).
6. Nikanor 1905, 1:140.
7. Origen, *Contra Celsum* 3.46 (Chadwick 1953, 160).
8. Augustine, *On Christian Doctrine* 2.40.60–61 (*NPNF*[1] 2:554).

Similarly, Saint Basil of Caesarea, in the epistle that has acquired the title *Address to Young Men, on How They Might Derive Benefit from Greek Literature*, advised his nephews not to avoid classical Greek literature, but to take away from it what was universally valid without succumbing to what was immoral or idolatrous.[9]

To be "instructed in all the wisdom" of the Greeks and Romans, and with the benefit of its insights into metaphysics and logic to find a valid expression for orthodox Christian teaching, was to become the ideal shared by Michael Psellus in the Greek East and Saint Thomas Aquinas in the Latin West.[10] Thomas's aphorism in the very first question of the *Summa theologica*, "grace does not abolish nature, but completes it" (*gratia non tollit naturam, sed perficit*),[11] meant that like Moses, to whom the revelation of God as Being was granted by the voice from the burning bush, the practitioner of Christian "sacred science" did not need to fear the valid findings of philosophy, science, and history, wherever they may have arisen, but could confidently study them as coming from the one true God who as the Creator was the source of both reason and revelation.

At the same time, in keeping with the defiant apostolic challenge, "Where is the wise man? Where is the scribe? Where is the debater of this age? Has not God made foolish the wisdom of the world?" (1 Cor. 1:20), the book of Acts makes it a point to describe the apostles Peter and John as "uneducated laymen," whose "fearlessness" did not come from their having been "taught all the wisdom of the Egyptians" or of the Greeks or even of the rabbis, but from their having been "associates of Jesus" (4:13 NJB). In the words of the troparion that is sung over and over at Pentecost, "Blessed art Thou, O Christ our God, who hast revealed the fishermen as most wise by sending down upon them the Holy Spirit; through them Thou didst draw the world into Thy net."

7:30–34 It does seem puzzling that Stephen's retelling of the revelation to Moses from the burning bush ignored the central formulation in this "towering text,"[12] the words "I am the one who is" (ἐγώ εἰμι ὁ ὤν) (Exod. 3:14 LXX), which, in the unpronounceable four consonants (Tetragrammaton) of the original Hebrew, were to become the foundation of the esoteric systems of mysteries in the Kabbalah—thus central for both Hellenistic and rabbinic Judaism.

7:37 Stephen repeats the prophecy in the book of Deuteronomy (Deut. 18:15, 18 LXX), by which Moses was understood as having himself predicted and promised that he was to be superseded (→3:25; →8:30–31; →21:13–14).

9. Basil of Caesarea, *Address to Young Men, on How They Might Derive Benefit from Greek Literature* (LCL 270:365–435).
10. *Chr. Trad.* 2:242–51; 3:284–93.
11. Thomas Aquinas, *Summa theologica* 1.1.8.
12. Murray 1964, 5.

7:39–42 It was supremely ironic that, having left Egypt at God's command and being encamped at Sinai to receive the revelation of God's law, the Israelites turned to the worship of the golden calf (→12:21–23; →19:28).

The Paradox of Sacred Space and Sacred Time

7:47–48 It was Solomon who built a house for him. Yet the Most High does not dwell in houses made with hands.

When the "angel" who was "the voice of the Lord," who is identified by the patristic tradition as the preexistent and preincarnate Son of God (→12:7),[13] said to Moses on the mountain, "Take off the shoes from your feet, for the place where you are standing is holy ground" (7:33, quoting Exod. 3:5 LXX), that was, in spite of the rejection of the heathen cult of "the high places" (τὰ ὑψηλά) (2 Chr. 14:2 LXX) as idolatrous, the designation of a particular space as holy, set aside from ordinary use and consecrated to the presence of the one true God. And when, later in the account of the book of Exodus, the voice of God issuing the Ten Commandments told the people of Israel to "remember the sabbath day, to keep it holy [ἀγιάζειν αὐτήν]," because "the Lord blessed the sabbath day and hallowed it [ἡγίασεν αὐτήν]" at the conclusion of the creation of heaven and earth (Exod. 20:8–11 LXX), that was the designation also of a particular time as consecrated. Early in the narrative of Acts, "Peter and John were going up to the temple at the hour of prayer, the ninth hour" (3:1). That was not only evidence of the persistence with which, even after the resurrection and ascension, the disciples of Jesus continued to regard themselves as observant Jews and as participants, not by adoption but by birthright, in the divine covenant with the people of Israel (→3:25); but it was also an expression of a paradoxical attitude toward both the idea of sacred space ("the temple") and the concept of sacred time ("*the* hour of prayer, the ninth hour") that has continued to characterize the belief and practice of the church ever since.[14]

That paradoxical attitude was visible above all in their relation to the cultic places and times of Jewish religious observance.[15] Earlier in this chapter, speaking about Abraham and the promised land, Stephen affirmed that "God ... promised to give it to him in possession and to his posterity after him"; but he called it "this land in which you are now living," nevertheless not their "possession," because the Romans were its real possessors (7:4–5). Just as Jesus was taunted with the cry, "You who would destroy the temple and build it in three days, save yourself!" (Matt. 27:40), so Stephen was subjected to the false accusation, "This man never ceases to speak words against this holy place and the law; for we have heard him say that this Jesus of Nazareth will destroy

13. Justin Martyr, *Dialogue with Trypho* 59 (*ANF* 1:226–27).
14. Bihler 1963, 161–78.
15. Bachmann 1980, 153–55.

this place" (6:13–14), and Paul was charged with having "tried to profane the temple" (24:6). The sacred spaces and sacred times of Judaism included not only the great temple of Solomon and the Holy Land itself with all its memorials of the promises of God and of the history of the people of Israel, but designated times such as "the sixth hour" (10:9) and "the ninth hour" (3:1; 10:3) and designated places throughout the Diaspora, where observant Jews would go, in obedience to the commandment to "remember the sabbath day, to keep it holy" (Exod. 20:8 LXX). Much of the activity of the apostles was concentrated in the Diaspora synagogue; συναγωγή was a Greek name for a Jewish sacred space (9:20; 13:5, 14; 14:1; 17:10; 18:19, 26; 19:8). But in addition to synagogues Judaism had other sacred spaces. At Philippi, therefore, Paul and his companions, apparently including Luke himself (→27:1), "on the sabbath day went outside the gate to the riverside, where we supposed there was a place of prayer [προσευχή]" (16:13, 16), using both the sacred time of Jewish ritual and a sacred place of Jewish worship to preach the gospel of Christ, just as at Corinth "he argued in the *synagogue* every *sabbath*" (18:4). As Gerhard A. Krodel points out, "the temple in Luke-Acts is the house of Jesus' Father (Luke 2:49), a house of worship and prayer (Luke 19:46), the place where Israel is called to worship God (Acts 7:7), the place where Jesus and the apostles prayed and taught (Luke 19:47; 21:37; Acts 3:1–26; 4:1; 5:20, 42), and it remains the place to which believers continued to go also after Stephen's martyrdom (21:22–26; 22:17; 24:18)."[16]

And so, Stephen quoted the Septuagint of the prophet Isaiah here (7:49–50):

Heaven is my throne,
and earth my footstool.
What house will you build for me, says the Lord,
or what is the place of my rest?
Did not my hand make all these things? (Isa. 66:1–2 LXX)

Stephen thus tells his Jewish audience that "the Most High does not dwell in houses made with hands" (7:48), which extended to every προσευχή and every synagogue—and even to the temple itself, which, with all its celebrated buildings (Matt. 24:1) and cherished liturgical associations, remained a "house made with hands." That was true in a special sense of idolatrous and polytheistic "holy places" such as "the temple of the great goddess Artemis . . . whom all Asia and the world worship" at Ephesus, said to contain "the sacred stone that fell from the sky" (19:27, 35). Therefore, using some of the same words, Paul repeated to the Greeks of Athens, and even reinforced, the statements of Stephen here to the Jews of Jerusalem: "The God who made the world and everything in it, being Lord of heaven and earth, does not live in shrines made by man" (17:24).

16. Krodel 1986, 152.

Authentic worship (→4:24–30), consequently, could be offered to the true God anytime and anywhere—on a housetop near Joppa (10:9) or on a sand beach at Tyre (21:5)—which implied that the spaces and times became sacred spaces and sacred times because of the prayer rather than vice versa.

But Luke the evangelist and historian, by contrast with other New Testament writers, took pains to locate the sacred events of the history of salvation on a publicly identifiable (→26:26) time line: the reign of the emperor Augustus (Luke 2:1–2) or of the emperor Tiberius (Luke 3:1) or of the emperor Claudius (11:28) or of the proconsul Gallio, who was the brother of philosopher Seneca (18:12). The particular times when those sacred events of salvation history took place acquired a derivative sacredness from them, and they were observed, "Pentecost" (πεντηκοστή) having originally been the Jewish Feast of Weeks (20:16)[17] but becoming eventually the Christian observance of the sending of the Holy Spirit.[18] Instead of the Sabbath when Moses was customarily read aloud in the synagogues (15:21), now it was "on the first day of the week, when we were gathered together to break bread" for the eucharistic service (→20:7), in remembrance and observance of that "first day of the week, at early dawn" (Luke 24:1) and the sacred event of the resurrection of Christ (→2:31). Such "gathering together to break bread" had an appointed time and an appointed place, and from a combination of historical and archeological evidence it seems that well before the activity of Constantine the builder in the early fourth century[19] there were such defined places, which could be the meaning of the enigmatic phrase "the church in their house" (1 Cor. 16:19). Even at Hagia Sophia in Constantinople or in the splendor of Saint Peter's in Rome and Saint Paul's in London, these words of Stephen have stood as a constant reminder: "Yet the Most High does not dwell in houses made with hands," not even in those made with Christian hands—"neither on this mountain nor in Jerusalem; . . . [for] God is spirit, and those who worship him must worship in spirit and truth" (John 4:21, 24).

The Imitation of Christ

7:59–60 As they were stoning Stephen, he prayed, "Lord Jesus, receive my spirit." And he knelt down and cried with a loud voice, "Lord, do not hold this sin against them." And when he had said this, he fell asleep.

Being in an altogether unique position as the writer both of the first history of the church and of one of the four canonical Gospels, Saint Luke was especially qualified to draw attention to the place of Christ as exemplar and example—exemplar of how God deals with humanity, example of how hu-

17. BDAG 796.
18. *PGL* 1060.
19. Eusebius, *Church History* 10.2–4 (*NPNF*[2] 1:370–78).

manity is to behave in response—and therefore to what the title of one of the most beloved books in all of Christian history, by Thomas à Kempis, called *The Imitation of Christ*, which, as he described it, consisted in a pattern of life that was far more profound than the simplistic application of the question "What would Jesus do?"

As one scholar notes, "The story of Stephen's death and its aftermath is modeled after the account of Jesus' passion. . . . The story of Stephen's martyrdom contains all the major generic components: cause and conspiracy (6:8–11); trial (6:12–7:53); condemnation (7:54); vindication and exaltation [of Jesus] (6:15 [7:55–56]); confession that Jesus is the Son of God (9:20)."[20] As the only one of the four evangelists to have recorded the word of Christ on the cross, "Father, into thy hands I commit my spirit!" (πάτερ, εἰς χεῖράς σου παρατίθεμαι τὸ πνεῦμά μου) (Luke 23:46), Luke does seem to have been drawing a parallel with Christ here (→14:22) when he had Stephen say as he followed Christ to an innocent death: "Lord Jesus, receive my spirit" (κύριε Ἰησοῦ, δέξαι τὸ πνεῦμά μου). Or, to put it negatively as well as more polemically, for Stephen to commit his spirit to the Lord Jesus when the Lord Jesus himself had committed his spirit to the Father was either an act of blatant idolatry or the acknowledgment of the κύριος Ἰησοῦς as the fitting recipient of the dying prayer of Stephen—and the fitting recipient of the spirit of the dying Stephen—because he was one with the Father (John 10:30), "one in being with the Father" (ὁμοούσιος τῷ πατρί), as the Council of Nicea confessed in 325.[21] As even a critic of this orthodox doctrine must acknowledge, "The straightest Jewish monotheism was an axiomatic dogma to Luke and to his predecessors, but neither he nor they ever questioned that Jesus, as well as the Father, was entitled to worship and adoration."[22] Therefore an early Christian homily could open with the admonition: "Brethren, it is fitting that you should think of Jesus Christ as of God";[23] and an early pagan account of Christians included the description of how "they had met regularly before dawn on a fixed day to chant verses alternately among themselves in honour of Christ as if to a god [*christo quasi deo*]."[24] "Let us then," one of the earliest Christian writers after the New Testament (and eventually himself a martyr) could admonish on the basis of the book of Acts, "be imitators of His patience; and if we suffer for His name's sake, let us glorify Him. For He has set us this example in Himself."[25]

But that supreme form of "the imitation of Christ," by which persecuting the church became tantamount to persecuting Christ because the church was the body of Christ (→9:4–5), was only the sublime consummation of all the other responses to the invitation of Jesus to follow his example, an invitation

20. Nickelsburg 2003, 82, 216.
21. Nicene Creed 2 (*CCF* 1:158–59).
22. Easton 1936, 38.
23. *2 Clement* 1 (*ANF* 10:251).
24. Pliny, *Letters* 10.96.7 (LCL 59:288–89).
25. Polycarp, *To the Philippians* 8 (*ANF* 1:35).

that not the evangelist Luke, but the evangelist Matthew recorded: "Take my yoke upon you, and learn from me" (Matt. 11:29). Because of all these responses, outsiders "recognized that they had been with Jesus" (4:13). It was "in the name of Jesus Christ" (6:8 TPR), by his power, and in imitation of his example that the apostles performed their miracles of healing (→6:8). Even when the apostles served as an example to their followers in turn, they did so in imitation of the example of Christ and in obedience to his precepts: "In all things," Paul could say to the Ephesian elders, "I have shown you that by so toiling one must help the weak, remembering the words of the Lord, for he himself said, 'The one who gives is blessed rather than the one who receives'" (20:35 TPR). As those who had been disciples now became teachers, they carried out an imitation of Christ the teacher, performed by his authority, which is why the authorities "charged them not to speak or teach at all in the name of Jesus" (4:18; 5:28). When that prohibition proved to be no more effective in the case of the disciples than it had been in the case of their Master, the disciples, like the Master, were the objects of an "ambush" (25:3). "Whatever they did in relation to Christ [ἐπὶ Χριστοῦ], they also do here," Theophylact explains.[26] Without changing a word, Luke's account of the arrest of Stephen here in Acts could have come directly from the passion story in the Gospels (cf. Matt. 26:59–61): "Then they secretly instigated men, who said, 'We have heard him speak blasphemous words against Moses and God.' And they stirred up the people and the elders and the scribes, and they came upon him and seized him and brought him before the council, and set up false witnesses who said, 'This man never ceases to speak words against this holy place and the law'" (6:11–13). Luke's emphasis in his Gospel on "Jerusalem" as the comprehensive token that stood for the entire suffering and death of Christ (Luke 9:51–53) had its equivalent here in Acts in the similar significance of "Jerusalem" for Paul (21:11–13; 22:18), in counterpoint with Rome (→28:14). The reproof issued to Paul in the narrative of Acts, "Would you revile God's high priest?" (23:4), is a reminder of the reproof issued to Jesus in the narrative of Saint John's Gospel, "Is that how you answer the high priest?" (John 18:22). In all these expressions of the imitation of Christ, even to the end (→14:22), they were fulfilling the summons: "If any man would come after me, let him deny himself and take up his cross daily and follow me" (Luke 9:23).

---

26. Theophylact, *Exposition of the Acts of the Apostles* 7.60 (PG 125:625).

ACTS 8

8:1 And Saul was consenting to his death. And on that day a great persecution arose against the church in Jerusalem.

The opening words of this addendum to the martyrology of Stephen form a one-sentence introduction to the transition (→9:15) from part one of Acts (chapters 1–8), which could carry the subtitle "The Disciples in Jerusalem," to part two, "Paul" (chapters 9–28), as well as a tantalizing anticipation of the next chapter on his conversion, raising but not answering, a host of questions about the psychological relation (→21:13–14) between what must have been an unforgettable experience, the death in faith (and for the faith) of the protomartyr Stephen (→14:22), whose "face was like the face of an angel" (6:15), and the experience of Saul (soon to be Paul) on the road to Damascus (→9:1–4).

8:2 If it was even necessary to explain, this description showed that having a faith in the resurrection of Christ (→2:31) and a hope of resurrection and eternal life (→23:8) was not inconsistent with expressing a "great lamentation" (κοπετός μέγας) at the death of a beloved brother or sister (→21:13–14).

8:8 TPR So there was great joy in that city.

Although the portrait of the early church here in the book of Acts does sometimes seem rather somber, references such as this relieve that emphasis (→21:13–14).

8:18–24 TPR Now when Simon saw that the Spirit was given through the laying on of the apostles' hands, he offered them money, saying, "Give me also this power, that any one on whom I lay my hands may receive the Holy Spirit." But Peter said to him, "Your silver perish with you, because you thought you could obtain the gift of God with money! You have neither part nor lot in this faith, for your heart is not right before God. Repent therefore of this wickedness of yours, and pray to the Lord that, if possible, the intent of your heart may be forgiven you. For I see that you are in the gall of bitterness and in the bond of iniquity." And Simon answered, "Pray for me to the Lord, that nothing of what you have said may come upon me."

This tawdry but really quite simple story has had far-reaching historical consequences, and in at least two respects:

1. The name Simon became an eponym for the sin—which was indeed sometimes labeled a "heresy"—of purchasing church offices for money.[1] It was often considerably more subtle than the blatant commercialism described here, and in some periods of church history, most notably perhaps in the later Middle Ages, it became epidemic.[2]
2. The person of Simon himself was associated by very early Christian writers with the origins of the Gnostic heresy. Justin Martyr reported that Simon was the subject of a statue erected by Samaritans with the inscription *Simoni deo sancto* ("To Simon the Holy God") and linked his name with those of Menander and Marcion as heresiarchs;[3] and Irenaeus, quoting at length from this chapter of Acts, attributed to him a Gnostic systematic theology.[4] Modern scholarly opinion continues to be divided about the accuracy of these reports.[5]

The Communication of Divine Revelation

8:25 TPR Now when Peter and John had testified and spoken the word of the Lord, they returned to Jerusalem, preaching the gospel to many villages of the Samaritans as they passed through.

This one sentence, "When Peter and John had *testified* [διαμαρτυράμενοι] and spoken *the word of the Lord* [τὸν λόγον τοῦ κυρίου], they returned to Jerusalem, *preaching the gospel* [εὐηγγελίζοντο] to many villages of the Samaritans as they passed through," brings together several though not all—for example, "all the words of this Life" (5:20)—of the ways of speaking in the theological vocabulary of Acts about the communication of divine revelation: testimony; the word (of God, of the Lord); preaching; the gospel. The Greek verb εὐαγγελίζεσθαι ("to preach the gospel") appears in fifteen passages of the book of Acts, five

1. A. Bride in *DTC* 14:2141–60.
2. *Chr. Trad.* 3:212–13; 4:94–96.
3. Justin Martyr, *First Apology* 26 (*ANF* 1:171).
4. Irenaeus, *Against Heresies* 1.23 (*ANF* 1:347–48).
5. J. Martin in *LTK* 8:768–69.

of these being in this eighth chapter alone (5:42; 8:4, 12, 25, 35, 40; 10:36; 11:20; 13:32; 14:7, 15, 21; 15:35; 16:10; 17:18), more often than in any other book of the New Testament, and the noun εὐαγγέλιον ("gospel") in two more passages (15:7; 20:24). The Anglo-Saxon noun "gospel," from "good" and "spell" meaning "good news,"[6] is, together with the noun and verb "worship" (→4:24–30),[7] which renders Greek verbs such as λατρεύειν, προσκυνεῖν, and σέβεσθαι, one of the treasures of theological English. Most other languages, including Latin with its derivative tongues as well as German and the Slavic languages, employ some version of the Greek εὐαγγέλιον for the former and either "cultus" (*le culte* in French) or "divine service" (*Gottesdienst* in German, *bogosluž<enie* in Russian) for the latter, whereas English seems to be the only modern language to have its own native words for both.

The difference noted earlier between the Gospels and Paul in their treatment of the relation between "all that Jesus did [ποιεῖν]" and "all that Jesus taught [διδάσκειν]" (1:1) is reflected in the dual meaning of the term "gospel" (εὐαγγέλιον). It is used, already in the New Testament itself, either to mean the full account of "all that Jesus did and taught," as the term is used at the opening of the Gospel of Mark, "the beginning of the gospel of Jesus Christ, the Son of God" (Mark 1:1), or to identify the message of salvation through the death and resurrection of Christ, as it appears here in Acts, "the gospel of the grace of God" (20:24), and is used at the opening of the Epistle to the Romans: "For I am not ashamed of the gospel; it is the power of God for salvation to every one who has faith. . . . For in it the righteousness of God is revealed through faith for faith" (Rom. 1:16–17). A failure to observe that distinction was responsible for the supposition, reported without comment by Jerome,[8] that Paul could have meant Luke's Gospel by the term "my gospel" (τὸ εὐαγγέλιόν μου) (Rom. 16:25), which, as is evident from the linkage with "the preaching of Jesus Christ" (τὸ κήρυγμα Ἰησοῦ Χριστοῦ), referred to the message rather than to one of the four books we call "the Gospels" (probably none of which was in existence yet). Strictly speaking, that commonly used plural "the Gospels" is not precise; rather, the term remains in the singular, and "the Gospel according to [Matthew, Mark, Luke, John]" more accurately reflects the usage of the church in speaking about them. With greater or lesser consistency, the editorial conventions of contemporary American literary usage (which are also being observed in this commentary) try to cope with this duality of meaning by capitalizing "Gospel" when it refers to one of the first four books of the New Testament but lowercasing "gospel" when it refers to the Christian message of grace and forgiveness through Christ, above all as this was proclaimed by Paul, just as "Exodus" is capitalized as a reference to the second

6. *OED* 6:697–98.
7. *OED* 20:575–77.
8. Jerome, *Lives of Illustrious Men* 7 (*NPNF*[2] 3:364).

book of Moses and written lowercase as a reference to the divine deliverance and escape of the people of Israel from captivity in Egypt.

Throughout Acts, the Scripture of the Law and the Prophets (→21:9–10), correctly understood and interpreted, was taken to be the word of God (→8:30–31); yet it would be more accurate to say that Scripture was to be understood and interpreted on the basis of the word of God, which was in turn verified by the Scripture: "They received the word with all eagerness, examining the scriptures daily to see if these things were so" (17:11). In Acts as in the rest of the New Testament—with the possible exception of the term "the other scriptures" (τὰς λοιπὰς γραφάς), which was used only once in speaking about the Epistles of Paul (2 Pet. 3:15–16 AV)—the term "Scripture," whether in the singular γραφή or in the plural γραφαί, referred to what Christians came to call the *Old* Testament. There was no New Testament term for what we now call "the New Testament," passages such as the eucharistic phrase "the new testament [ἡ καινὴ διαθήκη] in my blood" (1 Cor. 11:25 AV) being references to an event, not to a book, much less a collection of books. Yet it is essential to remember, even when this was not explicitly stipulated, that the authority of that Old Testament Scripture derived from the authority of the inspiring Holy Spirit. Beginning with its first chapter, Acts spoke of "this scripture . . . which the Holy Ghost by the mouth of David spake before" (1:16 TPR AV). It was this same inspiring Holy Spirit who came upon the apostles not only at Pentecost but throughout their ministry (→2:1): "And when they had prayed, the place in which they were gathered together was shaken; and they were all filled with the Holy Spirit and spoke the word of God with boldness to everyone who wanted to believe" (4:31 TPR). Also after the close of the New Testament and the death of the last apostle, the same inspiring Holy Spirit was abiding in the church and with the church, in keeping with the promise of Christ (John 16:13–14). That continuity of the divine inspiration of the word of God became the justification for the church to extend to the New Testament the attributes that the New Testament itself had predicated of the Old Testament, including the technical terms γραφή as the title now for the entire Christian Bible and θεόπνευστος ("inspired by God") (2 Tim. 3:16) as the divine attestation of its authority, the latter of which could also be used in describing the decision of an ecumenical church council.[9]

The distinction between Scripture and the word of the gospel was that the word of God in the gospel was primarily oral, because it did not come by reading, but "faith comes from what is heard, and what is heard comes by the preaching of Christ" (Rom. 10:17). The Ethiopian in the present chapter was reading the written word of God in the book of Isaiah (8:28); but only when Philip, "beginning with this scripture, *announced* the good news of Jesus [εὐηγγελίζετο τὸν Ἰησοῦν]" (8:35 TPR) did he ask for baptism and make confession of his faith "that Jesus Christ is the Son of God" (→8:37 TPR AV).

9. *PGL* 322–23, 630.

The promise was that Peter "will declare to you a message [ῥήματα, 'spoken words'] by which you will be saved, you and all your household" (11:14). The verb that went with "the word of God" in the book of Acts was not "write," but "speak" or "preach" or "proclaim" or "announce" or "teach" (4:31; 6:2; 11:19; 13:5, 46; 14:3, 25; 15:35–36; 18:11). And so, when Luke reported that "the word of God increased" (6:7 AV), that did not mean, as some simpleminded Bible readers are alleged to have concluded, that now another book of the New Testament had been written. The risen Christ commanded his disciples to "preach" (Mark 16:15), and therefore "the ministry of the word" to which, along with prayer (→4:24–30), the apostles were to devote themselves was the ministry of the oral word of God.

A special category in the doctrine of the word of God was "the word of the Lord," which referred to the words of or about Jesus the κύριος, as becomes evident in an interesting set of variant readings (→20:28a): where the RSV says that at Antioch "almost the whole city gathered to hear *the word of God*" (13:44 RSV), NA^{27} prefers "the word *of the Lord*," and the TPR reads: "The whole city gathered to hear Paul deliver *many words about the Lord* [Παύλου πολὺν λόγον ποιησαμένου περὶ τοῦ κυρίου]" (13:44 TPR). Later on, again at Antioch, we find "Paul and Barnabas . . . teaching and proclaiming *the word of the Lord*, with many others also"; and also in Antioch, "after some days Paul said to Barnabas, 'Come, let us return and visit the brethren in every city where we proclaimed *the word of the Lord* and see how they are'" (15:35–36). Between these visits to Antioch, it was at Lystra that "the Lord . . . bore witness to *the word of his grace*, granting signs and wonders to be done by their hands" (14:3). Curiously, however, when it comes to quoting the actual word of the Lord Jesus, no one anywhere in Acts quotes words that were attributed to Jesus in the Gospels. As part of "the gospel of the forty days" (→1:2–3), Jesus said to the disciples: "You heard from me, for John baptized with water, but before many days you shall be baptized with the Holy Spirit" (1:4–5); and Peter "remembered the word of the Lord, how he said, 'John baptized with water, but you shall be baptized with the Holy Spirit'" (11:16). Yet in his Gospel (Luke 3:16), in agreement with all three other Gospels (Matt. 3:11; Mark 1:8; John 1:33), Luke had attributed this saying to John the Baptist, not to Jesus. And Paul, in "remembering the words of the Lord, for he himself said, 'The one who gives is blessed rather than the one who receives'" (20:35 TPR), quoted a saying that is undoubtedly authentic and that has always been taken to be authentic, having been quoted as early as *1 Clement*,[10] but that does not in fact appear in any of the Gospels. In addition, the TPR contains, in the epistle from the apostolic council at Jerusalem communicating its decrees (15:29 TPR), the additional commandment (→16:4a): "And whatever you do not want to be done to you, do not do it to someone else . . . , as you are sustained by the Holy Spirit"; this was clearly a version of the Golden Rule of Jesus, which was known both from

10. *1 Clement* 2 (*ANF* 1:5).

Luke in the Sermon on the Plain (Luke 6:31) and from Matthew in the Sermon on the Mount (Matt. 7:12). In this context it also deserves to be pointed out that the first words of Jesus to have been written down anywhere (as far as we know) were not the Sermon on the Mount or any parable or even the Lord's Prayer, but the words of institution of the Eucharist, which are also the words of consecration: "This is my body which is for you. Do this in remembrance of me," and "This cup is the new covenant in my blood. Do this, as often as you drink it, in remembrance of me" (1 Cor. 11:24–25); they were written down by Saint Paul, addressing the church at Corinth, before the composition of any of our Gospels, at any rate in their present form.

"In Accordance with the Scriptures"

8:30–31 TPR So Philip came to him, and heard him reading Isaiah the prophet, and asked the eunuch, "Do you understand what you are reading?" And he said, "How can I understand, unless someone instructs me?"

A persistent theme throughout the book of Acts (and then throughout the history of the church) was, in one form or another, the Ethiopian's plaintive question to the Apostle Philip (in the fuller form given by the TPR): "How can I understand, unless some one instructs me" (πῶς δύναμαι γινώσκειν ἐὰν μή τις διδάξει με)? The authority of Scripture, and therefore the obligation to study and heed it, was a fundamental assumption that was shared by Jewish and Christian believers: Justin Martyr put into the mouth of his Jewish interlocutor, Trypho, the assertion that he would not "have tolerated your conversation, had you not referred everything to the Scriptures";[11] and Irenaeus gave credit to the acceptance of the authority of the Law and the Prophets for preparing hearers such as this Ethiopian to accept the apostolic message.[12] The Ethiopian here, who has often been taken to be a proselyte to Judaism,[13] "was reading Isaiah the prophet," apparently out loud, as was the general practice in late antiquity.[14] With Paul in attendance at the synagogue in Antioch of Pisidia, "the law and the prophets" were read as part of the prescribed liturgical observance (13:15). Indeed, "the scriptures of the prophets are read every sabbath" (13:27 TPR); and "from early generations," according to James here in Acts, "Moses has had in every city those who preach him, for he is read every sabbath in the synagogues" (15:21). In acknowledging this authority and in studying and interpreting this (Old Testament) Scripture, it was the ideal object of a Christian leader, no less than it was that of a Jewish leader,

11. Justin Martyr, *Dialogue with Trypho* 56 (*ANF* 1:224).
12. Irenaeus, *Against Heresies* 4.23.2 (*ANF* 1:494–95).
13. Beverly Roberts Gaventa in *ABD* 2:667.
14. "In antiquity silent reading was uncommon, not unknown"; Chadwick 1992, 93 n. 1, commenting on Augustine, *Confessions* 6.3.3.

to be "an eloquent man, and mighty in the scriptures" (λόγιος . . . δυνατὸς ὢν ἐν ταῖς γραφαῖς), as was said of the Jewish, and then Christian, leader Apollos of Alexandria (18:24 AV).

This kind of Bible study was necessary, but it was not sufficient. That was the burden of this encounter between Philip and the Ethiopian: "How can I understand, unless some one instructs me? . . . About whom, pray, does the prophet say this, about himself or about some one else?" "That he should at all know," Chrysostom observes, "either that the Prophets speak in different ways about different persons, or that they speak of themselves in another person—the question betokens a very thoughtful mind."[15] After the reading of Scripture at the Antiochean synagogue, Paul and his colleagues were asked if they "have any word of exhortation [λόγος παρακλήσεως] for the people" (13:15), to which they replied with what the NJB (*ad* 13:15) calls "the great inaugural discourse of Paul." This included not only the report that "the utterances of the prophets are read every sabbath," but the indictment that when Jesus came, "those who live in Jerusalem and their rulers . . . did not recognize him nor understand the utterances" that were being read and heard (13:27). Moses was indeed read aloud every Sabbath (15:21), but his law (→10:15), when it was read by itself, represented "a yoke which our fathers have not been able to bear" (15:10 TPR). Apollos was "mighty in the scriptures" (18:24 AV); nevertheless he needed to have those Scriptures, in which he was so mighty, explained to him by Aquila and Priscilla (→18:24–26b), a husband-and-wife team who were, as was Apollos himself, converts to the Way (→11:26) from Judaism.

For the Ethiopian, for Apollos, and for all the other readers of Scripture in Acts from chapter 1 to chapter 28, the understanding of Scripture became complete only when they had both read the prophecy and accepted its normative interpretation as applying to the crucified Messiah (→3:18): "God foretold it by the mouth of all the prophets that his Christ should suffer, and he has fulfilled it" (3:18 TPR). The authority of Moses, and of the Torah as the Scripture that he wrote, was great, but he had pointed beyond himself and the Torah (Deut. 18:15) to the prophet of whose future coming he spoke (3:22; 7:37). Therefore, as Luke had described earlier, "beginning with Moses and all the prophets, [the risen Christ] interpreted to them in all the scriptures the things concerning himself" (Luke 24:27). Whether it was the psalm (Ps. 69:25) about Judas (1:16–20) or the prophecy of Joel (Joel 2:28) about Pentecost (2:16–20), already in the first two chapters it was established that neither these nor the many other passages from Scripture to be quoted could make sense "unless some one instructs me." And so even in the closing paragraphs of the narrative, Paul was still "trying to convince them about Jesus both from the law of Moses and from the prophets" (28:23). From the title given to them by Saint Cyprian, who seemed to be quoting it from earlier usage, the Christian compilation of these Old Testament passages pertaining to Christ has come to

15. Chrysostom, *Homilies on Acts* 19 (*NPNF*[1] 11:122).

be called *Testimonies.*[16] These apparently took on a life of their own and were passed on by the process of tradition even to those who did not always bother to check the passages in their original contexts.

This early development raises a challenging question for all subsequent generations of interpreters: If *sola scriptura* was not enough for all these devoted readers of (Old Testament) Scripture without the normative interpretation that was provided by the apostolic witness, does the written codification of that apostolic witness, in turn, in the books of the New Testament by itself render obsolete the Ethiopian's question, "How can I understand, unless some one instructs me?" Or does the history of the church and of its controversies (→15:2) raise anew the Apostle Philip's question to the Ethiopian, "Do you understand what you are reading?" and thus give new meaning to the reply, "How can I understand, unless some one instructs me?" It is the consensus of Orthodox and Catholic teaching that the continuing apostolic witness of the church under the guidance of the Holy Spirit (→2:1), as this has been set forth in tradition, liturgy, and creed (→8:37; →16:4b), performs the same function for the interpretation of the "Scripture" (now consisting of both the Old and the New Testament) as it did for the "Scripture" when this consisted of only the Old Testament. In the words about Scripture and creed of Pope Leo, who is a saint on both the Western and the Eastern calendars: "A man who has not the most elementary understanding even of the creed itself can have learnt nothing from the sacred texts of the New and Old Testaments."[17]

Credo: "The Rule of Faith"

8:37 TPR AV And Philip said, "If thou believest with all thine heart, thou mayest [be baptized]." And he answered and said, "I believe that Jesus Christ is the Son of God [πιστεύω τὸν υἱὸν τοῦ θεοῦ εἶναι Ἰησοῦν Χριστόν; Vulgate: *credo Jesum Christum filium dei esse*]."

This creedal (or creedlike) declaration is one of the most significant among the many distinctive readings in the TPR of Acts[18] and "is perhaps the earliest form of baptismal creed."[19] From there it found its way into the Textus Receptus and thus into several of the most important later versions and translations, including the Latin Vulgate, Luther's German Bible, and the Authorized Version of the English Bible; but in the RSV and NRSV it is printed in a footnote as yet another textual variant among the many in Acts (→20:28a). Its textual status in

16. Cyprian, *Testimonies* (*ANF* 5:507–57).
17. Tome of Leo 1 (*CCF* 1:114).
18. Boismard 2000, 157 documents it in detail from manuscripts and ancient versions, including Latin, Ethiopic, Georgian, and Armenian, as well as from Cyprian and Augustine.
19. Kirsopp Lake and Henry J. Cadbury in Foakes Jackson and Lake 1979, 4:98.

the various available manuscripts was already a puzzle to earlier interpreters of Acts, too,[20] but in traditional church teaching it has been taken to be evidence of the creedal knowledge that was still to be required of a candidate as a prerequisite for adult baptism.[21] "When he confessed Jesus Christ to be the Son of God," and only then, as D. Bogolepov explains, "Philip baptized him."[22]

From the opening word in Latin of the Ethiopian's confession, of the Apostles' Creed in its original form, and of the Niceno-Constantinopolitan Creed in its eventual form (→24:24–25a; →26:18), such a statement is called credo or creed, the rule of faith.[23] According to the *Interpreters' Bible*, it was "evidently added under the influence of later baptismal practice," because the church could not yet have had a catechism or a creed.[24] But in the very next chapter of Acts, we are told in all the manuscripts and versions that directly after Paul's conversion and his baptism (9:18), "in the synagogues immediately he proclaimed Jesus, saying, 'He is the Son of God'" (9:20). One plausible explanation for the verbal parallel between the Ethiopian's confession and Paul's is that not "*later* baptismal practice" but primitive and consistent baptismal practice entailed the existence of such a catechism or creed, functioning as a rule of faith. Presumably it would have been in oral rather than in written form, because even three centuries later Saint Cyril of Jerusalem was still warning his catechumen hearers: "This summary I wish you both to commit to memory when I recite it, and to rehearse it with all diligence among yourselves, *not writing it out on paper*, but engraving it by the memory upon your heart."[25] But just because even then the creed was not usually being "written out on paper," should that be taken to mean that it was not there, or that in one or another form it had not been there all along?

There was in fact no single passage in the New Testament, not even the primitive creed or hymn quoted in Phil. 2:6–11, that encompassed the entire scope of the Christian confession, "the whole counsel of God" (πᾶσαν τὴν βουλὴν τοῦ θεοῦ) (20:27) in its full trinitarian structure and in all the successive but distinct stages of redemption history, as comprehensively as the statement of the church's faith in the Niceno-Constantinopolitan Creed and the Apostles' Creed would: creation, redemption, sanctification; preexistence as "God from God"; incarnation and birth from the Virgin Mary; humiliation, suffering, and crucifixion; exaltation, resurrection, and ascension; second coming. It was the intended function of the creed to bring together these elements and stages of redemptive history into a single confession, above all, at least initially, for the purposes of baptism (→22:16). In 1:11, for example, only the last two of these stages, the ascension and the second coming, were explicitly affirmed; but this

---

20. Bede, *Exposition of the Acts of the Apostles* 8 (PL 92:963).

21. Nikanor 1905, 1:175–76.

22. Bogolepov 1900, 428.

23. Pelikan 2003, 35–63.

24. Macgregor 1954, 10.

25. Cyril of Jerusalem, *Catechetical Lectures* 5.12 (*NPNF*[2] 7:32) (emphasis added); Quasten et al. 1951–86, 3:363–64.

should not be taken to mean that the apostolic community—or, in this case, the angel speaking to the apostolic community in 1:11—did not confess (or did not possess) the creed as a whole.

Therefore the modern exegetical practice of reading or interpreting any single passage of the New Testament outside the total context of that confession, or even of treating the confession as the unwarranted imposition of a creedal schema on the biblical text, can lead to distortion. In the words just quoted from the Tome of Leo of 449, "A man who has not the most elementary understanding even of the creed itself can have learned nothing from the sacred texts of the Old and New Testaments";[26] thus the "understanding of the creed itself" was taken to be the presupposition for "learning from the sacred texts," not necessarily the other way around. That also seems to be the sense of Luke's introduction to his Gospel, where he stated it as its purpose (and, by a not unwarranted extension, the purpose also of the book of Acts) "that you [Theophilus] may know the truth concerning the things of which you have been informed [περὶ ὧν κατηχήθης]" (Luke 1:4): Theophilus had already "been informed" through his initial instruction, whether or not it is anachronistic to refer to this instruction as a "creed" or a "catechism"—the verb Luke used here, κατηχήθης, was etymologically connected to κατήχησις ("catechesis")[27]—and now he needed to acquire further reliable knowledge.

The Christology of the book of Acts presents throughout some instances of this problem that seem quite puzzling, none more so than the words of Peter: "God *has made him* both Lord and Christ [καὶ κύριον αὐτὸν καὶ χριστὸν ἐποίησεν ὁ θεός], this Jesus whom you crucified" (2:36).[28] Taken in isolation from the total scope of the confession of the church as this was documented elsewhere in Scripture and as it was collected in the creed, these words could be read—and were being read, by some of the opponents of the Council of Nicea—to refute the statement of the creeds that he was "begotten not made" (γεννηθέντα οὐ ποιηθέντα)[29] and to say that one who had begun as no more than a man (ψιλὸς ἄνθρωπος) was "made Lord" by adoption and promoted to a higher-than-human status that he had not possessed before. In a lengthy response explaining this passage from Peter's sermon, Saint Athanasius argued that it was unimaginable that the same Peter who at Caesarea Philippi had been commended by Christ himself for voicing the confession that "you are the Christ, the Son of the living God" (Matt. 16:16), and therefore that he was nothing less than the Creator and a hypostasis of the consubstantial Trinity, should be described as saying here "that in his essence [οὐσία] the Logos was a work" or a creature, not very God of very God.[30] In the chapter of Acts follow-

26. Tome of Leo 1 (*CCF* 1:114).
27. *PGL* 732–33.
28. Hahn 1969, 106–8.
29. Nicene Creed 2 (*CCF* 1:158–59); Niceno-Constantinopolitan Creed 2 (*CCF* 1:162–63).
30. Athanasius, *Discourses against the Arians* 2.11–18 (*NPNF*[2] 4:354–57).

ing Peter's statement (3:15), Jesus, already in his crucifixion, was spoken of as "the Author [ἀρχηγός] of life, whom God raised from the dead" (→2:31). Acts likewise contains, almost en passant, what turned out to be one of the strongest statements anywhere in the Scriptures equating the Holy Spirit with God, by the simple syllogism: lying to the Holy Spirit means lying to God; therefore the Holy Spirit is God, or, as the Latin version of the Niceno-Constantinopolitan Creed says, "the Lord" (*dominus*) (→5:3–4). All of the constituent elements of the Niceno-Constantinopolitan Creed about the Trinity were, therefore, already present at one place or another, more or less inchoately, in the book of Acts.[31] What the councils did by their "dogmas" and "decrees" (→16:4b) was to find a way of confessing all at once and in a single formulary what was scattered in various passages of the Old and the New Testament—including this passage from the TPR of Acts, which was cited almost verbatim in the words of the Niceno-Constantinopolitan Creed when it confessed: "And [we believe] in one Lord Jesus Christ, the Son of God."[32]

8:39 TPR And when they came up out of the water, the Holy Spirit fell upon the eunuch, and an angel of the Lord took Philip away from him; the eunuch saw him no more, and went on his way rejoicing.

Other manuscripts of this text have the Holy Spirit rather than an angel taking Philip away, but here in the TPR the Holy Spirit remained with the newly baptized—and newly confessing—Ethiopian convert.

---

31. J. Bellamy in *DTC* 1:351.
32. Niceno-Constantinopolitan Creed 2 (*CCF* 1:163).

ACTS 9

A Grammar of Assent

9:1–4 TPR But Saul, still breathing threats and murder against the disciples of the Lord, went to the high priests and asked them for letters to the synagogues at Damascus, so that if he found any belonging to this Way, men or women, he might bring them bound to Jerusalem. Now as he journeyed he approached Damascus, and suddenly a light from heaven flashed around him. And he fell to the ground in a great trance [μετὰ πολλῆς ἐκστάσεως].

In the book that is generally recognized to be his most subtle—and, as its modern editor acknowledges, his "least accessible"[1]—*An Essay in Aid of a Grammar of Assent* of 1870 and following, with its eighth and final edition prepared by the author in 1889, John Henry Newman probed the delicate relations between proof and probability, and therefore between conversion and assent, in moving the mind toward an acceptance of the truth of divine revelation: "How it is that a conditional acceptance of a proposition,—such as is an act of inference,—is able to lead as it does, to an unconditional acceptance of it,—such as is assent."[2] In the course of his argument he also provided a basis for considering, historically and almost empirically, the phenomena that his American contemporary William James in his Gifford Lectures was to call "the varieties of religious experience," especially the difference between what James defined (specifically referring to the events described here in the ninth chapter of Acts) as "those striking instantaneous instances of which Saint Paul's is the most eminent, and in which . . . a complete division is established in the twinkling of an eye between the old life and the new" and what he called "the volitional type" of conversion, in which "the regenerative change is usually

1. Ian T. Ker in Newman 1985, v.
2. Newman 1985, 105.

gradual, and consists in the building up, piece by piece, of a new set of moral and spiritual habits."[3]

The book of Acts contains three separate tellings of the conversion of Saul:[4] this account by Luke, which opens the second part of the book of Acts that carries the nascent Christian movement from Jerusalem to Athens and Rome and into world history (→28:14); and then two recitations of the story in the first-person singular that are put into the mouth of Saint Paul himself, one addressed to a Jewish audience (22:1–16), the other to King Agrippa (26:9–19). In all three of them conversion is depicted as, in Tertullian's phrase, "a fortuitous encounter rather than a deliberate selection" by the other apostles,[5] a highly dramatic event of being instantaneously "born anew" (John 3:3) by a divine intervention. These accounts of Paul's conversion served Saint Augustine as a paradigm of unmerited grace: "Tell me, I beseech you," he could use it to argue against the Pelagians, "what good, Paul, while he was as yet Saul, willed, and not rather great evils, when breathing out slaughter he went, in horrible darkness of mind and madness, to lay waste the Christians? For what merits of a good will did God convert him by a marvelous and sudden calling from those evils to good things?"[6] Augustine could have appealed, as he did in the *Confessions*, to his own experience of God's "converting me to yourself" after "a profound self-examination": "As I was . . . weeping in the bitter agony of my heart, suddenly I heard a voice . . . repeating over and over again 'Pick up and read, pick up and read.' At once my countenance changed. . . . At once . . . it was as if a light of relief from all anxiety flooded into my heart. All the shadows of doubt were dispelled."[7] Both Paul's experience and Augustine's are reflected in Luther's autobiographical account, written a year before his death, of his "tower experience" (*Turmerlebnis*) as he struggled over the meaning of the *iustitia dei* said to be revealed in the gospel (Rom. 1:17), when, as he reported, "I felt that I was altogether born again and had entered paradise itself through open gates,"[8] as well as in John Wesley's report of his heart being "strangely warmed" at Aldersgate on 24 May 1738 as a consequence of the reading of Luther's preface to Romans[9]—and in the individual conversion experiences of thousands of believers during various of the "great awakenings," both individual and collective, that have taken place throughout Christian history (and not only in eighteenth-century and nineteenth-century America).

More often in the history of the gospel (and in the history being narrated here in Acts), however, conversion has rather been (to use the term employed by

---

3. James 1990, 201, 192.
4. Haenchen 1971, 318–29; Löning 1973, 14–19; also Marguerat 1999, 275–84, for a point-by-point comparison; and Jacob Kremer in Verheyden 1999, 329–55.
5. Tertullian, *Against Marcion* 5.1 (*ANF* 3:429).
6. Augustine, *Against Two Letters of the Pelagians* 1.19.37 (*NPNF*[1] 5:388).
7. Augustine, *Confessions* 8.12.28–30 (Chadwick 1992, 152–54).
8. Luther 1955, 34:337.
9. John Wesley in Outler 1964, 51–69.

William James) a more "gradual" process of becoming persuaded. For example, a later chapter of Acts (17:1–3 TPR) employs the same verb that Aristotle used throughout his *Rhetoric* (→24:1–2) to describe how "some were persuaded by the doctrine [ἐπείσθησαν τῇ διδαχῇ]" after "Paul . . . , as was his custom, . . . for three weeks . . . argued with them from the scriptures, explaining and proving that it was necessary for the Christ to suffer and to rise from the dead, and saying, 'This [Christ is] Jesus, whom I proclaim to you.'"

Whatever may be the differences in modality and in timing between these two paths to conversion—and whatever may be all the infinite gradations between them, as these become evident in the lives of the saints in every period of the history of the church—one popular way of differentiating between them, by ascribing the first to divine action and the second to human, does not find support in the text of the book of Acts, for conversion by a gradual process of persuasion is seen here to be fully as much the work of God as is conversion by an instantaneous and dramatic intervention. A test case was Lydia (16:14–15 TPR), "a worshiper of God" (σεβομένη τὸν θεόν)—which, together with "devout God-fearer" (εὐσεβὴς καὶ φοβούμενος τὸν θεόν) (10:2), was a quasitechnical term for a Gentile on the way toward becoming a proselyte to Judaism. At a designated place of prayer (→7:47–48), as Lydia "heard us . . . *the Lord opened her heart* to give heed to what was said by Paul . . . [and] she was baptized, with her entire household." On the basis of Ps. 59:10 Vulgate, *Deus meus, misericordia eius praeveniet me*, this modality of the divine initiative in conversion has acquired the label *gratia praeveniens* ("prevenient grace").[10]

In the context of the larger account of Luke-Acts, the singular "conversion" story with which that entire account begins is the annunciation of the Blessed Virgin Mary (Luke 1:26–28), which the Greek Orthodox liturgy and the Greek church fathers called her "evangelization" (εὐαγγελισμός).[11] Although the annunciation demonstrated, according to Saint Gregory of Nyssa, that "the power of the Godhead is an immense and immeasurable thing, while man is a weak atom,"[12] and although the Virgin Mary was divinely predestined and chosen (→13:48) to become the Theotokos, the Mother of God (→1:14), nevertheless the incarnation took place at her voluntary and unconstrained response to the angel (→12:7): "Behold, I am the handmaid of the Lord; let it be to me according to your word" (Luke 1:38). That was why, according to Dante and the Florentine tradition, the beginning of the new age of human history was to be dated from the annunciation rather than from the nativity.[13] In the words of Irenaeus about Eve and Mary, "If the former did disobey God, yet the latter

10. Dogmatic Decrees of the Council of Trent 6.5 (*CCF* 2:828); Eva Maria Faber in Lacoste 1998, 503.
11. *PGL* 559.
12. Gregory of Nyssa, *Letters* 17 (*NPNF*² 5:543–44).
13. Dante Alighieri, *Paradiso* 16.34–39.

was persuaded [*suasa est*] to be obedient to God, in order that the Virgin Mary might become the patroness of the virgin Eve."[14]

The Church as "the Body of Christ"

9:4–5 TPR And he fell to the ground in a great trance, and heard a voice saying to him, "Saul, Saul, why do you persecute me? It hurts you to kick against the goads." And he said, "Who are you, Lord?" And he said, "I am Jesus, whom you are persecuting."

Without anywhere actually invoking the Pauline title of the church as the body of Christ (Rom. 12:5; 1 Cor. 12:27; Eph. 1:23; 4:12; Col. 1:24; 2:19), the book of Acts here describes the risen and ascended Christ as answering the question of Saul, the persecutor of the church, "Who are you, Lord?" with the identification underlying that Pauline title, "I am Jesus, whom you are persecuting" (9:5), marking Saul as a successor of those who had tormented Jesus Christ in his passion and marking the church as the successor of Christ in his passion. As Origen explains these words, "Every one who betrays the disciples of Jesus is reckoned as betraying Jesus Himself";[15] and Bede explains: "He does not say, 'Why are you persecuting my members?' but 'Why are you persecuting me?' because he has been suffering from the wicked ones in his body, which is the church."[16] Saul—together with the long line of his descendants—may have supposed that he was attacking the miserable adherents of a wretched fringe movement (→14:22); but here the ultimate target of the rage and the violence (→28:31) identified himself as none less than "Jesus, whom you are persecuting."

The death of Stephen, to which "Saul was consenting" (8:1), carried out that identification. The "false witnesses" who said against Stephen, "This man never ceases to speak words against this holy place and the law; for we have heard him say that this Jesus of Nazareth will destroy this place'" (6:13–14), were the lineal descendants of the "false witnesses" who "came forward . . . and said [against Jesus], 'This fellow said, "I am able to destroy the temple of God, and to build it in three days"'" (Matt. 26:60–61). The Stephen who saw "the heavens opened, and the Son of man standing at the right hand of God" (7:56) stood in the succession of the Jesus to whom after his baptism "the heavens were opened and he saw the Spirit of God descending like a dove, and alighting on him" (Matt. 3:16). Here in Acts, Luke quotes the two dying prayers of Stephen, as the representative of the body of Christ whom Saul was persecuting, which hark back to two of the dying prayers of the person of Christ on the cross, as Luke, uniquely among the four evangelists, had quoted them

---

14. Irenaeus, *Against Heresies* 5.19.1 (*ANF* 1:547).
15. Origen, *Commentary on John* 12 (*ANF* 10:304).
16. Bede, *Exposition of the Acts of the Apostles* 9 (PL 92:963).

in his Gospel. Stephen's prayer, "Lord Jesus, receive my spirit" (→7:59–60) stood in the succession of Jesus' prayer: "Father, into thy hands I commit my spirit!" (Luke 23:46); and the prayer with which Stephen continued, "Lord, do not hold this sin against them" (7:60), also stood in the succession of Jesus' prayer on the cross: "Father, forgive them; for they know not what they do" (Luke 23:34).

But the church was the body of Christ here in Acts not only in his death, but already in his life, teaching, and ministry, by its "teaching and fellowship, the breaking of bread and prayer" (2:42 TPR). What Christ taught, before and after his resurrection, was what the church as his body continued to teach (→1:2–3). The baptism that he himself underwent (Luke 3:21–22) and then commanded (Matt. 28:19–20) was its requirement for admission (→22:16). The call to repentance that he issued from the beginning of his first message (Mark 1:15) became its summons to all (→26:20). As he in his earthly ministry performed signs and miracles of healing (2:22), so his body did also (→6:8), not by its own authority or power but "in the name of Jesus Christ of Nazareth" (3:6; 6:8 TPR). The breaking of bread that he instituted in the night of his betrayal was the gift of his true body and blood (→20:7). And the root meaning of the metaphor, the relation of the members of the body one to another and to Christ their head, was summarized in the description, "All who believed were together" (2:44–46), as this solidarity was expressed concretely in their mutual support (→11:29). About much of the narrative in Acts, whether positive or negative, therefore, one could observe with Chrysostom: "This is also what they said about Christ."[17]

9:10–14 Ananias was both a representative of the new community of faith into which Saul had now been plunged and an agent of the Christ whom Saul had been persecuting. Therefore Saul's first experience of the faith and of the community came through Ananias, who, after his understandable reluctance to have anything to do with "this man" on account of the "evil he has done to thy saints at Jerusalem" (9:13), was sent by "the Lord Jesus" to welcome him as "Brother Saul" (9:17).

Paul the "Chosen Instrument"

9:15 TPR This man is a chosen instrument of mine to carry my name before the Gentiles and kings and the sons of Israel.

Acts 9, and even verse 15 within this chapter, can serve as a dividing line between the two major sections of the Acts of the Apostles; as the parting words of Christ before the ascension, "You shall be my witnesses in Jerusalem and

17. Chrysostom, *Homilies on Acts* 15 (*NPNF*[1] 11:95).

in all Judea and Samaria and to the ends of the earth" (1:8), initially provided the charter to his eleven remaining disciples to look beyond the confines of the Holy City and the Holy Land toward the wider world, so now the choosing of Paul carried with it "a roving commission" to him toward the constituencies enumerated here. The title σκεῦος ἐκλογῆς is translated "chosen vessel" in the AV, "chosen instrument" in the RSV, and "instrument whom I have chosen" in the NRSV.[18] As in the familiar words "we have this treasure in earthen vessels" (2 Cor. 4:7), σκεῦος ("vessel") seems to carry connotations of passivity, as that which receives and contains, which would suit the Paul who in a mystical rapture (and in the passive voice) "was caught up into Paradise . . . and . . . heard things that cannot be told, which man may not utter" (2 Cor. 12:4), while the translation "instrument" connotes activity, "not only being faithful but being a teacher"[19]—which certainly does fit the Paul of Acts. In either case, however, Calvin's comments on the word apply: "The word 'instrument' doth show that men can do nothing, save inasmuch as God useth their industry at his pleasure. For if we be instruments, he alone is the author; the force and power to do is in his power alone."[20]

The order of "Gentiles" and "the sons of Israel" is reversed here from the actual sequence of the narrative in Acts, which opened in Jerusalem (1:4) and closed in Rome (28:14), began with Israel and turned to the Gentiles, as in the words of Paul and Barnabas to a Jewish audience: "It was necessary that the word of God should be spoken *first to you*. Since you thrust it from you, and judge yourselves unworthy of eternal life, behold, we turn to the Gentiles" (13:46). The same was true of the argument in Romans, where "the gospel . . . is the power of God for salvation to every one who has faith, to the Jew *first* and also to the Greek" (Rom. 1:16). The same reversal of sequence, however, had appeared already in the Nunc Dimittis of Simeon, which, it is interesting to note, was also recorded by Luke:

> A light for revelation to the Gentiles,
> and for glory to thy people Israel. (Luke 2:32)

It is not obvious what the significance of this reversal is. It could be no more than a literary device, or it could reflect Luke's special interest, whether or not he himself was a Gentile, as is generally supposed. But unlike the earlier sequence of venues, "in Jerusalem and in all Judea and Samaria and to the ends of the earth" (1:8), this catalog in 9:15, "the Gentiles and kings and the sons of Israel," does not correspond to the chronological sequence of Acts, where the mission began with Israel (→3:25) and then was directed to the Gentiles. Interposing the reference to "kings" here between the more conventional terms

18. Löning 1973, 32–43, compares the translations "instrument" and "vessel."
19. Theophylact, *Exposition of the Acts of the Apostles* 9.16 (PG 125:644).
20. Calvin 1949, 1:380.

"the Gentiles" and "the sons of Israel" was an anticipation of Paul's appearance before King Agrippa (25:13–26:32) and ultimately of his arrival in Rome to stand before Caesar himself (28:14), as well as a reference to the verse from the Psalter:

I also spoke of thy testimonies before kings,
and was not put to shame. (Ps. 119:46 LXX)

Confessors of the Reformation period took this verse as their motto when they stood before hostile rulers to bear testimony.[21]

In spite of this designation of Paul as the chosen apostle to the Gentiles here and in parallel passages, the book of Acts, when it was describing the council of the apostles in Jerusalem, placed into the mouth of Peter, not of Paul, the words: "A good while ago God made choice among us, *that the Gentiles by my mouth* should hear the word of the gospel, and believe" (15:7 TPR AV). One possible explanation may be that this referred to "the early days" before the conversion of Paul, who then took over this Gentile mission from Peter. Nevertheless, from the rather idealized narrative of the apostolic council in Acts 15 it would be difficult to envisage the scene between Peter and Paul as this was described by Paul himself: "When Cephas came to Antioch, I opposed him to his face [κατὰ πρόσωπον], because he stood condemned. . . . I said to Cephas before them all, 'If you, though a Jew, live like a Gentile and not like a Jew, how can you compel the Gentiles to live like Jews?'" (Gal. 2:11, 14).[22]

Even those who date the Acts of the Apostles in the first century are often far more reluctant than traditional exegesis has been to interpret its portrait of Paul on the basis of the Pauline Epistles. An outstanding instance of the problem is the Pauline doctrine of justification by faith (→13:38–39). When the Paul of Acts, speaking in the synagogue of Antioch of Pisidia, declared, "Through this man is preached unto you the forgiveness of sins: And by him all that *believed* are *justified* from all things, from which ye could not be justified by the *law* of Moses [ἀπὸ πάντων ὧν οὐκ ἠδυνήθητε ἐν νόμῳ Μωϋσέως δικαιωθῆναι, ἐν τούτῳ πᾶς ὁ πιστεύων δικαιοῦται]" (13:38–39 AV), does the use of the three Greek vocables νόμος ("law"), δικαιοῦν ("to justify"), and πιστεύειν ("to believe") as technical terms in the mouth of the Apostle Paul warrant an interpretation of these verses—and a translation—on the basis of the parallel passage written by him in the Epistle to the Romans, using the same vocables: "Therefore we conclude that a man is *justified* by *faith* without the deeds of the *law*" (λογιζόμεθα γὰρ δικαιοῦσθαι πίστει ἄνθρωπον χωρὶς ἔργων νόμου) (Rom. 3:28 AV)? The methodology underlying the present commentary on the Acts of the Apostles would seem to imply an affirmative answer to that question.

21. Pelikan 2003, 222.
22. See pp. 28–29 above.

9:17–19 TPR And laying his hand on him in the name of Jesus Christ he said, "Brother Saul, the Lord Jesus who appeared to you on the road by which you came, has sent me that you may regain your sight and be filled with the Holy Spirit." And something like scales fell from his eyes and immediately he regained his sight. Then he rose and was baptized, and took food and was strengthened.

The phrase "in the name of Jesus Christ" in the TPR makes it clear that by laying his "hand" (singular in the TPR) (→6:6) on Saul, Ananias was acting not on his own behalf, but on behalf of the Lord who was choosing Saul to be his instrument. A later version of this incident makes it clear that the light by which Saul had been blinded was no creature, but a divine energy (→22:6).

9:21 TPR And all who heard him were amazed, and said, "Is not this the man who made havoc in Jerusalem among all those who called on this name?"

This question calls dramatic attention to the unique position of Paul and to the total reversal of his life through divine intervention, from persecutor to persecuted (→14:22).

9:40 TPR Peter put all of them outside and knelt down and prayed; then turning to the body he said, "Tabitha, rise in the name of Jesus Christ." And she opened her eyes, and when she saw Peter she sat up.

The raising of Tabitha/Dorcas by Peter was more than yet another (→6:8) of the "many wonders and signs [that] were done through the apostles" (2:43), as they said at one of the earliest (3:6)—and again here, at least according to the TPR—"in the name of Jesus Christ." It was a striking instance of how the imitation of Christ (→7:59–60) could extend even to some of the minute details of his miracles. Commentators note the parallel between this account and Christ's raising of the daughter of the leader of the synagogue in Matt. 9:22–25. But it is especially Mark's account of that miracle that provides a detail that may be of special interest, for Mark has Jesus say, in Aramaic transliterated into the Greek alphabet, "'Talitha cumi [ταλιθα κουμι],' which means, 'Little girl, I say to you, arise'" (Mark 5:41); and here Luke has Peter say, using the Aramaic form of Dorcas's name, "Tabitha, rise" (Ταβιθά, ἀνάστηθι). If, as seems likely, the Gospel account had been transmitted orally, complete with the Aramaic phrase, before being written down, may it perhaps also seem possible that Luke was engaging in wordplay on the assonance between ταλιθα and Ταβιθά? The tender account of how "all the widows stood beside [Peter] weeping, and showing tunics and other garments which Dorcas made while she was with them" (9:39) gives us a glimpse into the early Christian practice of grieving over the faithful departed (→21:13–14).

ACTS 10

10:3–4 TPR He saw clearly in a vision an angel of God coming in and saying to him, "Cornelius." And he stared at him in terror, and said, "Who are you, Lord?"

In the course of explaining the fundamental revision of the ceremonial laws of Moses that had come about through the coming of Christ, the encounter of Cornelius and then the encounter of Peter involved at least two other theological topics. Once again, as was to happen throughout the narrative of Acts, a new truth was being communicated not (or at any rate not only) through a clarification and deepening of the meaning of the biblical text, as had been the case in the encounter of Philip with the Ethiopian (→8:30–31), but through special visions and private revelations, one to Cornelius (10:3–6) and then one to Peter three times over (10:11–16). These visions seem to have been self-authenticating (→16:9), for Peter's "doubts" (10:17) pertained to the meaning of the vision, not to its genuineness. And the agent of this revelation to Cornelius was not Christ himself, as he was in each of the three tellings of Paul's conversion on the road to Damascus (→9:1–4), but "an angel of God," superhuman but still a creature, whom Cornelius in his terror nevertheless addressed as "Lord" (κύριε) (→12:7), just as he seemed to regard Peter himself as somehow an object of divine worship until Peter disabused him of this idolatrous illusion (10:25–26). To Peter the revelation came not in the presence of an angel, as it would in his rescue from prison (12:7–9), but with a voice (10:13), which, from Peter's response "Lord" (10:14), was probably the voice of Jesus Christ, which he would have recognized, and then with a second voice, which was the voice of the Holy Spirit (10:19).

The "Yoke" of the Mosaic Law

10:15 What God has cleansed, you must not call common.

The "customs and controversies of the Jews," with which, according to Paul, King Agrippa was "especially familiar" (26:3), included not only the "controversies" between Jewish sects, in which "the Sadducees say that there is no resurrection, nor angel, nor spirit; but the Pharisees confess the existence of resurrection and angel and spirit" (23:8 TPR) and of which Paul was able to take such good advantage in his confession of the resurrection of Christ (→23:8), but the "customs" and laws of individual and corporate Jewish life: (1) the sacredness of the Sabbath and of the temple (→7:47–48) and the regulations governing circumcision and kosher food, but also (2) the fundamental moral prohibitions and commandments of the Decalogue, with no precise delineation of a distinction between moral and ceremonial laws even within the Decalogue itself (Exod. 20:8–11). As they had been entrusted to Moses by God and legislated by Moses for the people of Israel throughout the Pentateuch, these laws and customs were originally seen as an inseparable part of God's covenant with Israel established in the exodus from Egypt (→3:25), together with the divine promise of the Holy Land to the descendants of Abraham (→7:47–48). From the way Moses was celebrated as the recipient of the special revelation of God as well as of secular wisdom (→7:22), it should be obvious that for the writer of the book of Acts the law of Moses had come from God in its entirety (→25:8). Nevertheless, both in the book of Acts (15:10) and in the Epistle to the Galatians (5:1) the law was called a "yoke" (ζυγός), and Christian liberty was defined as freedom from the yoke of the Mosaic law.[1]

Even within the Jewish community of the first century AD, as the works of Philo of Alexandria and of Josephus document, there were "controversies" about these laws and "customs." At least some of the commands and prohibitions seemed to be ethnic in their enforceability only upon those who were physically part of the nation of Israel, or regional in their applicability only to those who dwelled in (though they no longer governed) "this land in which you are now living" (7:4). Although "no other narrative in Acts is given quite such epic treatment as the Cornelius episode,"[2] there are in fact several levels of philo-Judaic Gentiles encountered in the book of Acts, from someone like Cornelius in this chapter, who was "devout" (εὐσεβής) (10:2) or "upright and God-fearing" (δίκαιος καὶ φοβούμενος τὸν θεόν) (10:22), to someone who had become a "proselyte" (2:10; 6:5) in the full sense;[3] we are told in the Gospels, somewhat surprisingly, that "scribes and Pharisees . . . traverse sea and land to make a single proselyte" (Matt. 23:15). The persisting distinction that Jews themselves made between "Jews and proselytes" (2:10) does seem to imply some continuing differences of status, which would then have been perpetuated and even exacerbated when some of these proselytes switched their loyalties one more time to become Christians (16:5).

1. Jervell 1972, 133–51.
2. Wilson 1973, 177.
3. Bruce 1990, 252–53, with bibliography.

Some of those who had come to "the Way" of Jesus Christ (→11:26) from Judaism were insisting to those who had come to it directly from paganism without an intervening stage as Jewish proselytes "unless you are circumcised and walk in accordance with the custom of Moses, you cannot be saved" (15:1 TPR). Indeed, the preaching of Paul and Barnabas to the Gentiles was perceived as posing a threat even to those observant Jews who were not becoming Christians. The elders of the church at Jerusalem, who were themselves converts from Judaism to "the Way," reported to Paul: "Thou seest, brother, how many thousands of Jews there are which believe; and they are all zealous of the law: And they are informed of thee, that thou teachest *all the Jews which are among the Gentiles* to forsake Moses, saying that they ought not to circumcise their children, neither to walk after the customs" (21:20–22 TPR AV). And the Jews haled Paul before Gallio, the Roman proconsul of Achaia, with the accusation: "This man is persuading men to worship God contrary to the law" (18:13), referring by the term "law" to Roman law, but also to the law of God as this had been given to Moses (→25:8).

Initially, the response of the apostles to such challenges and charges was a series of accommodations and improvisations. Because his pupil Timothy was the offspring of a mixed marriage between a Jewish mother and a Greek father, Paul made the concession of circumcising him (16:1–3). But no such concession was called for in the case of another pupil, the Gentile Titus (Gal. 2:3). The compromise embodied in the four prohibitions set down by the decree of the apostolic council at Jerusalem, published in Acts 15, "to abstain [1] from the pollutions of idols and [2] from unchastity and [3] from what is strangled and [4] from blood" (15:20), seems, at least on the face of it, to have perpetuated the confusion between ceremonial law and moral law (→24:25b), putting "unchastity" (πορνεία) and "what is strangled" (τὸ πνικτόν) on the same level as abominations. The confusion is only compounded by the number of variants, unusually high even for the book of Acts (→20:28a), in this text of the decree (15:23–29) and in the text of it that appears in a later chapter (21:25), with the prohibition of "what is strangled" being a special problem in the manuscripts.[4] To clarify the relation between the ceremonial and the moral law, the TPR includes in the decree: "And whatever you do not want to be done to you, do not do it to someone else . . . , as you are sustained by the Holy Spirit" (15:29 TPR).

Even as these compromises were going on, however, the divine nullification and repeal of the Mosaic law was being promulgated in the most absolute of terms through the vision of Peter: "What *God* has cleansed [including reptiles and other ceremonially unclean foods forbidden in the law of Moses], *you* must not call common" (10:15).[5] The fundamental problem was, of course, that it was not Peter at all, but no one less than the Lord God of Israel speaking through

4. Barrett 1994–98, 2:735–36.
5. Tannehill 1990, 2:128–45.

Moses and the Mosaic law, who had "called" such foods "common"—and worse. Part of the pragmatic solution to this problem was to label it "mak[ing] trial of God by putting a yoke upon the neck of the disciples which our fathers have not been able to bear" (15:10 TPR): the law as it was now being interpreted by its would-be enforcers had never worked in the past, even for observant Jews, and it could not be made to work now, especially for nonobservant Gentile Christians. The positive side of this pragmatic case was to argue that if Gentile Christians who did not observe the Mosaic law had received "the same gift . . . as he gave to us when we believed in the Lord Jesus Christ, who was I that I could prohibit God from giving them the Holy Spirit?" (11:17 TPR).

The eventual solution, adumbrated but not yet sorted out in the apostolic "decrees" (δόγματα) (→16:4b) of the council of Jerusalem, was to be, as Saint Justin Martyr explained to Trypho the Jew,[6] a stratification of the law of Moses. The civil law was applicable only to Israel as a political entity (→25:11); the ceremonial law was applicable to Judaism as a liturgical community, but had been superseded by Christian eucharistic worship (→4:24–30; →20:7). But the moral law, much of which was known also to natural reason (→7:22; →25:8), was "not only permanently . . . reserved, but even amplified"[7] to be as binding on Christians now as it had ever been on Jews (→24:25b). If this moral law was to be called a "yoke," then it had to be in the positive sense in which Christ himself had invited and promised: "Take my yoke upon you, and learn from me. . . . For my yoke is easy, and my burden is light" (Matt. 11:29–30).

10:30 TPR I was fasting and keeping the ninth hour of prayer in my house; and behold, a man stood before me in bright apparel.

Once more the book of Acts makes reference to ascetic self-denial (→24:25b) and to the Jewish stated times for prayer (→7:47–48). The "man . . . in bright apparel" was an angel (→12:7).

The Unity and Equality of All Humanity before God

10:34–35 Truly I perceive that God shows no partiality [οὐκ ἔστιν προσωπολήμπτης ὁ θεός], but in every nation any one who fears him and does what is right is acceptable to him.

The confession "that God shows no partiality" (οὐκ ἔστιν προσωπολήμπτης ὁ θεός), and that therefore "partiality" (προσωπολημψία) (Rom. 2:11) or prejudice and "respect of persons" (AV) is contrary to the will of God, was for the book of Acts a direct corollary of its transcendent monotheism (→19:28). As Clement

6. Justin Martyr, *Dialogue with Trypho* 11–12 (*ANF* 1:199–200).
7. Tertullian, *On Monogamy* 7 (*ANF* 4:63–64).

of Alexandria argued, therefore, quoting these words of Peter, this "absence of respect of persons in God is not in time, but from eternity."[8] At the same time it was, however, accessible even outside the boundaries of historical revelation (→7:22). The classical symbol of such impartiality, also in Greek and Roman thought, was the figure of the goddess Justice, who was depicted as wearing a blindfold, not to keep her from seeing the facts but to assure that she would not be a "respecter of persons."

According to Paul's proclamation at Athens, it was not only Moses and the prophets, but "even some of your poets [who] have said, 'For we are indeed his offspring.' Being then God's offspring" (17:28–29); the ultimate ground for affirming the unity and equality of all humanity was the affirmation that opened most of the creeds, as already at the First Council of Nicea in 325: "We believe in one God the Father all-powerful, Maker of all things both seen and unseen."[9] Had Paul been addressing not a Greek audience in Athens but a Jewish one, he would have shifted the rhetorical definition of *pathos*, "the frame of mind of the audience" (→24:1–2), as he often did (→23:1), and quoted not "one of *your* poets," the third-century BC Aratus, but "one of *our* prophets," Malachi, who had asked: "Has not one God created us? Is there not one father of all of us? Why then has each of you deserted his brother to defile the covenant of your fathers?" (Mal. 2:10 LXX). The advocates of a strict Christocentrism sometimes argue that the Bible does not teach a universal fatherhood of God; but they are contradicted by passages such as these verses of Acts, as well as by the direct linkage between "the Father all-powerful" and "Maker" in the first article of the creed. As in Paul's argumentation at Athens, so also in Peter's confession here, there was a logical argument, from the premise "that God shows no partiality" to the conclusion about "any one" in "every nation."

The phrase "all things both seen and unseen" in the creed embraced not only all humanity but all creation, under a common Creator, but the doctrine of unity and equality based on the sovereign act of a common Creator became even more specific: "And hath made of one blood [ἐξ ἑνὸς αἵματος] all nations of men" (17:26 TPR AV).[10] Across and behind all the historical differences among "all nations," there was a unity of species that was a product of origin "from one" ancestor, or even "from one blood."[11] From his epistles, it was clearly Paul's view that "not all flesh [or blood] is alike, but there is one kind for men, another for animals, another for birds, and another for fish" (1 Cor. 15:39), but within these species there was not a difference. A common ancestry in Adam meant that "many died through one man's trespass" (Rom. 5:15), which was also a part of the doctrine of the unity and equality of all humanity before God in a shared misery.

8. Clement of Alexandria, *Stromata* 6.8 (*ANF* 2:494–95).
9. Nicene Creed 1 (*CCF* 1:159).
10. Bede, *Retractations on the Acts of the Apostles* 17 (PL 92:1026).
11. Barrett 1994–98, 2:842.

Yet it was not only the misery that was shared; it was also liberation from the misery that crossed all boundaries: "*In every nation* [ἐν παντὶ ἔθνει] any one who fears him and does what is right is acceptable to him [δεκτὸς αὐτῷ]." If then, so the argumentation ran, someone was good enough to be δεκτός and acceptable to God, by what right may we be more restrictive than the Almighty One, more judgmental of sin than the Holy One? As the voice in the vision said to Peter, "What God has cleansed, you must not call common" (10:16)—or even "*Whom* God has cleansed"—for "you yourselves know how unlawful it is for a Jew to associate with or to visit any one of another nation; but God has shown me that I should not call any man [μηδένα . . . ἄνθρωπον] common or unclean" (10:28).

Paul's version of this doctrine that God was not προσωπολήμπτης, in his message about unity and equality at Athens, continued from the teaching that he "hath made of one blood all nations of men for to dwell on all the face of the earth" to the concrete reality of historical disunity and inequality as defined by both space and time: "and hath determined the times before appointed, and the bounds of their habitation" (17:26 TPR AV). That concrete reality was a historical reality, but in the plot line of the Acts of the Apostles the emphasis was on how that concrete reality was transcended and ultimately overcome. No historical force more dramatically illustrates these "times before appointed" and these "bounds," together with the differences, inequalities, and conflicts that spring from them, than the phenomenon of language and of linguistic differentiation (→21:37). But the gift of the Holy Spirit (→2:1), as "a new creation" beyond historical differences (Gal. 6:15), brought with it a transcending even of this: "How is it," the observers at Pentecost exclaimed in skeptical amazement, "that we hear, each of us in his own native language?" (2:8).

The resistance of both Jews and Greeks here in Acts to such asseverations of the unity and equality of all humanity before God has been matched throughout human history—and throughout Christian history as well. But so has the confession of a God who is not προσωπολήμπτης, whose Holy Spirit establishes national churches and creates vernacular liturgies, all of which nevertheless affirm in their diversity "one, holy, catholic, and apostolic church."[12]

De servo arbitrio: Sin Defined as Captivity to the Devil

10:38 He went about doing good and healing all that were oppressed by the devil, for God was with him.

Fundamental to the portrayal of the atonement through the cross (→3:18) and resurrection (→2:31) of Christ as the drama of *Christus Victor* (→13:8–11) here in Acts is the diagnosis of the sinful situation of the human race as one

12. Niceno-Constantinopolitan Creed 9 (*CCF* 1:163).

of being captive to the tyranny of Satan and the demonic powers and of being "oppressed" by them.[13] This diagnosis needs to be put alongside the definition of sin as a pride that refuses to give God his proper glory (→12:21–23), because each of these diagnoses, as well as each of these images of the atonement, contains insights that correct and complement the other. As can be seen in the developments leading from Saint Augustine to the Synod of Orange in 529[14] and, a millennium later, in Luther's treatise of 1525 against Erasmus, *The Bondage of the Will* (*De servo arbitrio*),[15] Christian thought has needed to be careful not to cross the line between this diagnosis of the human condition and a Manichean determinism. "Ananias," Saint Peter exclaimed (5:3), "why has Satan filled your heart to lie to the Holy Spirit?" Yet this explanation of the sin of Ananias did not allow Ananias to cop a plea of demonic possession and to avoid accountability by claiming that he could not help doing what he did.[16] Saint Peter could also ask, "Was it not *at your disposal?*" (5:4), thereby evidently attributing free will to him, before Ananias was punished with death. But he did trace the sin to its Satanic origin. Here, a few chapters later, Saint Peter generalized this situation of Ananias as slave of Satan into the universal predicament of humanity, invoking a mouthful-sized Greek compound passive participle to speak of "all that were oppressed by the devil" (πάντας τοὺς καταδυναστευομένους ὑπὸ τοῦ διαβόλου), to all of whom Jesus brought his "healing" and liberating power (10:38). In the third and last of the accounts of the conversion of Saint Paul (→9:1–4), Jesus was described as identifying the purpose of the ministry to which he was summoning Saul: "to open their eyes, that they may turn from darkness to light and *from the power of Satan to God*" (26:18), because the force that Jesus in Saint Luke's Gospel called "the power of darkness" (Luke 22:53) was here identified as "the power of Satan" and God was identified as the "light" (→22:6) that triumphed over this power.

Acts is the only New Testament book in which someone is described as "us[ing] sorcery" (μαγεύων) (8:9 AV) and in which the pagan practice of "sorceries" (μαγείαι) (8:11 AV) is recounted. The "wise men from the East" (Matt. 2:1) of the Epiphany Gospel are indeed named μάγοι in the original Greek (Matt. 2:1, 7, 16), therefore "Magi"; but their μαγεία, presumably astrology, led them to the Christ Child. But here the μαγεία appears to be demonic both in its origin and in its outcome, so that the translation (in both RSV and NRSV) with the cognate English words "magic" and "magician" as these terms are used currently, summoning up as they do someone who performs tricks at a children's birthday party or at most the entertainment genius of a Harry Houdini, is far too benign. The AV's "sorcery," summoning up instead at least "The Sorcerer's

13. For an early interpretation of this passage in this way, see Origen, *Contra Celsum* 8.54 (Chadwick 1953, 492–93).
14. Doctrinal Chapters of the Synod of Orange (*CCF* 1:693–98).
15. *Chr. Trad.* 4:140–46.
16. Theophylact, *Exposition of the Acts of the Apostles* 5.6 (PG 125:585).

Apprentice" in Goethe's poem (and Walt Disney's *Fantasia*) and at most, also from Goethe, the *Walpurgisnacht* or Witches' Sabbath in *Faust*, is much more appropriate. In the epigram coined in the topic sentence of Shirley Jackson Case's *Origins of Christian Supernaturalism*, "The sky hung low in the ancient world" for both good and ill.[17]

The incident of the sorcerer Bar-Jesus/Elymas (13:6–12) represented a dramatic encounter between the power of *Christus Victor* and "the power of Satan" in the form of sorcery and black magic, an encounter in which "Saul, who is also called Paul, filled with the Holy Spirit, looked intently at him and said, 'You son of the devil, you enemy of all righteousness, full of all deceit and villainy, will you not stop making crooked the straight paths of the Lord?'" The encounter with Simon Magus (8:9–24) has been historically influential as the primary cautionary tale of the attempt to purchase the gifts of the Holy Spirit, especially ordination (→6:6) and is, as such, the etymological origin of the word "simony."[18] Simon Peter, addressing Simon Magus, defined his situation in the language of demonic oppression and captivity, with his powerful words: "It is plain to me that you are held in the bitterness of gall and the chains of sin" (8:23 NJB). At Philippi, Saint Luke recounts, apparently from his own recollection as one of these traveling companions (→27:1), that Saint Paul and his companions "were met by a slave girl who had a spirit of divination [πνεῦμα πύθωνος] and brought her owners much gain by soothsaying [μαντευομένη]." In response, "Paul was annoyed, and turned to the spirit and said, 'I charge you *in the name of Jesus Christ* to come out of her.' And it came out that very hour" (16:16–18 TPR). But this power could itself be subject to misuse by demonic powers. In a somewhat amusing episode (→12:13–16), some would-be imitators of Paul's power to command the spirits invented the exorcistic formula "I adjure you by the Jesus whom Paul preaches"; but the evil spirit, which apparently possessed greater cunning and more theological acumen than they gave it credit for, retorted to them, "Jesus I know, and Paul I know; but who are you?" The end result of this botched exorcism was the conversion of the sorcerers and the triumphant vindication of "the name of the Lord Jesus" over the demonic powers (19:13–19).

The centrality of this definition of sin as oppression by the devil is visible also in the final petition of the Lord's Prayer: as it is usually prayed, "Deliver us from evil" (ῥῦσαι ἡμᾶς ἀπὸ τοῦ πονηροῦ) (Matt. 6:13), which is missing from Luke's version (Luke 11:4). A majority of interpreters, both ancient and modern, take that final genitive to be masculine rather than neuter (though grammatically it could be either one), so that the NRSV fittingly replaces the neuter "deliver us from evil" of both the AV and the RSV with "rescue us from the evil one."

---

17. Case 1946, 1.
18. É. Amann in *DTC* 14:2130–40; A. Bride in *DTC* 14:2141–60.

10:39–41 TPR And we are his witnesses of what he did both in the country of the Jews and in Jerusalem. They put him to death by hanging him on a tree; but God raised him on the third day and made him manifest; not to all the people but to us who were chosen by God as witnesses, who ate and drank and associated with him after he rose from the dead.

The sharp distinction between "all the people" and "us who were chosen by God as witnesses" qualifies the potential implications of the claim, put forth several times in Acts, that the events of salvation had been "public" (→26:26).

10:44 The use of the verb "fell" (ἐπέπεσεν) in 10:44 and other passages of Acts serves to emphasize the sovereign freedom of the Holy Spirit to "blow where it wills" (John 3:8) beyond human control or manipulation (→2:1; 22:16).

ACTS 11

11:1–16 Peter's rehearsal of the vision that was described in the narrative of his meeting with Cornelius in the preceding chapter forms the basis for an evidentiary, almost empirical argument (→26:26). If God the Creator had seen fit to create and cleanse these creatures, they were not to be despised; similarly, if the Holy Spirit had seen fit to come (or "fall"; →2:1) upon these Gentiles with the gifts of grace when they believed—as had obviously happened—they were not to be despised either.

11:17 TPR If then God gave the same gift to them as he gave to us when we believed in the Lord Jesus Christ, who was I that I could prohibit God from giving them the Holy Spirit?

Instead of the words "that I could withstand God," the TPR has the more specific "that I could prohibit God from giving them the Holy Spirit," which was the very point of Peter's argument.

Grace Abounding

11:23 When he came and saw the grace of God, he was glad [ἰδὼν τὴν χάριν τοῦ θεοῦ, ἐχάρη].

Grace Abounding to the Chief of Sinners, or the Brief Relation of the Exceeding Mercy of God in Christ to His Poor Servant John Bunyan was published in 1666 by John Bunyan, who is better known for his *Pilgrim's Progress* of 1678/1684. But each of these two book titles could apply to both works, for what Pilgrim encountered in the course of his wanderings were not only all those strange creatures and amazing obstacles that he had to surmount, but the "grace abounding" by which he managed to surmount them. For similar reasons,

137

"grace abounding" would also form an apt subtitle for much of the history of the work of the Holy Spirit being recounted in the Acts of the Apostles.

The doctrine of grace has dominated much of the history of theological controversy, especially in the Latin West. It was central to the thought of Saint Augustine in his controversy with Pelagianism, as becomes evident from the titles of four treatises written in that controversy during the last fifteen years of his life: *On Nature and Grace*; *On the Grace of Christ, and on Original Sin*; *On Grace and Free Will*; and *On Rebuke and Grace*.[1] Building on this Augustinian doctrine and probing these same four relations of the doctrine of divine grace—to natural human capacity, to the doctrine of Christ, to human accountability and the freedom of the will, and to the language of rebuke and admonition that seemed to presuppose an ability to obey—medieval Scholasticism, above all in Thomas Aquinas, developed the doctrine of grace into an elaborate schema of distinctions and definitions, such as "prevenient" grace, "habitual" grace, and "actual" grace.[2] The Scholastic doctrine of grace, especially in the form that it had taken after Thomas, became in turn the object of Reformation polemics, as well as of continuing investigation within post-Reformation Roman Catholic theology.[3] Although much of this development was focused on the doctrine of grace in the Epistles of Saint Paul, above all Romans and Galatians, the data of the functioning of grace in the lives of persons that were uniquely provided by the biographical accounts in the book of Acts—and in a special way, by the conversion of Paul (→9:1–4)—were an essential component of the theological investigation.

In speaking about grace, Acts seems to use "the grace of God" (ἡ χάρις τοῦ θεοῦ) (11:23; 14:26) and "the grace of the Lord" (ἡ χάρις τοῦ κυρίου) (15:40), that is, the grace of Christ, interchangeably. Just as, in the language of Peter's accusation against Ananias and Sapphira, the interchangeability of lying "to the Holy Spirit" (5:3) and lying "to God" (5:4) supplied Saint Basil the Great with support from a seemingly unlikely source for the orthodox doctrine of the deity of the Holy Spirit (→5:3–4), so Luke's indiscriminate attribution of grace to "God" or to "the Lord" would seem to be of a piece with Stephen's being able to pray at his death, "Lord Jesus, receive my spirit" (7:59), even though the Lord Jesus himself, according to Luke's earlier report, had prayed at his own death, "Father, into thy hands I commit my spirit!" (Luke 23:46). Either these substitutions of "the Lord Jesus" for "God" were idolatry or they stood as a witness to the identity in being —ὁμοουσία, it came to be called at the Council of Nicea and the First Council of Constantinople, a new and controversial expression of a primitive and continuing affirmation[4]—between

1. *NPNF*[1] 5:121–51, 217–55, 443–65, 471–91.
2. J. van der Meersch in *DTC* 6:1554–1687.
3. *Chr. Trad.* 4:145–53, 375–85.
4. Nicene Creed 2 (*CCF* 1:158); Niceno-Constantinopolitan Creed 2 (*CCF* 1:162).

Christ and God (→7:59–60), even absent a full-blown creed confessing the dogma of the Trinity (→8:37).

The grace "of God" or "of the Lord," moreover, was described as not remaining statically within its divine source, but it could be said to be or to come or to rest dynamically "upon" (ἐπί) a body of believers as they "gave their testimony to the resurrection of the Lord Jesus" (4:33). Grace was, therefore, an active force in human history. As the traditional epistle pericope of the Western church for Christmas said, "the grace of God has appeared [ἐπεφάνη] for the salvation of all men" (Titus 2:11) in the historical incarnation and nativity of Jesus Christ. If the grace of God could be said to "appear," the corollary must be that in some sense it could also be "seen" (→16:9; →26:26). Acts reports here that the church in Jerusalem sent Barnabas to Antioch; and "when he came and *saw* the grace of God, he was glad [ἰδὼν τὴν χάριν τοῦ θεοῦ, ἐχάρη]" (11:23); this play on words in Greek between χάριν and ἐχάρη, technically known as paronomasia, is difficult to reproduce in English, unless perhaps in a combination of English and Latin one were to translate "When he saw the *gratia* of God, he was gratified." Earlier in the present chapter (11:17), the evidence that the grace of God had come to Gentile Christians no less than it had to Jewish Christians was seen as a powerful argument, indeed a clinching one, for the equality of all in the church.

The description of the visit of Barnabas to Antioch goes on: "And he exhorted them all to remain faithful to the Lord with steadfast purpose; for he was a good man, full of the Holy Spirit and of faith" (11:23–24). Therefore a further characteristic of grace as this was described in Acts was continuity (→2:42), as a later chapter indicates when it says that Paul and Barnabas "urged them to continue in the grace of God [προσμένειν τῇ χάριτι τοῦ θεοῦ]" (13:43). Despite some instances of its dramatic intrusion into history (→9:1–4), therefore, the grace that was transforming human lives and "turn[ing] the world upside down" (17:6) was a force for continuity in the life of the church and of the individual.

As such, "grace" was also that to which believers "commended" other believers when they had to part company (15:40), for a shorter time or until eternity (20:32). Even more specifically, the apostles at Antioch were "commended to the grace of God [παραδεδομένοι τῇ χάριτι τοῦ θεοῦ] for the work" (14:26). Either way, the grace of God is portrayed here as the dynamic of the Holy Spirit (→2:1) for "the work" (τὸ ἔργον) of the apostles and thus as the animating force in the life and history of the church.

The Given Name of Christ's Disciples

11:26 And in Antioch the disciples were for the first time called Christians [χρηματίσαι τε πρώτως ἐν Ἀντιοχείᾳ τοὺς μαθητὰς Χριστιανούς].

The dismissal of the apostolic movement and message by the Roman pro-consul Gallio, and by the many who have followed his example, into modern times, as little more than "bickering about words and names" (ζητήματα . . . περὶ λόγου καὶ ὀνομάτων) (18:15 NEB) trivialized the importance, which was symbolic but vastly more than symbolic, not only of "words" but also of "names" and of Christian identification in the narrative. It was "the *name* [τὸ ὄνομα] of God" that was not to be "taken in vain" (Exod. 20:7 LXX). The name for the disciples was "those who called on this name" (9:21), which was "the name of Jesus Christ of Nazareth, whom you crucified, whom God raised from the dead" (4:10). To this day, alongside the title "confession" in several languages,[5] the technical term for the divisions within Christendom, particularly in Anglo-American usage, is "denomination" (given name), which, according to the *Oxford English Dictionary*, is "now almost always" used with this meaning.[6] The title "Christian," which appears here, "does not intend to say that the disciples gave it to themselves, . . . but the appellation came from the pagans."[7] It is used again in Acts only at 26:28—and in only one other New Testament passage (1 Pet. 4:16). The significance of it as "the given name of the disciples" may be gauged by an examination of the two other terms that are used as "given names" for the disciples and the church in Acts: "sect" (αἵρεσις) by its opponents, and "the Way" (ἡ ὁδός) by its proponents. The two terms are combined in the words of Paul's apologia: "But this I confess [ὁμολογῶ] unto thee, that after the way which they call heresy [κατὰ τὴν ὁδὸν ἣν λέγουσιν αἵρεσιν], so worship I the God of my fathers, believing all things which are written in the law and in the prophets" (24:14 AV).

While the Greek word αἵρεσις is, as this translation in the AV also shows, the etymological origin of the English word "heresy," which in patristic usage gradually came to be distinguished from "sect" by being defined as "false doc-trine" rather than "schism,"[8] in New Testament usage it referred not, strictly speaking, to doctrinal error (→18:24–26a), but to "sect" or "party."[9] Here in Acts it is used for the Jewish parties of the Sadducees (5:17) and of the Pharisees (15:5), perhaps even for "the strictest party" among the latter (26:5); the party of the Essenes is not identified as such in the New Testament,[10] although the question of the relation of John the Baptist (→19:2–3) to the Essene sect has become a matter of great interest to recent New Testament scholars. When Paul was attacked as "a pestilent fellow, an agitator among all the Jews throughout the world, and a ringleader of the sect of the Nazarenes [πρωτοστάτην . . . τῆς τῶν Ναζωραίων αἱρέσεως]" (24:5), that could be a nomenclature that places this

5. Pelikan 2003, 62–63.
6. *OED* 4:459.
7. Loisy 1920, 469–70.
8. *PGL* 51.
9. BDAG 27–28.
10. John J. Collins in *ABD* 2:619–26.

sect of "Nazarenes" alongside Sadducees and Pharisees (and Essenes) in the taxonomy of contemporary Jewish movements. But when, in the final chapter of Acts, its Jewish enemies in Rome dismissed it with the comment, "with regard to this sect [περὶ . . . τῆς αἱρέσεως ταύτης] we know that everywhere it is spoken against" (28:22), the term, as the New Testament lexicon says, was being "used in malam partem,"[11] as was, apparently, the title "Christian" in the present passage.[12]

But by far the most intriguing term used in the New Testament, and specifically in the book of Acts, as a given name for the disciples of Jesus is "the Way" (ἡ ὁδός).[13] In addition to 24:14, just quoted, it appears in the following passages: before his conversion Saul asked the Jewish high priest for letters (→23:25), "so that if he found any belonging to the Way, men or women, he might bring them bound to Jerusalem" (9:2); after his conversion Paul had to deal with those who "were stubborn and disbelieved, speaking evil of the Way before the congregation" (19:9); at Ephesus "there arose no little stir concerning the Way," leading to the riot of the artisans (19:23); speaking "in the Hebrew language," that is, in Aramaic, Paul confessed to his Jewish audience that before his conversion he had "persecuted this Way to the death" (22:4); and Felix the governor is said to have had "a rather accurate knowledge of the Way" (24:22). At none of these passages is there any attempt to define "the Way" or to specify its content; it is simply taken for granted, on the assumption that the Greek reader Theophilus (1:2–3) could understand its meaning. The closest to a definition in early Christian literature does not appear in the New Testament at all, but in the contrast at the opening of the *Didache*, which does sound like an already existing topos: "Two ways there are, one of Life and one of Death, and there is a great difference between the Two Ways."[14]

Also because of the roots of this contrast in biblical usage—with phrases such as "the way of sinners" (ἡ ὁδὸς ἁμαρτωλῶν) (Ps. 1:1 LXX), "the way of truth" (ὁδὸς ἀληθείας) (Wis. 5:6 LXX), "the way of the Lord" (ἡ ὁδὸς κυρίου) (Wis. 5:7 LXX), or "I am the way" (ἐγώ εἰμι ἡ ὁδός) (John 14:6)—"the Way" continued to be used for the faith and for those who adhered to it.[15] It is noteworthy that the RSV and NRSV, despite their general reluctance to use capital letters as a confessional symbol, did capitalize "the Way." But the Latin nickname *Christianus*, which was first applied to the "sect" and the "Way" in Antioch by its adversaries, is the one that has stuck to it as a given name, becoming in every language (→21:37) the preeminent mark of identification for the disciples and the church in every age.

11. BADG 24.
12. See Conzelmann 1987, 88–89.
13. BDAG 691–92.
14. *Didache* 1 (ACW 6:15).
15. *PGL* 936.

Mutual Support among the Members of Christ's Family

11:29 And the disciples determined, every one according to his ability, to send relief to the brethren who lived in Judea.

Among all the different forms that the imitation of Christ (→7:59–60) took in the first generation after Pentecost, the action of "send[ing] relief to the brethren" is the one that was connected the most explicitly to his example and his commandment "that by so toiling one must help the weak, remembering the words of the Lord Jesus, how he said, 'The one who gives is blessed rather than the one who receives'" (20:35 TPR). Although those "words of the Lord Jesus" as such do not appear in any of our Gospels, the imperative that they express does, and repeatedly, perhaps nowhere more forcefully than in the solemn command-*cum*-promise: "Truly I tell you, just as you did it to one of the least of these who are members of my family, you did it to me" (Matt. 25:40 NRSV). The mutual support described here was part of a pattern throughout the Acts of the Apostles, both in the early chapters about the primitive Christian community in Jerusalem and in the later chapters about the ministry of Saint Paul.

The most complete exposition in the New Testament of the Christian rationale for such mutual support comes from Saint Paul's commendation of the churches in Macedonia to the church in Corinth:

> We want you to know, brethren, about the grace of God which has been shown in the churches of Macedonia, for in a severe test of affliction, their abundance of joy and their extreme poverty have overflowed in a wealth of liberality on their part. For they gave according to their means, as I can testify, and beyond their means, of their own free will, begging us earnestly for the favor of taking part in the relief of the saints—and this, not as we expected, but first they gave themselves to the Lord and to us by the will of God. . . .
>
> For you know the grace of our Lord Jesus Christ, that though he was rich, yet for your sake he became poor, so that by his poverty you might become rich. (2 Cor. 8:1–5, 9)

This passage contains all the chapter headings of the theological case for mutual support among the members of Christ's family, also as it is being described in the book of Acts:

1. Fundamental to this case was "the grace of our Lord Jesus Christ" (→11:23), the poverty not simply of the one who said, "Foxes have holes, and birds of the air have nests; but the Son of man has nowhere to lay his head" (Luke 9:58), but of the one who, "though he was rich, yet for your sake he became poor, so that by his poverty you might become rich." The poverty of Christ was predicated on his riches as the one who was able to claim, "All that the

Father has is mine" (John 16:15). Christian charity and "relief of the saints" was defined by this Christocentric inspiration and motivation of those who "first . . . gave themselves to the Lord," which set it apart from other private charity, as well as from the relief systems of the welfare state, whether in late antiquity or in modern times, which have used the power to tax as the means of providing assistance. Throughout Christian history, conversely, there has also been ample and frequent evidence of the possibility of someone who "has the world's goods and sees his brother in need, yet closes his heart against him," loving not "in deed and in truth" but only in "word or speech" (1 John 3:17–18).

2. Paul's words to the Corinthians provide another key to the accounts in Acts of the mutual support of the members of Christ's family, with their stipulation that in giving "according to their means . . . and beyond their means" the Macedonians acted "of their own free will [αὐθαίρετοι]." On the narrow basis solely of the descriptions earlier in Acts, "all who believed . . . had all things in common; and they sold their possessions and goods and distributed them to all" (2:44–45), and again, "there was not a needy person among them, for as many as were possessors of lands or houses sold them, and brought the proceeds of what was sold and laid it at the apostles' feet; and distribution was made to each as any had need" (4:34–35), it would be difficult to tell whether these were instances of contribution or of confiscation. But a careful review of the longest sustained account of the process, the tragic story of Ananias and Sapphira (5:1–11), makes it clear that the property and its proceeds remained "at your disposal" (ἐν τῇ σῇ ἐξουσίᾳ) (5:4), so that here, too, the support was an act of their own free will. The report in the immediately following chapter, that "the Hellenists murmured against the Hebrews because their widows were neglected in the daily distribution" (6:1), provides at least a glimpse into the practical difficulties attendant on such mutual support.

3. Significantly, the author of Acts prefaces that glimpse with the explanation that "in these days . . . the disciples were increasing in number" (6:1). This can be seen as an anticipation of the vast complications that were to follow in the subsequent centuries, when the sheer size and the geographical spread of the Christian movement made such a direct and simple response to famine as is described here difficult to administer, and then when the Christianization of the Roman Empire brought about the reallocation of responsibility for "mutual support among the members of Christ's family" between the state and the church and the monastic communities.[16]

---

16. Constantelos 1991, 1–32.

ACTS 12

12:1-3 TPR About that time King Herod laid violent hands upon some who belonged to the church in Judea. He killed John the brother of James with the sword; and when he saw that his attack upon the faithful pleased the Jews, he proceeded to arrest Peter also.

As if to make the point that the persecution had not ended with the conversion of Paul (→9:1–4), this martyrology in miniature adds more names to the roster—with many more to come in this and later centuries (→28:31).

"Both Seen and Unseen": The Angels as "Ministering Spirits"

12:7 TPR And behold, an angel of the Lord appeared to Peter, and a light shone in the cell; and he struck Peter on the side and woke him, saying "Get up quickly." And the chains fell off his hands.

Throughout the book of Acts the dramatis personae include not only God as Father (1:4), Son (→1:2–3), or Holy Spirit (→2:1), and human actors, including women and men (→18:24–26b), royalty and commoners, saints and villains, Jews and Gentiles, but in a special way the angels as "ministering spirits" (λειτουργικὰ πνεύματα) (Heb. 1:14). Indeed, together with the Epistle to the Hebrews, which is the source of that title for the angels but which is primarily concerned with them in order to distinguish Christ from them and to refute any "angel Christology," and the Revelation of Saint John the Divine, where their presence is visible and audible throughout, the book of Acts and the Gospel of Luke, taken together, assign to the angels a more prominent place than does any other part of the New Testament. Even a modern reader who may otherwise know very little else about the New Testament will usually recognize a reference to the angels in the Christmas story as it appears in the Gospel of Luke (Luke 2:8–14).

When the author explains parenthetically to Theophilus (1:1) and other Gentile readers who might not be acquainted with the sectarian and theological controversies within first-century Judaism, that "the Sadducees say that there is no resurrection, nor angel, nor spirit; but the Pharisees confess the existence of resurrection and angel and spirit" (23:8 TPR), he identifies a rhetorical (→24:1–2) opening wedge by which Paul, taking advantage of his own background as "a Pharisee, a son of Pharisees" (23:6), was able to divide and conquer by provoking "a dissension" (23:7) and could claim, "With respect to the hope and the resurrection of the dead I am on trial" (23:6), which he later described as "the hope of Israel" (28:20). At least in these three interrelated doctrines of angels, spirits, and resurrection, then, the church explicitly affirmed its continuity with the Pharisees. In spite of his pronouncing "woe to you!" upon them (Luke 11:42–44), the Jesus of Luke's Gospel, too, defended the Pharisees' doctrine (though without, to be sure, identifying it as such) against "some Sadducees, those who say there is no resurrection" (Luke 20:27)—as well as that there are no angels and no spirits.

In keeping with the form of the many other private revelations and visions in the account of the book of Acts (→16:9), the involvement of the angels, as described in some detail here in chapter 12, was not uniformly obvious or publicly verifiable (→26:26). While two chapters earlier the book seems to be making a special point of explaining that Cornelius, "centurion of what was known as the Italian Cohort" of the Roman army (10:1), "saw *clearly* [φανερῶς] in a vision an angel of God," at whom he "stared . . . in terror [ἔμφοβος], and said, 'Who are you, Lord?'" (10:3–4 TPR), in this present chapter Saint Peter, the prince of the apostles (→5:29a), nevertheless "did not know that what was done by the angel was real, for he thought he was seeing a vision" (12:9 TPR).

In asking "who are you?" Cornelius did address the angel as "Lord" (κύριε) (10:4 TPR); but the heretical phenomenon alluded to by Irenaeus,[1] and referred to and condemned elsewhere in the New Testament as an idolatrous "worship of angels" (Col. 2:18), does not seem to be involved, although it may be meant by the earlier reference in Stephen's sermon to the idolatrous "worship [of] the host of heaven" (7:42). The punishment of idolatry appears to be a particular mission of angels, for when, later in this chapter, King Herod allowed himself to be acclaimed with the shout of the people, "the sounds of a god, and not of man!" punishment was terrible and swift (→12:21–23; →19:28): "Immediately an angel of the Lord smote him, because he did not give God the glory; and coming down from the throne, he was eaten alive by worms and died" (12:22–23 TPR). This was a continuation of the angelic mission described in the Old Testament, where "the Lord smote the camp of the Assyrians, / and his angel wiped them out" (Sir. 48:21 LXX) because "the angel of the Lord

---

1. Irenaeus, *Against Heresies* 2.2 (*ANF* 1:361–62).

went forth, and slew a hundred and eighty-five thousand in the camp of the Assyrians; and when men arose early in the morning, behold, these were all dead bodies" (2 Kgs. 19:35 LXX/RSV).

But the principal mission and ministry of the angels here in Acts, as in the Gospel of Luke and the rest of the New Testament, was to act as bearers of divine revelations and of divine commands. Even the opponents of the Christian "Way" (→11:26) seemed to be ready to acknowledge them as such and to recognize the validity of their revelations (23:9). In the very first chapter, the significance of the ascension and the expectation of the second coming were explained to the apostles by "two men . . . in white robes" (1:10), whose ministry, like that of Luke's "two men . . . in dazzling apparel" at the resurrection (Luke 24:4), was to provide the disciples with the clue to what they could see but did not understand. When the apostles had been imprisoned, "at night an angel of the Lord opened the prison doors and brought them out and said, 'Go and stand in the temple and speak to the people all the words of this Life'" (5:19–20). As Peter himself recounted later (11:13), Cornelius was directed by the angel, whom he also called "a man . . . in bright apparel" (10:30), to establish contact with Peter (10:2–7). So thoroughly did this ministry of revelation and command define the mission of the angels that Stephen feels entitled to add it, as a kind of Christian targum, to the biography of Moses in the book of Exodus. Perhaps by extrapolation from the statement of the Old Testament text that he quotes (Exod. 3:2 LXX), "When forty years had passed, *an angel appeared to him* in the wilderness of Mount Sinai, in a flame of fire in a bush" (7:30), he identified the Ten Commandments that Moses received from God later on Mount Sinai as "the law *as delivered by angels*" (7:53). Christian exegetes have interpreted this "angel of the Lord" as the preexistent and preincarnate Son of God,[2] and therefore the burning bush that "was not consumed" (οὐ κατεκαίετο) (Exod. 3:2 LXX) as the typological representation of Mary the Theotokos and Ever-Virgin Mother of God (→1:14).[3] According to the TPR, the conclusion of the encounter between the Apostle Philip and the Ethiopian eunuch came when, after the eunuch's baptism and confession, "I believe that Jesus Christ is the Son of God" (8:37 TPR AV), "the Holy Spirit fell upon the eunuch, and an angel of the Lord took Philip away from him" (8:39 TPR), whereas according to other manuscripts it was "the Spirit of the Lord [who] caught up Philip" (8:39 RSV).

Two references to angels in the book of Acts have a special interest when seen by hindsight in the light of the subsequent development of doctrine. Not perhaps at the first reading of the words they "saw that [Stephen's] face was like the face of an angel" (6:15), but at some subsequent reading, the question does have to be asked: How could the members of the Jewish council (or Luke) have any conception of what "the face of an angel," illumined by the

---

2. Justin Martyr, *Dialogue with Trypho* 59 (*ANF* 1:226–27).
3. Daniélou 1960, 224.

uncreated light of God (→22:6), might have looked like in the first place? In the iconoclastic controversies of the eighth, ninth, and tenth centuries (→19:26), one of the crucial arguments cited by defenders of Christian images such as Saint John of Damascus[4] and Saint Theodore of Studios[5] was that in the same book of Exodus that contained the constantly cited prohibition of "graven images" (Exod. 20:4), Moses, at God's explicit command, had artisans make two cherubim out of gold: "The cherubim shall spread out their wings above, overshadowing the mercy seat with their wings; and their faces shall be toward each other [καὶ τὰ πρόσωπα αὐτῶν εἰς ἄλληλα]" (Exod. 25:20 LXX). Therefore the description in the Epistle to the Hebrews of "the cherubim of glory over-shadowing the mercy seat" (Heb. 9:5) would seem to have been based on this visual representation,[6] from which others, too, could have known what "the face of an angel" (πρόσωπον ἀγγέλου) (6:15) looked like.

In the final words of the present passage, after telling Rhoda "you are mad" because she claimed to have seen Peter, her fellow believers suggested that instead "it is his angel." The conventional linkage between "angel" and "spirit" (πνεῦμα) (23:8) could be cited in support of interpreting these words to mean no more than "it is his ghost." But for that meaning the perfectly good word πνεῦμα was available. Therefore various interpreters have seen in the phrase "*his* angel" a reference to the doctrine of individual guardian angels assigned to believers, as they have in the words of Jesus about children: "See that you do not despise one of these little ones; for I tell you that in heaven *their* angels always behold the face of my Father who is in heaven" (Matt. 18:10).[7]

Even from all these and other biblical references to angels taken together, it is a considerable distance to the speculative constructs of Pseudo-Dionysius the Areopagite (17:34) and of later Scholastics in both East and West about the ranks of the celestial hierarchy.[8] But it is a much longer way to the dismissal of angels altogether in so much of modern theology.

12:11 This description of Peter's having "c[o]me to himself," which seems to find a Lukan parallel in the description of how the prodigal son "came to himself" (Luke 15:17), adds a small clinical detail to the description of the divinely induced "trance" (ἔκστασις) (→16:9) as a phenomenon by which, in Chrysostom's words, "the soul, so to say, was caused to be out of the body (ἐξέστη)."[9]

4. John of Damascus, *Three Treatises on the Divine Images* 3.9, 24 (SVS 89–91).
5. Theodore of Studios, *On the Holy Icons* 1.5 (SVS 24–25).
6. Nicephorus, *Refutation* 2.8 (PG 100:348).
7. On the relation between Matt. 18:10 and Acts 12:13–15 and the idea of individual guardian angels, see Origen, *Commentary on Matthew* 27–28 (*ANF* 10:491).
8. *Chr. Trad.* 1:344–49; 2:141–42; 3:293–303.
9. Chrysostom, *Homilies on Acts* 22 (*NPNF*¹ 11:143).

A Humor That Is Not "Unseemly"

12:13–16 And when he knocked at the door of the gateway, a maid named Rhoda came to answer. Recognizing Peter's voice, in her joy she did not open the gate but ran in and told that Peter was standing at the gate. They said to her, "You are mad." But she insisted that it was so. They said, "It is his angel!" But Peter continued knocking; and when they opened, they saw him and were amazed.

When the New Testament warns not only against "filthiness" but against "foolish talking [and] jesting which are not seemly [ἃ οὐκ ἀνῆκεν]" (Eph. 5:4, my translation), a great deal depends on whether there should be a comma between the word "jesting" and the word "which," or, to put it grammatically, whether the relative clause is restrictive or nonrestrictive: does this passage condemn not only all μωρολογία but all εὐτραπελία as unseemly, or only the kind of εὐτραπελία that actually is unseemly in itself? Or, to speak of substance rather than of grammar, can there be a humor that is not unseemly by Christian standards? Outside the New Testament, εὐτραπελία was used in Greek "mostly in a good sense," to mean "wittiness" or "facetiousness."[10] Therefore Aristotle, praising as he usually did the golden mean between two extremes, identified wittiness as a "pleasantness in social amusement," while "the excess is Buffoonery and its possessor a buffoon; the deficient man may be called boorish, and his disposition Boorishness."[11] Elsewhere he spoke of "those . . . who are clever at making or taking a joke, for each has the same end in view as his neighbour, being able to take a joke and return it in good taste."[12] "Jesus wept" (John 11:35) has long enjoyed a mild celebrity of sorts as the shortest verse in the Bible, according to aficionados of the biblical version of Trivial Pursuit, who sometimes add, with knowing solemnity, that nowhere is there a corresponding verse reading "Jesus laughed" or even "Jesus smiled." Nevertheless, Clement of Alexandria, while warning against "excessive laughter," acknowledged that there was a place for "joking" in Christian behavior.[13] And as Philip Carrington acknowledges about Saint Luke in Acts: "There is an element in his writing which may *almost* be described as sentiment and humor."[14]

Thus it would seem difficult not to smile when reading this little anecdote about Rhoda, who in her excitement at hearing Peter's voice after his release from prison became so flustered that she forgot to let him in and left him to keep pounding on the door. Something very much like Aristotle's "pleasantness in the giving of amusement" also seems to be at work in Peter's response to the charge that the Pentecost event was the result of intoxication: "For these men

---

10. BDAG 414.
11. Aristotle, *Nicomachean Ethics* 2.7.11–13 1108a (LCL 73:103–5).
12. Aristotle, *Rhetoric* 2.4.13 1381a (LCL 193:197).
13. Clement of Alexandria, *Instructor* 2.8 (*ANF* 2:252).
14. Carrington 1957, 1:281 (emphasis added).

are not drunk, as you suppose, *since it is only the third hour of the day*," nine o'clock in the morning (2:15).

Similar humor seems to be at work in two other incidents. Long before there was Christian preaching, there had been warnings in classical rhetoric (→24:1–2) against long-windedness and in favor of achieving "brevity" by "expressing each separate idea [only] once, in simple terms, and by paying no attention to anything but clearness of expression";[15] and long after there was Christian preaching, the Mikado in the Gilbert and Sullivan opera propounded his doctrine of justice and condign punishment:

All prosy dull society sinners,
Who chatter and bleat and bore,
Are sent to hear sermons
From mystical Germans
Who preach from ten till four.[16]

In spite of his obvious admiration for Paul, Luke knew from his own experience how stubborn he could be (→21:13–14), and probably also how loquacious he was once he got started. In the light of the happy outcome, therefore, another smile would not seem to be unwarranted at the end of this story: "Paul . . . prolonged his speech *until midnight*. . . . And a young man named Eutychus was sitting in the window. He sank into a deep sleep as Paul talked *still longer*; and being overcome by sleep, he fell down from the third story and was taken up dead"; but it all turned out well (20:7–12). Even the demons seem to have been capable of Aristotle's "ready wit," as when an evil spirit, upon being accosted by some itinerant amateur exorcists with the formula "I adjure you by the Jesus whom Paul preaches," replied: "Jesus I know, and Paul I know; but who are you?" and then chased them all away (19:13–17).

Another incident in the same chapter of Acts, which was, Luke says in a litotes, "no little stir" (τάραχος οὐκ ὀλίγος) (19:23), does seem to warrant a reaction rather more vigorous than a mere smile, especially if the reader were to visualize it as a scene in a film or on television. There is almost a touch of slapstick in the description of the riot in Ephesus, as the rabble-rousing Demetrius harangued the artisans: "Now some cried one thing, some another; for the assembly was in confusion, *and most of them did not know why they had come together*" (19:32). What they did know for certain was that both their livelihood and their traditional faith were in danger from interlopers like Paul, Gaius, and Aristarcus. "But when they recognized that he was a Jew, *for about two hours* they all with one voice cried out, 'Great is Artemis of the Ephesians!'" (19:34). A later riot against Paul has some of the same quality to it: in response to the tribune's question about "who he was and what he had done,"

15. Cicero, *De partitione oratorica* 6.19 (LCL 349:327).
16. W. S. Gilbert and Arthur Sullivan, *The Mikado*, Act II.

the reaction of the mob was that "some in the crowd shouted one thing, some another; and he could not learn the facts because of the uproar" (21:33–34). An earlier scene would also benefit from being realized on stage or on film, the slightly comic spectacle of the priest of Zeus at Lystra, with his garlands and his "lowing herd, wind[ing] slowly o'er the lea,"[17] on their way to be sacrificed to Barnabas and Paul, the ultramonotheistic apostles of Jesus Christ who by an egregious case of mistaken identity had been taken to be, of all things, the Greek gods Zeus and Hermes made visible on earth (14:11–18).

All of this, even taken together, is of course still a far cry from making Acts into some sort of opera buffa, not to mention the kind of crudity and μωρολογία to which theatergoers of the time would have been accustomed and which one did not have to be a puritan like Tertullian to find objectionable and "unseemly."[18]

Sin Defined as "Refusing to Let God Be God"

12:21–23 TPR Herod put on his royal robes, took his seat upon the throne, and made an oration to them. And he so ingratiated himself with them that the people shouted, "The sounds of a god, and not of a man!" Immediately an angel of the Lord smote him, because he did not give God the glory; and coming down from the throne, he was eaten alive by worms and died.

In the terse but precise formula "he did not give God the glory" or NEB's "he had usurped the honour due to God" (οὐκ ἔδωκεν τὴν δόξαν τῷ θεῷ) Acts here defines the essence of sin as "the deflection of divine praise"[19] or, in Luther's striking phrase, "refusing to let God be God";[20] and in the grisly words that follow, "coming down from the throne, he was eaten alive by worms and died" (καταβὰς ἀπὸ τοῦ βήματος γενόμενος σκωληκόβρωτος ἔτι ζῶν ἐξέψυξεν), it describes the consequences of sin. The polysyllabic adjective σκωληκόβρωτος ("eaten by worms") appears nowhere else in the New Testament; but a very close parallel to such a divine punishment for precisely such an expression of "superhuman arrogance" (τὴν ὑπὲρ ἄνθρωπον ἀλαζονείαν) is described elsewhere in the Bible, as Antiochus Epiphanes "was brought down to earth . . . , making the power of God manifest to all" when "the ungodly man's body swarmed with worms" (2 Macc. 9:8–9 LXX/NRSV). In each case, as John Dryden (who translated Plutarch's *Lives*, including the life of Alexander the Great) said of the godlike Alexander:

> With ravished ears,
> The monarch hears;

17. Thomas Gray, "Elegy Written in a Country Churchyard" (1751), line 2.
18. Tertullian, *De spectaculis* (*ANF* 3:79–91).
19. Allen 1997, 110–14.
20. Watson 1949.

Assumes the god,
Affects to nod,
And seems to shake the spheres.[21]

Neither in Maccabees nor in Acts are the consequences of sin always depicted as either so instantaneous or so visibly drastic. Yet this vignette is by no means isolated in Acts; in fact, this seems to be the pattern for the book's description—and therefore definition—of sin, which can with no difficulty be extended to the seven deadly sins of later moral theology.[22] With the Gospels, including his own (Luke 22:47–48), Luke connects this definition of sin with the definition as oppression by the devil (→10:38) by documenting the traitorous sin of Judas Iscariot in the service of "the power of darkness" (Luke 22:53). But while Matthew's Gospel goes on to tell how Judas met his end by taking his own life (Matt. 27:3–10), Luke reserves that for his second volume, setting the pattern of "monstrous sin/odious punishment" that he would follow also here in the history of Herod: "Judas . . . was guide to those who arrested Jesus. . . . Now this man bought a field with the reward of his wickedness; and falling headlong he burst open in the middle and all his bowels gushed out" (1:16, 18), as "the power of darkness" came to claim its own at the end. Again, Ananias and Sapphira "kept back some" of what they represented to have been the entire "proceeds" from their sale of property; and almost immediately each of them "fell down and died"—first he, then she (5:1–11). But the text takes great care to define their sin as not a simple case of cheating on their capital-gains taxes, but of "lying to the Holy Spirit" (5:3), which meant lying to God himself (→5:3–4), and of "tempt[ing] the Spirit of the Lord" (5:9). Judas Iscariot, Ananias and Sapphira, King Herod—to each of these the words used here about Herod could be applied: "He did not give God the glory." In both the Old and the New Testament the essence of sin, therefore, is seen as idolatry, which manifested itself sometimes overtly and sometimes covertly, as "gross idolatry" or as "fine idolatry" (→19:28).[23]

On the basis of the description "and the people saw down to eat and drink, and rose up to play [παίζειν]" (Exod. 32:6 LXX/RSV), penitential preachers have often gone into prurient detail in depicting the bacchanalian sinfulness of the orgiastic revels of the Israelites while Moses was up on Mount Sinai, as a way of warning their hearers against "the lust of the flesh and the lust of the eyes and the pride of life" (1 John 2:16). But according to Acts, the penitential preacher Stephen, in his own retelling of the life of Moses (7:30–35), depicted their sin as one of being "perfectly happy with something they had made for themselves" and of suffering the immediate punishment that "God turned away from them and abandoned them to the worship of the army of heaven"

21. John Dryden, "Alexander's Feast; or, The Power of Music," lines 37–41.
22. Karl Rahner and R. Scholz in *LTK* 9:1178–83.
23. A. Michel in *DTC* 7:602–69.

(7:41–42 NJB); in other words, they "did not give God the glory." When, in response to such penitential preaching, Stephen's hearers were willing to murder him, with "Saul . . . consenting to his death" (8:1), Stephen, "full of the Holy Spirit, gazed into heaven and saw *the glory of God*," which they for their part were either spurning or usurping (7:55). Simon Magus attempted to buy the power of "the Spirit [that] was given through the laying on of the apostles' hands" (→6:6), in the process giving his name to that sin (8:18–19). But thereby he showed himself to be "in the gall of bitterness and in the bond of iniquity" (8:23), because by this attempt he manifested the same hubris that had earlier been responsible for his acquiring the divine epithet "that power of God which is called Great" (ἡ δύναμις τοῦ θεοῦ ἡ καλουμένη μεγάλη) (8:10); in other words, "he did not give God the glory."[24] Paul could denounce Elymas the sorcerer with the harshest possible epithets, "You son of the devil, you enemy of all righteousness, full of all deceit and villainy"—because "he did not give God the glory," but had on the contrary taken "the straight paths of the Lord" and managed to make them "crooked" (13:8–11). Even such social sins as slavery (16:16–19) and avarice earned similar epithets from the apostles not primarily on moral or socioethical grounds as such, but because they gave the glory not to God but to his creatures (→4:32). In the history of Christian doctrine, especially in the Latin West, this definition of sin became, in the hands of Saint Anselm of Canterbury, the foundation for a depiction of the atonement as an act of rendering *satisfactio* to the "honor" or *rectitudo* of God, which human sin had violated (→3:18). Another way of defining sin, as captivity to the oppression of the devil (→10:38) and of death, had, as its counterpart doctrine of redemption, the image of *Christus Victor* (→13:8–11).

---

24. Irenaeus, *Against Heresies* 1.23 (*ANF* 1:347–48).

ACTS 13

13:1–5 TPR Now there were in the church prophets and teachers, among them Barnabas, Simeon who was called Niger, Lucius of Cyrene, Manaen a member of the court of Herod the ruler, and Paul. While they were worshiping the Lord and fasting, the Holy Spirit said, "Set apart for me Barnabas and Paul for the work to which I have called them." Then after fasting and praying they laid their hands on them and sent them off. . . . They proclaimed the word of the Lord in the synagogues of the Jews.

As it also does elsewhere in the book of Acts, the title "prophet" here refers to a continuing office in the Christian church rather than, as it sometimes does in Acts (e.g., 2:16, 30), to a prophet of ancient Israel (→21:9–10). The close association between "worshiping the Lord" and "fasting" seems to have been a special concern of the writer of Acts (→24:25b), as do both the special manifestation of the Holy Spirit to reveal the divine purpose (→16:9) and the laying-on of hands to designate someone for a special task (→6:6), in this case the task of proclaiming "the word" as "the word of God" or "the word of the Lord" or "the word of the gospel" (→8:25). Even now, as they would to the end of the story (28:17–29), Paul and Barnabas did that "proclaiming" first of all "in the synagogues of the Jews" (→3:25; →7:47–48), even in a city such as Athens (17:17), where the most memorable audience for their proclamation consisted of Greeks in the agora, including some Epicurean and Stoic philosophers (→17:18).

Christus Victor

13:8–11 TPR Elymas the sorcerer (for that is the meaning of his name) withstood them, seeking to turn away the proconsul from the faith. But Paul, filled with the Holy Spirit, looked intently at him and said, "You son of the devil, you enemy of all righteousness, full of all deceit and villainy, will you not stop making crooked the straight paths of the Lord? And now, behold, the hand of the Lord is upon you, and you shall be blind and unable to see the sun for a time."

As the diagnosis and definition of sin as the failure to "give God the glory" and the refusal to let God be God (→12:21–23) would become, in Saint Anselm's *Cur deus homo* (*Why God Became Man*), the presupposition for an interpretation of the saving power of the cross as *satisfactio* and as the restoration of the *rectitudo* and honor of God, with the "for us" (*pro nobis*, ὑπὲρ ἡμῶν) of the Niceno-Constantinopolitan Creed[1] being taken in a meaning that came close to being "in our stead" (→3:18), so in the history of the doctrine of reconciliation through Christ a concentration instead on a diagnosis of sin as captivity to the devil and oppression by the devil (→10:38) has had as its soteriological counterpart the image of the atonement as *Christus Victor*.

In a continuation of the ministry of Jesus also before the crucifixion and resurrection (→7:59–60), most dramatically expressed in his victorious refutation, as he began his ministry (Matt. 4:1–11), of the three questions of the tempter during his temptation in the wilderness—"in those three questions," Dostoevsky said, "the whole subsequent history of mankind is, as it were, brought together into one whole, and foretold, and in them are united all the unsolved historical contradictions of human nature"[2]—the ministry of his apostles here in the book of Acts was portrayed as the ongoing conflict of *Christus Victor* with the demonic powers and as his victory over them. Jesus himself was represented in Acts as not only challenging Saul in Aramaic with the question, "Why do you persecute me?" (26:14), but then as giving him a commission specifically "to open their [Jews' and Gentiles'] eyes, that they may turn away from the darkness of Satan to God" (26:18 TPR). But, more precisely, the verb "they may turn away" (ἀποστρέψεσθαι) meant "they may be turned away," because power could be broken only by superior power—or by trickery. The occasional homiletical resort by various early Christian writers to the idea of Christ's having tricked the devil involved hopeless theological and moral contradictions,[3] and so strength conquered by superior strength was seen as the only acceptable image. "The darkness of Satan" and the tyranny of the devil, which in this passage had made Elymas the sorcerer a "son of the devil, . . . enemy of all righteousness, full of all deceit and villainy," could yield only to what Paul here called "the hand of the Lord . . . upon you" (χεὶρ κυρίου ἐπὶ σέ), a phrase redolent of the Septuagint, as in the threat: "If you do not listen to the voice of the Lord and if you resist the mouth of the Lord, the hand of the Lord will be upon you and upon your king [ἔσται χεὶρ κυρίου ἐπὶ ὑμᾶς καὶ ἐπὶ τὸν βασιλέα ὑμῶν]" (1 Sam. 12:15 LXX). What he meant by "the hand of the

---

1. Niceno-Constantinopolitan Creed 4 (*CCF* 1:162–63).
2. F. M. Dostoevsky, *The Brothers Karamazov* (trans. Constance Garnett), book V, chapter 5.
3. Seeberg 1953, 1:526–27.

Lord" was the power of the cross and resurrection of Christ (→3:18; →2:31). By it God broke the tyrannical hold of the demonic powers over humanity, "disarmed the principalities and powers and made a public example of them, triumphing over [θριαμβεύσας] them in him" (Col. 2:15), as a Roman general would achieve a conquest over his enemies and stage a triumph. As Stephen the protomartyr learned, "the fellowship with Jesus Christ in his suffering has as its counterpart the fellowship with the exalted Lord."[4]

Christus Victor went on to become what Gustaf Aulén called "the classic view" of the atoning work of Christ.[5] In Anselm's portrayal, by contrast, the apparent conflict in the mind of God between the requirements of his justice and the imperatives of his mercy could be resolved only if humanity could be represented before God by the suffering and death of one who was truly human (to make the death availing) and truly divine (to make the death availing universally). In effect, then, the formula of Saint Paul, "God was in Christ . . . reconciling the world to himself" (2 Cor. 5:19), was to be paraphrased by inversion to read, "The world was in Christ reconciling God to itself," with God as the object, as well as the author, of the reconciling action. But if "the world" and humanity in the world had to be seen as victim and as captive, "oppressed by the devil" (10:38), then the object of God's reconciling action in Christ had to be, as it was in 2 Cor. 5, the world and the tyrants under whose oppression humanity was suffering. One of these tyrants was sin, which had the power to "reign [βασιλεύειν] in your mortal bodies" and to "have dominion [κυριεύειν] over you" (Rom. 6:12–14), thus claiming for itself the dual titles of βασιλεύς and κύριος, which properly belonged to God alone, even though "there are many 'gods' and many 'lords'" (1 Cor. 8:5). The other tyrant and "the last enemy to be destroyed is death" (1 Cor. 15:26). "Destroying every rule and every authority and power" (1 Cor. 15:24) in a *mirabile duellum*, Christ the Victor saved from the oppression of the devil, of sin, and of death, not only by his crucifixion but by his resurrection, "trampling down death by death."[6] Therefore the resurrection was central to his saving action (→2:31), rather than being merely God's declaration that the sacrifice of the cross had availed and had made an acceptable act of satisfaction. In the language of the liturgy and of preaching, these two ways of speaking about the atonement have often been complementary rather than antithetical, as ways of describing the indescribable and of speaking about the ineffable (→17:23).

13:15 TPR After the reading of the law and the prophets, the rulers of the synagogue sent to them, saying, "Brethren, if you have any word of wisdom for the people, say it."

4. Eckey 2000, 1:181.
5. Aulén 1969.
6. Liturgy of Saint John Chrysostom I.A.5 (*CCF* 1:271).

The invitation from the rulers of the synagogue to present an exegesis of "the law and the prophets" (→8:30–31) was one that Paul accepted with alacrity, and Luke may have been connecting this scene with his earlier account of how Jesus took advantage of a similar opportunity to speak a "word of wisdom" and exhortation to the people of his home synagogue in Nazareth (Luke 4:16–30), though with less success than Paul and Barnabas seem to have met with here at Antioch of Pisidia, where "the people begged that these things might be told them the next sabbath" (13:42).

13:17–41 Luke presents another of the several capsule histories of the people of Israel throughout the book of Acts, the longest and most notable of which was Stephen's (7:2–53); but each was so constructed as to reach its climax—and the climax of the history of Israel—in the coming of Jesus, whom "God . . . brought to Israel [as] a Savior" (13:23) and as the crucified (→3:18) and resurrected (→2:31) Messiah, and thus to stake out a claim to continuity with God's ancient chosen people (→3:25).

13:24–25 TPR Before his coming John had preached a baptism of repentance to all the people of Israel. And as John was finishing his course, he said, "Who do you suppose that I am? I am not he. No, but after me one is coming, the sandals of whose feet I am not worthy to untie."

John the Baptizer and Forerunner (→19:2–3) was, together with Mary the Theotokos (→1:14), the principal sign of the continuity and the transition from the covenant with Israel to the new covenant (→3:25). As the only one of the four Gospels to report that there was speculation "concerning John, whether perhaps he were the Christ" (Luke 3:15), the Gospel of Luke had quoted this saying of John about Jesus (Luke 3:16).

13:27 TPR The scriptures of the prophets are read every sabbath.

Paul presented himself here as standing on common ground with his Jewish listeners, the common ground of the prophets, but as being more faithful than they were to the message of the prophets (→8:30–31). So also in the second century, Justin Martyr, in an autobiographical apologia, would describe himself as having passed beyond Plato and Pythagoras to the prophets of Israel: "Straightway a flame was kindled in my soul; and a love of the prophets, and of those men who are friends of Christ, possessed me; and . . . I found this philosophy alone to be safe and profitable."[7]

7. Justin Martyr, *Dialogue with Trypho* 8 (*ANF* 1:198).

The Language of Justification

13:38–39 AV Be it known unto you therefore, men and brethren, that through this man is preached unto you the forgiveness of sins: And by him all that believe are justified from all things, from which ye could not be justified by the law of Moses.

As if by some law of compensation, theological English, which has a special standing among languages (→21:37) in being blessed with its own words both for "gospel" (→8:25) and for "worship" (→4:24–30), for both of which many other languages are forced to employ loanwords or periphrastic constructions, also suffers under a severe linguistic-theological handicap in articulating the doctrine of justification and dealing with the crucial concept of δικαιοσύνη and the related adjective δίκαιος and verb δικαιοῦν, terms which it shares with both the Jewish and the classical tradition (→25:8). Lack of clarity about this concept of "justice/righteousness" and its complexity can lead to major confusion. That became evident in the history of the doctrine of justification, especially since the sixteenth-century Reformation. It was then that, although it had of course always been part of the language of the New Testament, above all of the Epistle to the Romans (Rom. 3–5), the doctrine became a central part of the theological agenda as it had not been in the preceding centuries, East or West, and was broadly defined as comprehending "to remit sins, to absolve from guilt and punishment, to receive into favor, and to pronounce a man just."[8]

Just as the English verb "to owe" (shared with other Germanic languages) has no corresponding noun while the English noun "debt" (from the Latin *debere*) has no corresponding verb, so from its Latin and Latinate roots English has the noun "justice," the adjective "just," and the verb "to justify" to translate those three Greek words, while from its Germanic roots it has the noun "righteousness" for δικαιοσύνη and the adjective "righteous" for δίκαιος—yet no corresponding Anglo-Saxon verb for δικαιοῦν except the periphrastic "to make righteous," so that "to justify" has had to serve. Gradually if not completely or consistently, "just" and "justice" have come to be used for the attributes of the judge, which is why we speak of "a just judge" and of "the justice system," while "righteous" and "righteousness" are used as attributes of the innocent defendant, or generally of the moral person in the sight of God, not of the judge in an official capacity—except when they are used indiscriminately as synonyms for "self-righteous" and "self-righteousness," as they sometimes tend to be in vernacular parlance (which, for the same mixture of good and bad reasons, often uses "sanctity" to mean "sanctimoniousness"). But early translations of the New Testament into English, up to and including the AV, often reflected the continuing force of the Vulgate (which could simply use *iustus, iustitia, iustificare* throughout) in blurring the distinction, as in, "Judge not according

8. Second Helvetic Confession 15.1 (*CCF* 2:486).

to the appearance, but judge righteous [where we should now probably say 'just'] judgment" (John 7:24 AV), or, conversely, "The just [where we should now probably say 'righteous'] shall live by faith" (Rom. 1:17 AV). Yet that gradual clarification still leaves the anomalous situation that "to justify" and "justification" belong etymologically to the term "justice," but theologically to the term "righteousness."

These problems in the language of justification make themselves evident in the statement here, πᾶς ὁ πιστεύων δικαιοῦται, which, while grammatically in the singular, is rendered "all that believe are justified" by the AV, but not by the RSV or the NRSV; for some reason they use the more general, less precise, and less theologically technical verb "freed" rather than the specific term "justified." The AV translation appears to be formulated in the light of parallel passages in the Pauline Epistles, especially Rom. 4:5–8 RSV:

> And to one who does not work but trusts him who *justifies* the ungodly, his faith is reckoned as righteousness. So also David pronounces a blessing upon the man to whom God reckons righteousness apart from works:

> "Blessed are those whose iniquities are forgiven, and whose sins are covered; blessed is the man against whom the Lord will not reckon his sin [Ps. 32:1–2]."

The specification of "not being able to be justified by the law of Moses" (οὐκ ἠδυνήθητε ἐν νόμῳ Μωϋσέως δικαιωθῆναι) also suggests a parallel to the Pauline doctrine in the argument of Romans.[9] Additional support for reading this passage in Acts as a reference specifically to the doctrine of justification by faith comes from the earlier usage of Saint Luke, who in the parable of the Pharisee and the Publican (which is unique to his Gospel) had Jesus say, not only in the AV but also in the RSV, that the Publican "went down to his house *justified* [κατέβη οὗτος δεδικαιωμένος] rather than the other" (Luke 18:14 RSV). It is not clear why "to justify" is not seen as too "Pauline" a translation for δικαιοῦν in a parable of Jesus in the Gospel of Luke, but seems to be seen that way in Luke's book of Acts, whose principal character is the Apostle Paul.[10]

That quotation from Ps. 32 in Rom. 4 also serves to define "justification" as the forgiveness of sin, a more frequent concept and term than "justification" in Acts, especially in its early "Petrine" chapters: "And Peter said to them, 'Repent, and be baptized every one of you in the name of Jesus Christ for the forgiveness of your sins" (2:38); "repent therefore, and turn again, that your sins may be blotted out" (3:19); "him God exalted by his glory as Leader and Savior, to give repentance to Israel and forgiveness of sins in him" (5:31 TPR). There is a theologically significant use of this theme again in a later chapter, in the third and last of the narratives of Paul's conversion (→9:1–4), where

9. Loisy 1920, 536.
10. Philip Vielhauer in Keck and Martyn 1966, 42–43.

Christ said to the newly converted Saul: "I send you . . . that they may receive forgiveness of sins and a place among those who are sanctified by faith in me [ἐν τοῖς ἡγιασμένοις πίστει τῇ εἰς ἐμέ]" (26:17–18). Although later theological usage, especially in the aftermath of the Reformation, distinguished sharply between the "justification" that precedes and the "sanctification" that follows,[11] the two terms often seem to be practically synonymous in Pauline usage, as in the pleonastic reversal of the conventional sequence: "But you were washed, you were sanctified, you were justified [ἀλλὰ ἀπελούσασθε, ἀλλὰ ἡγιάσθητε, ἀλλὰ ἐδικαιώθητε] in the name of the Lord Jesus Christ and in the Spirit of our God" (1 Cor. 6:11). It would seem that the two were being used as synonyms especially when, as here, the "sanctification" was said to have taken place "by faith," as elsewhere "justification" was described as having happened "by faith" (πίστει) (Rom. 3:28).

13:44 TPR On the following sabbath, almost the entire city gathered to hear Paul deliver many words about the Lord.

This description of "many words about the Lord" (→3:25; →8:25) is in confirmation of the report about the enthusiastic response to the preaching of Paul in Antioch of Pisidia on the previous Sabbath (13:42).

Foreknowledge/Election/Predestination

13:48 TPR And when the Gentiles heard this, they were glad and glorified the word of the Lord; and as many as were ordained to eternal life believed.

In his controversial "Second Epilogue" to *War and Peace,* Tolstoy vigorously argues the opposition between what he called "the law of inevitability" in history and the consciousness of "free will" (illusory, according to him) that has characterized the actors, and particularly the leaders, in human history (in this case, Napoleon). That opposition, in the form of the attempt to harmonize divine election and human volition, and the obligation to deal with it, has not only been a source of consternation to speculative theologians, but it may be said to constitute a major component of "the predicament of the Christian historian," including the first Christian historian, the author of the Acts of the Apostles (→27:1).

Although the text of Acts 15:18—"known unto God are all his works from the beginning of the world" (15:18 TPR AV)—does not have the full attestation of all the manuscripts (→20:28a), its doctrine did have the full attestation of all the biblical writers and was the theological presupposition also of the narrative of Acts. The complicated exposition of the doctrines of foreknowledge, elec-

---

11. For example, Belgic Confession 22–23 (*CCF* 2:416–17).

tion, and predestination in the Epistle to the Romans was by far the lengthiest formulation of those doctrines anywhere in the New Testament. There it formed part of Saint Paul's searching examination of God's historic covenant with the people of Israel (→3:25), which, both here and in other places, was transposed into a broader consideration of the predestinating action of God.

The preeminent object of that predestinating action of God here in Acts was Jesus Christ himself. In the history of Christian doctrine, theological doctrines of predestination have often gone astray by neglecting this fundamental principle. According to Saint Peter's sermon at Pentecost, the cross (→3:18) and the resurrection (→2:31) of Christ took place "according to the definite plan and foreknowledge of God" (τῇ ὡρισμένῃ βουλῇ καὶ προγνώσει τοῦ θεοῦ) (2:23). At one level, therefore, the actors in the drama of the crucifixion, even Judas Iscariot (1:16–20) and Pontius Pilate (→25:11) and ultimately Jesus Christ, were to be seen as part of that definite plan and foreknowledge; according to Peter's earlier words: "The scripture *had to be* fulfilled [ἔδει πληρωθῆναι], which the Holy Spirit spoke beforehand by the mouth of David, concerning Judas" (1:16). So central was the concept of this "definite plan" (βουλή) as a continuing preoccupation in the book of Acts that in his farewell to the Ephesian elders Paul could describe his entire ministry as one of "declaring to you the whole counsel of God [πᾶσαν τὴν βουλὴν τοῦ θεοῦ]" (20:27).

Saint Paul had good personal reasons to speak this way, according to Acts, because he himself is also portrayed here as the object of predestination by God (→9:15). In each of the three accounts of his conversion (→9:1–4), where the formulations vary considerably in their words but do have the same content, that was the theme: "This man is a chosen instrument [σκεῦος ἐκλογῆς] of mine" (9:15 TPR); "the God of our fathers appointed you" (22:14); "I have appeared to you for this purpose, to appoint you [προχειρίσασθαί σε]" (26:16). Each successive step of his apostolic activity, amid all the vicissitudes, was seen as a stage in carrying out that divine election: to the very end he went on preaching and teaching "with all boldness" (μετὰ πάσης παρρησίας) (28:31 NRSV), in the full confidence of his having been chosen. His colleagues, including Luke himself (→27:1), learned the limits of arguing with that sense of total confidence: "And when he would not be persuaded" (→9:1–4), Luke could recall, "we ceased and said, 'The will of the Lord be done'" (→21:13–14).

Regardless of whether it involved Jews or pagan Gentiles or Christian believers, the historical narrative invokes the authority of the predestinating action of God. Even to a philosophical audience that included Stoics and Epicureans, with their long-standing controversies over free will and determinism in human affairs (→17:18), Paul was able to say that in dealing with all nations, whether Gentiles or Jews, God had already, long before, "determined allotted periods [ὁρίσας προστεταγμένους καιρούς] and the boundaries of their habitation" (17:26). More particularly, the history of the Christian doctrine of predestination makes it obligatory to ask: Is it legitimate to read the present passage, in asserting that "as many as were ordained to eternal life [ὅσοι ἦσαν τεταγμένοι εἰς ζωὴν αἰώνιον] believed," as logically implying "and therefore no others," for in the formula of Romans, "those whom he foreknew he also predestined. . . . And those whom he predestined he also called" (Rom. 8:29–30)? Therefore Peter could issue that divine "call" to an ever-widening circle at the beginning of Acts, which was then carried out in the following chapters of the book: "For the promise is [1] to us and [2] to our children and [3] to all that are far off, [4] every one whom the Lord our God calls to him" (2:39 TPR)—in sum, "as many as were ordained to eternal life" (13:48). Nevertheless, in reaction to that call "some were convinced by what he said, while others disbelieved. So, as they disagreed among themselves, they departed" (28:24–25), leaving to later generations of Christian theologians the question of the connection, if any, not only between predestination and faith, but between their disbelieving and God's "ordaining."

ACTS 14

14:1–6 The violent reaction against the preaching of Paul and Barnabas, with which the narrative of the preceding chapter had concluded, prompting them to shake off the "dust from their feet" and transfer their preaching to Iconium (13:50–51), was waiting for them in Iconium as well. As Jesus had prophesied that his message would divide families (Luke 12:51–53), so here it divided the entire city, and once again the itinerant evangelists had to move, from Iconium to Lystra and Derbe.

14:7 TPR And they preached the gospel, and the entire populace was moved by their teaching.

It seems clear that whether it was called, as here, the "preach[ing] of the gospel" or "the word (of God, of the Lord)," the apostolic message was essentially the same (→8:25), with some adaptation to fit the rhetorical requirements of a particular audience, Jewish or Greek and Roman (→24:1–2).

"And Became Incarnate": Incarnation and *Theosis*

14:11–15 TPR When the crowds saw what Paul had done, they lifted up their voices, saying in Lycaonian, "The gods have come down to us in the likeness of men [οἱ θεοὶ ὁμοιωθέντες τοῖς ἀνθρώποις κατέβησαν πρὸς ἡμᾶς]." . . . But when the apostles Barnabas and Paul heard of it, they tore their garments and rushed out among the multitude, crying, "Men, why are you doing this? We also are men, of like nature with you, and bring you the gospel of God, so that you should turn from these vain things."

With at least a touch of humor (→12:13–16), and with an irony analogous to that by which it was the tragic and self-destructive hypocrisy of Ananias and Sapphira that provided an occasion for the Apostle Peter to confess the deity

162

of the Holy Spirit (→5:3–4), the attempt at a sacrifice to Paul and Barnabas, based on a failure to grasp the meaning of miracles as "signs" (→6:8), was the liturgical counterpart to a pagan confession of faith that was at one and the same time woefully misguided in its polytheism and idolatry[1] (→19:28) and yet in some curious and twisted sense "not far from the kingdom of God" (Mark 12:34) as an anticipation of the orthodox Christian doctrine that was to be confessed in the Niceno-Constantinopolitan Creed: "And became incarnate from the Holy Spirit and the Virgin Mary, became human" (καὶ σαρκωθέντα ἐκ πνεύματος ἁγίου καὶ Μαρίας τῆς παρθένου καὶ ἐνανθρωπήσαντα).[2]

When these Lystran pagans exclaimed, οἱ θεοὶ ὁμοιωθέντες τοῖς ἀνθρώποις κατέβησαν πρὸς ἡμᾶς, or whatever this creed may have sounded like in their arcane Lycaonian language (→21:37), which is translated in the RSV as "the gods have come down to us in the likeness of men!" even Christian orthodoxy must acknowledge that this reference to the divine as appearing "in the likeness of men" did bear at least a superficial resemblance to the Pauline language about God "sending his own Son in the likeness of sinful flesh [ἐν ὁμοιώματι σαρκὸς ἁμαρτίας]" (Rom. 8:3) and about the incarnation of the preexistent Christ as "being born in the likeness of men and being found in human form" (ἐν ὁμοιώματι ἀνθρώπων γενόμενος καὶ σχήματι εὑρεθεὶς ὡς ἄνθρωπος) (Phil. 2:7–8). The early Christian apologists, above all Origen in *Contra Celsum*, were at great pains to differentiate the Christian doctrine of the incarnation from such pagan myths of the Olympian deities roaming the earth in search of plunder and sex. "The power and divinity of God," Origen explained, "come to dwell among men through the man whom God wills to choose and in whom He finds room without any changing from one place to another or leaving His former place empty and filling another."[3] At the same time, the perennial danger of Docetism required the apologists to stress that "form" here was not meant as the antonym of "reality" and that this "human form" of Jesus Christ was not a mere form, but the flesh-and-blood reality of a complete human soul and body,[4] "who in every respect has been tempted as we are, yet without sin" (Heb. 4:15). That was why, during the controversies after the Council of Nicea, the term ὁμοιούσιος, in spite of its affinity with the apostle's term ὁμοίωμα,[5] was found to be an inadequate substitute for the council's term ὁμοούσιος.[6] It made much more than "one iota of difference" whether one answered the question, "Is the Divine that has appeared upon the earth and reunited man with God identical with the supreme Divine who rules heaven and earth, or is it a demigod?"[7] by affirming the first or the second of these propositions.

1. Nikanor 1905, 1:268–69.
2. Niceno-Constantinopolitan Creed 3 (*CCF* 1:162–63).
3. Origen, *Contra Celsum* 4.5 (Chadwick 1953, 187).
4. For example, Ignatius of Antioch, *Epistle to the Smyrneans* 1–4 (ACW 1:90–91).
5. Prestige 1956, 197–241.
6. *Chr. Trad.* 1:200–210.
7. Harnack 1957, 242 (translation revised).

And yet here, too, it does not seem unwarranted to take the riposte of Paul to the inscription on the Athenian statue to the unknown God, "Whom therefore you worship without knowing him, him I proclaim to you" (17:23 TPR), as implying that even this utterly pagan and hopelessly deluded response of the Lystrans to the preaching of Paul and Barnabas was a convoluted way for them to "seek the Divine, in the hope that they might feel after him and find him" (17:27 TPR). With a grammatically trivial but metaphysically overwhelming change from the plural to the singular, from "the gods have come down to us in the likeness of men!" to "God has come down to us in the likeness of a man!" their Lycaonian shout, so reminiscent and representative of "the Greek practice of making human beings into gods,"[8] sounded remarkably like the orthodox Christian rule of faith at Nicea and Chalcedon (→8:37).

And the apostolic response to that shout, once again employing the root ὁμοίο- to denote similarity or identity of nature, "We also are men, of like nature with you" (καὶ ἡμεῖς ὁμοιοπαθεῖς ἐσμεν ὑμῖν), when combined with the words of the incantation of the crowd, calls to mind the patristic axiom that God "was made man that we might be made God,"[9] the doctrine of *theosis*/ θέωσις, which was the central soteriological theme in the theology of Saint Athanasius and other Greek fathers. Thus Saint Basil the Great itemized the gifts that were the consequences of the incarnation of the Logos: "Knowledge of the future, understanding of mysteries, apprehension of hidden things, heavenly citizenship, a place in the choir of angels, endless joy in the presence of God, *becoming like God*, and, the highest of all desires, *becoming God*."[10] According to the patristic doctrine, the divine appeared in human form in the incarnation of the divine Logos, but then also, as a result, in the deification of those who adhered to him, who thereby became, in one of the most shattering formulas anywhere in the entire New Testament, "partakers of the divine nature" (θείας κοινωνοὶ φύσεως) (2 Pet. 1:4). In the words of Saint Gregory of Nazianzus the Theologian: "Man and God blended. They became a single whole, the stronger side predominating, in order that I might be made God *to the same extent* that he was made man."[11] Saint Athanasius was even willing to carry this bold assertion to its necessary if surprising consequence: "Because of our relationship to His body we too have become God's temple, and in consequence are made God's sons, *so that even in us the Lord is now worshipped*, and . . . as the Apostle says [1 Cor. 14:25], that God is in them of a truth."[12]

8. Theophylact, *Exposition of the Acts of the Apostles* 14.18 (PG 125:708).
9. Athanasius, *Incarnation of the Word* 54.3 (*NPNF*² 4:65).
10. Basil of Caesarea, *On the Holy Spirit* 9.23 (SVS 44) (emphasis added); Pelikan 1993, 317–18.
11. Gregory of Nazianzus, *Orations* 29.19 (SVS 86) (emphasis added).
12. Athanasius, *Discourses against the Arians* 1.43 (*NPNF*² 4:331).

"The Love Which Moves the Sun and the Other Stars"

14:15–17 TPR A living God who made the heaven and the earth and the sea and all that is in them. In past generations he allowed each nation of men to walk in its own ways; yet he did not leave himself without witness, for he did good and gave you from heaven rains and fruitful seasons, satisfying your hearts with food and gladness.

As if to emphasize that this severely monotheistic repudiation of the Olympian deities as nonexistent did not imply in any way at all the absence of the divine from the world or some proto-Marcionite disjunction between the Creator and the Redeemer, Paul moved immediately from the harshness of his question "Men, why are you doing this?" (14:15) into his most generous assessment anywhere of the witness of creation to the reality of God. Within the Christian apologetic enterprise as this was portrayed in the book of Acts (→26:26), the two scenes of Paul at Lystra here in chapter 14 and of Paul at Athens in chapter 17 are by far the most prominent, with the latter having become the more celebrated in the history of philosophical theology, also because of its brilliant use of apophatic theology to turn the negation of the inscription "to an unknown god" into the affirmation of metaphysical transcendence (→17:23). In both of them, according to Ulrich Wilckens, "Luke made use of a traditional outline of Gentile Christian missionary preaching," which contrasted with the preaching to Jews;[13] but the apologetic at Lystra contained two central elements in addition to those in the later apologetic at Athens.

Although Saint Paul somewhat obliquely "praised the Athenians"[14] by commenting "that in every way you are very religious" (17:22)—this translation of δεισιδαιμονεστέρους in the RSV apparently being preferable in this context to the "too superstitious" of the AV[15]—and although he did speak there (17:23) of "what . . . you *worship* [εὐσεβεῖτε]" (→4:24–30) and not only of their philosophical systems (→17:18), his discourse at Athens was primarily an exercise in the rhetoric of convincing intellectually, which may also account for "the more secular style of this speech."[16] This discourse at Lystra came much closer to the rhetoric of persuading existentially (→9:1–4; →24:1–2) when it spoke about God as (reversing the original order) (1) "satisfying your hearts with . . . gladness" (εὐφροσύνης τὰς καρδίας ὑμῶν), (2) "filling you with food" (NRSV) (ἐμπιπλῶν τροφῆς), and (3) giving "you from heaven rains and fruitful seasons" (οὐρανόθεν ὑμῖν ὑετοὺς διδοὺς καὶ καιροὺς καρποφόρους).

This appeal to the testimony of the natural world in the rain and the seasons, which was at best only implicit in the Athenian discourse, came much closer to the reasoning in the cardinal text of Saint Paul for what has come to

13. Wilckens 1961, 99.
14. Bogolepov 1900, 454.
15. Barrett 1994–98, 2:835–36; BDAG 216.
16. Kirsopp Lake and Henry J. Cadbury in Foakes Jackson and Lake 1979, 4:209.

be called, more or less satisfactorily (and probably less rather than more), "the natural knowledge of God," as it was invoked for example by the Greek church fathers[17] and by Saint Thomas Aquinas[18]: "The invisible things of him from the creation of the world [ἀπὸ κτίσεως κόσμου, meaning 'ever since the creation' chronologically or perhaps, by some interpretations, 'on the basis of the creation' logically] are clearly seen, being understood by [through] the things that are made, even his eternal power and Godhead" (Rom. 1:20 AV). Significantly, this passage in Rom. 1 in the context of the argument of the first two chapters was intended to show, by means of an alpha privative, that human beings are "without excuse" (ἀναπολογήτους), while this passage in Acts 14 was intended to show, by means of another alpha privative, that God was "not . . . without witness" (οὐκ ἀμάρτυρον)—which, to be sure, finally did come down to the same thing, because it meant also that human beings were "without excuse," since they could not plead that they did not know the witness and the will of God when they were violating it.

It was, however, as the Epistle to the Hebrews insisted, not by any such apologetic proofs but "*by faith we understand* that the world was created by the word of God, so that what is seen was made out of things which do not appear" (Heb. 11:3); by insisting that "faith" could "understand," the words πίστει νοοῦμεν united the πίστις and the νοῦς that had stood in disjunction for the cosmology of Plato in the *Timaeus*.[19] But by putting this positive connotation on the witness of creation and thus emphasizing the continuity between the love of God as Creator and the love of God as Redeemer, the Lystran apologetic reached backward and forward: backward to Scripture, not only to the solemn majesty of the creation story in the opening chapter of Genesis (→17:24–25a), but to the words of the Psalter:

> The heavens are telling the glory of God;
>   and the firmament proclaims his handiwork.
> Day to day pours forth speech,
>   and night to night declares knowledge.
> There are no speeches or words,
>   of which their voices are not heard.
> Their voice has goes out into all the earth,
>   and their words to the ends of the world. (Ps. 19:1–4 LXX)

It reached backward to the Wisdom of Solomon:

> If through delight in the beauty of these things men assumed them to be gods,
> let them know how much better than these is their Lord,
> for the author of beauty created them.

17. Pelikan 1993, 65–66.
18. Thomas Aquinas, *Summa theologica* 1.2.2.
19. Plato, *Timaeus* 29c–d (LCL 234:53–55); Pelikan 1997, 89–90.

And if men were amazed at their power and working,
let them perceive from them
how much more powerful is he who formed them.
For from the greatness and beauty of created things
comes a corresponding perception of their Creator. (Wis. 13:3–5 LXX/RSV)

And this apologetic reached forward to the history of Christian art and literature celebrating the created world, as summarized once and for all in the ceiling frescoes of the Sistine Chapel painted by Michelangelo and in the closing lines of Dante's *Divine Comedy*:

But now was turning my desire and will,
Even as a wheel that equally is moved,
The Love which moves the sun and the other stars.[20]

14:21 TPR When they had preached the gospel to the people in that city and had made many disciples.

The TPR's additional explanation, "the people in that city," forms a more precise counterpart to the phrase "many disciples."

The Cost of Discipleship

14:22 Strengthening the souls of the disciples, exhorting them to continue in the faith, and saying that through many tribulations we must enter the kingdom of God.

The ultimate expression of the concept of "the imitation of Christ" (→7:59–60) as a moral imperative in the book of Acts was to pay the final price of "the cost of discipleship" and to follow him on the way of the cross all the way to a martyr's death, by which the universally shared Christian experience of being "united with him in a death like his" (Rom. 6:5) through baptism (→22:16) took its supreme form. The death of every Christian martyr was, as the death of Christ was in a qualitatively unique way (→3:18), the divine response to the human violence that sought either to coerce faith or to compel a denial of the faith (→28:31), whether this violence came from a mob or from a (more or less) legally constituted political authority, be this Herod or Nero or Pontius Pilate—or Adolf Hitler or Joseph Stalin (→25:11).

These words of reassurance from Paul and Barnabas, "that through many tribulations we must enter the kingdom of God," which already in the second century were being quoted as a saying of Jesus himself,[21] come three short verses

20. Dante Alighieri, *Paradiso* 33.143–45 (trans. Henry Wadsworth Longfellow).
21. *Letter of Barnabas* 7 (*ANF* 1:142).

after the report that Paul, having just been literally "idolized" in Lystra as the pagan deity Hermes, was set upon by a lynch mob, who "stoned Paul and dragged him out of the city, supposing that he was dead" (14:19). Two chapters earlier stands the report that "King Herod laid violent hands upon some who belonged to the church in Judea. He killed John the brother of James with the sword" (12:1–2 TPR). But the normative example of martyrdom in Acts, and in all of early Christian literature, was the death of Saint Stephen, the protomartyr "who, of all men, was the first to follow the footsteps of the martyrdom of the Lord, being the first that was slain for confessing Christ,"[22] which was told by Saint Luke with a noble simplicity:

> But he, full of the Holy Spirit, gazed into heaven and saw the glory of God, and Jesus standing at the right hand of God; and he said, "Behold, I see the heavens opened, and the Son of man standing at the right hand of God." But they cried out with a loud voice and stopped their ears and rushed together upon him. Then they cast him out of the city and stoned him; and the witnesses laid down their garments at the feet of a young man named Saul. And as they were stoning Stephen, he prayed, "Lord Jesus, receive my spirit." And he knelt down and cried out with a loud voice, "Lord, do not hold this sin against them." And when he had said this, he fell asleep. (7:55–60)

Stephen was identified by the Greek neologism "*the proto*martyr" (ὁ πρωτομάρτυς)[23] in early Christian literature, because his death served as a model for the deaths of later martyrs, and even for the martyrologies coming out of those deaths such as the *Martyrdom of Polycarp*.[24] This is evident from the retelling of Saint Polycarp's death by Eusebius,[25] who earlier had identified Saint Stephen as "first, after the Lord, . . . to receive the crown, corresponding to his name [the Greek word στέφανος means 'crown'],[26] which belongs to the martyrs of Christ."[27]

Eusebius was able to use the word μάρτυρες as a quasitechnical term for "martyrs," from which it is of course derived; but when the same plural μάρτυρες appeared in the story of Stephen itself (7:58), it referred to the persecutors rather than to the martyrs! As the church would find out already in the days of Eusebius, and even more sharply in the experience of Saint Augustine, it was, despite its attractiveness as an apologetic and rhetorical device, naïve to appeal to martyrdom as a public vindication (→26:26) of the truth of the gospel, because the champions of error could be at least as willing to die for their cause as were orthodox believers. In his conflict with Donatism, therefore, Saint Augustine emphasized that in the

22. Irenaeus, *Against Heresies* 3.12.10 (*ANF* 1:434).
23. *PGL* 1200.
24. *ANF* 1:39–44.
25. Eusebius, *Church History* 4.15 (*NPNF*² 1:188–93).
26. *PGL* 1258.
27. Eusebius, *Church History* 2.1.1 (*NPNF*² 1:104).

Beatitudes Christ had specified, "Blessed are those who are persecuted *for righteousness' sake*, for theirs is the kingdom of heaven" (Matt. 5:10), not identifying persecution as such to be either the guarantee of the promise of the kingdom or the proof for the correctness of their teachings.[28] That was why Christ said of Paul here in Acts, not simply "I will show him how much he must suffer," but "I will show him how much he must suffer *for the sake of my name*" (9:16). After all, others than true believers in Christ could also suffer persecution from the Roman rulers (18:2), who might therefore have the right to be called "equal opportunity oppressors." Although it was "through *many* tribulations" that "we must enter the kingdom of God," then, it was not through just *any* tribulations, but through those that were suffered for the sake of the name (→11:26). That was the key to the theological definition of martyrdom.[29] The clarification of this definition acquired new relevance for all the churches during the twentieth century, with the death of martyrs like the author of the book that in its first English translation bore the title *The Cost of Discipleship*, Dietrich Bonhoeffer, under Nazi persecution in Germany, and of the "neomartyrs" under Communist persecution in Soviet Russia. Although precise statistics are unavailable, it has been estimated that more Christians may have died for the faith during the twentieth century than during all the preceding centuries combined.

14:23 And when they had appointed elders for them in every church, with prayer and fasting they committed them to the Lord in whom they believed.

The precise meaning of the title "elder" is left unspecified (→6:2–4). What is specified is the central function of prayer and worship (→4:24–30), as well as its linkage with the ascetic practice of fasting (→24:25b).

14:25–26 TPR And when they had spoken the word in Perga, they went down to Attalia, preaching the gospel to them; and from there they sailed to Antioch, where they had been commended to the grace of God for the work which they had fulfilled.

From the beginning of this chapter (14:1) to its conclusion (14:27), "speaking the word" was the theme (→8:25).

28. Augustine, *On the Correction of the Donatists* 2.11 (*NPNF*¹ 4:637).
29. R. Hedde in *DTC* 10:220–54.

ACTS 15

Controversy and Polemics

15:2 Paul and Barnabas had no small dissension and debate with them.

The earlier description of an ideal (or even idealized) harmony in the adherence of the first generation of believers to the criteria of apostolic continuity—"doctrine, fellowship, breaking of bread, prayer" (→2:42)—did not preclude the rise of disagreement within the community; nor should it obscure the role of controversy and polemics, in this first generation and ever since, as the provocation for a theological clarification to which, at least humanly speaking, the church could not (or, at any rate, probably would not) have come without it.

In virtually every chapter of the book of Acts there is evidence of ongoing theological disagreement, at the surface or hovering just beneath it. In its own way, this disagreement is a measure of the seriousness with which the apostolic generation took questions of theology and principle (→18:24–26a), as well as of the perennial nature of such fundamental issues as grace and free will (→9:1–4), reason and revelation (→7:22; →17:23), the interpretation of Scripture (→8:30–31), and predestination (→13:48). At least by hindsight, it is possible to see here in Acts previews and intimations of coming theological controversies, some of which would not erupt until many centuries later in the history of Christian doctrine. The difference between the ongoing process of the church's teaching through preaching, liturgy, and catechesis on one hand and the authority of the formal and official statements and promulgations of the church on the other hand, as these are exemplified in the present chapter by the decrees of the apostolic council of Jerusalem (→15:28)—and therefore the difference between (in the eventual senses of the two terms) "apostolic tradition" and "apostolic dogma" (→16:4b)—has been formulated in the distinction between the ordinary magisterium and the extraordinary magisterium

ACT S

of the church.[1] That distinction is also an effort to counterbalance an exclusive emphasis, whether by its proponents or by its critics (or, for that matter, by later historians of doctrine), on the official formulations of creed (→8:37) and dogma (→16:4b) without paying due attention to the "ordinary" and ongoing function of the teaching authority.

Within the ordinary magisterium there has been the continuous practice of what one Reformation confession calls "the mutual conversation and consolation of brethren,"[2] which also involved, when need arose, disagreement and fraternal correction. A particularly winsome example of this appears a little later in Acts in the case of Apollos (→18:24–26b). Although he already "taught accurately [ἀκριβῶς] the things concerning Jesus," it became necessary for "Priscilla and Aquila" (18:26), when they heard him speak, to "[take] him aside and explain . . . the Way of God to him more accurately [ἀκριβέστερον]" (NRSV), and on that basis to write a letter of recommendation (→23:25) for him to the disciples over in Achaia. The "explaining" and controversy was handled with the utmost discretion: "they took him aside [προσελάβοντο]" privately, without, as the modern saying goes, "making a federal [or an apostolic] case out of it," and the cultivation of the ordinary magisterium through the ongoing process of "the mutual conversation and consolation of brethren" was able to go on, without resort to council, creed, or further controversy.

Obviously there have been occasions when this was not enough and when more formal procedures of litigation and appeal became necessary. The litotes here, "had no small dissension and debate" (γενομένης δὲ στάσεως καὶ ζητήσεως οὐκ ὀλιγῆς), compels us to try to imagine the intensity of the controversy. We have no small basis for such imagining in Saint Paul's own very strong report elsewhere (→9:15)—which is unmediated by Saint Luke, but also remains unreported by him, to the puzzlement also of orthodox interpreters[3]—of his encounter on this very same issue with Saint Peter not at Jerusalem but at Antioch (Gal. 2:11, 14): "I opposed him to his face, because he stood condemned. . . . When I saw that they were not straightforward about the truth of the gospel, I said to Cephas before them all, 'If you, though a Jew, live like a Gentile and not like a Jew, how can you compel the Gentiles to live like Jews?'" This "dissension and debate" between Peter and Paul having been inconclusive, the appellate procedure moved to another level, and the question was remanded to "the apostles and the elders"—whatever the distinction between these two may have implied at this stage (→6:2–4)—at Jerusalem.

But it turns out that there, too, the question could not be decided until "after there had been much debate [πολλῆς . . . ζητήσεως]" (15:7). The fifth ecumenical council, held at Constantinople in 553, was to formulate the classic theological defense for this reliance of the church on debate:

1. Rahner and Vorgrimler 1965, 268–69; Karl Rahner in *LTK* 6:884–90.
2. Smalcald Articles 3.4 (*CCF* 2:142).
3. Bogolepov 1900, 446 n.

The holy fathers . . . have followed the examples of antiquity. They dealt with heresies and current problems by debate in common, since it was established as certain that when the disputed question is set out by each side in communal discussions, the light of truth drives out the shadows of lying. The truth cannot be made clear in any other way when there are debates about questions of faith, since everyone requires the assistance of his neighbor.[4]

Then the ordinary magisterium led to the extraordinary magisterium; and, as at Constantinople in 553, the body of dogma has been, in one sense, "increased" in the sheer number of words required for a complete statement of the church's teaching, although in another sense it remained the same (→16:4b), for it also remained true throughout this process that "they continued stedfastly in the apostles' doctrine" (2:42 AV).

At the same time Acts draws a fundamental distinction between this species of controversy and two other kinds of disagreement with which it has repeatedly been equated (and confused) throughout church history. Later in this same chapter (15:39), another controversy—and another kind of controversy—arose, also involving Paul and Barnabas, but with each other, "not over a matter of faith,"[5] but over the advisability of being accompanied on their missionary journey by John Mark, who apparently was a kinsman to Barnabas (Col. 4:10). Whether or not there was intended to be any theological significance in the variation of terminology between the στάσις καὶ ζήτησις of 15:2 and the παροξυσμός of 15:39,[6] it is true here, too, that it was "a sharp contention, so that they separated from each other." But the disagreement did not call for either a doctrinal condemnation or an appeal to the apostolic council. Yet another kind of controversy is described in the dismissive comment of Gallio, proconsul of Achaia: "some bickering about words and names" (18:15 NEB). There are certainly enough genuine instances of such bickering in Christian theological history to justify the constant suspicion that it is always a clear and present danger (→18:15); but as has been noted earlier (→14:11–15), the difference between ὁμοούσιος and ὁμοιούσιος after the Council of Nicea is only one instance of how shallow it was, and is, to rule out a doctrinal controversy on the grounds that this is always the case.

The Historical "Economies" of the Living God

15:8–9 And God who knows the heart bore witness to them, giving them the Holy Spirit just as he did to us; and he made no distinction between us and them, but cleansed their hearts by faith.

4. Decrees of the Second Council of Constantinople (*CCF* 1:187).
5. Theophylact, *Exposition of the Acts of the Apostles* 16 (PG 125:724).
6. BDAG 940, 428–29, 780.

A version of the rule of faith (→8:37) that has been recorded by Tertullian confesses "that there is in fact one God, but that under the dispensation which we call 'economy' there is also a Son of this one God."[7] That principle of "economy" (οἰκονομία) is a continuing theme of the book of Acts: "Observe God's providential management" (θέα τοῦ θεοῦ τὴν οἰκονομίαν), Chrysostom says about the entire book.[8] These four middle chapters of the narrative, from chapter 14 through chapter 17, articulate the interpretation of human history as the "economies" or "dispensations" or "providential management" of the living "God who knows the heart." Here and elsewhere, one of the most powerful titles to be employed by the language of biblical monotheism (→19:28) in articulating the contrast between the one true God and all the idols was to speak of "a living God who made the heaven and the earth and the sea and all that is in them" (14:15), or in this verse, of the "God who knows the heart" (ὁ καρδιογνώστης θεός), or of "the God who made the world and everything in it, being Lord of heaven and earth" (→17:24–29), for "it is a fearful thing to fall into the hands of the living God" (Heb. 10:31). And therefore because, in the formula of Luke Timothy Johnson quoted earlier, "Luke's Apology is . . . in the broadest sense a theodicy. His purpose is to defend God's activity in the world,"[9] this interpretation of history aptly summarized the central theme of that "apology." To be able to speak about the historical actions of God in a way that did not compromise the doctrine of divine transcendence (→17:23), Greek church fathers such as Saint Athanasius developed the distinction between "theology" and "economy," the former being seen as the doctrine of the divine essence (οὐσία) as Trinity and the latter as the understanding of the historical way of God (οἰκονομία) in relation to the world and the human race. Explaining on the basis of the distinction between theology and economy such problematic statements as the one here in Acts 2:36, "God *has made* [ἐποίησεν] him both Lord and Christ, this Jesus whom you crucified," Saint Athanasius argued: "The Son is not a work, but in Essence indeed the Father's offspring, while in the Economy, according to the good pleasure of the Father, He was on our behalf made, and consists as man."[10]

As an interpretation of history, this doctrine of divine economy entailed a unique perspective on the human past. The ground of the divine economy in the past was the confession of God as Creator (→17:24–29). More specifically, it was based on the historic covenant of God with the people of Israel, which was now extended but also reaffirmed through the coming of Christ (→3:25). But in the light of this covenant and of the sovereign and exclusivistic claims that the apostles made here in Acts, such as "there is salvation in no one else, for there is no other name under heaven given among men by which we

7. Tertullian, *Adversus Praxean* 2.1 (*CCF* 1:56).
8. Chrysostom, *Homilies on Acts* 24 (*NPNF*[1] 11:155).
9. Johnson 1992, 7.
10. Athanasius, *Discourses against the Arians* 2.14.11 (*NPNF*[2] 4:354).

must be saved" (4:12), it may be a theological surprise to find them quoted as speaking as they did about the centuries and generations that had gone before (→3:21), particularly in the two apologetic addresses of Saint Paul in Lystra (14:15–17) and in Athens (17:22–31): "In past generations," Saint Paul said at Lystra, "he allowed all the nations to walk in their own ways" (14:16); and again at Athens, "The times of ignorance God overlooked" (17:30). "Respecting former sins of ignorance," according to Hermas, "God alone is able to heal them."[11] This did not imply that God was absent from his created world and its history (→14:15–17), but, on the contrary, that he was willing to "overlook" (ὑπεροράν) (RSV) or to "wink at" (AV) the aberrations of that past as "the times of ignorance" (τοὺς . . . χρόνους τῆς ἀγνοίας).

Yet that permissiveness had its limits in the divine economy. Both in Athens and in Lystra Saint Paul accompanied his statement with an existential summons and call to account: "*But now* he commands all men everywhere to repent" (17:30); "that you should turn from these vain things [of idolatry] to a living God" (14:15). The historical action of God in the present made this period of history one that moved from the economy of χρόνος, time as sequence and "time of ignorance" (17:30), to the economy of καιρός, time as "the acceptable time": "Behold, now is the acceptable time" (ἰδοὺ νῦν καιρὸς εὐπρόσδεκτος)! (2 Cor. 6:2). The most sagacious recognition in the narrative of Acts of this moral imperative to pay attention to the divine economies was put into the mouth of Rabbi Gamaliel, who, after rehearsing some other events of the recent Jewish past, warned his fellow members of the Jewish council: "If this authority comes from human will, its power will fail" (5:39 TPR).

But just as the description of the historical economy of the past as "times of ignorance" led to the identification of the historical economy of the present as the καιρός of "but now," so that identification in turn moved directly into the historical economy of the future: "But now he commands all men everywhere to repent, because he has fixed a day on which he will judge the world in righteousness by a man whom he has appointed, and of this he has given assurance to all men by raising him from the dead" (17:30–31). As the living "God who knows the heart," God had promised and would accomplish an age of renewal, in fulfillment of ancient prophecy, in which, among other novelties, Gentiles, and not only Israelites, were said to be "called by my name" (Amos 9:11–12 LXX; Jer. 12:15 LXX; Isa. 45:21 LXX) (→13:48; →20:28a):

> After this I will return,
> and I will rebuild the dwelling of David, which has fallen:
> I will rebuild its ruins,
> and I will set it up,
> that the rest of men may seek the Lord,
> and all the Gentiles who are called by my name,

11. Shepherd of Hermas Similitude 5.7 (*ANF* 2:36).

says the Lord.
Known from of old is his work. (15:16–18 TPR)

"From of old" and "but now," taken together, were a confession of all the historical economies of God, as they were comprehended in the affirmation of the psalmist: "My times [οἱ καιροί μου] are in thy hand" (Ps. 31:15 LXX/RSV).

15:10 TPR A yoke . . . which our fathers have not been able to bear.

The use of the metaphor of a "yoke" to describe a law of Moses that had been given by God (→10:15), while predominantly negative in this context, could also carry with it a positive connotation (Matt. 11:30).

Authority *at* Church Councils and the Authority *of* Church Councils

15:28 It has seemed good to the Holy Spirit and to us.

This entire chapter has served throughout Christian history as a model for decision-making in the church[12] and as a charter both for authority *at* church councils and for the authority *of* church councils. Therefore these very words, "it has seemed good to the Holy Spirit and to us," identifying the voice of a council with the voice and will of the Holy Spirit and not "something human,"[13] were quoted by later councils and confessions, including some Protestant ones.[14] The theological understanding of church councils underwent a vigorous revival of interest in the West when Pope John XXIII, citing the authority of a special inspiration of the Holy Spirit (→16:9), convoked the Second Vatican Council (1962–65) on 25 January 1959; it had long been a constituent element in the characteristically Eastern understanding of church authority.[15] This definition of councils involved several fundamental components, all of which were at work already in this, the first "council of the church," and were made explicit here in chapter 15 of the Acts of the Apostles.[16]

Historically, a council has become necessary in the life and teaching of the church when there arose "no small dissension and debate" (γενομένης δὲ στάσεως καὶ ζητήσεως οὐκ ὀλιγῆς) (15:2) that had reached the point of not being manageable through the usual instrumentalities of theological and administrative adjudication operating in the process that has come to be called the ordinary magisterium of the church (→15:2). In the case of each of those seven councils whose authority as "ecumenical" is acknowledged by both the East and the

---

12. Johnson 1983.
13. Theophylact, *Exposition of the Acts of the Apostles* 15.37 (PG 125:721).
14. Pelikan 2003, 100 n. 44.
15. Pelikan 2003, 413–19.
16. Darù 2001, 122–40.

West, there was chiefly one "dissension and debate," and "no small" one at that, which precipitated the calling of the council and dominated its proceedings:

1. At the First Council of Nicea (325), it was the doctrine that the Son of God is identical in being (ὁμοούσιος) with the Father.
2. At the First Council of Constantinople (381), it was the relation of the Holy Spirit to the Father and the Son, and therefore the dogma of the Holy Trinity.
3. At the Council of Ephesus (431), it was the inseparability of the man Jesus from the Logos, and therefore the propriety of calling the Blessed Virgin Mary "Theotokos [θεοτόκος], Mother of God" (→1:14).
4. At the Council of Chalcedon (451), it was the relation in the person of Jesus Christ of the two natures, "which undergo no confusion, no change, no division, no separation [ἀσυγχύτως, ἀτρέπτως, ἀδιαιρέτως, ἀχωρίστως]."
5. At the Second Council of Constantinople (553), it was the distinction between the two wills of the one incarnate Logos.
6. At the Third Council of Constantinople (680–81), it was the attribution to each nature in Christ of its own "center of action" (ἐνέργεια) (→22:6), in opposition to the idea that there was a single center of action in Christ that was divine and human at the same time.
7. At the Second Council of Nicea (787), it was the long and bitter "dissension and debate" over the use of images in the church (→19:26).

Alongside these central issues, each council also took up and adjudicated a host of other disagreements, especially disciplinary and jurisdictional ones (→16:4a), for example, the relation between the authority of Old Rome and New Rome at both Constantinople I in 381 and Chalcedon in 451.[17]

Seen within the total context of the book of Acts, the apostolic council set a pattern for the authority *at* church councils that has repeatedly itself become the occasion for "no small dissension and debate." It would be understandable if a reader of only the first two chapters of Acts concluded—as many readers not only of the first two chapters of Acts, but of the entire New Testament have—that the mouthpiece of the postresurrection church was the Apostle Peter (→5:29a), the "rock" on which Christ had promised to build a church against which the gates of hell would not be able to prevail (Matt. 16:18). According to the TPR it was (apparently) Peter alone who nominated the candidates, one of whom was to be chosen by lot as the successor to Judas (1:23 TPR); and Peter is indeed the first speaker to be identified by name also here at the council (15:7–11), but as a prominent participant among other participants, not as a monarch or even, for now, as *primus inter pares*. Yet the decision was rendered by the Apostle James, "brother of the Lord" (→1:14), who, after introducing his opinion with the words "brethren, listen to me" (ἄνδρες ἀδελφοί,

17. Pelikan 2003, 106–7.

ἀκούσατέ μου) (15:13), announced: "Therefore *my judgment is* [διὸ ἐγὼ κρίνω] that we should not trouble those of the Gentiles who turn to God" (15:19); "this (James) was bishop, as they say," Chrysostom the bishop explains dryly, "and therefore he speaks last."[18] Last or not, however, his function was made clear by the earlier description of the entire proceeding, "the apostles and the elders gathered together [συνήχθησαν] to consider this matter" (15:6), and then in the next chapter by the summary description of the judgment of the council as "the decisions which had been reached by the apostles and elders who were at Jerusalem" (16:4)—by all of them in concert together, neither by James alone nor by Peter alone.

With the authority of these "apostles and elders who were [in attendance at the council] at Jerusalem," these "decisions" carried the weight of δόγματα, which is what they were called (→16:4b). Yet the chapter also spoke of "the consent of the whole church" (15:22 NRSV); that notion of "consent" was the basis for the later theological doctrine that a council's authority must also take into account the phenomenon of "reception," which is defined by Yves Congar as

> the process by means of which a church (body) truly takes over as its own a resolution that it did not originate as to its self, and acknowledges the measure it promulgates as a rule applicable to its own life. . . . It includes a degree of consent, and possibly of judgment, in which the life of a body is expressed which brings into play its own, original spiritual resources.[19]

The outstanding negative example of the workings of "reception" in the early centuries of the church was the Synod of Ephesus of 449. Although, considered a priori, it might have appeared to be carrying the credentials of "apostolicity" and therefore the criteria of an "ecumenical council" at least as much as its acknowledgedly "ecumenical" predecessor in Ephesus eighteen years earlier had, it nevertheless did not achieve reception and stands in the history books and in the law of the church as, in the epithet that was pinned on it by Pope Saint Leo, "the robber synod of Ephesus" (*latrocinium ephesinum*).[20]

15:29 TPR And whatever you do not want to be done to you, do not do it to someone else . . . , as you are sustained by the Holy Spirit.

Transmitted by the TPR but not by other manuscript traditions (→20:28a), this paraphrase of the Golden Rule of Jesus (Luke 6:31; Matt. 7:12) belonged to another version of the canon law promulgated by the apostolic council (→16:4a).

18. Chrysostom, *Homilies on Acts* 33 (*NPNF*[1] 11:205).
19. Quoted in Pelikan 2003, 256.
20. Pelikan 2003, 258–59.

was attributed individually to Saint James read: "To abstain [1] from the pollutions of idols and [2] from unchastity and [3] from what is strangled and [4]
from blood" (15:20). A slightly different (and apparently final) version, which
was incorporated into the official epistle (→23:25) that was addressed by the
council to the church at Antioch, read: "That you abstain [1] from what has
been sacrificed to idols and [2] from blood and [3] from what is strangled and
[4] from unchastity. If you keep yourselves from these, you will do well" (15:29).
The account given to Paul by "the brethren" at Jerusalem, Jewish converts to
the Way (→11:26), quoting that epistle, was identical in wording to it: "As for
the Gentiles who have believed, we have sent a letter with our judgment that
they should abstain [1] from what has been sacrificed to idols and [2] from
blood and [3] from what is strangled and [4] from unchastity" (21:25). But
in all three of these versions, the third taboo, "from what is strangled" (καὶ
τοῦ πνικτοῦ or καὶ πνικτῶν or καὶ πνικτόν), is omitted in the TPR, which instead inserts into the first two of these a version of the Golden Rule from the
teaching of Jesus (Luke 6:31; Matt. 7:12): "And whatever you do not want to
be done to you, do not do it to someone else . . . , as you are sustained by the
Holy Spirit"; the clause "from unchastity" also lacks universal attestation in the
manuscripts. But these attempts to clarify and simplify the text of the decrees
have not prevailed in most of the manuscripts, in the modern critical editions
of the Greek text, or in the several twentieth-century translations of the book
of Acts into English (RSV, NRSV, NJB, NEB, REB), which have instead added
various explanatory footnotes about the textual history.

Taken at face value, then, the two texts of the decrees represent what looks
like a combination of prohibitions of several kinds, all of them seemingly put
on the same level of permanent authority. "From the pollutions of idols" (τῶν
ἀλισγημάτων τῶν εἰδώλων) as it stands could be read a warning against the sin
of idolatry (→19:28), which was a violation of the commandment that Jesus
had called "the greatest and first" (Matt. 22:38 NJB): "You shall love the Lord
your God from your whole heart and from your whole soul and from your
whole power" (Deut. 6:5 LXX). "From unchastity" (τῆς πορνείας) seems to be
a repetition of the universally binding commandment: "You shall not commit adultery" (οὐ μοιχεύσεις) (Exod. 20:14 LXX/RSV), numbered fifth in the
Decalogue by most Protestants and by Eastern Orthodox, but sixth by Roman
Catholics and by Lutherans. The prohibitions "from what is strangled and from
blood" repeated some of the ceremonial provisions of the Mosaic law (→10:15).
Some commentators seek to clarify this combination by relating it to what one
reference manual defines on the basis of the Talmud as the "seven Noahide prohibitions: idol worship, taking God's name in vain, murder, prohibited sexual
activity, theft, eating flesh from a living animal, and the obligation to enforce
laws," which pertained not only to the law and covenant that were issued through
Moses on Mount Sinai, but to the law and covenant that had been given already
to Noah and that were therefore binding on the entire human race, as descended

from Noah, rather than only on the covenant people of Israel.[5] There are also parallels in the Qur'an.[6]

Looked at in the light of its historical outcome rather than of its talmudic or other sources, however, this combination raises, more clearly perhaps than does any other passage in the New Testament, the question of canon law, for it seems to bundle together the normative biblical doctrine of monotheism ("idolatry"), the unchangeable moral law of the sanctity of marriage ("unchastity"), and two ceremonial-canonical provisions from Leviticus ("what is strangled" and "blood"). Already in the New Testament discussion that is headed "Concerning food offered to idols" (περὶ . . . τῶν εἰδωλοθύτων) (1 Cor. 8:1), these latter provisions seem to have been treated as changeable in the sense that the provisions of canon law are changeable, with the issue being good "order" (1 Cor. 14:40) and offense to the weak (Rom. 14:21), rather than as the absolute commandments and prohibitions of God; and they have not been enforced even as ecclesiastical practice, much less as divine law, through most of church history.

From the deliberations of the apostolic council at Jerusalem it does become clear that, in spite of its strictures against the continued enforcement of the ceremonial laws of the book of Leviticus (→10:15), the apostolic church (and the postapostolic church in any age) would not be able to get along without canon law. If it was a binding apostolic imperative that both in the liturgy and in the housekeeping of the church "all things should be done decently and in order [εὐσχημόνως καὶ κατὰ τάξιν]" (1 Cor. 14:40), then it was both permissible and necessary for the church to legislate the specific provisions of that "order" and, over and over again, to revise those provisions in the light of subsequent experience and need. In denouncing the accumulated legalism of church institutions, reformers have repeatedly acted as though the true church could dispense with canon law. On 10 December 1520 Luther burned not only the bull of Pope Leo X condemning him and his writings, but Gratian's *Corpus of the Canon Law*; ten years later, in 1530, he found himself, as a consultant to the secular authorities together with his faculty colleagues, compelled to deal with "marriage matters" (*Ehesachen*) and to cite the very same *Canon Law* of Gratian as an authority.[7]

Even when it does not profess to be based on Scripture, canon law, as formulated for example by a church council, claims the right to demand that members of the church "observe" (φυλάσσειν) and obey it, because the voice of the church as mother is the voice of God, even more than are the commandments of human parents to their children.[8] In the realm of civil law, too

---

5. Emmanuel Rackman, Michael Broyde, and Amy Lynne Fishkin in Neusner et al. 1999, 1:347.
6. Bruce 1990, 346.
7. Pelikan 1968, 98–112.
8. Confession of Dositheus 2 (*CCF* 1:616).

(→25:11), "he who resists the authorities resists what God has appointed, and those who resist will incur judgment" (Rom. 13:2). Yet unlike "obedien[ce] to the faith" (6:7), which was obedience to the authority of divine revelation itself (→24:24–25a), this obedience to canon law or civil law (or even parental law) was always limited rather than absolute; and one of the most frequently quoted passages from the entire book of Acts throughout Christian history has been the overriding authority of the principle that "we must obey God rather than men," which at times has even been applied to rules legislated by the church (→5:29b).

Apostolic Tradition and Apostolic Dogma

16:4b They traditioned the dogmas of the apostles for observance [παρεδίδοσαν ... φυλάσσειν τὰ δόγματα ... τῶν ἀποστόλων].

Although it appears to be missing from the TPR,[9] 16:4 contains in Greek two terms that in subsequent times were to figure prominently in the authority structure of Christian doctrine: the verb παραδιδόναι ("to deliver"), from which comes the noun παράδοσις ("tradition") and therefore the admittedly rare English verb "to tradition";[10] and δόγμα, the noun for an official "decree"—therefore the technical terms both for "apostolic tradition" and for "apostolic dogma." But each of these terms can also carry a strongly pejorative sense—it is not simply a bit of etymological miscellany to point out that the English words "tradition" and "traitor" both have the same root, in the Latin verb *tradere*[11]—and both of them required considerable further development before reaching the full sense that they were to acquire in the lexicon of the church.

Like the English word "deliver," which is often used to translate it in versions of the English Bible, παραδιδόναι is in itself neutral, depending on the context for specific meaning: thus in one chapter of the Gospel of Matthew it was employed for Judas's "delivering" Christ to his enemies (Matt. 10:4), and in the next for the Father's "delivering all things" to the Son (Matt. 11:27). In the corpus of Luke-Acts (as well as in the other Gospels), it was the standard term for the betrayal of Jesus by Judas Iscariot, who "conferred with the chief priests and officers how he might betray him [παραδῷ αὐτόν]" (Luke 22:4); here in Acts, therefore, Peter accused the Jews of having "delivered up and denied" (παρεδώκατε καὶ ἠρνήσασθε) Jesus (3:13). Also in the more specific sense of "tradition," its connotation depended on just what was being traditioned. Therefore the accusation against Stephen was based on the allegation of his having said "that this Jesus of Nazareth . . . will change the customs which Moses delivered [παρέδωκεν] to us" (6:14). What this accusation was really

9. Boismard 2000, 264.
10. *OED* 18:354.
11. *OED* 18:353–54, 374.

defending was not what Moses had actually delivered from God, but what they themselves, on the basis of this original law, had identified as what Moses delivered, "the tradition of the elders" (ἡ παράδοσις τῶν πρεσβυτέρων) (Matt. 15:2), so that Jesus could counter their accusations with the question (Matt. 15:3), "And why do you transgress the commandment of God for the sake of your tradition [διὰ τὴν παράδοσιν ὑμῶν]?"

In the context of the present verse, however, what was being traditioned was not only positive; it was apostolic and carried the authority of a council of the church (→15:28). The process that the word "tradition" described in this passage, moreover, was seen not as a single act of traditioning, but as one that was being repeated over and over "as they went on their way through the cities," to each of which they "delivered . . . for observance" what they had received from the apostles. Luke wrote this as one who, being a convert to the gospel, had himself been the recipient and beneficiary of such a process of traditioning and had then become its bearer as an evangelist and historian. Together with others (not otherwise identified) who "have undertaken to draw up an account of the events that have happened among us," he knew himself to be "following the traditions handed down to us [καθὼς παρέδοσαν ἡμῖν] by the original eyewitnesses and servants of the Gospel" (Luke 1:1–2 NEB) and to be delivering them in turn to Theophilus and all of his other readers until the present day.

That set the essential content of the doctrine of tradition, which was not a single action but a process. It was succinctly defined in the conclusion of the doctrinal decree of the Council of Chalcedon of 451: "Just as [1] the prophets [in the Old Testament] taught us from the beginning about him, and as [2] the Lord Jesus Christ [in the Gospels] himself instructed us, and as [3] the creed of the fathers handed it down to us [τὸ τῶν πατέρων ἡμῖν παραδέδωκε σύμβολον]."[12] The σύμβολον referred to here was in the first instance the Nicene Creed of 325 and the Niceno-Constantinopolitan Creed adopted in 381, taken together. But the process of traditioning went on, so that this very decree of Chalcedon itself became in turn an essential component of it for the centuries that followed. Tradition and Scripture were not seen as separate, as they came to be treated in later controversies, but as continuous and ongoing and interpenetrating—and apostolic: Old Testament, New Testament, councils and creeds (→1:2–3).

The meaning of the Greek word δόγμα, too, varied with its context. Luke-Acts uses it a total of three times, here and in two other places, both of which identified a decree of the Roman powers that be (→25:11): the "decree [which] went out from Caesar Augustus that all the world should be enrolled" (Luke 2:1), which served as the prelude to the Lukan account of the nativity of Jesus; and the accusation that the followers of the Way (→11:26) "are all acting against the decrees of Caesar [ἀπέναντι τῶν δογμάτων Καίσαρος], saying that there is

12. Definition of Faith of the Council of Chalcedon 25–27 (CCF 1:181).

another king, Jesus" (17:7), where it is missing from the TPR, which has simply ἀπέναντι τοῦ Καίσαρος. The two instances of the word δόγμα in the Pauline Epistles both were negative in their connotation: "the law of commandments and ordinances" (τὸν νόμον τῶν ἐντολῶν ἐν δόγμασιν) (Eph. 2:15); and "the bond which stood against us with its legal demands" (τὸ καθ' ἡμῶν χειρόγραφον τοῖς δόγμασιν) (Col. 2:14). In the Septuagint and other Greek versions of the Old Testament, it was used more often by the book of Daniel, usually for the laws of the Medes and Persians, than by all the other books combined. Which leaves the present passage as the only one of the five appearances of the word δόγμα in the New Testament where it is used about something pertaining to the Christian faith—because the ones who issued these particular δόγματα were not emperors but the apostles.

In their content, these "decisions" or "decrees" of the apostles and elders at Jerusalem belonged more to Christian observance than to Christian doctrine and, among kinds of observance, mostly to what came eventually to be known as canon law (→16:4a). But "dogma," like "tradition," is in the first instance more the identification of a process than of a content: whatever the apostles had decreed, like whatever the apostles had handed down, was *eo ipso* authoritative. That went on including legislation about liturgical and moral observance, about episcopal jurisdiction, and about politics both ecclesiastical and civil. But from the first ecumenical council onward, it also included doctrine, the faith as the *fides quae creditur* (→24:24–25a), and the "decrees" (δόγματα) of the councils that pertained to the rule of faith (→8:37). Because the decrees of the seven ecumenical councils were decrees of imperial councils, three of them (the second, the fifth, and the sixth) having been held in Constantinople itself (381, 553, 680–81), the designation "the decrees of Caesar" (τὰ δόγματα Καίσαρος) (17:7), who was now not Nero but Constantine and his Christian successors, could be used to refer to the officially defined and promulgated apostolic teachings of the church as these were embodied in the apostolic tradition.

Innovative—indeed revolutionary—though it certainly was to have Caesar enforcing the authority of apostolic teaching as dogma, the notion of accepting authoritative teaching as handed down by tradition was itself an apostolic one and could be described, for example by the Apostle Paul, as a "whole-hearted obedience to the pattern of teaching which was handed on [or: traditioned] to you [εἰς ὃν παρεδόθητε τύπον διδαχῆς]" (Rom. 6:17 NEB margin).

Visions and Private Revelations

16:9 TPR And in a vision there appeared to Paul, as though a man of Macedonia [were standing] before him, pleading and saying: "Come over to Macedonia and help us."

The emphasis of Acts on the authority of Old Testament Scripture and of its normative interpretation (→8:30–31) and on the finality of the revelation in Jesus Christ (→3:21; →18:24–26a) must not be permitted to obscure the evidence that from the second chapter to the second-to-last chapter, the Acts of the Apostles is replete with visions, trances, and private revelations. Indeed, the only book of the New Testament that makes more of these special disclosures of the will of God is, as might be expected, the Revelation of Saint John, with its many parallels to the prophetic books of Ezekiel and Daniel. The book of Acts at the outset (2:17–21) appropriated for the church the prophecy of Joel (Joel 2:28 LXX):

> And in the last days it shall be, God declares,
> that I will pour out my Spirit upon all flesh,
> and your sons and your daughters shall prophesy,
> and your old men shall dream dreams [ἐνύπνια ἐνυπνιασθήσονται],
> and your young men shall see visions [ὁράσεις ὄψονται].

Having done so, Acts then sets out to provide more than ample documentation throughout the balance of its narrative that all of these were precisely what had happened. Even its technical vocabulary substantiates this impression: the word ὅραμα ("vision") occurs twelve times in the entire New Testament, one of these in the Gospel of Matthew (17:9) and eleven of them in Acts (7:31; 9:10, 12; 10:3, 17, 19; 11:5; 12:9; 16:9, 10; 18:9), in addition to the related term ὅρασις (2:17); the report of 16:16 that a slave girl had "a spirit of divination" (πνεῦμα πύθωνα) is a unique instance of a title that had traditionally been associated with the Delphic oracle;[13] and Paul's account, "When I had returned to Jerusalem and was praying in the temple, I fell into a trance [ἐν ἐκστάσει] and saw him [Jesus] saying to me" (22:17–18), invokes yet another loanword borrowed from the language of soothsaying and the mystery religions.[14] "What means this expression, ἔκστασις, 'trance'?" Chrysostom could ask in commenting on this last passage: "There was presented to him a kind of spiritual view (θεωρία): the soul, so to say, was caused to be out of the body (ἐξέστη)."[15] It was, Theophylact explains, expanding on Chrysostom, "that which goes beyond sense-perception" (τὸ ἔξω τῶν αἰσθητῶν).[16]

The most transforming of all the visions in Acts certainly must be Saul's encounter with the risen Christ on the road to Damascus (→9:1–4), which is the only one that is narrated three times (9:1–19; 22:1–16; 26:9–19), although the visions of Cornelius (10:3–7; 10:30–33) and of Peter on the roof (10:10–22; 11:4–18) are told twice each. Additional visions to Ananias (9:10–16) and to Paul himself (22:17–18) give further emphasis to the vision of the Damascus

13. BDAG 896–97.
14. BDAG 309.
15. Chrysostom, *Homilies on Acts* 22 (*NPNF*[1] 11:143).
16. Theophylact, *Exposition of the Acts of the Apostles* 10.16 (PG 125:657).

road. At least two other visions to Paul were intended to encourage him in difficulty: "And the Lord said to Paul one night in a vision, 'Do not be afraid, but speak and do not be silent; for I am with you, and no man shall attack you to harm you; for I have many people in this city" (18:9–10); and, "This very night there stood by me an angel of the God to whom I belong and whom I worship, and he said, 'Do not be afraid, Paul; you must stand before Caesar; and lo, God has granted you all those who sail with you'" (27:23–24). But here in chapter 16 there are—in the sharpest possible contrast with the pathetic slave girl who is to be described a few verses later (16:16), whose special gift, whether it was of demonic origin or not (→10:38), had made her the victim of exploitation—three separate special revelations in succession: the prohibition by the Holy Spirit (16:6), the prohibition by "the Spirit of Jesus" (16:7), and the Macedonian vision to come over and preach the gospel (16:9). (It does not seem entirely clear whether the term "as though" [ὡσεί] in the TPR of this verse is intended to qualify the objectivity of the vision in some significant manner.)[17] Also prohibitory in its import was the revelation given to the disciples in Tyre—for some reason it was not given directly to Paul—that he should not go on to Jerusalem (21:4). The words of Joel quoted by Peter at Pentecost, "and they shall prophesy" (2:18), certainly referred to all of these visions, trances, and private revelations as a fulfillment of the prediction; but they also, by the use of the verb προφητεύειν,[18] referred to a special continuity that prophecy, as an ongoing part of the church's ministry, had not only with the prophet Joel, but with all the prophets of ancient Israel (→21:9–10).

At least two of the responses to these special revelations and visions are also theologically important. One was Paul's description to King Agrippa of his own response to the Damascus experience: "I was not disobedient to the heavenly vision" (26:19). This made it clear that a vision did not merely provide special information, but that it commanded obedience, the same kind of obedience that "the faith" itself did (6:7; Rom. 1:5; 16:26). The other was the explanation of Peter's rescue from prison by the angel: "He did not know that what was done by the angel was real, but thought he was seeing a vision" (12:9). This seems to suggest a fundamental ontological difference of some sort between a "vision" (ὅραμα) and what was "real" (ἀληθές), which may also be the import of the TPR's use of ὡσεί here.

The most dramatic event of this genre in the life and ministry of Paul—exceeded in the entire New Testament only by the visions of John the Theologian on the Isle of Patmos—does not appear as part of the narrative in Acts at all, but is an autobiographical excursus introduced into Paul's correspondence with the church at Corinth. It deserves to be quoted in full:

17. Boismard 2000, 266.
18. BDAG 890.

186

I know a man in Christ who fourteen years ago was caught up to the third heaven—whether in the body or out of the body I do not know, God knows. And I know that this man was caught up into Paradise—whether in the body or out of the body I do not know, God knows—and he heard things that cannot be told, which man may not utter. (2 Cor. 12:2–4)

As in Paul's address at Athens, these paradoxical negations, "things that cannot be told, which man may not utter" (ἄρρητα ῥήματα ἃ οὐκ ἐξὸν ἀνθρώπῳ λαλῆσαι), were a way of speaking about a metaphysical transcendence (→17:23). As a way of putting such visions into their proper place, Paul adds: "And to keep me from being too elated by the abundance of revelations, a thorn was given me in the flesh, a messenger of Satan, to harass me" (2 Cor. 12:7).

There is no indication here or elsewhere in the book of Acts that there would ever come a point in the history of the church when such visions and special revelations would cease. And in fact they did not cease. Not only the visions of the seer of Patmos, but the Shepherd of Hermas, who in his sleep was "carried away" and heard voices revealing the will of God,[19] and Eusebius's claim that the emperor Constantine "saw with his own eyes the trophy of a cross of light in the heavens, above the sun, and bearing the inscription, CONQUER BY THIS"[20]—these and countless other accounts of revelations granted especially to mystics and hermits, which are standard features of the lives of the saints, are evidence of that. At the same time, the condemnation of Montanism not only for what it taught but for what it claimed as a prerogative does signal the problematic nature of postapostolic and postbiblical revelations.[21]

16:10–11 Immediately we sought to go on into Macedonia, concluding that God had called us to preach the gospel to them. Setting sail therefore from Troas, we made a direct voyage to Samothrace.

This is the first instance where the author of Acts speaks in the first-person plural. These so-called we-passages have fascinated readers of the book, as evidence that the author, who elsewhere, in his Gospel, claimed to be relying on others as "eyewitnesses" for his account of the life of Jesus (Luke 1:2), had himself been an eyewitness to some of the events he reported here in the later chapters of the Acts of the Apostles (→27:1; →28:14).

16:13 The term προσευχή, translated here as "a place of prayer," refers to a gathering place for Jewish worship (→7:47–48).

16:15 TPR She was baptized, with her entire household.

19. Shepherd of Hermas Vision 1.1 (*ANF* 2:9).
20. Eusebius, *Life of Constantine* 28 (*NPNF*² 1:490).
21. *Chr. Trad.* 1:97–108.

The reading in TPR, πᾶς ὁ οἶκος αὐτῆς, rather than simply ὁ οἶκος αὐτῆς as other manuscript traditions have it, does seem to be relevant to the question of the baptism of infants (→9:1–4; →22:16).

16:16–19 This vignette is a human interest story of value for its own sake, but it is also evidence of a more far-reaching encounter with the murky world of supernatural and demonic powers (→4:24–30; →4:32; →7:47–48; →13:8–11; →19:28).

16:20 These men are Jews and they are disturbing our city.

The accusation that the apostles were guilty of disturbing the peace was apparently meant by Saint Luke to be ironic, considering the actions that were contemplated and taken against them (→3:25; →25:11).

16:25–34 Running throughout the narrative of the book of Acts is a polemic against the use of violence and coercion—in this case, the violence that the jailer wanted to perpetrate on himself (→4:24–30; →6:8; →21:13–14; →22:16; →24:24–25b; →26:20; →28:31).

16:35–39 They have beaten us publicly, uncondemned, men who are Roman citizens.

This encounter was another turning point in the story of Paul, for with his words here the appeal to the authority of Caesar in Rome was set in motion (22:25–28; 25:11–12).

ACTS 17

17:1–4 It was Paul's "custom" (τὸ εἰωθός), also in a Greek city such as Thessalonica, to begin his visit by holding sessions with his fellow Jews at the synagogue. There he would present his biblical arguments for the distinctive Christian interpretation of the Messiah as one who had to suffer and be raised from the dead and for the identification of this suffering and resurrected Christ with the historical figure of Jesus of Nazareth, "whom I proclaim to you" (→3:18; →9:1–4; →24:1–2).

17:5–9 Once again it is the familiar pattern of not only opposition but rioting and physical violence. This time, all of that is accompanied by the charge—which would in fact become a much more accurate historical description in the next three centuries than these "low fellows from the dregs of the populace" (17:5 NEB) could have had any way of knowing at the time—that "these men . . . have turned the world [τὴν οἰκουμένην] upside down." As a result of the conversion of the emperor Constantine within less than three centuries after this riot, the οἰκουμένη of the Roman Empire was being ruled by a Caesar who was indeed himself "saying that there is another king, Jesus" (17:7), and even a Caesar who was insisting through the Council of Nicea (and, by some accounts, also *to* the Council of Nicea), whatever the state of his own spiritual life may in fact have been as a still unbaptized believer,[1] that this same Jesus was "ὁμοούσιος with the Father"[2] (→4:32; →16:4a; →25:11; →28:31).

17:11 NJB Here the Jews were more noble-minded than those in Thessalonica, and they welcomed the word very readily; every day they studied the scriptures to check whether it was true.

1. Meyendorff 1989, 6–7.
2. Nicene Creed 2 (*CCF* 1:158–59).

The example of these "more noble-minded" (εὐγενέστεροι) Jews at the synagogue in Beroea, who "every day . . . studied the scriptures to check whether it was true," would appear to be not only commended here on its own account, but also recommended as a model for Christian believers to follow (→8:25; →8:30–31; →28:14).

17:16 The disgust and anger of any faithful Jew at the artifacts and practices of pagan idolatry was not in any way lessened by being converted to the Christian "Way" (→11:26).[3] If anything, Paul was eager to show that his newly acquired faith in Jesus as Lord and Christ was completely consistent with the strict monotheism of his Jewish upbringing (→19:28).

Christian Theology in Encounter with Greco-Roman Philosophy

17:18 Some also of the Epicurean and Stoic philosophers met him.

In the *Exposition of the Chapters of the Acts of the Apostles* attributed to Pamphilus, the theme of Acts 17 chapter is given as: "Of the inscription on the altar at Athens, and of the philosophic preaching and piety of Paul";[4] and Cassiodorus describes the message as "celestial philosophy."[5] The most profound point both of the affinity and of the difference between Christian theology (whether it be seen as "preaching" or as "piety") and its Gentile context was not to be found in the dramatic confrontations with the Greco-Roman polytheism of myths and theogonies, which the church rejected unequivocally (→14:11–15), but in the encounter with Greco-Roman philosophy. As Werner Jaeger was in a position to say, being a scholar both of classical philosophy and of patristic theology, "When we stop to consider for a moment with what a Greek could compare the phenomenon of Jewish-Christian monotheism we find nothing but philosophy in Greek thought that corresponds to it."[6] And as he had said elsewhere, "The Greek spirit reached its highest *religious* development, not in the cults of the gods . . . but chiefly in philosophy, assisted by the Greek gift for constructing systematic theories of the universe."[7] In this as in so many other aspects of its message (→3:25), early Christianity was following the example of Hellenistic Judaism, in which Moses had become, for Philo and Josephus, the model of the faithful prophet of the one true God of Israel who could nevertheless appreciate and appropriate "the wisdom of the Egyptians" and of the Greeks (→7:22) as coming ultimately from the same one true God. That

3. Pelikan 1990, 54–57.
4. Pamphilus, *Exposition of the Chapters of the Acts of the Apostles* Z (*ANF* 6:167).
5. Cassiodorus, *Commentary on the Acts of the Apostles* 43 (PL 70:1395–96).
6. Jaeger 1961, 29.
7. Jaeger 1939–44, 2:43 (emphasis added).

was the reason Pamphilus could also speak of "the philosophic preaching and piety of Paul."

The two systems of Greek philosophy mentioned here by name were Stoicism and Epicureanism (→23:8); according to Bede, the reason for selecting these two philosophical systems was that the Epicureans located human happiness only in the pleasures of the body and the Stoics only in the virtue of the soul, but "the apostle condemns them both, because just as man consists of soul and body, so happiness must be found in both."[8] These were also, according to Clement of Alexandria, the specific schools of philosophy that Paul had in mind when he warned, "See to it that no one makes a prey of you by philosophy" (Col. 2:8)—"branding not all philosophy, but the Epicurean, which Paul mentioned in the Acts of the Apostles, which abolishes providence and deifies pleasure, . . . the Stoics also, [who] say not well that the Deity, being a body, pervades the vilest matter."[9] Of the two, the Stoic has been far more important in the history of Christian theology than has the Epicurean.[10] Thus later in this chapter, as Stephen G. Wilson points out in commenting on "in him we live and move and have our being" in verse 28, all three of these verbs, "ζῶμεν, ἐσμέν, and in particular κινούμεθα, recall Stoic ideas."[11] At some later point there even arose an apocryphal correspondence between Saint Paul and Roman Stoic philosopher Seneca, which seems to have misled even so perceptive a historical scholar as Saint Jerome into placing Seneca (because he was executed by his erstwhile pupil Nero) "in the category of saints" and Christian martyrs.[12] Not mentioned by Jerome, though it might have seemed to be a contribution to his thesis, is the coincidental historical fact that Gallio (Annaeus Novatus), proconsul of Achaia, who appears in the following chapter of the narrative of the book of Acts (18:12–17) as a protector of Paul's civil rights (→25:16) but certainly not as a supporter of his teachings, which he dismissed as "questions about words and names and your own law" (→18:15), was Seneca's brother.[13] Such a concept as "conscience" (συνείδησις) (→23:1) has frequently (though not universally) been seen as demonstrating some degree of affinity between Stoic and Christian thought.[14] Particularly in the form that Stoicism took on in its Latin career, as documented above all in the works of Cicero, who was deeply under Stoic influence though he cannot be classified as a consistent Stoic, it served to provide Christian theology with at least some of its vocabulary and conceptual framework. The widely influential book on Christian ethics composed by Saint Ambrose of Milan, *On the Duties of the Clergy* (*De officiis*

---

8. Bede, *Exposition of the Acts of the Apostles* 17 (PL 92:979).

9. Clement of Alexandria, *Stromata* 1.11 (*ANF* 2:311).

10. Colish 1985.

11. Wilson 1973, 207.

12. Jerome, *Lives of Illustrious Men* 12 (*NPNF*[2] 3:365).

13. Arnaldo Momigliano and Miriam T. Griffin in *OCD* 95; Kirsopp Lake in Foakes Jackson and Lake 1979, 5:462.

14. See the bibliography in BDAG 967–68.

ministrorum),[15] took that title from the no less influential book of Cicero (→27:3); and Augustine could claim that it was the reading of Cicero's (now lost) treatise *Hortensius* that "changed my feelings. It altered my prayers, Lord, to be towards you yourself. It gave me different values and priorities."[16]

But as Edwin Hatch says of early Christianity, "on its ethical side it had ... large elements in common with reformed Stoicism; on its theological side it moved in harmony with the new movements of Platonism."[17] The place of Stoicism—not to say of Epicureanism—in the Christian encounter with classical philosophy is vastly overshadowed by the dominance of Platonism (Middle Platonism, Neoplatonism) during the early centuries in both East and West, perhaps above all because of its doctrine of immortality, and then of Aristotelianism especially during the Latin Middle Ages. Seen in relation to this chapter of Acts, that entire development is not without a certain irony, for, of the resident philosophers, "when they heard of the resurrection of the dead, some mocked; but others said, 'We will hear you again about this'" (17:32). But in the sixth century another apocryphal body of writings would surface, combining Christian and Neoplatonic thinking and fathered upon the only Athenian man mentioned by name in this chapter as "among" those who "joined him and believed, [namely] Dionysius the Areopagite" (17:32–33); both in the original Greek and in Latin translation, the writings of the Pseudo-Dionysius would provide Christian philosophizing with quasiapostolic credentials.[18]

Two of Plato's dialogues were especially important for documenting this supposed affinity with the gospel. The *Phaedo*, his exposition of the doctrine of the immortality of the soul, provided some of the presupposition for the treatise *On the Soul and the Resurrection* by Saint Gregory of Nyssa (→3:21), a dialogue put into the mouth of his sister Macrina, in which the Platonic idea of the immortality of the soul and the Christian idea of the resurrection of the body were combined into a single view, which was then, already in the title, equated with the teachings of Saint Paul; it is with good reason that a modern scholarly study of this treatise bears the title *Phaedo Christianus*.[19] The other Platonic dialogue to enjoy a long afterlife in Christian thought was the *Timaeus*, which would turn out to be the only writing of Plato that was available, albeit in a fragmentary and "crabbed" Latin translation,[20] during the Western Middle Ages. Once again following in the train of Philo and Hellenistic Judaism, early Christian fathers read this Platonic treatise in "counterpoint" with the Septuagint translation of the first chapters of the book of Genesis to formulate their doctrine of creation.[21] As a result of this process, in Georges V.

15. *NPNF*[2] 10:1–89.
16. Augustine, *Confessions* 3.4.7 (Chadwick 1992, 39).
17. Hatch 1957, 238.
18. *Chr. Trad.* 1:344–49; Pelikan 1987, 11–24.
19. Apostolopoulos 1986.
20. Henry Chadwick and Mark Julian Edwards in *OCD* 316.
21. Pelikan 1997.

Florovsky's pithy formula, "the idea which [Gregory of Nazianzus] expresses in Platonic language is not itself Platonic," and Basil of Caesarea "did not so much adapt Neoplatonism as overcome it."[22]

All of this made the problematics analyzed in the monograph *Platonisme des pères* by Plotinus scholar René Arnou[23] the ineluctable starting point for any theology in the East or in the West that strove to be traditional, and it made the task of extricating that tradition from its Neoplatonic involvement one of the primary assignments to which Thomas Aquinas had to address himself.[24] This represents a long journey indeed from this brief and evidently inconclusive encounter of the Apostle Paul with "some . . . of the Epicurean and Stoic philosophers," and from his warning (whichever Greek—or perhaps Gnostic—systems he may have had in mind), "See to it that no one makes a prey of you by philosophy and empty deceit, according to human tradition, according to the elemental spirits of the universe [κατὰ τὰ στοιχεῖα τοῦ κόσμου]" (Col. 2:8), where the use of the classical term στοιχεῖα, which was so loaded with it own philosophical and religious baggage,[25] presages the impossibility, documented throughout the history of the tortured relation between Christian theology and every school of philosophy, of denouncing philosophy without becoming involved in it.

17:19 AV May we know what this new doctrine, whereof thou speakest is?

The translation "new doctrine" in the AV aligns this question of the Greeks with the attention to "doctrine" in the primitive apostolic community (→2:42) and with the continuing Christian insistence on "accuracy" in doctrine (→18:24–26a).

Apophatic Theology: Negation as the Affirmation of Metaphysical Transcendence

17:23 TPR "To an unknown God": whom therefore you worship without knowing him, him I proclaim to you.

According to this, "the most wonderful passage in the book of Acts . . . full of truth,"[26] Saint Paul, after having toured a "city . . . full of idols" (17:16), stood before the Athenians on the Areopagus (AV: "Mars' Hill"), where "under the open heaven the supreme council would gather."[27] Yet it was not in all the sublime

22. Florovsky 1972–89, 7:119, 107.
23. R. Arnou in *DTC* 12:2258–2392.
24. Gilson 1926.
25. BDAG 946, with bibliography.
26. Harnack 1961, 383.
27. Lopuchin 1895, 655.

creations of Greek architecture, sculpture, and mosaic that were surrounding him (→19:26); nor in the (literally) "fabulous" and polytheistic myths and cults of the gods of Mount Olympus (→19:28); nor yet in the foreshadowings of the cross of Christ that were anticipated by the redemptive suffering of characters such as Oedipus in the Greek tragedies of Sophocles or by the Homeric image of Odysseus with his hands bound to the mast to save his fellows as Christ's were bound to the cross;[28] nor even in the positive and often monotheistic-sounding speculations of the Greek philosophers, and above all of Socrates and Plato, that have so often proved to be almost irresistible to Christian speculation and apologetics (→17:18)—it was not, at least in the first instance, in any of these that he found his point of contact with the Athenians and specifically with their ways of worship, but in a presumably faceless and nameless and mythless (as well as being still unknown to archeology) "altar with this inscription, 'To an unknown God [ἀγνώστῳ θεῷ].'"[29] As Calvin notes in his commentary on this passage, "Paul doth not in this place commend that which the men of Athens had done; but taketh from their affection, though it were corrupt, free matter for teaching."[30] The classic New Testament definition of faith as, at one and the same time, "the assurance of things hoped for, the conviction of things not seen" (ἐλπιζομένων ὑπόστασις, πραγμάτων ἔλεγχος οὐ βλεπομένων) (Heb. 11:1), brings together in one sentence the affirmation/κατάφασις of "assurance" and the negation/ἀπόφασις of "not seen" as appropriate ways of speaking about transcendent reality. Thus, in George Leonard Prestige's warning, "Though the Fathers in speaking of the ineffable being of God tended to use abstract forms which are outwardly expressive of a negative meaning, nevertheless their minds were far from being bounded by merely negative conceptions. The negative forms are enriched with an infinite wealth of positive association."[31]

Quoting the favorite text of Hellenistic writers from Plato's *Timaeus*, "To discover the Maker and Father of this Universe were a task indeed; and having discovered Him, to declare Him unto all men were a thing impossible,"[32] Clement of Alexandria argued:

> Since the first principle of everything is difficult to find out, the absolutely first and oldest principle, which is the cause of all other things being and having been, is difficult to exhibit. For how can that be expressed which is neither genus, nor difference, nor species, nor individual, nor number? . . . And if we name it, we do not do so properly, terming it either the One, or the Good, or Mind, or Absolute Being, or Father, or God, or Creator, or Lord. We speak not

28. Clement of Alexandria, *Exhortation to the Greeks* 12.118.4 (*ANF* 2:205), quoting Homer, *Odyssey* 12.160–64 (LCL 104:443).

29. Norden 1913, 56–83; Kirsopp Lake in Foakes Jackson and Lake 1979, 5:240–46 on pagan parallels and Christian exegesis.

30. Calvin 1949, 2:157.

31. Prestige 1956, 4.

32. Plato, *Timaeus* 28c (LCL 234:51); see also p. 166 above.

as supplying His name; but for want, we use good names, in order that the mind may have these as points of support, so as not to err in other respects. For each one by itself does not express God; but all together are indicative of the power of the Omnipotent.

And that, he concluded, was what Paul had meant by his use of the Athenian inscription "To an unknown God."[33]

This fundamental insight into the nature of language about God was worked out with special trenchancy by "the Four Cappadocians": Saint Gregory of Nazianzus the Theologian, Saint Basil the Great, Saint Gregory of Nyssa, and Saint Macrina, sister of the latter two.[34] They were provoked to this insight by the presumptuous claims that were attributed to—or being made by—fourth-century Christian heretic Eunomius: "God knows no more of his own substance than we do; nor is this more known to him, and less to us: but whatever we know about the Divine substance [οὐσία], that precisely is known to God; and on the other hand, whatever he knows, the same also you will find without any difference in us."[35] To the contrary, on the basis of the statement of Scripture (Wis. 13:5 LXX) that "the greatness and beauty of created things analogically [ἀναλόγως] give us an idea of their Creator," they insisted that the knowledge of God, also in revelation, was only "analogical" and that it was therefore, in Saint Basil's formula, both "incomprehensible to man's reason" (also to the human reason of the believer) and "unutterable by man's voice" (also by the orthodox human voice, even in the orthodox liturgy).[36] "Thou art called the Word, and Thou art above Word; Thou art above Light, yet art named Light," Gregory the Theologian prayed.[37] Negative, apophatic language was called for in speaking about metaphysically transcendent reality: "Incorporeal, purely immaterial, and indivisible . . . boundless in power, of unlimited greatness, generous in goodness, whom time cannot measure."[38]

The linguistic usage of the book of Acts, above all here in this speech of the Apostle Paul to the Athenians with its "finesse,"[39] corroborated this Cappadocian view of apophatic language as the affirmation of metaphysical transcendence.[40] To stress how God transcended all space and time (→7:47–48) and all created reality, he insisted on four closely interrelated propositions: (1) that God "does not live in shrines made by man"; (2) that the dependency between God and man was not mutual but all in one direction, because God was not

33. Clement of Alexandria, *Stromata* 5.12 (*ANF* 2:462–64).
34. Pelikan 1993, 40–56, 200–214.
35. Eunomius, as quoted in Socrates Scholasticus, *Ecclesiastical History* 4.7 (*NPNF*² 2:98).
36. Basil of Caesarea, *Hexaemeron* 2.2 (*NPNF*² 8:60).
37. Gregory of Nazianzus, *Orations* 37.4 (*NPNF*² 7:339).
38. Basil of Caesarea, *On the Holy Spirit* 9.22 (SVS 42–43).
39. Morgenthaler 1949, 1:93.
40. Nikanor 1905, 1:323–25.

"served by human hands, as though he needed anything"; (3) that the efforts of human art (or of human language) to depict God, howsoever beautiful the results might be, were useless, because God was not "like gold, or silver, or stone, a representation formed by the art and imagination of man" (→19:26); and yet (4) that the Transcendent One was not remote, as this emphasis on "the wholly Other" seemed to suggest (→14:15–17), but rather that God was "not far from each one of us." Even where the language as such was not strictly apophatic, moreover, its meaning could be. Insisting in affirmative, "cataphatic" language, against the foolish attempt of the Lystrans to worship Paul as Hermes and Barnabas as Zeus, that "we also are men, of like nature with you [ὁμοιοπαθεῖς . . . ὑμῖν]" (14:15) necessarily meant that the one true God was not "of like nature"; acknowledging the "God who knows the heart" (ὁ καρδιογνώστης θεός) (15:8) entailed admitting that the one true God not only knows vastly more than we do or can, but does so by an altogether different way of knowing. Therefore the best formula even for asserting the transcendence of the universal love and regard of God for all humanity was the apophatic formula of saying with Peter: "Truly I perceive that God shows no partiality [οὐκ ἔστιν προσωπολήμπτης ὁ θεός]" (10:34), because this universal love and regard, like all of the "judgments" and "ways" of God—be they negative or affirmative—had to be confessed to be "unsearchable" (ἀνεξεραύνητα) and "inscrutable" (ἀνεξιχνίαστοι) (Rom. 11:33).

In all of these formulations, apophatic language, the language of negation, was a way of declaring the biblical doctrine that God not only exceeds quantitatively, but transcends qualitatively, all the knowable attributes, which it is permissible therefore to predicate of the Deity only "analogically" (ἀναλόγως) (Wis. 13:5 LXX).

"One God the Father, All-Powerful Maker"

17:24–29 TPR The God who made the world and everything in it, being Lord of heaven and earth . . . made from one blood the entire race of men . . . that they should seek the Deity, in the hope that they might feel after him and find him. Yet he is not far from each one of us, for "In him we live and move and have our being"; as even some among you have said, "For we are indeed his offspring." Being then God's offspring, we ought not to think that the Deity is like gold, or silver, or stone, a representation by the art and imagination of man.

The first article of the Niceno-Constantinopolitan Creed, of the Apostles' Creed—and of many, perhaps most, other ancient (or modern) creedal affirmations (→8:37)—is the declaration of faith in God the Father and the Creator.[41]

41. Pelikan 2003, 544–46.

This declaration of faith is also the subject of the first verse of the first chapter of the first book of the Jewish and Christian Scriptures.

That helps to explain its place in the theology of the book of Acts. When addressing the Christian message to those who had the Jewish Scripture, the disciples did not begin with that first article, but with the specific history and covenant of the people of Israel (→3:25): "The God of glory appeared to our father Abraham," Stephen said as he opened his historical discourse to a Jewish audience (7:2); "the God of this people Israel chose our fathers and made the people great," Paul said when he was speaking to "men of Israel, and you that fear God" (13:16–17). The reason was that in the book of Genesis, seen as the first book of the people of Israel, the creation story in the first chapter formed the framework of, and was the presupposition for, the history of the covenant. That also helps to account for its tantalizing brevity and inadequacy as a cosmogony: even for the astronomy of preclassical antiquity, "he made the stars also" (Gen. 1:16)—separated from the rest of the sentence in English translation by a semicolon—would be inadequate as an explanation for the existence and scope of the stars that were beyond counting (Gen. 15:5).

Therefore it was only in the two "apologetic" addresses to Greco-Roman audiences that the book of Acts gave the doctrine of creation proper treatment in its own right. In the first of those addresses, at Lystra, the emphasis was on the testimony of the creation to the glory and the love of the Creator (→14:15–17): "He did not leave himself without witness, for he did good and gave you from heaven rains and fruitful seasons, satisfying your hearts with food and gladness" (14:17). At Lystra, the announcement of "a living God who made the heaven and the earth and the sea and all that is in them" (14:15) was even presented as a message of "the gospel" (εὐαγγέλιον) (→8:25): εὐαγγελιζόμενοι ὑμᾶς, Paul and Barnabas were able to say about it.

Here in this second apologetic, at Athens, the emphasis was on the two main themes of the doctrine of creation, the creation of the universe and the creation of the human race: "[1] The God who made the world and everything in it, being Lord of heaven and earth, does not live in shrines made by man, nor is he served by human hands, as though he needed anything, [2] since he himself gives to all men life and breath and everything. And he made from one blood the entire race of men [ἐξ ἑνὸς αἵματος πᾶν γένος ἀνθρώπων (TPR)] to live on all the face of the earth, having determined allotted periods and the boundaries of their habitation, that they should seek the Deity [τὸ θεῖον (TPR)], in the hope that they might feel after him and find him" (→10:34–35):

1. Significantly, this identification of the living God as, in the words of the creed, the "All-Powerful Maker" of "the world and everything in it," to which is specifically added here "the sea" (→27:24), made no reference to the creation story in Genesis or to the details of the six days. Whether these were taken to refer to entire eons (as some of the Greek patristic tradition interpreted them), or to six normal days (as Saint Thomas

197

Aquinas read them), or to an instantaneous divine act (as Saint Augustine took them), their central meaning was that "the God who made the world and everything in it [is] Lord of heaven and earth." Creation was, therefore, seen as a free act of a sovereign God who made the world and everything in it not because he was in need of it, but because

> Our God is in the heaven above;
> in the heaven and on earth
> he does whatever he pleases. (Ps. 115:3 LXX)

Nor was creation seen only as a single act "in the beginning" (Gen. 1:1), but as that by which God the Creator was constituted "Lord of heaven and earth" and the all-knowing Lord of history (→13:48). Explaining this doctrine to a Greco-Roman pagan audience required moving immediately from it to a rejection of idolatry and polytheism (→19:28): this Creator-God "does not live in shrines made by man, nor is he served by human hands, as though he needed anything" (→7:47–48), and hence "we ought not to think that the Deity is like gold, or silver, or stone, a representation by the art and imagination of man" (→19:26).

2. In the Genesis story the account of the six days served to introduce the account of the creation of the human race, as Saint Basil's *Hexaemeron*[42] led naturally to Saint Gregory of Nyssa's *On the Making of Man*.[43] Here, too, Paul moved directly to the message that God "himself gives to all men life and breath and everything." And once again creation was more than a doctrine of historical origins, for this Creator-God was active in human history (→15:8–9), but always with the purpose "that they should seek the Deity, in the hope that they might feel after him and find him." With that emphasis here in the Athenian apologetic Paul made a direct connection to the earlier Lystran apologetic and its doctrine of the witness of creation.

17:30–32 The times of ignorance God overlooked, but now he commands all men everywhere to repent, because he has fixed a day on which he will judge the world in righteousness by a man whom he has appointed, and of this he has given assurance to all men by raising him from the dead.

Whether, with TPR, we read παριδών or, with most other manuscripts, ὑπεριδών, both verbs carry the meaning "overlook, take no notice of, disregard,"[44] and emphasize the generosity of the divine "economy" (→2:24–32; →3:21; →14:11–15; →15:8–9; →23:8).

---

42. *NPNF*[2] 8:51–107; Quasten et al. 1951–86, 3:216–18.
43. *NPNF*[2] 5:386–427; Quasten et al. 1951–86, 3:263–64.
44. BDAG 780, 1034.

ACTS 18

18:1–2 Among the books of the New Testament, only Luke-Acts mentions any of the Roman emperors by name (→25:11).

18:5, 28 As in the preceding chapter and throughout, a major burden of Paul's message was the interpretation of the Law and the Prophets to show that Jesus, who died and was raised from the dead, was the promised Messiah (→3:18).

18:6 Together with the words of the high priest earlier (5:28), the words of Paul here, "Your blood be upon your heads!" continue a way of speaking that is best known from the cry, "His blood be on us and on our children!" (Matt. 27:25).

18:8 TPR A certain ruler of the synagogue named Crispus believed in the Lord with his entire household, and a great multitude of Corinthians, hearing the word of the Lord, were baptized, believing God in the name of Jesus Christ [πιστεύοντες τῷ θεῷ ἐν τῷ ὀνόματι Ἰησοῦ Χριστοῦ].

The question whether this "entire household" who believed and then were baptized included infants has made this text one of the points of contention for the doctrine of baptism (→22:16). The believing and the baptizing were closely tied to the hearing of "the word of the Lord" (→8:25), and the "believing" would seem to refer not to "the faith that is believed" (*fides quae creditur*) (→24:24–25a), but to "the faith by which one believes" (*fides qua creditur*) (→26:18).

18:9–10 This is yet another instance when a vision served as the means of a special revelation (→16:9).

18:13 Countering the stock accusation that his gospel undercut the authority of the law of Moses, Paul consistently presented it as "the hope of Israel" (→9:1–4; →24:1–2).

Theological "Bickering about Words and Names"

18:15 NEB If it is some bickering about words and names and your Jewish law, you may see to it yourselves; I have no mind to be a judge of these matters.

By the same kind of instructive juxtaposition that brings the hope of an ἀποκατάστασις πάντων as universal restoration (→3:21) into close proximity with the assertion of salvation as a gift that is available exclusively in the "name" of Jesus Christ (4:12), compelling a dialectical consideration of each in the light of the other, this dismissal of theological controversy (→15:2) as "some bickering about words and names," and as nothing more than that despite the "spiritual" significance of names especially in the biblical tradition,[1] appears immediately before the most specific discussion in Acts, and one of the most specific anywhere in the New Testament, of the threefold imperative of doctrinal ἀκρίβεια as precision (→18:24–26a): (1) clarifying and specifying the substance of the faith as *fides quae creditur* (→24:24–25a); (2) getting the words of the creed and confession right, which included the explanation of why they were not mere words (→8:37); and (3) setting straight someone who did not understand (→15:2) and did not get the content right (→11:26).

This is not the only instance in Acts of a political figure who was called in to adjudicate questions of Christian doctrine that he could not understand or even take seriously. In a later chapter, as part of an introduction that classical rhetoric (→24:1–2) prescribed in Latin as *captatio benevolentiae*, Paul appealed to King Agrippa as one who was "especially familiar with all customs and controversies of the Jews" (26:2–3). There was probably no "controversy of the Jews" mentioned in Acts that was more fundamental than that between the Pharisees and the Sadducees over immortality and resurrection: "For the Sadducees say that there is no resurrection, nor angel, nor spirit; but the Pharisees confess the existence of resurrection and angel and spirit" (23:8 TPR). Yet in addressing this same King Agrippa, Festus the Roman governor could describe such "bickering about words and names" this way: "When the accusers stood up, they brought no charges in his [Paul's] case of such evils as I supposed, but they had certain points of dispute with him about their own superstition [ζητήματα . . . τινα περὶ τῆς ἰδίας δεισιδαιμονίας] and about one Jesus, who was dead, but whom Paul asserted to be alive. Being at a loss to investigate these questions, I asked whether he wished to go to Jerusalem and be tried there regarding them," probably before a court of his Jewish peers who were the only

---

1. Bede, *Retractations on the Acts of the Apostles* 10 (PL 92:1018).

ones who had the competency and theological expertise to adjudicate questions "about their own superstition" (25:17–27). In the event, Saint Paul appealed instead to the tribunal of Caesar (→25:11).

It is not necessary to share this—or any other—"superstition" to recognize that "mere bickering about words and names" is often not "mere" at all. In American constitutional law, for example, a lawyer's argument or a Supreme Court decision often turns precisely on the meaning of a single word. Because the Constitution repeatedly frames its prescriptions with the word "shall," Justice Joseph Story in 1816 could insist that there was a basic and decisive difference between "shall" and "may," on which the entire force of an article of the Constitution rested.[2] It is difficult to avoid the generalization that differences over the meaning of terms tend to be vital to those to whom the issues involved are themselves vital, but that they are no more than "bickering about words and names" to those who, like Claudius Lysius (23:28–29) or Festus or Agrippa, stand outside "the hermeneutical circle."

That said, it must also be freely admitted that there truly has been much "bickering about words and names" in the history of Christian theology, what Saint Gregory of Nazianzus, quoting the First Epistle to Timothy, called "profane and vain babblings and contradictions of the Knowledge falsely so-called, and strife of words, which lead to no useful result."[3] This tendency has been recognized also by those who take Christian doctrine with the utmost seriousness and who strenuously insist on the necessity for ἀκρίβεια in its formulation. It is salutary to recall that in spinning out some of the most elaborate speculation on the doctrine of the Trinity ever composed, Saint Augustine explained that he had done this not to presume to describe this mystery as though he were speaking from the mind of God, but so as not to be altogether silent, and he begged forgiveness where his speculations had gone too far.[4] Perhaps the most dramatic present-day illustration of this is in the relation between "Chalcedonian" and "non-Chalcedonian" churches. In a schism that has endured three times as long as has the division between Roman Catholicism and Protestantism, the formulation of the doctrine of the two natures in Christ by the Council of Chalcedon in 451 as united with "no confusion, no change, no division, no separation"[5] has divided the main body of Orthodox and Catholic Christendom from the so-called Monophysites ("a single nature") such as the Church of Armenia.[6] But as the twentieth century was closing, a series of reconciliatory understandings were reached which expressed the "determined conviction that because of the fundamental common faith in God and in Jesus Christ, the controversies and unhappy divisions which sometimes have followed

2. Justice Joseph Story, *Martin v. Hunter's Lessee*, 14 U.S. 327–28 (1816).
3. Gregory of Nazianzus, *Orations* 27.1 (SVS 25), quoting 1 Tim. 6:20 and 6:4.
4. Augustine, *On the Trinity* 5.9.10; 15.28.51 (*NPNF*[1] 3:92, 227–28).
5. Definition of Faith of the Council of Chalcedon 18 (*CCF* 1:181).
6. *Chr. Trad.* 2:37–90.

upon the divergent ways in expressing it . . . should not continue to influence the life and witness of the church today."[7] The name "Monophysite" has all but disappeared from the theological vocabulary, being replaced by "Oriental Orthodox" (as distinguished from "Eastern Orthodox"). The conclusion to be drawn from these developments is not that doctrine or doctrinal formulation is always tantamount to "bickering about words and names," but that "divisions following upon divergent ways in expressing" rather than upon genuine and substantive divergence in doctrine do remain a clear and present danger.

"Accuracy" in the Confession of Christian Doctrine

18:24–26a Now a Jew named Apollos [TPR: Apollonius], a native of Alexandria, came to Ephesus. He was an eloquent man, well versed in the scriptures. He had been instructed in the way of the Lord; and being fervent in spirit, he spoke and taught accurately the things concerning Jesus, though he knew only the baptism of John. He began to speak boldly in the synagogue; but when Priscilla and Aquila heard him, they [TPR: when Aquila heard him, he] took him and expounded to him the way of God more accurately.

Implicit in "the faith" as *fides quae creditur* (→24:24–25a) was the requirement that to be truly "well versed in the scriptures," including their correct interpretation (→8:30–31), as Apollos was said to be here, one "taught accurately" (ἐδίδασκεν ἀκριβῶς), as Apollos was said to be doing here on the basis of his already having "been instructed in the way of the Lord," as this instruction was contained in "the traditions handed down to us by the original eyewitnesses and servants of the Gospel" (Luke 1:2 NEB) and in the rule of faith, whatever its form may have been at the time (→8:37). But therefore one was also expected to teach "more accurately" (ἀκριβέστερον) after correction, as Apollos was said here to have learned to do. The moral corollary of the faithful adherence to the Way (→11:26), therefore, was the readiness to "destroy arguments and every proud obstacle to the knowledge of God, and take every thought captive to obey Christ, being ready to punish every disobedience" (2 Cor. 10:5–6), which included, though it was by no means confined to, the teaching of church doctrine.[8]

Such seriousness about doctrine may be seen as underlying the priorities in the normative description of the primitive community of believers after Pentecost: "And they continued stedfastly in the apostles' *doctrine* [διδαχῇ]" (2:42 AV). The most important question facing the community in those first weeks and months after Pentecost was: Would the quantum increase in membership brought about by the sudden addition of some 3,000 new believers

---

7. Common Declaration of Pope John Paul II and Karekin I, Catholicos of the Church of Armenia (*CCF* 3:869).

8. Origen, *On First Principles* 3.2.4 (*ANF* 4:331–32).

(2:41) to the 120 or so previously identified as "disciples" (μαθηταί) (1:15), and then the qualitative changes that this entailed, fundamentally alter or redefine the very nature of the movement? Or were there ways to ensure—invoking the later terminology of the Niceno-Constantinopolitan Creed[9]—that in the process of becoming "catholic" the church would continue to be "apostolic," as well as "one" and "holy"? Fundamentally, the answer to that question was the coming of the Holy Spirit (→2:1), in keeping with the promise of Christ to the disciples (John 16:12–14) that the Spirit would at one and the same time "glorify" him by recalling what Christ had taught and done in the past and would for the future lead them into the whole truth by teaching them what they had not been capable of receiving before. But the means by which the Holy Spirit accomplished this were the ones enumerated in the four criteria of apostolic continuity (→2:42): apostolic "doctrine" (διδαχή), apostolic "fellowship" (κοινωνία) (→11:29), apostolic "breaking of bread" (→20:7) and the other sacraments (→22:16), and apostolic "prayer" and worship (→4:24–30). But the first among these four criteria, in this listing at any rate, was "doctrine."

"Doctrine" would, moreover, continue to be seen as a distinctive characteristic of the movement, whether the reactions to it were positive or negative. Sergius Paulus manifested an interest in hearing "the word of God," and he witnessed the encounter between the apostles and the sorcerer named Bar-Jesus or Elymas (→13:8–11). But instead of dismissing the encounter in the way that Pharaoh had waved aside the encounter between his sorcerers and Aaron (Exod. 7:10–13), Sergius Paulus, "when he saw what was done, believed, being astonished at the doctrine of the Lord [ἐκπλησσόμενος ἐπὶ τῇ διδαχῇ τοῦ κυρίου]" (13:12 AV). But "doctrine" could have a negative impact as well. When Paul came to Athens and encountered Epicurean and Stoic philosophers, "some said, 'What would this babbler say?' Others said, 'He seems to be a preacher of foreign divinities [ξένων δαιμονίων δοκεῖ καταγγελεὺς εἶναι]'—because he preached Jesus and the resurrection" (→17:18). Whatever their impression of the "babbler" and of the content of his message may have been initially, under direct questioning on the Areopagus it all came down once again to "doctrine": "May we know what *this new doctrine* [καινὴ . . . διδαχή], whereof thou speakest, is? For thou bringest certain strange things to our ears: we would know therefore what these things mean" (17:19–20 AV).

Another form of negative impact of "doctrine," and in some respects one that was even more dangerous than rejecting it, was trivializing it, by the glib dismissal, "We will hear you on this subject some other time" (17:32 NEB). Significantly, two instances of this particular reaction in the narrative of the book of Acts came from political figures (→25:11), who seemed not only to reason (correctly) that questions of doctrine were outside their official purview (→28:31), but also that they were by definition purely technical, "merely theological," and therefore irrelevant. Gallio refused to intervene in the dispute

9. Niceno-Constantinopolitan Creed 9 (*CCF* 1:163).

between Paul and the Jews, on the grounds that their disagreement was "bickering about words and names and your Jewish law" (18:15 NEB). Similarly, Festus reported to King Agrippa that the dispute of the Jews with Paul involved "certain points of dispute with him about their own superstition and about one Jesus, who was dead, but whom Paul asserted to be alive." Caught as he was within the box of raison d'état, Festus concluded that he was "at a loss how to investigate these questions" (25:18–20). There was a certain similarity, but also a profound difference, between these political reactions to the doctrine of the resurrection of Christ (→2:31) and the philosophical ones (17:32).

Being as important as it obviously was to the early Christian community, "doctrine" called for the concern with "accuracy" (ἀκρίβεια) that was manifested by Aquila (and Priscilla; →18:24–26b), and then (after correction) by Apollos, in this narrative. Conversely, departure from such accuracy, particularly after appropriate instruction and admonition, was a matter of enormous gravity. That was what made controversy about doctrine (→15:2) such serious business, altogether different in kind from even "sharp contention" about procedure and administration (15:37–39). Therefore in the scene that is personally the most touching (→21:13–14) in the entire narrative of Acts, Paul not only expressed, more deeply than anywhere else in Acts, his personal feelings for the elders of Ephesus; but he also warned them—in language that is reminiscent of his warnings to the Romans about those who "cause divisions and offences contrary to the doctrine which ye have learned" (Rom. 16:17 AV) and to Timothy about "deceitful spirits and doctrines of demons" (1 Tim. 4:1)—of the grave danger of false doctrine: "And from among your own selves will arise men *speaking perverse things* [λαλοῦντες διεστραμμένα], to draw away the disciples after them" (20:30). In the light of such concern for doctrine and its correctness (ἀκρίβεια), the preoccupation of the later church councils with heresy and with the precise formulation of the church's teachings does not seem to have been an aberration, for in the formula of the Synod of Constantinople of 1351, "In a confession, accuracy [ἀκρίβεια] in all respects is preserved and required."[10]

The Ministry of Women

18:24–26b A Jew named Apollos, a native of Alexandria [TPR: Apollonius of Alexandria]. . . . When Priscilla and Aquila heard him, they [TPR: When Aquila heard him, he] took him and expounded to him the way of God more accurately.

The absence of the name Priscilla from this passage in the TPR is one of the grounds for ascribing to it an "antifeminist" bias[11] (although it should

10. Synod of Constantinople (1351) Tome 7 (*CCF* 1:338).
11. Witherington 1984.

be noted that the TPR does include "and their daughters" (καὶ αἱ θυγατέρες αὐτῶν) as "prophesying" at 2:17 and the account of the daughters of Philip who were "prophesying" at 21:9–10). Not only is Priscilla's name included in the Alexandrian Text of this passage, but it comes first.

In the case of the λόγιος Apollos (TPR: Apollonius of Alexandria), who is familiar also from Paul's reference to him in his denunciation of party spirit at Corinth (1 Cor. 1:12), the function of instructing a man and introducing more "accuracy" (ἀκρίβεια) into his theology (→18:24–26a), even though he was admittedly "eloquent . . . , well versed in the scriptures" and already "taught accurately the things concerning Jesus" (18:24–25), was carried out jointly by Priscilla and her husband Aquila (listed in that order here), who together "took him and expounded to him the way of God more accurately" (προσελάβοντο αὐτὸν καὶ ἀκριβέστερον αὐτῷ ἐξέθεντο τὴν ὁδὸν τοῦ θεοῦ), the verbs here being plural, though singular in the TPR (18:26).

Throughout his two-volume work, and especially at the beginning of his Gospel and again at its conclusion, the author of Luke-Acts seems to have made a special point of celebrating the ministry of women and of hearing and recording also treble voices.[12] That is uniquely true of the voice of the Blessed Virgin Mary, whom the Liturgy of Saint John Chrysostom celebrates as "higher than the cherubim, more glorious beyond compare than the seraphim"[13]—and also more glorious than the disciples and apostles (→1:14). The Magnificat (Luke 1:47–55) was an act of prophesying in both senses, not only of predicting what was to come in time but also of proclaiming what preeminently and eternally is.

Moreover, it was a treble voice, that of Mary's kinswoman Elizabeth, that anticipated not only the central clauses of the most widely used of all Marian prayers, the Ave Maria, whose opening words also come from the salutation of the angel (→12:7) in the Vulgate of Luke, *Ave Maria, gratia plena* (Luke 1:28 Vulgate), but what John Henry Newman admitted to be "an addition, greater perhaps than any before or since, to the letter of the primitive faith,"[14] the designation of the Virgin Mary as Theotokos, Mother of God, by the Third Ecumenical Council, the Council of Ephesus in 431.[15] It was from Elizabeth that there came "a loud cry, 'Blessed are you among women, and blessed is the fruit of your womb! And why is this granted me, that *the mother of my Lord* should come to me?'" (Luke 1:42–43), especially if Greek ὁ κύριος μου ("my Lord") is taken to be a rendering of the Hebrew and Aramaic *Adonai* ("my Lord") as a substitute for the Tetragrammaton *YHWH*.

At the conclusion of his Gospel, Luke made a point of specifying that after the resurrection of Christ "it was Mary Magdalene and Joanna and Mary the

12. Cadbury 1958, 263–65; Witherington 1998, 334–39.
13. Liturgy of Saint John Chrysostom II.F.6 (*CCF* 1:288).
14. Newman 1989, 303.
15. Formula of Union of the Council of Ephesus (*CCF* 1:168–70).

mother of James and *the other women with them who told this to the apostles*"
(Luke 24:10); this made them, in a term employed (though sparingly) by both
Augustine and Jerome, *apostolorum apostolae* ("female apostles to the male
apostles").[16]

In some passages of the New Testament, the desire for "inclusive language"
has prompted the translators of the NRSV, for example, to add "and sisters"
where the original has only "brothers," therefore to translate ἰδόντες παρεκάλεσαν
τοὺς ἀδελφούς with "when they had seen and encouraged *the brothers and sisters* there" (16:40 NRSV). Nevertheless it is unavoidably clear both from the
original words in the second chapter of Joel and from the quotation of them in
the sermon of Peter at Pentecost that it was to be "sons *and daughters*" (2:17)
and "both men *and women*" (2:18) on whom God "will pour out my Spirit"
and who "shall prophesy." Conversely, the opposition to the Way (→11:26)
likewise involved persecution by "the devout women of high standing and the
leading men of the city" without gender discrimination (13:50).

At the same time, all of the original twelve (→5:29a) "whom he had chosen"
(1:2) in his sovereign authority, which transcended the prejudices and practices
of his own time (or any other time), were men. And when the apostasy of
Judas presented the body of the apostles with the need to assign his ἐπισκοπή
(Ps. 109:8 LXX) to another, and in the process presented them with a unique
opportunity to begin to redress the gender balance and undo the damage, the
specification for the choice explicitly stipulated that it must be "one of the
men [τῶν . . . ἀνδρῶν] who have accompanied us during all the time that the
Lord Jesus went in and out among us" (1:21). In keeping with that stipulation
"they [TPR: he] put forward two, Joseph called Barsabbas, who was surnamed
Justus, and Matthias" (1:23)—and neither Mary Magdalene nor even Mary
the Mother of God (→1:14).

Any interpretation of the ministry of women that strives to be responsible
to the authority of Holy Scripture and of living tradition, rather than to take
the easy way of uncritically following either the safety of the status quo or the
trendiness of the Zeitgeist, does seem to be obliged to find a way to encompass
and to come to terms with both—not one but both—of these theological reali-
ties in the text of the book of Acts.

---

16. Blaise and Chirat 1954, 89.

ACTS 19

19:1 TPR Although Paul of his own counsel wanted to go to Jerusalem, the Spirit told him to cross over into Asia. Passing through the upper country, he came to Ephesus.

The first sentence of 19:1 is unique to the TPR, and evidently picks up the narrative of an earlier chapter, in which Paul and Silas were "forbidden by the Holy Spirit to speak the word in Asia" (16:6). Although the thrust of the second half of Acts is clearly directed to Europe—Athens in chapter 17 and above all Rome in chapter 28—"Asia," that is, Asia Minor, is essential to the plan, overriding any personal preferences of Paul "of his own counsel" (κατὰ τὴν ἰδίαν βουλήν) to go to Jerusalem, for what mattered was not his personal preferences, but "the whole βουλή of God" (20:27).

The Abiding Theological Significance of Saint John the Forerunner

19:2–3 TPR He said to the disciples, "Did you receive the Holy Spirit when you believed?" But they said to him, "No, we have never even heard that some have received the Holy Spirit." Paul said to them, "Then have you been baptized?" They said, "Into the baptism of John."

A reader coming to the book of Acts from the reading of the Gospel of Luke, as Theophilus (1:1) would have done (Luke 1:3), would find many profound elements of continuity between the two narratives (→1:2–3; →6:8; →7:59–60); but one element of continuity for which the Gospel would not have prepared him was the prominent place still being occupied by Saint John the Baptist, the "Forerunner" (ὁ πρόδρομος), here in the narrative of Acts.[1]

---

1. Wilckens 1961, 101–5.

Although the life of Saint John the Baptist figures prominently in each of the Gospels, Saint Luke's is the only Gospel that tells how it began: Saint Matthew has the annunciation to Joseph of the coming birth of Jesus to Mary (Matt. 1:18–25), but introduces John the Baptist as full grown (Matt. 3:1); but Saint Luke, who describes the annunciation as being addressed by the angel Gabriel to the Virgin Mary rather than to Joseph (Luke 1:26–38), leads up to it with a parallel annunciation (unique to his Gospel) by the angel Gabriel to Zechariah of the impending birth of his son John (Luke 1:8–23), including the prescription that "you shall call his name John" (Luke 1:13, 63), and then brings the two expectant mothers together in the visitation of Mary to her "relative" (συγγενίς) Elizabeth (Luke 1:36). This visit was the occasion for the Magnificat (Luke 1:39–56), which in a few patristic citations of these verses is even attributed to Elizabeth. The only detailed account of John's martyrdom (→14:22) at the behest of King Herod, including Jesus' reaction to it, is in Saint Matthew (Matt. 14:1–13); after a mention of Herod's imprisonment of John (Luke 3:19–20), Saint Luke's only specific reference to this martyrdom, which is Herod's question, "John I beheaded; but who is this about whom I hear such things?" (Luke 9:9), treats it as a fait accompli and uses it to speak about Jesus rather than about John. Unique to Saint Luke's Gospel, on the other hand, is the report that "the people were filled with expectation, and all were questioning in their hearts concerning John, whether he might be the Messiah" (Luke 3:15 NRSV).

That report may perhaps be seen as a presage and an explanation of the apparently widespread survival of what almost seems to have been a continuing cult of John, in some kind of combination—a paradoxical combination, as it would certainly have to seem to later orthodox Christians—with an adherence to Jesus as the Messiah. Here in Ephesus, for example, Saint Paul "found some *disciples*" (τινας μαθητάς), evidently meaning "disciples of Jesus Christ," whom he addressed as ones who earlier had become *believers*, presumably believers in Jesus Christ. Despite these titles, they had nevertheless been baptized only into the baptism of John. In the preceding chapter that combination produces this surprising, almost shocking, anticlimax in the description of Apollos of Alexandria (18:24–25): "He was an eloquent man, well versed in the scriptures," who "had been instructed in the way of the Lord; and being fervent in spirit, he spoke and taught accurately [ἐδίδασκεν ἀκριβῶς] the things concerning Jesus"—and yet Apollos "knew only the baptism of John" (ἐπιστάμενος μόνον τὸ βάπτισμα Ἰωάννου). This provided the occasion for Priscilla and Aquila to "[take] him and expound . . . to him the way of God more accurately" (→18:24–26b). From the context of the book of Acts as a whole, including the discussion between Saint Paul and the disciples in Ephesus here in chapter 19, it seems justifiable to conclude that such a "more accurate" explanation would have had to include a clarification of (1) the historical and epoch-defining position of John, (2) his function as the "forerunner" (ὁ πρόδρομος), and (3) the theological significance of his baptism—a more than trivial course correction:

1. As Luke Timothy Johnson observes, "Luke uses the baptism of John to demarcate the beginning of Jesus' ministry," both in the book of Acts and in his Gospel.[2] He does so here in Acts at the very beginning, when the basic qualification of the candidates to replace Judas was said to be "one of the men [ἀνδρῶν] [→18:24–26b] who have accompanied us during all the time that the Lord Jesus went in and out among us, *beginning from the baptism of John*" (1:21–22), which apparently means "beginning from the time of Jesus' own baptism by John." Again, Saint Peter dates the beginning of the preaching of the "good news of peace" with "the baptism which John preached: how God anointed Jesus of Nazareth with the Holy Spirit and with power" (10:36–38). This connection between the baptism of Jesus at the hands of Saint John the Forerunner and his being anointed with the Holy Spirit and with power appears already in Saint Luke's Gospel (Luke 3:21–22), where it is followed immediately by the report that thereupon "Jesus . . . began his ministry" (Luke 3:23). The historical and epoch-defining position of John is identified by Jesus in Saint Luke's Gospel: "The law and the prophets were until John; since then the good news of the kingdom of God is preached [εὐαγγελίζεται]" (Luke 16:16). And it is Saint Luke who has Jesus reinforce that historical position with the declaration, "I tell you, among those born of women none is greater than John," and then, lest that be misinterpreted (as it obviously would be and probably was), quickly with the clarification of John's relation to the new epoch: "Yet he who is least in the kingdom of God is greater than he" (Luke 7:28).

2. The title "the forerunner" (ὁ πρόδρομος) became the standard way of identifying John the Baptist in patristic literature[3] and on icons. On the iconostasis of an Orthodox church, the Forerunner is shown in the *Deēsis* (δέησις) on one side of Christ, with the Theotokos on the other side.[4] The title "forerunner" appears in only one passage of the New Testament (Heb. 6:20), where it does not refer to John as the forerunner of Jesus, but to Jesus himself as "a forerunner on our behalf, having become a high priest for ever after the order of Melchizedek." But as a verb rather than a noun, the substance of the title is anticipated in the Gospel of Luke by the promise of the angel Gabriel to John's father Zechariah:

> And he will turn many of the sons of Israel to the Lord their God,
> and *he will go before him* [προσελεύσεται ἐνώπιον αὐτοῦ] in the spirit and
> power of Elijah. (Luke 1:16–17)

2. Johnson 1992, 37.
3. *PGL* 1144.
4. Pelikan 1990, 122–28; Onasch and Schnieper 1997, 228.

The title is also anticipated by the Baptist's promising that "he who is mightier than I is coming" (Luke 3:16). Here in Acts the identification of that function of John as forerunner is put not into his mouth, as it is in Luke's Gospel (Luke 3:15), but is transferred into the words of Jesus to the disciples immediately before the ascension (1:5), and then into Saint Peter's recollection of the words as words of Jesus (11:16). Saint Paul expands on it in his message at Antioch of Pisidia, this time reversing that process by transferring a question attributed to Jesus in the Gospels (Matt. 16:15) to John: "As John was finishing his course, he said, 'What do you suppose that I am?'" and then answering the question with a saying that is attributed to John in the Gospel (Luke 3:16), "I am not he. No, but after me one is coming [ἔρχεται μετ' ἐμέ], the sandals of whose feet I am not worthy to untie" (13:25).

3. But as is evident from the reference to "John's baptism" in almost every mention of him in Acts, including the present one, and from the (almost uniquely Christian) surname ὁ βαπτιστής, which could even be used as a title for him without his personal name,[5] it was not primarily the person of John as, by contrast with Jesus (Luke 7:33–34), the supreme embodiment of the ascetic ideal within the New Testament (→24:25b) that marked him and made him special, nor yet his message of repentance (→26:20), which earned him such notoriety and brought on his martyrdom, but specifically the baptism he administered to "the multitudes that came out to be baptized by him" (Luke 3:7), which would include Jesus among "all the people [who] were baptized" (Luke 3:21–22). This passage in chapter 19 and most of the other references show that for the author of Acts and for the persons portrayed in Acts, the central question about the baptism practiced by John was how it differed from the baptism subsequently commanded by Christ; this would continue to be a central theological question about the baptism of John, as, for example, between the Protestant Reformers and the Council of Trent.[6] One point of differentiation was specified by the very first reference to it in Acts, which is the words of Jesus: "Which, he said, 'you have heard from me, for John baptized with water, but before many days you shall be baptized with the Holy Spirit'" (1:5); those words were repeated later almost verbatim by Peter as "the word of the Lord" (11:16). John's water baptism was thus a foreshadowing of the fullness of the Spirit baptism that was about to come at Pentecost (→2:1), and the conjunction "but" (δέ) in both places seems to indicate not only a contrast between the two baptisms but also the overshadowing of the first by the second. At the same time it was, of course, also the case that not only did "John baptize with water," but so did the church (2:38–39; 8:36), in obedience

5. BDAG 165; *PGL* 288.
6. H. Houbant in *DTC* 8:646–56.

to the command and great commission of Christ (Matt. 28:19–20). Similarly, Paul's characterization of the baptism of John as "a baptism of repentance to all the people of Israel" (βάπτισμα μετανοίας παντὶ τῷ λαῷ Ἰσραήλ) (13:24) is clearly meant to contrast it with what was to come "after" John. But the appearance, near the beginning of the book of Acts, of the formula "repent, and be baptized every one of you in the name of Jesus Christ for the forgiveness of your sins; and you shall receive the gift of the Holy Spirit" (2:38), would argue for the interpretation that the emphasis of the contrast in Paul's characterization was not on the term "repentance" but on "the people of Israel," because John had addressed his summons chiefly to Jews, except perhaps for the "soldiers" described by Saint Luke (Luke 3:14), while Jesus' command to make disciples and baptize (→1:2–3) now encompassed "all nations" (Matt. 28:19), whose "universal restoration" (ἀποκατάστασις) and inclusion in the kingdom of God was the burden of the book of Acts (→3:21)—yet always in association, through Christ, with the unbreakable covenant already conferred by God upon the people of Israel (→3:25) and with "the hope of Israel," which, to the very end, Paul insisted was the real reason that he was "bound with this chain" (28:20).

19:8 "The kingdom of God" is identified here as the theme of Paul's preaching; yet the phrase "the kingdom of God" was far less prominent in Paul's Epistles than it was in the Gospels (→28:23). On the other hand, the phrase "spoke boldly, arguing and pleading" is a recognizable characterization of the Paul who is repeatedly described as possessing great powers of persuasion and a burning desire to communicate (→9:1–4; →24:1–2).

19:9 "The Way" is a standard term in Acts for speaking about the Christian movement (→11:26).

19:11–20 Paul is depicted here as having shared in the extraordinary powers of Peter, Stephen, and other apostles, powers that were made only more special by this pathetic—and slightly humorous—attempt to imitate them (→6:8; →13:8–11; →28:14).

19:21 Now after these events Paul resolved in the Spirit to pass through Macedonia and Achaia and go to Jerusalem, saying, "After I have been there, I must also see Rome."

In this saying of Paul, more pithily than in any other single sentence, the book of Acts shows itself to be "a tale of two cities," Jerusalem and Rome (→22:27; →28:14).

Images of the Divine?

19:26 TPR Saying that gods made with human hands are not gods [λέγων ὅτι οὐκ εἰσὶν θεοὶ οἱ διὰ χειρῶν ἀνθρώπων γινόμενοι].

Paul's denunciation in Athens of the pagan idea "that the Deity is like gold, or silver, or stone, a representation by the art and imagination of man [χαράγματι τέχνης καὶ ἐνθυμήσεως ἀνθρώπου]" (17:29)—which was brought on when "his spirit was provoked within him as he saw that the city was full of idols" (17:16), because "nowhere else were so many objects of worship to be seen" as there in Athens[7]—was an expression of the unanimous disgust and consistent horror of Jewish and Christian monotheism at the sight of idolatry and polytheism (→19:28). Already at Lystra, the sight of "the priest of Zeus" wanting to bring sacrifices to him and Barnabas as though they were Hermes and Zeus, "the gods . . . come down to us in the likeness of men," had the effect that Barnabas and Paul "tore their garments and rushed out among the multitude, crying, 'Men, why are you doing this!'" (14:11–15). And here he seems to have acquired a measure of notoriety for "saying that gods made with human hands are not gods."

In this revulsion they stood in unbroken continuity with the prophets and psalms of Israel:

> The idols of the nations are silver and gold,
> > the work of men's hands [ἔργα χειρῶν ἀνθρώπων].
> They have a mouth, but do not speak;
> > they have eyes, but do not see. . . .
> Those who make them are like them;
> > so are all who trust in them. (Ps. 115:4–5, 8 LXX)

With exquisite sarcasm the prophet Isaiah portrayed what Paul was to describe as idolatrous "representation by the art and imagination of man" at work, as a craftsman fells a tree, warms himself by its fire and bakes his bread over it, "and the rest of it he makes into a graven god, and falls down to it and prays to it and says, 'Deliver me, for thou art my god!'" (Isa. 44:12–17 LXX).

This revulsion at pagan images and rejection of their underlying assumptions remained central to the Christian case against paganism during the following centuries. On the basis of the Second Commandment, "You shall not make for yourself an idol, or any likeness of anything that is in heaven above, or that is in the earth beneath, or that is in the water under the earth; you shall not bow down to them or serve them; for I the Lord your God am a jealous God" (Exod. 20:4–5 LXX), Clement of Alexandria drew the sharpest possible contrast between image-making and authentic worship when he maintained that "the image is only dead matter shaped by the craftsman's hand. But *we*

---

7. Chrysostom, *Homilies on Acts* 38 (*NPNF*[1] 11:232).

have no sensible [i.e., tangible] image [made] of sensible matter, but an image that is perceived by the mind alone—the God, who alone is truly God."[8] When the empress Constantia, having become a Christian, asked church historian Eusebius to have an image of Jesus Christ produced for her, he replied: "I do not know what has impelled you to command that an image of our Savior be drawn. Which image of Christ do you want? Is it a true and unchangeable one, portraying his countenance truly, or the one which he assumed on our behalf when he took on the appearance of the form of a slave [Phil. 2:7]?" Whichever choice she made in that dilemma, the very idea of imaging Christ was a contradiction in terms.[9]

And yet meanwhile the very same church that was denouncing idolatry had itself begun to create images—of saints, of angels, of Mary the Theotokos (→1:14), and even of Jesus Christ, though not of the Godhead as such. Just when and where became one of the principal points of conflict in the iconoclastic controversies of the eighth and ninth centuries. In addition to the pedagogical argument that images of Christ and the saints could serve as Gospels in color and as "Bibles for the illiterate" who could not read biblical narratives and saints' lives for themselves, the most sophisticated theological argument that there could legitimately be Christian images and, to use Paul's phrase, "representation[s] by the art and imagination of man" (17:29) was that since the issuance of the Second Commandment God himself had provided the human race with an accurate and authentic Image, for the sake of whom he had prohibited all those inauthentic images.[10] Paul taught in the Epistle to the Colossians (1) that Christ was from eternity "the image of the invisible God" (εἰκὼν τοῦ θεοῦ τοῦ ἀοράτου) (Col. 1:15) and (2) that in Jesus Christ "the whole fulness of deity dwells bodily" (κατοικεῖ πᾶν τὸ πλήρωμα τῆς θεότητος σωματικῶς) (Col. 2:9). The full implications of that "dual proclamation" (διπλοῦν κήρυγμα), as Saint Athanasius termed it,[11] became the subject matter of the decrees of the first six ecumenical councils, first confessing the dogma of the Trinity and therefore the full deity of the Son, and then affirming the relation between that full deity of the Son and the no less fully human nature of the man Jesus. In response to Eusebius's dilemma, therefore, the seventh ecumenical council, at Nicea in 787, followed those six councils when it asserted the legitimacy of images of Christ on the basis of the doctrine of *communicatio idiomatum* (→20:28b): the one Lord Jesus Christ in two natures could be imaged, because his divine nature dwelt σωματικῶς in the imageable and circumscribed form of his human nature.[12] That was why the Blessed Virgin Mary was indeed Theotokos, Mother of God (→1:14), and could be imaged, as could the apostles and

8. Clement of Alexandria, *Exhortation to the Greeks* 4.51.6 (*ANF* 2:186).
9. Florovsky 1972–89, 2:101–19.
10. Pelikan 1990, 67–98.
11. Athanasius, *Against Apollinarius* 1 (PG 26:1112).
12. *Chr. Trad.* 2:129–30.

the other saints. The imaging of the angels, who were by their nature invisible but who did assume visible forms as required, also here in the narratives of the book of Acts (7:30; 10:3), so that they could actually be referred to as "men" (1:10), is of special interest here in Acts, because of report that "gazing at [Saint Stephen the protomartyr, on trial for his life], all who sat in the council saw that his face was like the face of an angel" (6:15), for how could they have known what "the face of an angel" looked like unless it had been imaged and portrayed somewhere through "representation by the art and imagination of man" (17:29) already in Judaism (→12:7)?

"We Believe in One God": Monotheism in Conflict with Polytheism and Idolatry

19:28 Great is Artemis of the Ephesians!

The book of Acts is not only the one New Testament book that describes in great detail the Christian conflict with magic, sorcery, superstition, and the other Satanic powers (→13:8–11), but also the one in which we can see with the greatest clarity the opposition of biblical monotheism to Greco-Roman polytheism and idolatry in action, "not only to popular Hellenistic folk religion (cf. 14:11) but to the idolatry of pantheistic Stoicism and other philosophies as well."[13] Luke also tells us more about Greco-Roman religion than any other New Testament writer, even the Apostle Paul. This is the only New Testament book to refer to any pagan deities by name: Zeus and Hermes in an earlier chapter (14:12–13)[14] and Artemis here (19:23–35). (All three of these were rendered in the Vulgate and then in the AV by their Roman names, Jupiter, Mercury, and Diana, just as at 17:22 "the Areopagus" [ὁ Ἄρειος πάγος] became "Mars' Hill" in the AV.) It is also the only book to mention the mysterious and nameless ἄγνωστος θεός honored by the Athenians (→17:23), which is indeed the solitary instance in the New Testament of the word ἄγνωστος. In the case of the goddess Artemis, this account of the perceived threat posed by the missionary work of the apostles to the lucrative commerce in golden idols also provides insight into the combination of religious worship and civic pride that was associated with the cult of local deities (or of local manifestations of the Olympic deities). As with the slave girl who was being exploited for the purposes of divination (16:16–19), so here with the rioting goldsmiths, the apostles seem, much to the regret of later Christian activists and social reformers, to have been concerned exclusively with the religious rather than with the socioeconomic dimension of the situation (→4:32).

13. Krodel 1986, 337.
14. The reference to "Hermes" in Rom. 16:14 is to a human being (and a Christian at that) bearing that name.

But the worship of the Olympians Zeus and Hermes (14:8–18) affected the apostles even more personally, evoking not only the disgust that Jewish Christians instinctively felt whenever they found a place "full of idols" (κατείδωλον) (17:16), but the shock of finding that they themselves were being made the objects of idolatrous worship. That phenomenon appears at three distinct points in the narrative of Acts. Cornelius, though "a devout man who feared God with all his household, gave alms liberally to the people, and prayed constantly to God" (10:2), was so overwhelmed at meeting Peter that he "fell down at his feet and worshiped him. But Peter lifted him up, saying, 'Stand up; I too am a man just like you'" (10:25–26 TPR). At Lystra, Barnabas and Paul reacted by tearing their clothes, rushing out into the crowd, and shouting, "We also are men, of like nature with you" (14:11–15). And at Malta, the fickle natives saw the attack of the viper on Paul as evidence that "no doubt this man is a murderer" (28:4), and then "changed their minds" 180 degrees to see his survival of the venomous attack as evidence "that he was a god" (28:6). This readiness of the superficial rabble to make an idol of a mere mortal expressed itself with disastrous consequences in the case of King Herod, whom they hailed with the cry, "The sounds of a god, and not of man!" Because Herod did not react to this idolization with rejection as the apostles did, but in complete contrast with them failed to "give God the glory," the result was that "an angel of the Lord smote him, . . . and coming down from the throne, he was eaten alive by worms and died" (12:21–23 TPR).

The supreme cautionary tale for all time of the confrontation between biblical monotheism and idolatry happened at Mount Sinai. After the one true God, on the basis of the covenant (→3:25), had led the people of Israel out of polytheistic Egypt and while he was engaged in giving the law to his servant Moses on the mountain, they "thrust him aside, and in their hearts they turned to Egypt, saying to Aaron, 'Make for us gods to go before us; as for this Moses who led us out from the land of Egypt, we do not know what has become of him.' And they made a calf in those days, and offered a sacrifice to the idol and rejoiced in the works of their hands" (7:39–41). It was, on the other hand, the precise opposite of this idolatry when the dying protomartyr Stephen "prayed, 'Lord Jesus, receive my spirit'" (7:59) to the Lord Jesus who, when dying, had prayed, "Father, into thy hands I commit my spirit!" (Luke 23:46)—for that was a confession of the one true God (→8:37).

ACTS 20

20:5-6 Luke here records another of the we-passages, even, according to some interpreters, a sailor's travelogue-journal (→27:1; →27:24; →28:14), although it is not clear whether that includes the visits to Macedonia (20:1) and to Greece (20:2).

The Breaking of Bread

20:7 On the first day of the week, . . . we were gathered together to break bread.

This is one of the five references in the Acts of the Apostles (2:42, 46; 20:7, 11; 27:35) to "the breaking of bread" (ἡ κλάσις τοῦ ἄρτου), but it is probably safer and "more accurate" (ἀκριβέστερον) (18:26) to interpret at least one and perhaps as many as three of these in a noneucharistic sense.

When, in the maritime travelogue with which the book concludes, Paul "took bread, and giving thanks to God in the presence of all he broke it and began to eat" (λαβὼν ἄρτον εὐχαρίστησεν τῷ θεῷ ἐνώπιον πάντων καὶ κλάσας ἤρξατο ἐσθίειν) (27:35), there are enough parallels to the four accounts of the institution of the Lord's Supper by Christ on the night in which he was betrayed (Matt. 26:26–29; Mark 14:22–26; Luke 22:14–20; 1 Cor. 11:23–26), and especially of the last of these accounts (which was almost certainly the first to be written down)—"took bread," "gave thanks," "broke it"—to remind any reader of the Eucharist. But such parallels can be misleading, for εὐχαριστεῖν is also the verb that Luke puts into the mouth of the Pharisee who was moved to "thank [God] that I am not like other men" (Luke 18:11). In the context, moreover, this use of εὐχαριστεῖν is part of the account of how "Paul urged them all to take some food" (27:33), because "it will give you strength" (27:34)—"them all" and "in the presence of all" both referring to the motley crew of his shipmates, which

216

would seem to have included a majority of nonbelievers as well as "some other prisoners [and] a centurion of the Augustan Cohort" (27:1), who would not have been eligible to share in the eucharistic breaking of bread. From the way he elsewhere restricted the celebration and reception of the Lord's Supper (1 Cor. 11:27–34), it would appear that he was not celebrating it as part of his admonition to all his shipmates to take some nourishment after the shipwreck.

Similarly, the description of the early Christian community, "and day by day, attending the temple together and breaking bread in their homes, they partook of food with glad and generous hearts" (2:46), does carry a reminder of the clearly eucharistic reference to "the breaking of bread" a few verses earlier (2:42); Paul's words about "the church in their house" (1 Cor. 16:19) suggest that there is a contrast between their "attending the temple together" as Jews and their "breaking bread [of the Eucharist] in their homes" as Christians (→7:47–48), because "the household . . . will increasingly be mentioned as the locus for cult activities."[1] Then the words "they partook of food with glad and generous hearts" would have to be a reference to an *agapē* meal in the home as the setting for the Eucharist. On the other hand, it does seem somewhat forced to read the general words "they partook of food with glad and generous hearts" in this passage in so narrow and specifically "sacramental" a way. The reference here in chapter 20 a few verses later, "and when Paul had gone up and had broken bread and eaten" (20:11), coming right after the present verse, would then have to be taken to mean that in addition to (or instead of) the communal Eucharist of this verse Paul celebrated a private Mass, which does seem to be an extremely anachronistic straining of the sense of both verses.

But exclusion of one, two, or three of these reference makes the two remaining passages about the breaking of bread all the more precious. Together with doctrine, fellowship, and prayer, "the breaking of bread" was one of the four marks of apostolic continuity defined earlier (→2:42). It does seem curious that, along with the Eucharist, there is no explicit reference among these four criteria to baptism, which is much more prominent in Acts than is the Eucharist (→22:16). But if it is a legitimate exegesis of a reference to one of the saving events of the life, death, and resurrection of Christ to extrapolate from it to the entire kerygma as set out in the rule of faith rather than to invoke the argument from silence as a limitation (→8:37), it could also be legitimate, in a consideration of the forces of continuity that made the church "one, holy, catholic, and apostolic" (→2:42), to take "the breaking of bread" as broadly as possible to include, in addition to the Eucharist itself, the still inchoate but already developing sacramental system, therefore at this point at least baptism (→22:16), the laying-on of hands as it would eventually become part both of chrismation-confirmation and of ordination (→6:6), and the forgiveness of postbaptismal sins through penance and absolution (→26:20), with, eventually, matrimony as "sacrament" (μυστήριον) (Eph. 5:32).

1. Johnson 1992, 59.

Not a part of the book of Acts, but appropriately seen as a kind of preface to it, the concluding chapter of the Gospel according to Saint Luke serves as a transition from what in the opening verse of Acts Luke calls "all that Jesus began to do and teach" (1:1) to the narratives about the apostles. And therefore when, in that concluding chapter of his Gospel, he describes how as Jesus "was at table with them, he took the bread and blessed, and broke it, and gave it to them" (Luke 24:30), Luke is preparing that transition. Even and especially after the ascension, when Jesus was no longer visible to them in physical form (→1:11), it would remain more true than ever, throughout Acts and for all time to come, that "he was known to them in the breaking of the bread" (ἐγνώσθη αὐτοῖς ἐν τῇ κλάσει τοῦ ἄρτου) (Luke 24:35).

20:7–12 This serious, potentially tragic, episode does have a touch of humor in it (→12:13–16).

20:17 Those who are identified by the title "elder" (πρεσβύτερος) in 20:17 seem to be the same ones who are identified by the title "bishop" (ἐπίσκοπος) a few verses later (20:28), leading to the conclusion of the Lima Text, quoted earlier, that "the New Testament does not describe a single pattern of ministry which might serve as a blueprint or continuing norm for all future ministry in the church. . . . [Only] during the second and third centuries, a threefold pattern of bishop, presbyter, and deacon became established as the pattern of ordained ministry throughout the church"[2] (→6:2–4).

20:21 Testifying both to Jews and to Greeks of repentance to God and of faith in our Lord Jesus Christ.

The linkage here in Paul's ministry between "repentance" (μετάνοια) and "faith" (πίστις) could trace its continuity all the way back to the inauguration (Mark 1:15) of the ministry of Jesus (→26:18; →28:14).

20:24 The gospel of the grace of God.

As was his practice also in the epistles, Paul was using "gospel" here to refer to the message of salvation, not (as in the titles of the first four books of the New Testament) to the narrative of the life and teachings of Jesus (→6:2–4; →8:25).

20:25 Luke provides another reference to "the kingdom" of God as the content of Paul's preaching, even though it is not prominent in his epistles (→28:23).

2. Lima Text: Baptism, Eucharist, Ministry 3.19 (*CCF* 3:832).

20:27 I did not shrink from declaring to you the whole counsel of God.

The emphasis here on "the *whole* counsel" (πᾶσαν τὴν βουλήν) would suggest that part of "accuracy" (ἀκρίβεια) in the presentation of the Christian message was the obligation not only not to pervert it, but also not to omit some part of it, for heresy has often been a concentration on one aspect, in itself correct, of "the whole counsel," at the expense of the message "as a whole" (καθ᾽ ὅλον)—the etymology of "catholic" (→8:37; →13:48; →18:24–26a).

The Theological Import of Textual Variants

20:28a variant To shepherd the church [of God/of the Lord/of the Lord and God] that he obtained with [the blood of his own/his own blood/his blood/the blood of his own Son]. [ποιμαίνειν τὴν ἐκκλησίαν τοῦ (θεοῦ/κυρίου/κυρίου καὶ θεοῦ), ἣν περιεποιήσατο διὰ (τοῦ αἵματος τοῦ ἰδίου/ἰδίου αἵματος/αἵματος αὐτοῦ/αἵματος τοῦ ἰδίου υἱοῦ)].

Even beyond 20:28, the book of Acts probably contains more textual variants with theological significance than any other book of the Bible, for example, in the decrees of the apostolic council at Jerusalem (→16:4a); most of these textual variants receive individual attention here as part of the commentary on the particular verses where they occur, and therefore are not itemized at this *locus communis*. In addition, as the introduction explained, the Greek text of Acts has been transmitted in two "editions"; one of these, conventionally identified as the "Western Text" but labeled here *textus a patribus receptus* (TPR), does not really fall into the category of ordinary textual variants, but of alternative recensions. It is the one that is regularly being cited here, in keeping with the charge to the commentaries in the series to be "based upon the final form of the text, taken in its canonical context." Likewise, the New Testament, in turn, contains more textual variants—at least partly because it comes in so many more manuscripts—than any other book of Greek and Roman antiquity, probably more than any other book of any historical period.

But except perhaps for the creedal and theological implications of the reading of the TPR, "I believe that Jesus Christ is the Son of God" (→8:37), the present verse is probably the most egregious instance in the entire book of Acts of the theological and dogmatic puzzles that textual criticism can pose. In this one infinitive with object plus relative clause there is a bewildering array of alternate readings, which have considerable theological significance, above all for the doctrine of the relation between the human nature and the divine nature in the one hypostasis of Jesus Christ. Following the textual variants that underlie the AV, the phrase reads: "to feed the church of *God*, which he hath purchased with *his own* blood"; and the Vulgate has *pascere ecclesiam dei, quam acquisivit sanguine suo*. If those readings are to be accepted, such a way of speaking seems to provide unequivocal legitimation for ascribing "blood" to "God," through the interchange of attributes between the divine and the human natures of the one incarnate Son of God (→20:28b).

The textual variants in an even more celebrated passage of the New Testament likewise affect the legitimacy of attributing to "God" the qualities and actions that are predicated of the incarnate Logos and Son of God: "No one has ever seen God. It is *God the only Son*, who is close to the Father's heart, who has made him known" (John 1:18 NRSV). The NRSV's rendering, "God the only Son," translates the Greek reading μονογενὴς θεός (lit., "the only begotten God"); but some manuscripts read ὁ μονογενὴς υἱός ("the only begotten Son"). The former reading does raise theological difficulties for some interpreters, because it appears to posit the equation of "Son" and "God" as unambiguously as does the Nicene Creed with its terminology identifying Jesus Christ the Son as "God from God, light from light, true God from true God" (θεὸν ἐκ θεοῦ, φῶς ἐκ φωτός, θεὸν ἀληθινὸν ἐκ θεοῦ ἀληθινοῦ).[3] It was also the standard way of quoting this passage in such an expositor of the Nicene faith as Gregory of Nyssa.[4] Although it has the weight of the manuscript evidence in its favor and is therefore the reading given in NA[27], modern exegetes and many modern translations have tended to resist its implications.[5] Even the RSV still had "the only Son," with "God" only supplied in a footnote as being contained in "other ancient authorities"; but the NRSV, while still persisting in the RSV's preference for "only" to the AV's "only begotten" as the English for μονογενής,[6] put the translation "God" into the body of the text and relegated the translation of the less "Nicene"-sounding textual variants to a footnote.

There are other such instances of textual variants with theological import in other passages of the New Testament, and they call for careful study.[7] It remains, however, a useful reminder that although textual variants have provided endless particular fuel to theological disputes, of which indeed some of them are themselves a reflection, most textual variants have little or no theological significance in and of themselves; many of them are little more than, for example, fluctuations between τὰ Ἱεροσόλυμα and ἡ Ἱερουσαλήμ as Greek transliterations of the Hebrew and Aramaic name for "Jerusalem." To be sure, even such trivial differences do have a bearing on the understanding of what could be meant by the claim that the Hebrew and Greek text of the Scriptures is "immediately inspired by God, and, by his singular care and providence, *kept pure* in all ages," as the Westminster Confession of Faith and other confessions teach.[8] If, as this doctrine of biblical inspiration insists, that "singular care and providence" of God directed (or even "dictated") the selection of every single word and the composition of every sentence of the original, it must be asked

3. Nicene Creed 2 (*CCF* 1:158–59).
4. Pelikan 1993, 224–25.
5. McReynolds 1981; Fennema 1985, 124–35.
6. On the relation between these translations, see BDAG 658.
7. See Epp and Fee 1981 for discussions of the most significant of these.
8. Westminster Confession of Faith 1.8 (*CCF* 2:607).

why, in keeping the text "pure in all ages," it did not extend to the preservation of all those words and sentences in their original and inspired formulations, down to the individual letters.

"One Christ, One Son, One Lord"

20:28b AV To feed the church of God, which he hath purchased with his own blood.

If, in trying to decide the immensely complicated textual problems raised by this verse (→20:28a), one follows the venerable principle *lectio difficilior praeferenda est* ("the reading that is more difficult to account for is the one to be preferred"), on the reasonable grounds that a scribe would more probably have "corrected" a difficult text by simplifying it than by complicating it still further, it should be translated as the AV translated it: "the church of God, which he hath purchased with his own blood," leaving to the exegetes and the theologians the assignment of explaining how God could be said to have "blood." Their performance of that assignment has led to the doctrine of *communicatio idiomatum* ("interchange of the properties"; ἀντίδοσις τῶν ἰδιομάτων),[9] by which properties or actions belonging to one nature of Christ may be attributed to, or predicated of, the other nature, because of the unity of the single person of the God-man. "He does not hesitate to speak of 'the blood of God,'" Bede explains, "on account of the unity of the person in the two natures of the one Jesus Christ."[10]

This way of speaking about "the blood of God," visible for example already in Tertullian,[11] is not only the source of the old-fashioned English oath "God's blood!"[12] but is reflected elsewhere in the New Testament: "God is light. . . . If we walk in the light, as he is in the light . . . the blood of Jesus Christ his Son [τὸ αἷμα Ἰησοῦ Χριστοῦ τοῦ υἱοῦ αὐτοῦ] cleanseth us from all sin" (1 John 1:5, 7 AV). A similar predication occurs elsewhere in Saint Luke's oeuvre. Saint Elizabeth, mother of Saint John the Forerunner (→19:2–3), greeted the Blessed Virgin Mary as "the mother of my Lord" (Luke 1:43). This becomes the biblical foundation for the liturgical and dogmatic title "Theotokos": "Mother of God" or "the one who gave birth to the one who is God" (→1:14), which was legislated to be the official dogmatic language of the church by the Council of Ephesus in 431: "Therefore we confess one Christ, one Son, one Lord. According to this understanding of the unconfused union, we confess the Holy Virgin to be the Mother of God [θεοτόκον] because God the Word took flesh

9. *ODCC* 386.
10. Bede, *Exposition of the Acts of the Apostles* 20 (PL 92:986).
11. Tertullian, *To His Wife* 3 (*ANF* 4:46).
12. *OED* 2:302.

221

and became man and from his very conception united to himself the temple he took from her."[13]

But in some passages of the New Testament the interchange works in the opposite direction as well, when properties that are appropriate to the divine nature are attached to the human nature, once again because of the unity of the person of the God-man. The most well-known instance of this occurs in the familiar creedal hymn of Saint Paul, which may be based on an even earlier confession (→8:37): "That at the name of Jesus every knee should bow, in heaven and on earth and under the earth, and every tongue confess that Jesus Christ is Lord, to the glory of God the Father" (Phil. 2:10–11). It is the human and earthly name "Jesus" (Ἰησοῦς), which was given to him by the angel of the annunciation (Luke 1:31)—and which was the name Joshua, the successor of Moses, in the Septuagint as well as in one passage of the book of Acts (7:45) and at least one other place in the New Testament (Heb. 4:8)—that is here made the object of adoration by the entire created cosmos.

Reflection on such biblical usage, particularly by Greek theologians such as Saint Cyril of Alexandria, produced the *communicatio idiomatum* as a formula that simultaneously safeguards the confession of the Niceno-Constantinopolitan Creed in "*one Lord* Jesus Christ"[14] and yet distinguishes between the actions or properties that are appropriate to one nature and those that are appropriate to the other. Pope Saint Leo the Great, in his Tome of 449 addressed to the Council of Chalcedon, set down the classic statement of the distinction: "It does not belong to the same nature to weep out of deep-felt pity for a dead friend, and to call him back to life again at the word of command [John 11:35–44]," because only the human nature could do the first and only the divine nature could do the second and yet the actions are both attributed to the single person of the incarnate Logos.[15] The Council of Chalcedon itself two years later provided the comprehensive and apophatic (→17:23) formulation: "One and the same Christ, Son, Lord, Only begotten, acknowledged in two natures which undergo no confusion, no change, no division, no separation" (ἕνα καὶ τὸν αὐτὸν Χριστὸν υἱὸν κύριον μονογενῆ, ἐν δύο φύσεσιν ἀσυγχύτως, ἀτρέπτως, ἀδιαιρέτως, ἀχωρίστως γνωριζόμενον).[16]

Clearly the confession of the church both at Ephesus and at Chalcedon was intent on preserving, with the utmost "accuracy" (ἀκρίβεια) (→18:24–26a), the faith of the creed in "*one* Lord Jesus Christ," whose unity of person makes it not only a permissible way of speaking, but a required way of confessing, to declare that the Blessed Virgin Mary is the Mother of God or even (if that is what this text says after all the variants of all the manuscripts have been sorted out) that "God" had redeemed the church "with his own blood."

13. Formula of Union of the Council of Ephesus (*CCF* 1:168–71).
14. Niceno-Constantinopolitan Creed 2 (*CCF* 1:163).
15. Tome of Leo 9 (*CCF* 1:117–18).
16. Definition of Faith of the Council of Chalcedon 16–18 (*CCF* 1:180–81).

20:35 TPR The one who gives is blessed rather than the one who receives [μακάριος ὁ διδῶν μᾶλλον ἢ ὁ λαμβάνων].

This saying of Jesus does not appear in any of our four Gospels, and Luke does not include it in his own "orderly account" of "the things which have been accomplished among us, just as they were delivered to us by those who from the beginning were eyewitnesses and ministers of the word" (Luke 1:1–3). Nevertheless, as an agraphon it has carried great authority, being quoted by one of the very earliest of ancient Christian writers, Saint Clement of Rome,[17] perhaps because it may have been part of "the gospel of the forty days" (→1:2–3).

20:37–38 TPR They all wept and embraced him and kissed him, most of all because he said, "You will never see my face again."

This is one of the most tender scenes anywhere in the New Testament, providing as it does at least a glimpse of the personality of the apostle as well as of the bonds of affection between him and his devoted congregants (→21:13–14; →27:3).

---

17. *1 Clement* 2.1 (ACW 1:10).

ACTS 21

21:1–3 From Miletus to Cos to Rhodes to Patara to Cyprus to Tyre—these six ports take only three verses, but they took many weeks of sailing (→27:24).

21:4 As so often in this narrative, a decisive turning point came as the consequence of a vision or special revelation of Christ or of the Holy Spirit or of an angel (→16:9).

21:5 Prayer was not confined to special appointed places (or times), but could take place anywhere (→4:24–30; →7:47–48).

"Who Spoke [and Speaks] through the Prophets"

21:9–10 TPR He had four unmarried daughters, who prophesied. While we were staying for some days, a prophet named Agabus came down from Judea.

The title of this *locus communis* is a quotation from the Niceno-Constantinopolitan Creed, referring to the Holy Spirit: "who spoke through the prophets."[1] In his Pentecost sermon (2:14–46), Peter quoted the book of the prophet Joel (Joel 2:28 LXX):

> And in the last days it shall be, God declares,
> that I will pour out my Spirit upon all flesh,
> and your sons and your daughters shall prophesy,
> and your young men shall see visions,
> and your old men shall dream dreams. (2:17)

---

1. Niceno-Constantinopolitan Creed 8 (*CCF* 1:163).

When he did so, he was using the writings of one of the Hebrew prophets to vindicate the authority not of the major and minor prophets who were canonized in Scripture and did not need to have their authority vindicated, to this audience at any rate, but of a phenomenon—even of an office of the ministry (→6:2–4)—within the early Christian community, the gift of prophecy. In addition to the intermittent visions, trances, and private revelations that were granted to one or another individual from time to time and under special circumstances in the course of the narrative of Acts (→16:9), the title προφήτης was employed for certain persons on a continuing basis. And if the omission of the name Priscilla from an earlier chapter (18:26 TPR) is taken to be evidence for "antifeminist tendencies" in the distinctive readings of the TPR,[2] those tendencies do not seem to have prevented the TPR from ascribing to women here not the very private taking aside of a brother to explain "the way of God more accurately," but the highly public function of "prophesying" (προφητεύουσαι).

Acts 13 contained the report that "there were in the church prophets and teachers [προφῆται καὶ διδάσκαλοι]" (13:1 TPR), with no clear indication of what the relation between the "prophets" and the "teachers" was nor whether "Barnabas, Simeon who was called Niger, Lucius of Cyrene, Manaen a member of the court of Herod the tetrarch, and Paul" were all five to be seen as holding both titles. In the roster of offices and titles given in the Letter to the Ephesians, "[1] some ... apostles, [2] some prophets, [3] some evangelists, [4] some pastors and teachers" (Eph. 4:11), it would seem from the language that "prophets" and "teachers" were distinct from each other, more so than were "pastors" and "teachers," who could be lumped together under the fourth category without a separate "some" (τούς) for the "teachers." The inclusion of "apostles" as the first office and of "prophets" as the second also suggests to many interpreters that the earlier statement in Ephesians about the church as being "built upon the foundation of the apostles and prophets, Christ Jesus himself being the cornerstone" (Eph. 2:20) did not refer to the authority of the two Testaments—"apostles" standing for the New Testament, "prophets" for the Old Testament—as it has often been taken, especially in the arguments of the Reformation period about the authority of Scripture,[3] but to two continuing modes of ministry in the church. When chapter 13 immediately went on to say, "While they were worshiping the Lord and fasting, the Holy Spirit said, 'Set apart for me Barnabas and Saul for the work to which I have called them'" (13:2), it clearly seems to be that they were to be functioning as "prophets," conveyors of specific and topical instructions from the Holy Spirit, which had been granted to them as they were worshiping (→4:24–30) and fasting (→24:25b).

2. Witherington 1984.
3. For example, Westminster Confession of Faith 1.2, 10 (*CCF* 2:606, 608).

On the other hand, there are other instances of the title "prophets" in Acts that raise questions about any precise distinction between "prophets" and "teachers." As Calvin says, commenting on chapter 2, "this word *prophesy* doth signify nothing else save only the rare and excellent gift of understanding."[4] The warning of Agabus to Paul here in chapter 21—complete with a symbolic gesture of binding with Paul's "girdle" (ζώνη), which was reminiscent of the symbolic "girdle" (περίζωμα) that had been employed by the Hebrew prophet Jeremiah (Jer. 13:1–11 LXX)—emphasized the "prophetic" and even "predictive" component. So did the earlier report that "Agabus stood up and foretold by the Spirit [ἐσήμανεν διὰ τοῦ πνεύματος] that there would be a great famine over all the world" (11:28). Yet there does not seem to have been anything especially predictive or prophetic, despite the specification that they "were themselves prophets" (καὶ αὐτοὶ προφῆται ὄντες), about the description that "Judas and Silas . . . exhorted the brethren with many words and strengthened them" (15:32).

It does not seem possible on the basis of the existing documentary evidence to date with any precision the decline (or even eventual disappearance) of this distinct "prophetic" office from the range of ministries in the church. But the evidence does suggest that the Montanist movement, with its claims to be "the new prophecy," was a major factor in bringing such a change. Hippolytus of Rome took the saying of Jesus that "the law and the prophets were until John; since then the good news of the kingdom of God is preached" (Luke 16:16) as a periodization of the successive revelations of the word of God: "the law," "the prophets," "the good news" of the gospel about the kingdom of God. Stretching the boundaries of the periodization and with a wordplay on the name "John," Hippolytus located the terminus ad quem of prophecy not in John the Baptizer and Forerunner (→19:2–3) but in John the writer of the Apocalypse. "Prophets" now referred to biblical prophets, not to prophets in the church.[5] And "built upon the foundation of the apostles and prophets" did refer to the authority of the Scriptures (→8:30–31)—though only in the context of the total system of authority and continuity, which included the authority of tradition (→16:4a), of the ministerial and episcopal office (→6:2–4), of the creed as rule of faith (→8:37), and of the councils of the church (→15:28).[6]

Religious Affections

21:13–14 TPR Paul said to us, "What are you doing, weeping and throwing my heart into disorder [θορυβοῦντες]? For I am ready not only to be imprisoned, but to die for the name of my Lord Jesus."

4. Calvin 1949, 1:87.
5. *Chr. Trad.* 1:97–108.
6. *Chr. Trad.* 2:8–36.

Intimidation, threats, tears, heartbreak, stubbornness, resignation—even in purely human terms, this dramatic confrontation of Paul with his friends (who, it seems from the repeated use of the first-person plural, even one extra time in the TPR, must have included Luke himself) over the risks involved in his going to Jerusalem is an especially striking description of what Jonathan Edwards, in his 1746 classic treatise, labeled "religious affections," which is an element of biblical language and style that deserves careful attention even and especially in a theological commentary, where it can all too easily be overshadowed by dogma and creed.

The Epistles of Paul (→23:25) constitute a special, if not unique, literary genre (of which Augustine's *Confessions* may be seen as a further development), because of their combination of didactic with affective language, and their frequent use of affective language for didactic purposes: Paul the believer was for Paul the writer—and even for Paul the apostle—a case study of the gospel in action. Among these epistles, the Epistles to the Galatians and to the Philippians are in this respect in a class unto themselves, the first for its theological and rhetorical use of indignation to make a didactic point (Gal. 3:1) and the second for its celebration of his beloved readers as "my joy and crown" (Phil. 4:1).

The theological standing of the religious affections was elevated to a normative position in the dogmatics of Friedrich Daniel Ernst Schleiermacher, *The Christian Faith*, originally published in 1821–22, where (in thesis 30) he posited the distinction around which he built the structure of the entire work: "All the propositions which the doctrine of the Christian faith is to bring forward can be comprehended either as descriptions of conditions of human life [*Beschreibungen menschlicher Lebenszustände*], or as concepts of divine attributes and ways of dealing, or as statements concerning the constitution of the world; and all three forms have always coexisted side by side."[7] By making the first of these, as he went on to explain in the next thesis, his fundamental form of speaking about all doctrines, Schleiermacher recast each of the major dogmas of the Christian tradition, from the nature of God to eschatology, in the terms that were dictated by the "feeling of absolute dependence," reading off the doctrines from their reflection in Christian feeling and experience, almost as though he were painting a self-portrait by using a mirror. But the theologies of Gregory of Nazianzus, of Augustine—not only in the *Confessions* but in *On the Trinity*, in a speculative psychological construct of breathtaking scope—as well as of Bonaventure and Luther show that even when it was not so radically conceived, the affective element has provided an important lens for viewing and interpreting Christian faith and doctrine.

Both the portrayal of Joseph, David, and Elijah in its biblical models and the accounts of Pericles and Julius Caesar in its classical predecessors implied that the Acts of the Apostles, being in its literary design a historical and biographi-

7. Schleiermacher 1960, 1:163.

cal narrative, was obliged to portray the religious affections—or else to make its dramatis personae into robots. Among these religious affections, the most fundamental of all was the experience that Rudolf Otto, apparently coining the word for German and other modern languages, calls the sense of the "numinous," the experience of awe in the presence of the transcendent *mysterium tremendum*. The biblical precedents for it were the prophet Isaiah "pricked to the heart" because "I am only a human being, and my eyes have seen the King, the Lord of hosts" (Isa. 6:5 LXX), the prophet Jeremiah overwhelmed at the summons to speak in the name of the Lord because he was still "a mere lad" (νεώτερος) (Jer. 1:6 LXX), and above all Moses standing on "holy ground" (γῆ ἁγία) at the burning bush (Exod. 3:5 LXX). Recalling that scene as part of his miniature biography of Moses, Stephen described how, "when Moses saw it he wondered at the sight" and "trembled and did not dare to look," because he was standing on "holy ground" in the presence of "the God of Abraham and of Isaac and of Jacob" (7:31–32). In language also reminiscent of that scene, Acts described as a man "in terror" (ἔμφοβος) the Roman centurion Cornelius when he was accosted by "an angel of God coming in and saying to him, 'Cornelius'" (10:1–8).

The religious affections come through in the accounts that Acts gives us of actions, and especially of controversies and confrontations, and in its depictions of the enemies of the Way (→11:26). Having described in his Gospel how the opponents of Christ "were urgent" and fierce against him (Luke 23:5), Luke went on to portray their rage and violence (→28:31) as it was turned against his followers (→7:59–60). In the course of the narrative, the supreme embodiment of such rage was "Saul, still breathing threats and murder against the disciples of the Lord [ἐμπνέων ἀπειλῆς καὶ φόνου εἰς τοὺς μαθητὰς τοῦ κυρίου]" (9:1). His conversion (→9:1–4) drastically modified such behavior, but it did nothing to bank the fires of religious affection and zeal within him that had produced it. Saul the persecutor was, moreover, only reflecting the rage that he shared with others, who, "when they heard this were enraged and wanted to kill them" (5:33), or "when they heard these things were enraged, and ground their teeth against" Stephen (7:54) and not only "wanted to kill" him but did, and wanted to kill many others besides—including now Saul the persecutor who had become Paul the follower of Jesus (→14:22; →28:31).

The venting of such violent rage and the martyrdom to which it led are described as evoking grief and lamentation among the believers, which were, in Calvin's words, a "profession of faith and godliness in their lamentation."[8] When the Apostle Paul urged the Thessalonians "concerning those who are asleep" not to "grieve as others do who have no hope" (1 Thess. 4:13), he was not forbidding grief as such. There were, it would seem from these words, two kinds of grieving, one without hope and the other with hope—just as, for that matter, there were two kinds of anger, so that he did not command, "Do not

8. Calvin 1949, 1:326–27.

become angry," but "Be angry but do not sin; do not let the sun go down on your anger" (Eph. 4:26). Paul's "solemn protestation"[9] in his farewell to the presbyters of Ephesus was an illustration of how those who did have Christian hope could nevertheless grieve: "They all wept and embraced him and kissed him, most of all because he said, 'You will never see my face again'" (20:37–38 TPR);[10] "so much did they love him, such was their affection towards him."[11] In what may be called our earliest description of a Christian funeral, Acts describes how, after the martyrdom of Stephen, "devout men buried Stephen, and made great lamentation [κοπετὸν μέγαν] over him" (8:2). Once again in the following chapter, after the death of the seamstress Dorcas, "all the widows stood beside [Peter] weeping, and showing tunics and other garments which Dorcas made while she was with them" (9:39).

Corresponding to those two kinds of grieving is the distinction between authentic Christian "joy" (χαρά)[12] and mere "pleasure" (ἡδονή), which, in the New Testament and even elsewhere, is employed "usu[ally] in a bad sense: (evil) pleasure, lust."[13] The high place occupied by joy among the religious affections is indicated by the grammatical coordination in the description "and the disciples were filled with joy and with the Holy Spirit" (οἵ τε μαθηταὶ ἐπληροῦντο χαρᾶς καὶ πνεύματος ἁγίου) (13:52), also because of the regular association of the Holy Spirit with the concept of "fullness" (πλήρωμα) (→2:1). "Joy" as a noun appears again when the report of the conversion of the Gentiles "gave great joy [χαρὰν μεγάλην] to all the brethren" (15:3).[14] As a result of the exorcisms and other sign miracles (→6:8) performed by Philip in Samaria, "there was much joy in that city" (8:8). When Rhoda heard the voice of Peter at the gate after the angel had set him free from imprisonment, "in her joy [ἀπὸ τῆς χαρᾶς] she did not open the gate but ran in and told that Peter was standing at the gate" (→12:13–16). In some of the most telling references to the religious affection of joy, however, it is the verb "to rejoice" (χαίρειν or ἀγαλλιᾶσθαι) rather than the noun that is employed, because such a joy was not a passive emotion but an active experience. After his baptism, the Ethiopian eunuch "went on his way rejoicing [χαίρων]" (8:39). "When [Barnabas] came and saw the grace of God, he was glad" (11:23), which in Greek involves an untranslatable play on the words (paronomasia) for "grace" and "was glad": ἰδὼν τὴν χάριν τοῦ θεοῦ, ἐχάρη. As a result of the announcement by Paul and Barnabas that they were turning to the Gentile mission, "when the Gentiles heard this, they were glad [ἔχαιρον] and glorified the word of God" (13:48); similarly, the jailer "rejoiced [ἠγαλλιάσατο, the same verb that Luke put into the mouth of the Blessed Virgin

9. Loisy 1920, 775.
10. Tannehill 1990, 2:252–67.
11. Chrysostom, *Homilies on Acts* 45 (*NPNF*[1] 11:273).
12. BDAG 1077.
13. BADG 344.
14. Harnack 1909, 277–81.

Mary at the opening of the Magnificat in Luke 1:47] with all his household that he had believed in God" (16:34).

But according to the second verse of the present passage Paul manifested another "religious affection," for which readers of his epistles, especially Galatians, should not be entirely unprepared: a fierce sense of determination, which was sometimes difficult to distinguish from just plain stubbornness. One almost expects a "sigh" (στεναγμός) in the sentence, "And when he would not be persuaded, we ceased and said, 'The will of the Lord be done.'" This is a true-to-life portrayal of the man who could exclaim: "But even if we, or an angel from heaven, should preach to you a gospel contrary to that which we preached to you, let him be accursed" (Gal. 1:8). So is the description of the reaction from him and Barnabas to the opposition they encountered in Antioch of Pisidia, "But they shook off the dust from their feet against them" (13:51), which was in literal obedience to the command of Jesus, as also reported by Luke, "And wherever they do not receive you, when you leave that town shake off the dust from your feet as a testimony against them" (Luke 9:5). When combined with the growing insistence on "accuracy" (ἀκρίβεια) in the confession of doctrine (→18:24–26a) and with the increasing precision of the rule of faith (→8:37), whatever its form may have been, this helps to explain the vehemence with which perceived aberrations from the rule of faith, whether by Marcion in the second century or Paul of Samosata in the third or Arius in the fourth, were opposed by orthodox theologians and church councils.

21:17–18 In succeeding verses this text speaks of "the brethren" (οἱ ἀδελφοί) and of "all the elders" (πάντες . . . οἱ πρεσβύτεροι), without defining either category or distinguishing between them (→6:2–4).

21:20–21 This charge accused Paul of extending even to observant Jews who were not Christian believers the radical interpretation of the Mosaic law that he was applying to Gentile converts (→10:15).

21:31 They were trying to kill him.

This fierce, indeed lethal, opposition to Paul continued to the end of the narrative in Acts (→28:31), and according to tradition well beyond, ending only with his martyrdom.

"Debtor to Greek": Language and Languages

21:37 Do you know Greek?

Of all the writers to whom the books of the New Testament were attributed by the early traditions of the church, only the writer of Luke-Acts was usually identified as a Gentile (though, according to some, a proselyte to Judaism before he became a Christian) and therefore as one who could understand as from within not only the Greek language, but both Greco-Roman religion, including magic, sorcery, and superstition (→19:28), and classical culture, literature, and philosophy (→17:18). He writes Greek as one to whom the language was native.[15] The heroine of John Henry Newman's *Callista*, a highly educated Greek pagan, found Luke's prose to be "the writing of a provincial Greek, elegant however, and marked with that simplicity which was to her taste the elementary idea of a classic author," all of which contributed to her conversion (which was followed immediately by her martyrdom).[16]

There are few studies more fascinating than the comparison of languages, whether by merchants or diplomats or scholars or tourists, and few discoveries more exciting than learning a new language and gradually (and never perfectly) acquiring some degree of mastery in it. The special qualities of each language, whether spoken or written, and its ability to express the nuances of thought and feeling can be matched only by the power of music—which is why the cliché calls music "the universal language." Yet this esthetic appeal of language and of languages may easily obscure the infinite mischief that the diversity of languages has wrought between enemies, between friends, between lovers, between generations, between nations—and between churches.

The gospel went on to be spoken and written in more than two thousand languages, some of them with alphabets that were invented for that purpose. Here in chapter 21 of Acts Paul is portrayed as having been able to put his virtuoso abilities as a linguist to good use, as his knowledge of Greek exonerated him of the suspicion that he was an Egyptian terrorist, and then his ability to switch effortlessly from Greek to Aramaic gave him instant access to a Jewish audience. There is no indication, here or elsewhere, whether he knew Latin, and he wrote his Epistle to the Romans in Greek, as he could of course have been expected to do at that time. When at Lystra the astonished natives shouted "in [the] Lycaonian [language], 'The gods have come down to us in the likeness of men!'" (14:11), they were speaking in what the standard lexicon of the New Testament is still compelled to define as "a dialect spoken in Lycaonia, no longer known."[17]

Nevertheless, the history of the church seems in many respects to be the continuation not of the day of Pentecost at all, as Acts seems to want to portray it, but of the tower of Babel, as tensions caused by linguistic differences have repeatedly become a reenactment of the scene here in Acts when "the Hellenists murmured against the Hebrews" (6:1). Although it is dangerous to exaggerate the reciprocal linguistic tone deafness of the Latin church and the Greek church

15. Cadbury 1958, 113–26. J. de Zwaan in Foakes Jackson and Lake 1979, 2:30–65 provides an informative linguistic analysis.
16. Newman 1962, 180.
17. BDAG 604.

as a factor in the eventual schism between them—Eastern Christendom was not exclusively Greek, but polyglot from the very beginning, and even more so after the ninth century with the Christianization of the Slavs—the identification of the faith with a particular culture or language of origin has been a particular bane for missionary churches or for immigrant churches in a new culture, and the experimentation involved in linguistic acculturation has precipitated major theological conflicts such as the seventeenth-century Chinese Rites controversy in Roman Catholicism[18] and analogous controversies in other churches over the use of pagan terminology for Christian concepts (→19:28).

But no discussion of language as a theological question would be complete without attention to the privileged status that is held, or should be held, by the original languages of Scripture. When, at least partly under the sway of Renaissance humanism, the sixteenth-century Protestant Reformers singled out "the Old Testament in Hebrew (which was the native language of the people of God of old), and the New Testament in Greek (which, at the time of the writing of it, was most generally known to the nations)"[19] as the ultimate arbiter of Christian doctrine and morals, they were according to the original Hebrew and Greek texts a primary authority that pertained to any other version of the text of Scripture only derivatively. Even the Septuagint, which was the "Old Testament" for the writers of the Greek "New Testament," including Luke here in the Acts of the Apostles, had to abdicate its privileged position, and the Latin Vulgate even more. As a consequence, the ability to interpret the Scriptures on the basis of the original languages became, in many Reformation and post-Reformation churches, a requirement for ordination to the ministry of preaching the word and especially for the theological exegesis of the Bible.

But when Saint Paul called himself a "debtor . . . to the Greeks" (Rom. 1:14 AV) and thus also to Greek as a language, that is a reminder that there is a fundamental difference—a philological difference that becomes a theological difference—between the place of Hebrew and the place of Greek in Christian theology: the Hebrew Bible is the oldest (and virtually the sole) surviving sample of Hebrew; but the Greek Bible, both the Septuagint and the New Testament, stands on the shoulders of many centuries of pagan Greek literature, history, and philosophy. Both in translating the Hebrew text of the Old Testament into Greek and in articulating the newness of the gospel in the New Testament, the fundamental assumption was that the Greek language was pliable enough to accommodate a radically novel message without doing violence to it. But as the history of Christian theology and philosophy demonstrates, the continuity and the discontinuity of Christian Greek with classical and Hellenistic Greek would continue to challenge Christians both when they spoke Greek and when, repeatedly throughout the centuries of church history, "they . . . began to speak

18. J. Brucker in *DTC* 2:2364–91.
19. Westminster Confession of Faith 1.8 (*CCF* 2:607).

with other tongues, as the Spirit gave them utterance" (2:4), even and especially when such speaking did not involve glossolalia but translation.

21:40 Here as elsewhere in Acts (22:2; 26:14) and at other places in the New Testament (John 5:2; 19:13, 17, 20), the phrase "in the Hebrew language" (τῇ Ἑβραΐδι διαλέκτῳ) does not mean the Hebrew that was written and spoken by Moses and the prophets, but Aramaic, the related yet altogether distinct Semitic language that was spoken in Palestine in the first century and that Paul spoke along with Greek.

ACTS 22

22:1 Speaking here as a Jew to other Jews (→3:25), Paul delivers the first of five apologias (→23:1) in this and the following chapters, for himself and for the Christian cause (→24:1–2).

22:2 Here again, "Hebrew" is actually Aramaic (→21:37).

22:3 Gamaliel was described earlier (5:34–40) as having advised his fellow members of the Sanhedrin not to persecute the nascent Christian movement, but to leave the outcome to God (→3:25; →23:1).

22:4 Paul was still referring to the gospel and its adherents as "the Way" (→11:26).

"The Uncreated Light" as a Divine Energy

22:6 About noon a great light from heaven suddenly shone about me [ἐκ τοῦ οὐρανοῦ περιαστράψαι φῶς ἱκανον περὶ ἐμέ].

The three accounts that the book of Acts gives of the miraculous conversion of Saul on the road to Damascus (→9:1–4), which differ from one another in various details, all make a point of calling attention to the extraordinary light that overwhelmed him with its brightness. The first account of this light, which Luke includes as part of his own narrative, is the simplest of the three: "Suddenly a light from heaven flashed around him" (ἐξαίφνης τε αὐτὸν περιήστραψεν φῶς ἐκ τοῦ οὐρανοῦ) (9:3). Next, this account here in chapter 22 by Paul himself, speaking to a Jewish audience, basically repeats that version, with the addition that it took place "about noon." But in the third account, also attributed to Paul, this time defending himself before King Agrippa, he elaborates on the light still further: "At midday, O king, I saw on the way a light from heaven, brighter than the sun [οὐρανόθεν ὑπὲρ τὴν λαμπρότητα τοῦ ἡλίου . . . φῶς], shining round me and those who journeyed with me" (26:13). This appears to suggest that no one had ever seen a light in all creation that was "brighter than the sun." Therefore this has been taken to belong to metaphysics rather than simply to physics, as a reference to an "uncreated light."

Saint Luke writes about this miraculous light in these three passages of Acts after having spoken in his "first book," in which he "dealt with all that Jesus began to do and teach" (1:1), about the related miracle of the transfiguration of Jesus: "The appearance of his countenance was altered, and his raiment became dazzling white [λευκὸς ἐξαστράπτων]" (Luke 9:29). Saint Matthew says that "his face shone like the sun, and his garments became white as light" (Matt. 17:2). But Saint Mark's account of the light at the transfiguration (whether or not, as is usually supposed in modern New Testament scholarship, it is the earliest of the three to be written down, and whether or not Saint Luke was acquainted with it in writing his own) comes closer than either Luke's or Matthew's does to serving as a commentary on the "light from heaven, brighter than the sun" in Luke's final telling of the conversion of Saul: "And he was transfigured before them, and his garments became glistening, intensely white [στίλβοντα λευκὰ λίαν], as no fuller on earth could bleach them" (Mark 9:2–3). There does seem to be a parallel between Mark's description, "intensely white, as no fuller on earth could bleach them," and Luke's description, "a light from heaven, brighter than the sun, shining round me"—a light of heaven not of earth, and transcendent in its whiteness and brilliance.

The biblical precedent for this unique light is found in the account of Moses speaking face to face with the Lord on Mount Sinai, so that when he descended from the mountain his face shone with a brilliance that was beyond human endurance to behold and he had to veil it when he spoke with the people of Israel (Exod. 34:29–35). For Saint Paul, the immediate significance of "such splendor that the Israelites could not look at Moses' face because of its brightness, fading as this was," was to serve as an allegory for the relation between the law and the gospel (2 Cor. 3:7–8); but this divine light on Mount Sinai stood in close connection with the divine light on Mount Tabor at the transfiguration of Christ—and with the divine light that overwhelmed Paul on the Damascus road.

But if it was truly "divine" and "uncreated" and not "fading," therefore falling on God's side of the line of demarcation between Creator and creature, that raised the question: Where did this light fit into the doctrine of the divine and into the orthodox trinitarian metaphysics of the one οὐσία and the three ὑποστάσεις? It could not be part of the divine οὐσία, for it was supremely visible, but "no one has ever seen God" (John 1:18). And it could not be one of the three ὑποστάσεις of Father, Son, and Holy Spirit, much less a fourth ὑπόστασις! To find a way of speaking about this with a fitting ἀκρίβεια (→18:24–26a), the Cappadocians (→17:23) took up an earlier theological theme and spoke of a divine "energy" or "principle of action" (ἐνέργεια).[1] That concept was then formulated by the sixth ecumenical council in 680/681, which decreed that as there were two natures in Christ and two wills in Christ, one divine and the other human, so there also had to be "two natural principles of action,"[2] one for each nature rather than a single one for the one person of Christ. This definition was applied to the uncreated light above all by Saint Gregory Palamas in his defense and exposition of the teachings of Hesychasm: as it was granted for example on Mount Tabor, revelation was "not according to essence [οὐσία], for no one has ever seen or spoken the nature of God, but according to the grace and power and energy which is common to the Father and the Son and the Holy Spirit."[3] This definition of the uncreated light as divine "principle of action" or "energy" was legislated as dogma, for the East at any rate, by the Synods of Constantinople in 1341 and 1351.[4] Nevertheless, as liturgy if not as dogma, the doctrine of the uncreated and eternal divine light has found even wider distribution in the West than in the East, in the prayer of the Requiem Mass: *Requiescant in pace, et lux perpetua luceat eis.*

22:14–15 The twin themes of the confessional imperative (→4:20) and of divine election (→13:48) come through in this version of the commission delivered by Ananias to Saul who would be called Paul.

"We Acknowledge One Baptism for the Forgiving of Sins"

22:16 Rise and be baptized, and wash away your sins, calling on his name.

As is evident from the passages about baptism throughout the book of Acts as well as from those dealing with the breaking of bread (→20:7), neither the Acts of the Apostles nor the rest of the New Testament contains a presentation of the doctrine of the sacraments as such, a *tractatus de sacramentis in genere* as the topic was to be entitled by the Western medieval Scholastics, but only of one "sacrament" at a time, and then without invoking that term, except perhaps for the use of μυστήριον in Eph. 5:32, which came to be used as a proof text for the sacramentality of holy matrimony.[5] Although the Gospel of Matthew closes with the command to baptize (Matt. 28:19), which is also contained in the "long ending" of the Gospel of Mark (Mark 16:16), and the Gospel of John includes the imperative of being born of water and the Spirit (John 3:5), there is no explicit reference to Christian baptism in the Gospel of Luke, but only to the baptism by John the Forerunner (→19:2–3). But that

1. *PGL* 470–73.
2. Exposition of Faith of the Third Council of Constantinople (*CCF* 1:227).
3. Gregory Palamas Confession of the Orthodox Faith 3 (*CCF* 1:376).
4. Synodical Tome of 1341 (*CCF* 1:320–33); Synodical Tome of 1351 (*CCF* 1:334–74).
5. Dogmatic Decrees of the Council of Trent 24.11 (*CCF* 2:868).

lacuna is more than compensated for by the prominence of baptism in Acts, which discusses it more frequently and at greater length than does either the Epistle to the Romans (Rom. 6:3–11) or the Epistle to Titus (Titus 3:4–8), both of which have figured importantly as proof texts in many catechetical and theological discussions of baptism.[6]

The unique position of Luke among the evangelists as the only one of the four who continued his narrative into the next generation suggests that his descriptions of Christian baptism here in Acts all hark back to his description of the baptism of Jesus in his Gospel (Luke 3:21–22). Commemorated as "the Theophany" (τά θεοφάνια) on the sixth of January,[7] the baptism of Jesus "appears very early in Christian art and is elaborately developed later in connection with the feast day hymns and baptismal rites."[8] The identification of the baptized neophyte with the baptized Christ was represented architecturally by his dominant figure on the dome of the baptistery.[9] Each subsequent reference to baptism in the book of Acts, such as this one, is also connected to the earliest mention of Christian baptism in Acts, which comes in Peter's appeal at the end of his Pentecost homily and which contains all the components of church doctrine on baptism: "[1] Repent, and [2] be baptized every one of you [3] in the name of Jesus Christ [4] for the forgiveness of your sins; [5] and you shall receive the gift of the Holy Spirit. [6] For the promise is to you and to your children and to all that are far off, every one whom the Lord our God calls to him" (2:38):

1. Peter's summons, "repent" (μετανοήσατε), is a reminder that as Jesus himself had "not come to call the righteous, but sinners to repentance" (Luke 5:32), so the preaching of his apostles throughout Acts was a summons to repent (→26:20): with its etymology in νοῦς ("mind"), the imperative μετανοήσατε called upon the hearer to "acquire a new mind." From the coordination in the two imperative verbs with which, in the Gospel of Mark, the proclamation of Jesus opened, "repent, and believe in the gospel" (Mark 1:15), it is clear that such repenting in the full sense of the word included faith, seen as *fides qua creditur*, the faith with which one believes (→26:18). Such repentance with faith was, moreover, seen as prerequisite to baptism: "Repent, and [καί] be baptized." In the case of Lydia, "the Lord opened her heart to give heed to what was said by Paul," and then "she was baptized, with her entire household [πᾶς ὁ οἶκος αὐτῆς]" (16:14–15 TPR). But the *fides quae creditur*, the faith that one believes and that the church believes, teaches, and confesses (→24:24–25a), was also inseparable from baptism. Whatever may be the textual status

6. For example, Heidelberg Catechism 70–71 (*CCF* 2:442).
7. *PGL* 642; Sophocles 1870, 578–79.
8. Onasch and Schnieper 1997, 107.
9. Kostof 1965, 86–89.

(→20:28a) of the creedal confession of the Ethiopian, "I believe that Jesus Christ is the Son of God" (→8:37 TPR AV), the unequivocal judgment of Hans Lietzmann stands: "It is indisputable that the root of all creeds is the formula of belief pronounced by the baptizand, or pronounced in his hearing and assented to by him, before his baptism."[10]

2. The case of the Ethiopian also suggests that when the preaching of the word had generated repentance and faith, the immediate reaction was the question, "See, here is water! What is to prevent my being baptized?" (8:36), which was followed, immediately in turn, by the administration of baptism. The cause célèbre of this immediacy of sequence in Acts was Saul who became Paul: he was interrupted in his journey on the road to Damascus by the appearing of Christ, "and when his eyes were opened, he could see nothing" (9:8); but after three days "he regained his sight. Then he rose and was baptized" (9:18). Here, in a later recital of those events, Paul quoted his newfound brother Ananias as having urged him: "And now why do you wait? Rise and be baptized, and wash away your sins, calling on his name" (22:16). In the light of Paul's disclaimer to the Corinthians, "Christ did not send me to baptize but to preach the gospel" (1 Cor. 1:17), it is intriguing to note that nowhere here in Acts is he portrayed as having baptized anyone; rather, in every passage of Acts where that might be implied (e.g., 16:15, 33; 18:8; 19:5), the verb is—ambiguously—put into the passive voice, with no agent or minister of the baptizing specified.

3. It is even more intriguing to ask, in the light of the magisterial and normative command of the ascending Christ as reported by Matthew, "baptizing them in the name of the Father and of the Son and of the Holy Spirit" (Matt. 28:19),[11] why Peter at Pentecost calls upon his hearers to "be baptized every one of you *in the name of Jesus Christ.*" That goes on, indeed, to become the formula "through the entire text of this book," as orthodox catholic interpreters are also obliged to admit.[12] Those who knew only the baptism of John were told that they had to be upgraded into the fullness of baptism; and "on hearing this, they were baptized in the name of the Lord Jesus" (19:5), with no suggestion of the eventual orthodox position that "the full fullness" of baptism was nothing short of baptism in the name of the Holy Trinity, even though they had acknowledged, "No, we have never even heard that there is a Holy Spirit" (19:2 RSV), or at least, "No, we have never even heard that some have received the Holy Spirit" (19:2 TPR). The interpretation is made more complex by the report (8:16–17) that the believers in Samaria "had only been baptized in the name of the Lord Jesus," which was also inadequate, but that what

10. Quoted in Pelikan 2003, 383.
11. Basil of Caesarea, *On the Holy Spirit* 17–18, 43–44 (SVS 70–71).
12. Bede, *Exposition of the Acts of the Apostles* 10 (PL 92:970).

then made it adequate was not the invocation of the Trinity, as the great commission would seem to imply (Matt. 28:19), but the laying-on of hands (→6:6). Theologians have long been vexed by the question whether a baptism performed "in the name of Jesus" and without the recitation of the trinitarian formula would still be valid now.[13]

4. The instructions given to Paul at his conversion, as he reported them here, speaking in Aramaic and to a Jewish audience, were: "And now why do you wait? Rise and be baptized, and *wash away your sins*, calling on his name" (22:16). In Peter's formula at Pentecost, the prepositional phrase in English, "for the forgiveness of your sins," renders the prepositional phrase in Greek, εἰς ἄφεσιν τῶν ἁμαρτιῶν ὑμῶν, the preposition εἰς being used here as a "marker of goals" or "to denote purpose."[14] To the recurring objection of those who reject the orthodox doctrine of sacramental grace that works *ex opere operato*[15] and who insist that the sacraments do not convey the forgiveness of sins but only announce it—which does seem reminiscent of the objection of the scribes and Pharisees, as reported by Saint Luke, "Who can forgive sins but God only?" (Luke 5:21)—the tenor of the preposition εἰς here would appear to be that the God who alone can forgive sins had, in sovereign freedom, chosen to attach that forgiveness to the means of grace, and specifically to baptism, in a connection described by the Epistle to Titus: "He saved us, not because of deeds done by us in righteousness, but in virtue of his own mercy, by the washing of regeneration and renewal in the Holy Spirit" (Titus 3:5). The connection between "be baptized" and "wash away your sins" acquired special importance as the baptism of infants, whensoever it may have begun, increasingly became normal Christian practice: Which "sins" could this baptism be said to "wash away" in infants? The definitive answer came from Saint Cyprian of Carthage, who, in urging that baptism take place within a few days after birth, spoke of "an infant, who, being lately born, has not sinned, except in that, being born after the flesh according to Adam, he has contracted the contagion [*contagium*] of the ancient death at its earliest birth."[16] In his conflict with the Pelagians, Saint Augustine elaborated this formula of Cyprian's into the doctrine of original sin in the form in which it has dominated Western theology, Protestant as well as Roman Catholic, ever since.[17] And in opposition to Donatism he affirmed that the church could be confessed as "one, *holy*, catholic, and apostolic" (→4:32),[18] not because of the empirical holiness

13. J. Bellamy in *DTC* 2:172.
14. BDAG 290.
15. Rahner and Vorgrimler 1965, 325–26.
16. Cyprian, *Epistles* 58.5 (*ANF* 5:354).
17. *Chr. Trad.* 1:313–18.
18. Niceno-Constantinopolitan Creed 9 (*CCF* 1:163).

of its members or its clergy or its hierarchs, all of which have proved to be notoriously fragile, but because of the holiness conferred by the sacraments, beginning with holy baptism.[19]

5. The passage from the Epistle to Titus continues: "Which he poured out upon us richly through Jesus Christ our Savior, so that we might be justified by his grace and become heirs in hope of eternal life. The saying is sure" (Titus 3:6–8). These words form an exact parallel to the "sure" promise enunciated by Peter: "And you shall receive the gift of the Holy Spirit." In keeping with the unique emphasis of Luke-Acts on the work of the Holy Spirit (→2:1), which seems if anything to be heightened in the TPR,[20] the gift of the Holy Spirit and the reception of holy baptism often stand in close relation to each other; but the relation is not a simple one. As the question of Peter indicated when he asked, "Can any one forbid water for baptizing these people who have received the Holy Spirit just as we have?" (10:47), there were instances where, as an earlier verse says, "the Holy Spirit fell upon all who heard the word" (10:44) without (or before) their receiving baptism—though it should be noted that they *had* "heard the word." Yet another chronological sequence was at work in the encounter of Paul in Ephesus (19:1–7). To his question "did you receive the Holy Spirit when you believed?" they replied in the negative, apparently because they had received only the baptism of John. Thereupon "they were baptized in the name of the Lord Jesus. *And when Paul had laid his hands upon them,* the Holy Spirit came on them." Between the conferral of baptism and the conferral of the Holy Spirit came, at any rate in their case, the laying-on of hands (→6:6).

6. In the light of the closing words of Peter's homily—"for the promise is to you and to your children and to all that are far off, every one whom the Lord our God calls to him"—and of the controversies that began with the Anabaptists of the Reformation period but have continued into the modern period, the question of the baptism of children must be raised, though it cannot be answered definitively solely on the basis of Acts. Defenders of the legitimacy of baptizing children have argued, on the basis of this passage and others, that if the gospel represented, as Peter's delineation of the ever-widening circle of divine grace (→13:48) made clear, the inclusion of those who had previously been excluded but not the exclusion of those who had previously been included, the New Testament equivalent and expansion of the rite of initiation by circumcision "for your children" was baptism. Therefore Acts 16 specifies that Lydia "was baptized, *with her household* [ὁ οἶκος αὐτῆς]" (16:15) or perhaps even, as TPR has it, "her *entire* household" (πᾶς ὁ οἶκος αὐτῆς) (16:15 TPR); and in a later verse the repentant jailer, who had been saved by the apostles

19. *Chr. Trad.* 1:307–18.
20. Black 1981.

from suicide, "was baptized at once *with all his family* [οἱ αὐτοῦ πάντες]" (16:33). And yet, when the author of Acts would have had perhaps his best opportunity to make this point, he reports concerning the former followers of Simon Magus (→13:8–11), "They were baptized, both men and women" (8:12), with no mention of children, even though in a later chapter he makes a point of specifying that at Tyre "they all, *with wives and children*, brought us on our way" (21:5)—an argument from silence perhaps, but not one that is easily dismissed, especially in the light of the statistical regularity with which, in the narrative of Acts, faith precedes baptism.

22:17–18 The original Greek of "trance" here is ἔκστασις, which connects Paul's account with the other instances of trances, dreams, and special revelations throughout the book of Acts and beyond (→4:24–30; →7:47–48; →7:59–60; →16:9) and perhaps also with the office of "prophets" and "prophetesses" (→21:9–10).

22:22 The cumulative pattern of violent uproar and lynch mobs is continued here (→28:31).

"One, Holy, *Catholic*, and Apostolic Church": "Every Native Land a Foreign Land"

22:27 TPR So the tribune came and asked him, "Are you a Roman citizen?" He said, "I am."

Each of these five verses (22:25–29) contains, in the RSV, the word "Roman citizen" (Ῥωμαῖος) or "citizen" or "citizenship" (πολιτεία). The words of the tribune, "I bought this citizenship for a large sum," give a measure of the estimation in which this status was held, both by those who could claim it and by those who could not; and Paul's boast, "but I was born a citizen," takes advantage of it as a counterweight to the balance of the power relation between captor and captive.

The stage was set for this encounter during the imprisonment of Paul and Silas at Philippi, which was the scene not only of the repentance and conversion of their jailer (16:30–31) in the aftermath of "a great earthquake" (16:26) and of his contemplated suicide (16:27), but of the first recorded disclosure that Paul held Roman citizenship. The xenophobic accusation of the slaveowners against him and Silas charged that "these men are Jews" and that "they advocate customs which it is not lawful for *us Romans* to accept or practice [ἃ οὐκ ἔξεστιν ἡμῖν . . . Ῥωμαίοις οὖσιν]" (16:21–22). That seemed to provide excuse enough for both the "crowd" and the "magistrates" to rough them up by "inflict[ing] many blows upon them" (16:23) and then to clap them into jail.

But when, for whatever reason, the magistrates thought better of it and gave orders for Paul and Silas to be released but without drawing attention to them, Paul dropped the bombshell of his (and Silas's) Roman citizenship almost en passant: "They have beaten us *publicly*, uncondemned, men who are Roman citizens [ἀνθρώπους Ῥωμαίους ὑπάρχοντας], and have thrown us into prison; and do they now cast us out *secretly*?" (16:37). It did the trick, because it put, if not the fear of the Lord then at least the fear of Caesar, into the magistrates, who came in person and apologized, escorting them out of the city rather than "casting" them out (16:38–39).

In the event, this was a turning point for Paul, and therefore for the plot of the book of Acts. Having played the Roman card so effectively at Philippi, Paul now employed it again at Jerusalem, once more en passant: "Is it lawful for you to scourge a man who is a Roman citizen, and uncondemned?" Apparently this stratagem of citing the civil rights of a Roman citizen saved him from being scourged—this time, at any rate, although in his *historia calamitatum* to the Corinthians he reported not only that on five separate occasions he had been beaten by Jews with thirty-nine strokes (to avoid the maximum of forty that had been set by the law of Moses; Deut. 25:3), but that "three times I have been beaten with rods," presumably by the Roman authorities (2 Cor. 11:24–25). More importantly, it provided the grounds for taking advantage of the appellate procedure open to him as a Roman citizen in the provinces: although already here in Palestine he was "standing before Caesar's tribunal, where I ought to be tried" (25:10), he invoked the two-word formula: Καίσαρα ἐπικαλοῦμαι ("I appeal to Caesar") (25:11). And under Roman law Festus had no alternative but to honor the decision: "You have appealed to Caesar; to Caesar you shall go" (25:12).

Visiting Rome and bearing witness there had long been part of Paul's plan (19:21)—and, more importantly, of Christ's plan for Paul (23:11). But as he wrote to the believers in Rome, he had "so often been hindered from coming to you" (Rom. 15:22) by the vicissitudes recounted in Acts and by a great many more that do not appear in the accounts of Acts (2 Cor. 11:23–28). Humanly speaking, therefore, it was Paul's arrest and then his appeal to the tribunal of Caesar at Rome that finally made it possible. And this, in turn, was made possible by his being a Roman citizen, "with all the rights and privileges thereunto appertaining" as the saying goes, which were considerable. By the time the Acts of the Apostles was written, whenever that was, the political situation of Christian believers, whether they were Roman citizens or not, had degenerated still further, making this emphasis on Paul's Roman citizenship a part of the apologetic grand design of the book (→26:26; →28:14).

Nevertheless, those who suspected Paul the Roman citizen of divided loyalty did have a point, as the persecutions, particularly those under the emperors Decius and Diocletian, were to show. "Our citizenship [ἡμῶν . . . τὸ πολίτευμα] is in heaven," Paul the Roman citizen could write, in the only passage of the New Testament where the word πολίτευμα occurs (Phil. 3:20 NRSV), although the related πολιτεία appears here (→25:11). When a later Roman proconsul demanded that Polycarp "take the oath" and "revile Christ" as the price of his freedom, "Polycarp replied: 'For six and eighty years I have been serving Him, and He has done no wrong to me; how, then, dare I blaspheme my King who has saved me!'"[21] The *Letter to Diognetus* is commonly also dated in the second century, in the setting of the pagan Roman Empire; but it would continue to express this tension when the Roman Empire became Christian, and no less when it was succeeded by the modern nation-state:

> Christians are not distinguished from the rest of mankind by either country, speech, or customs; the fact is, they nowhere settle in cities of their own; they use no peculiar language; they cultivate no eccentric mode of life. . . . Yet while they dwell in both Greek and non-Greek cities, as each one's lot was cast, and conform to the customs of the country in dress, food, and mode of life in general, the whole tenor of their way of living stamps it as worthy of admiration and admittedly extraordinary. They reside in their respective countries, but only as aliens. They take part in everything as citizens and put up with everything as foreigners. *Every foreign land is their home, and every home a foreign land.*[22]

Already in the first chapter of Acts, therefore after the reference to Jerusalem and then to "all Judea and Samaria," all of which together did not amount to much more than a tiny "corner" (26:26) of the Roman Empire and of the then-known world, it does seem to be something of an anticlimax in reverse to add, not Syria or Egypt, but "unto the uttermost part of the earth" (1:8 AV). What can that phrase be understood to have meant geographically in the immediate context, to an author who could write about "a decree [that] went out from Caesar Augustus that *all the world* should be enrolled" (Luke 2:1), meaning the οἰκουμένη of the "civilized world" of the Roman Empire, or who could identify "devout men *from every nation under heaven*" living in Jerusalem (2:5), or who could describe how "*all the residents of Asia [Minor]* heard the word of the Lord, both Jews and Greeks" (19:10)? Regardless of the answer, its meaning has expanded with each new "discovery" or exploration or conquest and (which has often been the same thing) with each new expansion of the Christian mission to another nation and with each new translation of the Bible into another language. There is, therefore, undeniably some sense in which "catholic" as an attribute of the church does carry an almost statistical connotation, so that the fulfillment, already within human history, of the eschatological vision of "a great multitude which no man could number, from every nation, from all tribes and peoples and tongues" (Rev. 7:9), as faith in the gospel has spread to all the continents and to the islands of the sea, is also the concrete realization of the catholicity that was predicated of the church already in some of its earliest creeds.[23] Therefore Acts could even invoke a

21. *Martyrdom of Polycarp* 9.3 (ACW 6:94).
22. *Letter to Diognetus* 5.1–5 (ACW 6:138–39) (emphasis added).
23. Apostles' Creed 9 (*CCF* 1:669).

statistical-*cum*-theological coordination: "So the churches were strengthened in the faith, and they increased in numbers daily" (16:5).

There is, nevertheless, also a certain specious triumphalism about any doctrine of "church growth" that seems to make its universality and catholicity a thing to be measured or quantified, for in the dark hours between the crucifixion and the resurrection, when, as Christian thinkers in various periods have said, there was a "church of one," the "Lady full of grace" to whom, as the Paschal troparion puts it, "the angel cried aloud, 'Rejoice, O Virgin, in the resurrection of your Son,'" she was already, as the troparion goes on to confess, the universal "Zion" and the catholic "new Jerusalem" (→1:14).

ACTS 23

The Testimony of a "Good Conscience"

23:1 I have lived before God in all good conscience up to this day.

It is a measure of the "afflictions, hardships, calamities, beatings, imprisonments, tumults" (2 Cor. 6:4–5) of Saint Paul's ministry that this is only one in a series of speeches delivered by him in self-defense, which appear here in five successive chapters of the Acts of the Apostles:[1]

1. to a Jewish audience, speaking in Aramaic (22:3–21);
2. to the Jewish Sanhedrin (23:1–6), interrupted by various outbursts;
3. to Felix, Roman governor of Judea (24:10–21), in response to the official indictment as stated by Tertullus the lawyer-orator (ῥήτωρ) (24:2–8);
4. to Porcius Festus, another Roman governor of Judea (25:8–11);
5. to King Agrippa (26:2–23);

These apologias are, also because of the variation in the audience, excellent examples of how the classic Aristotelian definition of "*pathos*, the frame of mind of the audience,"[2] shifted in Christian rhetoric as it was being addressed to Jews or to Gentiles (→24:1–2); and it is instructive to pay attention both to the differences and to the common elements between the apologias, as in the present one.

"Brethren, I have lived before God in all *good* conscience [πάσῃ συνειδήσει ἀγαθῇ] up to this day" was his description here to a Jewish audience. In the following chapter, speaking now to a Gentile audience, which included a Roman governor and a Roman attorney, he characterized his moral stance as that of one

---

1. Bruce W. Winter in Winter and Clarke 1993–94, 1:305–36; O'Toole 1978.
2. Aristotle, *Rhetoric* 2.2–11 1378a–88b (LCL 193:173–247).

who "always take[s] pains to have a *clear* conscience [ἀπρόσκοπον συνείδησιν] toward God and toward men" (24:16). In the first he was speaking to an audience who would have known the testimony of a troubled conscience very well, from the confession of David:

> I know my transgressions,
>   and my sin is ever before me.
> Against thee, thee only, have I sinned,
>   and done that which is evil in thy sight,
> so that thou art justified [δικαιωθῇς] in thy sentence
>   and victorious in thy judgment. (Ps. 51:3–4 LXX)

In the second he was addressing those who could remember the conscience or δαίμων of Socrates, who had described it to his own accusers as "something divine and spiritual [that] comes to me. . . . I have had this from my childhood; it is a sort of voice that comes to me, and when it comes it always holds me back from what I am thinking of doing, but never urges me forward."[3]

These two formulations of the doctrine of conscience by Paul differed from each other in two respects, both of which may be theologically significant. The more obvious one is that to Jewish hearers, claiming, as he consistently did to everyone, "that according to the Way, which they call a sect, I worship the God of our fathers, believing everything laid down by the law or written in the prophets" (24:14), in other words, that the Christian "Way" was a (or, now, *the*) form of worshiping the God of Israel, the point of reference for what he said about his conscience was the God of his and their fathers, and only that God. But to Gentile hearers, with whom his theistic point of contact was not the affirmative one of the shared covenant with Israel (→3:25) but the negative one of the apophatic theology (→17:23) of the "unknown God," whom they "ignorantly worship" (17:23 AV), he stated a dual point of reference, "toward God and toward men," so that even if they did not have in common at least a minimal doctrine of God, not to speak of the revelation of God to Moses, it could be their common humanity (→10:34–35) that provided a sufficient ground for him to vindicate his conscience.

The second difference was more subtle, and it may or may not be important theologically, depending, at least in part, on whether the Pauline Epistles have a primary role in interpreting the theology of Acts, as for example on the doctrine of justification by faith (→13:38–39). It is to be found in the two related but distinct adjectives that Paul employed in speaking about his conscience: to Jews he called it "good" (ἀγαθός); to Gentiles he referred to it as "clear" (ἀπρόσκοπος), the same adjective that was employed in his admonition: "Give no offense [ἀπρόσκοποι] to Jews or to Greeks or to the church of God" (1 Cor. 10:32). In stating his argument for the universality of sin and divine

---

3. Plato, *Apology of Socrates* 31d (LCL 36:115).

judgment, as a consequence of which "you have no excuse, O man, whoever you are" (Rom. 2:1), he based his case against Jews on the revealed law of Moses, which he charged them with affirming in theory but disobeying in fact (Rom. 2:17–24). But he based his case against the "Gentiles who have not the law" on the law that was "written on their hearts"—and on "their conscience [which] also bears witness" (Rom. 2:14–15). Addressing the latter audience, therefore, he felt entitled here in Acts to lay claim to a "*clear* conscience," which for his current forensic and rhetorical purposes was sufficient. But addressing the former audience, whose revealed law "speaks to those who are under the law, so that every mouth may be stopped, and the whole world may be held accountable to God" (Rom. 3:19), including as part of "the whole accountable world" Paul the Jew and Christian, it was "a *good* conscience" that he could say he had, one that was good because of the forgiveness of sins, which he described in the words of Ps. 32:1–2, a biblical authority that he shared with them:

> Blessed are those whose iniquities are forgiven, and whose sins are covered; blessed is the man against whom the Lord will not reckon his sin. (Rom. 4:7–8)

But this conscience of Paul's, whether he was speaking before both God and man or only before God, and whether he was describing it as "clear" or as "good" (or finally as both), was one over which, as he could say, "I always take pains" (ἀσκῶ . . . διὰ παντός) (24:16), one that required constant and scrupulous attention from him; the Greek for "to take pains" was ἀσκεῖν, which was the root of the word "ascetic" (→24:25b). In traditional Christian usage, the admonition "examine yourselves" (2 Cor. 13:5) has been seen as an examination of conscience, above all in preparation for receiving "the body and blood of the Lord" in the Lord's Supper not "unworthily" (ἀναξίως) (1 Cor. 11:27–28 AV). The results of that self-examination become evident throughout Acts (→26:20), but most of all in his detailed summary of his apostolic ministry to the elders of Ephesus, where he could claim "that I am innocent of the blood of all of you" (20:26) and that "I coveted no one's silver or gold or apparel" (20:33)—both of these related to the "accusing" (Rom. 2:15) function of conscience. And positively, his catalog of his "good" or "clear" conscience to the Ephesian elders consisted of (1) the description of the moral responsibility he had exercised over himself and for others ("you yourselves know that these hands ministered to my necessities, and to those who were with me"); (2) the identification of the special needs of those who had a particular claim on the consciences of their fellows ("in all things I have shown you that by so toiling one must help the weak"); and (3) the divine imperative of the example (→7:59–60) and of the command of Christ ("the words of the Lord, for he himself said, 'The one who gives is blessed rather than the one who receives'"; 20:35 TPR).

23:3 This flash of Paul's hot temper is by no means an isolated instance in Luke's portrait of him (→21:13–14).

"We Look Forward to a Resurrection of the Dead and Life in the Age to Come"

23:8 TPR The Pharisees confess the existence of resurrection and angel and spirit.

The closing words of the Niceno-Constantinopolitan Creed, "We [later: "I"; →26:18] look forward to a resurrection of the dead and life in the age to come,"[4] summarized an eschatology that was at one and the same time distinctively Christian and yet to some extent a common element shared with the other traditions, the Jewish theology (→3:25) and the Greek philosophy (→17:18), with which Christian thought was in dialogue throughout the book of Acts and then throughout Christian history.

Already in the opening scene of the book Christian eschatology set itself apart from contemporary Jewish eschatology. If, as the disciples finally came to believe and understand through "the gospel of the forty days" (→1:2–3), Jesus truly was the Messiah, although a "crucified Messiah" (→3:18), he could now be expected to do what the Messiah was to do. And "so when they had come together, they asked him, 'Lord, is it at this time that you will bring about the restoration [ἀποκαταστάθήσῃ], and when will the kingdom of Israel be?'" (1:6 TPR). The rebuff, "No one can know the time or season which the Father has fixed by his own authority. But you shall receive power when the Holy Spirit has come upon you" (1:7–8), substituted the kingdom that would come through the Holy Spirit (→28:23) for the "restored kingdom" of the expectations that they shared with at least some of their Jewish coreligionists, for "when the disciples pose the eschatological question, Jesus directs them away from apocalyptic speculation to their responsibility to proclaim the gospel."[5]

Yet this must not be taken to be a repudiation of Jewish eschatology in its entirety. To the contrary, Paul asserted a massive continuity between the Christian hope he now professed and the particular brand of Jewish theology in which he had been reared, calling himself "a Pharisee, a son of Pharisees."[6] As such, he took the side of the Pharisees against the Sadducees; "for the Sadducees say that there is no resurrection, nor angel, nor spirit; but the Pharisees confess the existence of resurrection and angel and spirit." Jesus had already clashed with the Sadducees over the same question, proving "the resurrection of the dead" from the word that came to Moses out of the burning bush (Exod. 3:6): "I am the God of Abraham, and the God of Isaac, and the God of Jacob." Because "he is not God of the dead, but of the living," it followed that Abraham, Isaac, and Jacob must still have been living, and therefore that there was a resurrection of the dead. Those who, like the Sadducees, denied

4. Niceno-Constantinopolitan Creed 11–12 (*CCF* 1:163); Niceno-Constantinopolitan Creed: Western Recension 11–12 (*CCF* 1:673).
5. Nickelsburg 2003, 140.
6. Rakocy 2000, 151–54.

the resurrection of the dead, therefore, "know neither the scriptures nor the power of God" (Matt. 22:29–32).

This interpretation of a continuity with Pharisaic Judaism made Paul's present situation all the more ironic, as he said before King Agrippa: "And now I stand here on trial for hope in the promise made by God to our fathers, to which our twelve tribes hope to attain, as they earnestly worship night and day. And for this hope I am accused by Jews, O king!" (26:6–7). And earlier, before Felix the governor, he posited the same continuity between the Christian "Way, which they call a sect [αἵρεσις]" (→11:26) and the "worship [of] the God of our fathers," which necessarily entailed "believing everything laid down by the law or written in the prophets," including "a hope in God which these themselves accept, that there will be a resurrection of both the just and the unjust" (24:14–15). In relation to both of these groups of Jewish accusers, therefore, he could ask the rhetorical question: "Why is it thought incredible by any of you that God raises the dead?" (26:8).

On quite different grounds he would have been able to put the same rhetorical question to his Greek audiences, or at least to some parts of them: "Why is it thought incredible by any of *you*" that the dead live on? At Athens "some also of the Epicurean and Stoic philosophers met him," but by historical hindsight one might wish that, on this issue at any rate, it had been Neoplatonic philosophers instead (→17:18), for, as the *Oxford Classical Dictionary* points out, "it was also the Epicureans, among the philosophers, who most resolutely opposed the idea of an immortal psyche."[7] On the other hand, it was in the Platonic philosophical tradition, rooted in the *Phaedo* and the *Meno*, that the idea of the immortality of the soul was most unambiguously affirmed, an idea that became part of Christian anthropology and therefore of Christian eschatology, which defined the resurrection of the dead as (in the words of the Apostles' Creed) "the resurrection of the body" or "resurrection of the flesh" (*carnis resurrectio*)[8] and as its reunion with the immortal soul, which could not die and did not need to be brought back to life. There was no reference to this idea of immortality in Paul's address on the Areopagus, whose eschatology consisted in the doctrine that God "has fixed a day on which he will judge the world in righteousness" and in the message that God "has given assurance to all men" of this doctrine "by raising [Jesus] from the dead." Like the parties of Pharisees and the Sadducees in his Jewish audiences, then, there were also two—though, typically, more noncommittal—parties here at Athens: "Now when they heard of the resurrection of the dead, some mocked; but others said, 'We will hear you again about this. [And let's do lunch sometime!]'" (17:31–32).

It is noteworthy in that report (though invisible in uninflected English) that it was not, or not only, the resurrection of Christ at which they mocked, but "the resurrection of [all] the dead" (ἀνάστασις νεκρῶν: genitive plural). Paul's

7. Christopher J. Rowe in *OCD* 1428.
8. Apostles' Creed 11 (*CCF* 1:669).

reference was to the resurrection specifically of Jesus Christ, but it prompted this reaction to the general doctrine of resurrection. If the disciples "annoyed" the Sadducees because "they were teaching the people and proclaiming Jesus in the resurrection of the dead" (4:1–2 TPR), two alternative linkages seem possible: it was the resurrection of Jesus that made the general doctrine of resurrection credible, and/or the resurrection of Jesus was not credible except for a general doctrine of resurrection. Both in the eschatology of Acts and in the most complete statement of the doctrine anywhere in the New Testament, 1 Cor. 15, as well as in the subsequent history of Christian doctrine from the very outset,[9] there is some evidence for either of these alternative interpretations (→2:31).

23:11 The following night the Lord stood by him and said, "Take courage, for as you have testified about me at Jerusalem, so you must bear witness also at Rome."

The Rome to whose authority Paul had appealed as a Roman citizen (→22:27) was also the world capital where the universal significance of the gospel for all of world history would be made manifest (→28:14).

23:12–24 The widespread religious practice of taking a vow, which was known in both Jewish and pagan observance and would become a central component of Christian asceticism, was here being placed into the service of coercion and violence (→3:25; →21:35; →24:25b; →28:31).

Epistles—Jewish, Roman, and Christian

23:25 And he wrote a letter.

In addition to rhetoric (→24:1–2), especially the rhetoric of self-defense (→23:1), another classical literary genre adopted by the Christians and put to special use was the epistle: twenty-one of the twenty-seven books in the New Testament canon—all except the four Gospels, this book of Acts, and Revelation—are epistles; and even the last of these is cast in the form of seven letters to seven churches (Rev. 1:11). In the liturgies of most churches a reading from one of these (sometimes designated "the apostle") stands alongside a reading from one of the Gospels (plus, in many cases, a reading from the Old Testament) to form the "lessons" or pericopes prescribed for a Sunday or holiday. As a leading reference work puts it:

9. *Chr. Trad.* 1:47–52, 149–50.

The letter is one of the most common and socially significant kinds of written text from antiquity. Extant letters represent every level of Greco-Roman society from Egyptian peasants to Roman emperors. The letter served the most basic needs of day-to-day communication and the most highly developed art and ideology. The letter is also arguably the most important, and certainly the most prevalent type of literature in early Christianity.[10]

The epistle would continue to be prevalent as a type of literature: some of the most important theological essays of various church fathers in both East and West were written in the form of letters, which, like the epistles of the New Testament, took a local audience and a topical question as the occasion for an exposition that carried universal theological implications.[11] It is not surprising, then, that letters should also be as prominent as they are in the Acts of the Apostles and that as a historical narrative the book of Acts should be the only place in the New Testament where we get a broader sense of the epistle in context.

The epistle as a Jewish literary form had appeared already in the Old Testament: most prominently in the book of Ezra, which contained a "letter written in Aramaic and translated" (Ezra 4:7 LXX/RSV) that was addressed to Artaxerxes (Ezra 4:11–16), his response to that letter (Ezra 4:17–22), and a letter addressed to Darius (Ezra 5:7–17); and then in the books of the Maccabees, where letters from Antiochus Epiphanes commanding idolatry and abomination set up the plot of the narrative (1 Macc. 1:44–51) and appealed for support from the Jews (2 Macc. 9:19–27) and where a letter written by Judas Maccabeus cemented the alliance between Israel and Rome (1 Macc. 8:23–32). Here in Acts there are two mentions of Jewish epistles, both of which refer to official documents and both of which involve the person of Saul/Paul. The preface to the first of the three accounts of his conversion (→9:1–4) explained that his persecution of the believers was not only the personal animus of one who was "breathing threats and murder against the disciples of the Lord," but that, desiring official authorization for these "threats and murder," he "went to the high priest and asked him for letters to the synagogues of Damascus, so that if he found any belonging to the Way, men or women, he might bring them bound to Jerusalem" (9:1–2). It was apparently similar letters of indictment that the local leaders of the Jews in Rome had in mind when they told Paul, "We have received no letters from Judea about you" (28:21), although there was plenty of reason, even absent such letters, for their harboring suspicions about "this sect" (28:22).

10. Stanley K. Stowers in *ABD* 4:290.
11. For example, Cyprian, *Epistles* 62 (*ANF* 5:358–64), on the Eucharist; Basil of Caesarea, *Address to Young Men, on How They Might Derive Benefit from Greek Literature* (LCL 270:365–435), on reason and revelation; Augustine, *Letters* 164 (*NPNF*[1] 1:515–21), on the descent of Christ into Hades.

Neither of these mentions of Jewish letters about Paul included any text, but this official letter about him from the Roman tribune Claudius Lysias to the Roman governor Felix was framed in the standard Roman epistolary form: "Claudius Lysias to his Excellency the governor Felix, greeting [χαίρειν]" (23:26–30)—although, as has been pointed out, Paul did not use this common formula of salutation in his own letters.[12] Later in the legal proceedings, the Roman governor Festus explained the need to have an official letter of transmittal to accompany the prisoner, who had invoked his right as a Roman citizen (→22:27) to appeal to the tribunal of Caesar (→25:11): "As he himself appealed to the emperor, I decided to send him. But I have nothing definite to write to my lord about him. Therefore I have brought him before you, and, especially before you, King Agrippa, that after we have examined him, I may have something to write" (25:25–26). Roman standards of what we now call "due process of law" (→25:16) required such written documentation.

That official dimension of the letter, which was evident in both the Jewish and the Roman epistles, applied to the Christian epistle as well, transmitting the "decisions [δόγματα] which had been reached by the apostles and elders who were at Jerusalem" (→16:4b). After the deliberations of the council at Jerusalem, the Apostle James, in his capacity as official spokesman (→15:28), expressed his "judgment that we should not trouble those of the Gentiles who turn to God, but should *write to them*" (15:19–20). What follows a few verses later is the text of the official letter (15:23–29). The obvious intent in writing it down was to leave no ambiguity, or, as Festus would say, to have a "definite" (ἀσφαλές) (25:26) formulation—which makes it all the more ironic that this decree of the apostolic council should have turned out to be one of the more textually ambiguous portions of a book that has more than its share of textual ambiguities and variants (→20:28a).

Yet what the book of Acts does not tell us about Christian epistles is more important than what it does tell us, for, quite surprisingly, we have no direct references to the Epistles of Paul,[13] which have probably had more of an impact on subsequent history than all of his missionary journeys and speeches combined (and, perhaps, than all other letters ever written by anyone else). Repeatedly, the narrative seems to provide an opportunity for such a reference, but each time we are left to wonder whether the epistles were written earlier or later, as well as just where they were composed. From the judgment of public opinion quoted by Paul himself, "his letters are weighty and strong, but his bodily presence is weak, and his speech of no account" (2 Cor. 10:9–10), it would seem that they were being circulated. At some later point they were even collected (2 Pet. 3:15–16), and the possibility exists that the book of Acts helped to provide the stimulus for collecting them.[14] Of the Pauline Epistles

12. Barrett 1994–98, 2:740.
13. Hemer 1989, 244–76.
14. John Knox in Keck and Martyn 1966, 279–87.

addressed to cities and territories (→28:14), only Colossians has no reference point in Acts, and of the individual persons to whom Paul wrote epistles, neither Titus nor Philemon is mentioned. The following recipients of Pauline Letters are mentioned in Acts:

New Testament Book	References in Acts
Romans	2:10; 18:2; 19:21; 23:11; 28:14, 16
1–2 Corinthians	18:1; 19:1
Galatians	16:6; 18:23
Ephesians	18:19, 21, 24; 19:1, 17, 26, 35; 20:16–17
Philippians	16:12; 20:6
1–2 Thessalonians	17:1, 11, 13; 27:2
1–2 Timothy	16:1, 3; 17:14–15; 18:5; 19:22; 20:4

ACTS 24

The Christian Appropriation of Classical Rhetoric

24:1–2, 10 And after five days the high priest Ananias came down with some elders and a spokesman [ῥήτωρ], one Tertullus. They laid before the governor their case against Paul; and when he was called, Tertullus began to accuse [κατηγορεῖν] him.... And when the governor had motioned to him to speak, Paul replied: "Realizing that for many years you have been judge over this nation, I cheerfully make my defense [ἀπολογοῦμαι]."

The encounter with Greco-Roman philosophy (→17:18) has, for understandable reasons, predominated in most discussions of the relation between "Christianity and classical culture,"[1] as well as in the debates over the concept of "the Hellenization of Christianity."[2] But at least equally as important, also because the preaching of the word of God has been so central throughout the life and history of the church (→8:25) even in those centuries when philosophy was largely neglected, was the process by which classical rhetoric was adapted to Christian purposes.[3] The appearance here (and only here) of the noun ῥήτωρ and the use of the verb ἀπολογεῖσθαι (which is confined, apart from this and five other passages in Acts [19:33; 25:8; 26:1, 2, 24], to Saint Paul [Rom. 2:15 and 2 Cor. 12:19] and, in the Gospels, only to Luke [Luke 12:11 and 21:14]), as technical terms from the vocabulary of classical and Hellenistic rhetoric, is a measure of that importance.[4]

Theophilus and the other Hellenistic readers to whom the Acts of the Apostles was originally addressed would have been familiar with the public practice of

1. Cochrane 1944; Nock 1972, 2:676–81; Pelikan 1993.
2. Glawe 1912.
3. Philip E. Satterthwaite in Winter and Clarke 1993–94, 1:337–80.
4. Witherington 1998, 116–24.

rhetoric in the Roman courts and in political life, as well as with the standard device, employed by Greek and Roman historians, of embedding set speeches into a historical narrative as a way of moving the story along and of commenting on it.[5] This device, which has often been compared to the function of the chorus in the Greek tragedies of Sophocles and Aeschylus, did not pretend to be quoting the *ipsissima verba* of the actors and was not understood by its readers as doing so. Thucydides spelled out his historiographical method in candid detail:

> As to the speeches that were made by different men, . . . it has been difficult to recall with strict accuracy the words actually spoken, both for me as regards that which I myself heard, and for those who from various sources have brought me reports. Therefore the speeches are given in the language in which, as it seemed to me, the several speakers would express, on the subjects under consideration, the sentiments most befitting the occasion, though at the same time I have adhered as closely as possible to the general sense of what was actually said.[6]

Therefore, as Alfred Zimmern says of the funeral oration of Pericles in the *Peloponnesian War* of Thucydides, "It is not, of course, the speech which Pericles delivered. . . . But there is no reason to doubt that Thucydides had heard his hero speak. . . . We may feel with confidence that he has given us, with the added color of his own experience, not merely the inner thought but much of the language of Pericles. So that here we can listen, as in all fine works of interpretation, to two great spirits at once."[7]

Combining this rhetorical quality of being "an eloquent man" (ἀνὴρ λόγιος) with his biblical erudition (18:24), Apollos, a Hellenistic Jew who had become a Christian, seems to have been so "eloquent" that, presumably against his will, one of the contending parties in the church at Corinth took his name as its standard (1 Cor. 1:12). The repercussions of this—or perhaps of his own dismal results in Athens (17:22–34)—may be audible in Saint Paul's disclaimer, addressed to the church in Corinth, of any pretensions of being known as one who "proclaimed to you the testimony of God in lofty words or wisdom" (1 Cor. 2:1). Nevertheless, each of the many speeches in Acts[8]—specifically, the early homilies by Saint Peter (2:14–36; 3:12–26; 10:34–43; 15:7–11), the full-length historical dissertation of Saint Stephen (7:2–53), the allocution of Saint James on behalf of the apostolic council (15:13–21), and the several exhortations by Saint Paul, whether addressed to Jews (13:16–41; 22:1–21; 28:17–20), to Gentiles (14:14–18; 17:22–31; 24:10–21; 26:1–23), or to Christians (20:18–35)—can

5. Plümacher 1972, 33–38.
6. Thucydides, *Peloponnesian War* 1.22.1 (LCL 108:39).
7. Zimmern 1931, 199.
8. See, above all, the classic monograph of Dibelius 1949, with the comments of Nock 1972, 2:828–32; Henry J. Cadbury in Foakes Jackson and Lake 1979, 5:402–27; and Gasque 1974.

be understood better on the basis of rhetorical analysis. The components of a persuasive speech, according to Aristotle's classic definition of categories in his *Rhetoric*, were three: "the character of the speaker" (often labeled, though not by him, *ethos*); "the frame of mind of the audience" (*pathos*); and "the structure of the argument" (*logos*). These categories were as applicable to Christian rhetorical discourse as they were to rhetorical discourse generally, both because of the nature of language and because of the universality of the need to persuade.[9] The axiom of Thomas Aquinas about the functioning of reason in relation to revelation, "grace does not abolish nature, but completes it"[10] (→7:22), held here as well. Therefore when, in consecutive chapters, Acts says that "some of them were persuaded [ἐπείσθησαν]" (17:4), or it quotes Paul's opponents as attacking him on the grounds that "this man is persuading [ἀναπείθει] men to worship God contrary to the law" (18:13), or it describes how Paul "spoke boldly, arguing and pleading [διαλεγόμενος καὶ πείθων] about the kingdom of God" (19:8), it is employing the same verb that Aristotle and other Greek rhetoricians used when they spoke, as Aristotle did in the very definition of rhetoric, of "the existing means of persuasion."[11] Here in Acts and in the rest of Scripture, the mysterious relation between such "persuading" and the converting initiative of the Holy Spirit is neither psychologized (→9:1–4) nor resolved by recourse to a deterministic or fatalistic theory that would negate the role of free will (→13:48), but left to stand as a mystery: "O the depths of the riches and wisdom and knowledge of God! How unsearchable are his judgments and how inscrutable his ways!" (Rom. 11:33).

The demonic potential of rhetoric and oratory, against which Greco-Roman thinkers from Socrates (according to Plato's *Gorgias* and *Phaedrus*) to Cicero had warned, made itself evident in the narrative of Acts above all in the case of King Herod (12:21–23 TPR), who "on an appointed day put on his royal robes, took his seat upon the throne, and made an oration [ἐδημηγόρει] to them. And . . . the people shouted, 'The sounds of a god, and not of man!' Immediately an angel of the Lord smote him, because he did not give God the glory; and . . . he was eaten alive by worms and died" (→12:21–23).

24:6–8 TPR He even tried to profane the temple, but we seized him, and we would have judged him according to our law. But the chief captain Lysias came and with great violence took him out of our hands, commanding his accusers to come before you.

With his fellow Christians, Paul went on honoring the temple in Jerusalem as holy ground (→7:47–48), but that was regarded by his accusers as profanation because he used it to "proclaim Jesus in the resurrection from the dead"

9. Pelikan 2000.
10. Thomas Aquinas, *Summa theologica* 1.1.8.
11. Aristotle, *Rhetoric* 1.1.14 1355b (LCL 193:13).

(4:1–2 TPR). And what they regarded here as the "great violence" (→28:31) with which Paul was taken out of their hands and summoned before a duly constituted court was in fact the observance of the Roman standard of the due process of law (→25:16).

24:14 AV I confess unto thee, that after the way which they call heresy, so worship I the God of my fathers, believing all things which are written in the law and in the prophets.

The "confessional imperative" (→4:20) continues to be central to the portrait of Paul in Acts, even in the opening word of this sentence, "I confess" (ὁμολογῶ), as does the insistence on a continuity between "the way which they call heresy" and the traditional Jewish faith in "the God of my fathers" (→3:25), which had been laid down "in the law and in the prophets" of the Jewish Scriptures (→8:30–31).

24:16 Here Paul speaks of a "*clear* conscience toward God and toward men," whereas earlier he had referred to it as "a *good* conscience" (→23:1).

24:21 Not only was confessing "the resurrection of the dead" (→23:8) and of Jesus Christ (→2:31) to be the core of the Christian gospel, but the first half of this confession was a fundamental point of division within Judaism itself, separating the Sadducees from the Pharisees, who "confess the existence of resurrection and angel and spirit" (23:7–8 TPR) and with whom therefore the gospel was in agreement on this point.

"We Believe": *Fides quae creditur*

24:24–25a AV He sent for Paul, and heard him concerning the faith in Christ. And as he reasoned of [1] righteousness, [2] temperance, and [3] judgment to come. . . .

When the primitive apostolic rule of faith, which had begun to acquire a creedal-catechetical format quite early, if only orally (→8:37), was finally codified by the fourth-century councils of the church (→15:28) into a normative and enforceable creed, its opening word in Greek, both at Nicea in 325 and again at Constantinople in 381, was πιστεύομεν ("we believe") in the plural.[12] But probably because of the use of this "Nicene Creed" as a baptismal symbol in the East, the plural was changed to a singular, πιστεύω ("I believe"), which persisted, also in the usage of the Latin Church, even when this creed served as the confession of faith in the liturgy of the Eucharist (although in the West

12. Nicene Creed 1 (*CCF* 1:158); Niceno-Constantinopolitan Creed 1 (*CCF* 1:162).

it was the Apostles' Creed that was confessed at baptism).[13] The existence of these two formularies, "We believe" and "I believe," side by side makes it possible, without arbitrarily turning a distinction into a difference, to give consideration both to πίστις as the faith of the church ("we believe") and to πίστις as the faith of the person ("I believe").[14] Moreover, "We believe," the faith of the church—seen as "what the church of Jesus Christ believes, teaches, and confesses on the basis of the word of God"[15] to be its doctrinal "rule of faith" (*regula fidei*) in all centuries and what it has gone on believing, and its contents, "the faith that is believed" (*fides quae creditur*)—may be treated here in distinction from "the faith by which one believes" (*fides qua creditur*), epitomized in the formula "I believe" (→26:18). The former, *fides quae creditur*, is often translated in English as "believing *that*," expressed in Greek with an infinitive, as in 8:37 TPR, or with the conjunction ὅτι ("that"), as in Rom. 10:9, "If you confess with your lips that Jesus is Lord and believe in your heart that [ὅτι] God raised him from the dead," where "believing" and "confessing" are coordinated (→4:20). The latter, *fides qua creditur*, is expressed in Greek by a dative (Gen. 15:6 LXX; Rom. 4:3) or by a genitive (Rom. 3:22) or by a preposition, sometimes ἐπί (16:31) but more usually εἰς.

Theological usage in English (→8:25) has, though with less than perfect consistency, tended to formulate this distinction by using "faith" with the definite article, as "*the* faith," when referring to the *fides quae creditur*, and without the article, simply as "faith," when referring to the *fides qua creditur*. Perhaps the clearest illustration of the distinction in the New Testament is the admonition: "I found it necessary to write appealing to you to contend for *the* faith which was once for all delivered to the saints" (Jude 3), where the definite article in English translates the definite article in Greek: τῇ ἅπαξ παραδοθείσῃ τοῖς ἁγίοις πίστει. But there are other passages in the New Testament, also in Acts, in which the Greek uses the definite article while undeniably referring to that faith with which one believes in Christ Jesus (*fides qua creditur*) and in which therefore "faith" without the article is the appropriate rendering in English, as for example in the words of Saint Peter: "And his name, by faith in his name [ἐπὶ τῇ πίστει τοῦ ὀνόματος αὐτοῦ], has made this man strong whom you see and know; and the faith which is through Jesus [ἡ πίστις ἡ δι᾽ αὐτοῦ] has given the man this perfect health in the presence of you all" (3:16).

The present passage is a nice illustration of the problem. Is τῆς εἰς Χριστὸν Ἰησοῦν πίστεως, with the definite article in Greek, to be translated in English without the definite article (so RSV) as "faith in Christ Jesus," therefore presumably as referring to *fides qua creditur*, or with the definite article (so AV) as "*the* faith in Christ Jesus," referring to that faith which, in the company of the church through the ages, one believes and affirms about Jesus Christ (*fides quae*

13. Pelikan 2003, 37, 50.
14. D. Kirn in *RE* 6:680.
15. *Chr. Trad.* 1:1.

creditur), "that Jesus is the Son of God" (8:37 TPR AV) or "that Jesus Christ is Lord" (Phil. 2:11)? In "and the word of God increased; and the number of the disciples multiplied greatly in Jerusalem, and a great many of the priests were obedient to the faith" (6:7), both RSV and NRSV, and not only AV, do translate ὑπήκουον τῇ πίστει as "became/were obedient to *the* faith," which in the context could mean the shared faith as content, *fides quae creditur.* The same is true in the description of Paul and Barnabas "strengthening the souls of the disciples, exhorting them to continue in *the* faith, and saying that through many tribulations we must enter the kingdom of God" (14:22).

A decision about which of the two meanings, "faith" or "the faith," is at work in the present passage also affects the interpretation and even the translation of the words that immediately follow, as the text goes on to specify: "He discussed περὶ δικαιοσύνης καὶ ἐγκρατείας καὶ τοῦ κρίματος τοῦ μέλλοντος." If he was discussing "*the* faith" as the faith that is believed and confessed by the church, then δικαιοσύνη can mean the righteousness that comes, according to Saint Paul, through justification by faith (→13:38–39); and it should not be translated, as it is in the NEB, with "morals," which would, however, be acceptable if πίστις here means *fides qua creditur,* as the translators of the NEB have evidently understood it.

Ascetic Discipline and Self-Denial

24:25b NJB He began to treat of . . . self-control [περὶ . . . ἐγκρατείας].

By inserting καὶ ἐγκρατείας between δικαιοσύνη and κρίμα here, the book of Acts serves notice that in the first century and in the twenty-first, as well as in the centuries in between, "faith in Jesus Christ" (→24:24–25a) and the righteousness it brings through justification (→13:38–39) has set itself apart from "the lust of the flesh and the lust of the eyes and the pride of life" (1 John 2:16) by summoning the disciples of Christ to be "the salt of the earth" (Matt. 5:13) and to practice a life of ascetic discipline and self-control.[16] This self-denial extends to all of human life, including the treatment of wealth and possessions (→4:32), and it includes avoidance of all seven of what came eventually to be identified as the seven deadly sins (→12:21–23).

In that connection the commentators have long puzzled over the decree of the apostolic council itemizing the catalog of the Mosaic prohibitions that were still binding on believers, including Gentile believers. Even after sorting out the confused textual transmission of the decree (→20:28a), these prohibitions came to four in number: "to abstain [1] from the pollutions of idols and [2] from unchastity and [3] from what is strangled and [4] from blood" (15:20). By any taxonomy or stratification of the Mosaic law (→25:8), the appearance of

---

16. On ἐγκράτεια, see the parallels listed in Tarazi 2001, 268 n. 19.

"unchastity" "fornication" (πορνεία) as the second of the four, the other three being "ceremonial law" rather than "moral law" in any definition or classification, does not seem to make sense, unless it is seen as not only a general moral precept but more specifically an ascetic one or specifically as a prohibition of such pagan practices as consorting with temple prostitutes.

As Henry J. Cadbury points out, "it is in Luke's writings only that we get the frequent combination of fasting and prayer."[17] Without the testimony of the book of Acts, the case for the importance of fasting in the discipline of the Christian life would be difficult to make specifically from the New Testament[18]—also because the one saying of Jesus that has often been quoted in support of the practice, "this kind [of demon] can come forth by nothing, but by prayer *and fasting*" (Mark 9:29 AV), lacks those final two words in the best manuscripts (→20:28a). A similar negative tone is found in the discussion of fasting in the Sermon on the Mount:

> And when you fast, do not look dismal, like the hypocrites, for they disfigure their faces that their fasting may be seen by men. Truly, I say to you, they have received their reward. But when you fast, anoint your head and wash your face, that your fasting may not be seen by men but by your Father who is in secret; and your Father who sees in secret will reward you. (Matt. 6:16–18)

This obviously negative tone has sometimes obscured the point that this is a condemnation not of fasting, but of the hypocrisy so often associated with it. Indeed, the rightness of fasting seems to be presupposed in the iteration of "when you fast" or even "whenever you fast," namely, "as you should rather than as the hypocrites do."[19]

Acts was no less harsh in its language about hypocrisy, as when Paul in the preceding chapter denounced the high priest for ordering that he be struck on the mouth: "God shall strike you, you whitewashed wall! Are you sitting to judge me according to the law, and yet contrary to the law you order me to be struck?" (23:3). But such language was notably absent from its many references to fasting; as Chrysostom summarizes it, "A great, yes a great good is fasting: it is circumscribed by no limits. When need was to ordain, then they fast: and to them while fasting, the Spirit spake."[20] In keeping with their adherence to the covenant of God with the people of Israel (→3:25), which was a continuing part of the life of the apostolic community despite the drastic reconfiguration of the Mosaic law (→10:15), the fasting that was so prominent an element in Jewish observance of the law (Joel 1:14; 2:12) continued to figure in the practice of Christian discipline. "The days of Unleavened Bread" continued to be marked on the Christian calendar (20:6), as did "*the* fast" (ἡ νηστεία)

17. Cadbury 1958, 269.
18. See Tertullian, *On Fasting* 8 (*ANF* 4:107).
19. Augustine, *Our Lord's Sermon on the Mount* 2.12.40–42 (*NPNF*[1] 6:47–48).
20. Chrysostom, *Homilies on Acts* 27 (*NPNF*[1] 11:176).

(27:9). It was part of the initiation of Saul the persecutor into his new life as Paul the "chosen instrument" (→9:15) that he "neither ate nor drank" (9:9); only after his baptism was he permitted to break that fast (9:19). Fasting was the accompaniment for the further specification of his call to the apostolic ministry: "While they were worshiping the Lord *and fasting*, the Holy Spirit said, 'Set apart for me Barnabas and Paul for the work to which I have called them.' Then after *fasting* and praying they laid their hands on them [→6:6] and sent them off" (13:2–3 TPR). It also accompanied a further extension of the apostolic ministry to presbyters: "And when they had appointed elders for them in every church, with prayer *and fasting* they committed them to the Lord in whom they believed" (14:23).

This practice of ἐγκράτεια as abstention from food in ascetic self-discipline went on to become a constituent element of the Christian life for all believers, as the Jewish "fast" (27:9) evolved into the Christian Lent—or, rather, "Lents" in the plural, with "Advent" also being called "Lent." In spite of an insensitivity to the essentially Christian roots of this asceticism that could lead him to his "astonishing" final comment, "One is astonished at how small a role explicitly Christian considerations played. . . . What was fundamentally at work is an idea that was not Christian, but came out of the mystery religions," Karl Holl shows that the growth of the four seasons of fasting in the Byzantine church eventually meant that there were more fasting days than nonfasting days on the calendar of the church year.[21] Another expression of ἐγκράτεια was celibacy and abstention from sex—either "for a season, that you may devote yourselves to prayer" (1 Cor. 7:5), or for a lifetime. In some portions of the early church, celibacy may even have been required as a prerequisite for baptism.[22] But for centuries compulsory celibacy was not a rule for the clergy, or even for bishops: Saint Peter was married (Luke 4:38–39; 1 Cor. 9:5); Saint Gregory of Nyssa was married;[23] and Gregory of Nazianzus the Elder, father of Saint Gregory the Theologian, was a bishop.[24] Nevertheless, the imperative of ἐγκράτεια also in this respect acquired institutional form with the rise of Christian monasticism.

Yet ascetic practice and vows could also have a darker side in Acts (23:11–13): "Behold fasting the mother of murder!" Chrysostom exclaims.[25] This darker side becomes evident from the principal etymological derivative of the word ἐγκράτεια, which is "Encratite," as a party label to mark the heresy of contempt for divine creations such as food and sexuality.[26] The Encratites were described by Saint Irenaeus: "Those who are called Encratites . . . preached against marriage, thus setting aside the original creation of God, and indirectly blaming

21. Holl 1928, 155–203.
22. Vööbus 1951.
23. Quasten et al. 1951–86, 3:254.
24. Gregory of Nazianzus, *Orations* 18 (*NPNF*[2] 7:255–69).
25. Chrysostom, *Homilies on Acts* 49 (*NPNF*[1] 11:293).
26. H. Rahner in *LTK* 3:892–93; *ODCC* 545.

Him who made the male and female for the propagation of the human race."[27] The dualistic attitudes to which an extremist interpretation of Jewish laws of kosher could occasionally lead were not confined to Judaism, but took a far more virulent form in Christianity. Therefore it has repeatedly become necessary, in the canon law of the church (→16:4a) and, when that proved to be insufficient, in movements of protest and reformation, to address to Christian ascetics the reminder spoken to Peter: "What God has cleansed, you must not call common" or profane (10:15)—whether food or drink or sex or property or money (→4:32).

24:25c And future judgment.

The third constituent element of "the faith" as *fides quae creditur* here was eschatology (→23:8).

---

27. Irenaeus, *Against Heresies* 1.28.1 (*ANF* 1:353).

ACTS 25

25:3 This "ambush" (ἐνέδρα) is yet another illustration of how much of the narrative in the book of Acts is taken up with violence, plots, and intrigue—"shipwreck[s], . . . journeys, . . . danger, . . . toil and hardship" (2 Cor. 11:25–27)—and a great deal more (→7:59–60; →28:31).

The Law of Reason, the Law of Nations, the Law of God

25:8, 27 Paul said . . . , "Neither against the law of the Jews, nor against the temple, nor against Caesar have I offended at all." . . . Festus said, . . . "It seems to me unreasonable, in sending a prisoner, not to indicate the charges against him."

From the topics of all three *loci communes* in this twenty-fifth chapter it is evident that this is, in some respects, the most political chapter of the book of Acts, or at least the one in which there is the most attention to questions of politics and of law. Together with "wisdom" (σοφία, *sapientia*) (→7:22) and "justice" (δικαιοσύνη, *iustitia*) (→13:38–39), the concept of "law" (νόμος, *lex, ius*) (→10:15) occupied a dominant position both in the Jewish scheme of revelation and in the Greek and Roman worldviews. All three of these concepts, therefore, shaped the vocabulary of the Christian witness from the beginning. Each of them, moreover, stood in a special relation to another concept that was held in common by all these traditions, the concept of "reason" (λόγος, *ratio*). Juxtaposing these two statements this way from the opposite ends of this twenty-fifth chapter, the first reporting the words of Paul and the second reporting the words of Festus the Roman governor, calls attention, in the concept of law, to the complex interrelation between the law of reason, the law of nations, and the law of God: in biblical teaching these were not identical, nor were they mutually exclusive.

Already within Greco-Roman jurisprudence and philosophy, the possibility—indeed, the undeniable reality—of conflicts between the first two, the law of reason and the law of nations, was a serious issue. Traditional Greek and Roman law, whether traced to Solon among the Greeks or to the Law of the Twelve Tables among the Romans, had inherited a multitude of regulations and customs. Michael H. Crawford deals with these at length, and even in his summary article their complexity and their variety of origin are manifest.[1] It was manifestly impossible to find any philosophical justification for many of these, beyond the rational requirements of pragmatic necessity. But unless the difference between the law of nations and the law of reason represented an outright contradiction, it was the counsel of philosopher-statesmen such as Cicero, most explicitly perhaps in *De legibus* (only portions of which have survived), to go along with the law even while recognizing that "the most foolish notion of all is the belief that everything is just which is found in the customs or laws of nations."[2] All of that became even more complicated with the introduction of the Hebrew notion of a—or, rather, *the*—revealed law of God (→5:29b) and then of the Christian reinterpretation of this revealed law (→3:25; →10:15).

As the Sixth Amendment in the Bill of Rights of the United States Constitution shows with its provision "in all criminal prosecutions, the accused shall enjoy the right . . . to be informed of the nature and cause of the accusation," Festus might have said, "It seems to me *unconstitutional*, in sending a prisoner, not to indicate the charges against him," for the origins of the Sixth Amendment can be traced to the Roman constitution and Roman law.[3] The tern "unconstitutional," moreover, would make sense in a Roman context, even though the Roman "constitution" was not spelled out as explicitly as the American Constitution is.[4]

Invoking instead the criterion of what was "unreasonable" (ἄλογον) introduced the principle of the law of reason, not in the first instance as a source of positive law but as a test by which positive law could be judged and which it was obliged not to violate. The natural-law tradition in Christian thought has found support for this criterion in the apostle's answer to the problem of good (which is in many ways more difficult and challenging than is the problem of evil): "When Gentiles who have not the law [of Moses] do by nature [φύσει] what the law requires, they are a law to themselves, even though they do not have the law. They show that what the law requires is written on their hearts" (Rom. 2:14–15).

1. Michael H. Crawford in *OCD* 848–53, based on his 1996 edition of *Roman Statutes*.
2. Cicero, *On the Laws* 1.15–16 (LCL 213:343–47).
3. See the helpful discussion by Henry J. Cadbury in Foakes Jackson and Lake 1979, 5:297–338.
4. Lintott 1999.

Even so generous an estimate of the law of reason or natural law as these words of Paul to the Romans, however, has never been taken to preclude the necessity of positive law and the law of nations. Therefore Paul insisted here that he had not "offended" "against Caesar at all." The Greek verb he used for "offended" was ἁμαρτάνειν, which in the Septuagint—"against thee only have I sinned" (σοὶ μόνῳ ἥμαρτον), the psalm confesses (Ps. 51:4 LXX)—and in New Testament Greek was the standard word for "to commit sin."[5] In addition to its implication for the Christian understanding of political authority as such (→25:11), this statement in its context referred specifically to Roman law and therefore to the consistent claim especially of Luke-Acts that "the Way" (→11:26) did not represent a violation of the law but was legitimate. It was also consistent with Paul's reference to an "immorality . . . of a kind that is not found even among pagans" (1 Cor. 5:1), contrary both to Roman law and to Jewish law (Lev. 18:7–8). Even this positive attitude to Roman law was inadequate as a preparation for the political and legal revolution effected by the emperors Constantine and Theodosius in the fourth century, when "offend[ing]" "against Caesar" came increasingly to mean committing blasphemy or heresy against Christian orthodoxy or violating Christian morality. Yet it is at least intriguing, and perhaps significant, that the codification of the Roman law, including the law of pagan Rome, was not the work of Caesar Augustus or of the philosopher-emperor Marcus Aurelius, but of the Christian emperor Justinian, building on the foundation of jurisprudence laid by the Christian emperor Theodosius. This suggests that the positive attitude to Roman law visible here must have rested in fact on a substantial theological base.

Paul's defense against the charge of having "offended" "against Caesar" came after his earlier disclaimer of not having offended "against the law of the Jews, [or] against the temple." This was of a piece with the attitude both toward "the law of the Jews" (→3:25) and toward "the temple" (→7:47–48) throughout the Acts of the Apostles, for what Paul here called "the law of the Jews" was in fact the law of God, the "living oracles" (λόγια ζῶντα) (7:38), "the law as delivered by angels" (7:53) as Stephen called it. As such, the moral law was eternal, and it had to be invoked both against the political authorities and against the religious hierarchy: "We must obey God rather than men" (→5:29b). Both in its confrontations with the concrete laws of many different nations during many periods of history and in its ordered philosophical and theological reflection on the nature of law and on the relation between the law of reason, the law of nations, and the law of God, Christian thought has shaped not only the conscience (→23:1) but the legal systems of many traditions. But the tension between these three species of "law" has also been responsible for some of the more radical expressions of Christian obedience—which have often entailed disobedience to a specific human authority in the name of the still higher authority of the law and the will of God (→14:22).

5. BDAG 49–50.

"Under Pontius Pilate": "The Powers That Be"

25:11 I appeal to Caesar [Καίσαρα ἐπικαλοῦμαι].

It is another of the many historical ironies of the Christian message (→5:3–4) that of all the famous ancient Romans—Julius Caesar or Cicero or Vergil—none has achieved even nearly the universal name recognition of an otherwise obscure provincial gauleiter named Pontius Pilate, who has the distinction—which he shares with, of all people, the Blessed Virgin Mary (→1:14), and with no other human creature—of having his name recited every day all over the world in the Nicene Creed (as well as in the Apostles' Creed): σταυρωθέντα ὑπὲρ ἡμῶν ἐπὶ Ποντίου Πιλάτου (*crucifixus etiam pro nobis sub Pontio Pilato*, "crucified on our behalf under Pontius Pilate"[6] (→3:18). And it is no less ironic that of all the Roman emperors—three of whom are mentioned by name in the New Testament (though only in Luke-Acts), namely, Augustus (Luke 2:1), Tiberius (Luke 3:1), and Claudius (11:28; 18:2), in addition to the title "emperor" (σεβαστός) here (25:25)—it should happen to have been one of the most notorious (and anti-Christian) Caesars, Nero, who, though not mentioned by name, was the emperor when Saint Paul, writing to Christian believers in Rome, laid down the rule: "Let every soul be subject unto the higher powers. For there is no power but of God: the powers that be are ordained of God. Whosoever therefore resisteth the power, resisteth the ordinance of God" (Rom. 13:1–2 AV). The Christians who suffered persecution and martyrdom (→14:22) under Nero, and then under the grim line of his successors from Decius to Stalin, had good reason to puzzle over what could conceivably have been meant by the words with which Saint Paul continued, "For rulers are not a terror to good works, but to the evil" (Rom. 13:3 AV). Could this be taken to mean that when rulers stopped being a terror to evil works and became a terror to good works instead, they lost their legitimacy? So it has repeatedly been construed in the debates throughout Christian history over the permissibility of tyrannicide.[7]

Just as the language of the Christian eucharistic liturgy about eating the body of the Son of God and drinking his blood (→20:7) led pagan critics of the church to accuse believers of cannibalism,[8] so, too, the political metaphors of Christian language (→22:27; →27:24), such as the declaration of Saint Paul that "our citizenship [ἡμῶν . . . τὸ πολίτευμα] is in heaven" (Phil. 3:20 NRSV), and, above all, the emphasis on the preaching of the "kingdom of God" (→28:23) led those same critics to accuse them of sedition. This accusation comes through, perhaps most explicitly anywhere in the New Testament, in the charge, "They are all acting against the decrees of Caesar, saying that there is another king, Jesus" (17:7); "the decrees of Caesar" did not countenance allegiance to another king, but only to Caesar as divine, while the "decrees" (δόγματα) (→16:4b) of Jesus

---

6. Niceno-Constantinopolitan Creed 4 (*CCF* 1:162–63).
7. A. Bride in *DTC* 15:1988–2016.
8. Tertullian, *Apology* 7 (*ANF* 3:23).

did not countenance allegiance to any other god, including Caesar (→19:26). Further to the same point was the charge: "These men are Jews and they are disturbing our city. They advocate customs which it is not lawful for us Romans to accept or practice" (16:20–21).

The Christian defense against such accusations took several major forms, at least two of which figure prominently in Acts.[9] The first, in elaboration of Saint Paul's exhortation, "the powers that be are ordained of God," was to emphasize the Christian pledge of allegiance to legitimate government, including the government of Caesar, in which, as a matter of fact, Saint Paul held citizenship. On that basis he claimed his civil rights to complain to the Roman magistrates: "They have beaten us publicly, uncondemned, men who are Roman citizens, and have thrown us into prison; and do they now cast us out secretly?" (16:37). And he could interrupt the centurion who, to make him tell the truth, was about to have him scourged: "Is it lawful for you to scourge a man who is a Roman citizen, and uncondemned?" (22:25). The rightness of that exercise of civic prerogative was acknowledged also by the letter of Claudius Lysias to the governor Felix: "This man was seized by the Jews, and was about to be killed by them, when I came upon them with the soldiers and rescued him, having learned that he was a Roman citizen" (23:27). This was a right to which, as a Roman citizen without political allegiance to some other earthly ruler, Saint Paul was fully entitled.

The other response was, while recognizing the legitimate claims of "the powers that be," to reject any ultimate claims by any rulers, whether in the temporal or in the spiritual realm, as illegitimate, indeed as blasphemous (→5:29b). Such a twofold stance was taken to be an act of obedience to the command of Jesus: "Render therefore to Caesar the things that are Caesar's, and to God the things that are God's" (Matt. 22:21). Together with many other aspects of Christian obedience, this twofold stance would face the need of fundamental reconsideration when, in the fourth century, Caesar was suddenly a Christian, although, as the anomaly was trenchantly summarized by John Meyendorff, "he did not share in the sacramental life and the liturgical celebrations of the Church until his last moments," and yet "no single human being in history has contributed, directly or indirectly, to the conversion of so many to the Christian faith."[10] But after initially welcoming the intervention of Constantine Caesar in support of the orthodoxy decreed by the Council of Nicea, "Athanasius moved ... to an insistence ... upon the complete independence of a council from the emperor," even an orthodox Christian emperor.[11] And in most of the centuries since, while reciting the name Pontius Pilate in its two most universal creeds, the Niceno-Constantinopolitan Creed and the Apostles' Creed, and reading about "the powers that be" in its New Testament, the church has frequently

9. Maddox 1985, 91–99.
10. Meyendorff 1989, 6–7.
11. George Huntston Williams, quoted in Pelikan 2003, 229–30.

had more than enough reason to consider—and to reconsider—its relation to those powers.

"Due Process"

25:16 TPR I answered them that it was not the custom of the Romans to give up any one to destruction [εἰς ἀπώλειαν] before the accused met the accusers face to face, and had opportunity to make his defense concerning the charge laid against him.

The setting of these actions (→18:15; →23:25; →28:14; →28:31) in the context of a "court" and a "tribunal" (βῆμα) is a reminder of the prominence of law throughout the narrative of Acts, of Jewish law (→10:15) especially in the first half and of Roman law (→25:8) especially in the second.[12] "Observe," comments Chrysostom, "how, when [Paul] discourses to those that are without, he does not decline availing himself of the aids afforded by the laws."[13] This emphasis on law implied that the narrative had to pay attention also to the concept of due process.[14] As in the Constitution of the United States, "The central aim of due process doctrine is to assure fair procedure when the government imposes a burden on an individual. The doctrine seeks to [1] prevent arbitrary government, [2] avoid mistaken deprivations, [3] allow persons to know about and respond to charges against them, and [4] promote a sense of the legitimacy of official behavior."[15] Although, according to the same authority, "the concept of due process derives from the Magna Carta (1215), the great charter of English liberties," both of these ancient legal systems, the Jewish and the Roman, already had their own doctrines of due process and paid attention to these same four civil and legal rights, which were therefore an important feature also of the legal proceedings in Acts:

1. The need to *prevent arbitrary government* comes through in the message of the town clerk of Ephesus to "Demetrius and the craftsmen with him," who found that their livelihood as goldsmiths and artisans of idols was being threatened by the monotheistic message of the apostles and who threatened to lynch the threatening intruders: "The courts are open, and there are proconsuls" (ἀγοραῖοι ἄγονται καὶ ἀνθύπατοί εἰσιν) (19:38). If these failed to give satisfaction, moreover, there was a prescribed appellate procedure: "But if you seek anything further, it shall be settled in the regular assembly" (19:39). Instead of following due process, however, the goldsmiths were running amok—"in confusion . . . for about two hours"

12. Sherwin-White 1963.
13. Chrysostom, *Homilies on Acts* 47 (*NPNF*[1] 11:282).
14. Morgenthaler 1949, 2:33–34.
15. Thomas O. Sargentich in Hall 1992, 236.

(19:32, 34) through the streets—shouting "Great is Artemis of the Ephesians!" (→12:13–16). If this went on, the town clerk warned, "we are in danger of being charged with rioting today, there being no cause that we can give to justify this commotion" (19:40).

2. The obligation to *avoid mistaken deprivations* has often been the result of having made such mistakes in the past. Urging his colleagues to ponder the lessons of recent mistakes, Gamaliel the rabbi, who had once been the teacher of Saul in the Jewish law (22:3), took that lesson to be: "In the present case I tell you, keep away from these men and let them alone; for if this authority comes from human will, its power will fail; but if it is of God, you will not be able to overthrow them. You might even be found opposing God!" (5:38–39 TPR). Due process, therefore, was a protection not only of the accused but of the accusers from the consequences of their own folly.

3. The due process requirement to *allow persons to know about and respond to charges against them* was formulated in so many words by Festus when he explained to Agrippa how he had in turn explained to the chief priests and elders "that it was not the custom of the Romans [οὐκ ἔστιν ἔθος Ῥωμαίοις] to give up any one before the accused met the accusers face to face, and had opportunity to make his defense concerning the charge laid against him" (25:16). Indeed, it was, as the same chapter goes on to explain, "unreasonable, in sending a prisoner, not to indicate the charges against him" (25:27).

4. The duty of officials, by observing due process, to *promote a sense of the legitimacy of official behavior* was cited by Tertullus the ῥήτωρ in his advice to Felix the Roman governor: "By examining him yourself you will be able to learn from him about everything of which we accuse him" (24:8). But the supreme instance of reliance on due process that Luke documents was the trial of Jesus under Pontius Pilate (→25:11), where he seemed to be intent on establishing "the legitimacy of official behavior." Therefore Peter could speak to the Jewish people about "Jesus, whom you delivered up and denied in the presence of Pilate, when he had decided to release him" (3:13), even though he added, in partial exculpation, "that you acted in ignorance, as did also your rulers" (3:17). Because both Jewish law and Roman law had a doctrine of due process, both the legal process (Jewish and Roman) against Jesus and the subsequent action (also Jewish and Roman) against his disciples in their imitation of him (→7:59–60) must be judged in the light of that doctrine of jurisprudence.

ACTS 26

26:2–3 Paul's apologia begins with the standard introduction to a rhetorical statement of one's case before a judge (→23:1; →24:1–2). It includes the acknowledgment that King Agrippa II, unlike many other rulers and magistrates under Roman rule such as Pontius Pilate (→25:11), could be counted on to understand internal Jewish affairs, as became evident in his defense of the Jews to Emperor Claudius.[1]

26:5–8 This argument seeks to turn the case against the accusers by representing Paul, the accused, as the real champion of "hope in the promise made by God to our fathers, . . . and for this hope I am accused by Jews!" As he had earlier, Paul was laying claim to a continuity with Pharisaism that had not been abolished by his conversion to the name and Way of Jesus Christ (→9:1–4), because, as observed earlier, "the Pharisees confess the existence of resurrection and angel and spirit" (23:8 TPR), making him closer to this party of Judaism than it itself was to the other parties of Judaism, particularly the Sadducees, on this vital element of Jewish eschatological doctrine (→23:8).

26:9–18 This is the third and last of the narrations of Paul's conversion (→9:1–4); like the second (22:1–16), it takes the form of an autobiographical account, following the outline of the previous tellings but displaying some interesting variations.

26:13 A light from heaven, brighter than the sun.

Like the light of the transfiguration of Christ, this is being described here as a more than natural phenomenon and as more than a creature, "uncreated

---

1. David C. Braund in *ABD* 1:99–100.

light," which has been interpreted, in the Cappadocians and then especially in Byzantine theology, as a divine "principle of action" (ἐνέργεια) (→22:6).

26:14 As it does elsewhere in the usage of the book of Acts, "the Hebrew language" apparently means Aramaic (→21:37).

"I Believe": *Fides qua creditur*

26:18 That they may receive forgiveness of sins and a place among those who are sanctified by faith in me.

Because of the way the terms "faith" and "to believe" are used in biblical and ecclesiastical language, there has developed a theological distinction between two ways of using "faith" (πίστις):[2] either "*the* faith which was once for all delivered to the saints" (Jude 3), *fides quae creditur* (→24:24–25a), which is "believed, taught, and confessed"[3] by the church in the creed when it says "we believe"; or "faith" (often without the article in English), referring to a personal and existential *fides qua creditur*, which is avowed by the believer who says "I believe." Such a distinction, which sought to distinguish without separating, was made necessary by statements such as "you believe that God is one; you do well. Even the demons believe—and shudder" (Jas. 2:19). If the demons could be said to "believe," this must mean that they were orthodox in their *fides quae creditur*, even though they were in hell because they lacked the *fides qua creditur*. At the same time, a passage-by-passage comparison does lead to the recognition that in many places, whether here in the book of Acts or elsewhere, it is not at all clear which sense of the word predominates and that the distinction must in any case not be allowed to become a difference.

Nevertheless, there are some verses in Acts where personal, saving "faith" as *fides qua creditur* is definitely the primary subject, rather than the faith and confession of the church, *fides quae creditur*. One such is this statement of Christ to Saint Paul, here in the third of the three versions of the history of the conversion of Saul (→9:1–4), about "those who are sanctified by faith in me." Although this final phrase, "by faith in me," does employ the definite article in Greek, πίστει τῇ εἰς ἐμέ, this was a "faith in," not a "faith that," because it was said to carry with it the power to "sanctify" (ἁγιάζειν) and to "justify" (δικαιοῦν) the believers, which is a central feature of the argument in the Epistle to the Romans regarding "the righteousness of God through faith in Jesus Christ for all who believe" (δικαιοσύνη δὲ θεοῦ διὰ πίστεως Ἰησοῦ Χριστοῦ εἰς πάντας τοὺς πιστεύοντας) (Rom. 3:22).

2. D. Kirn in *RE* 6:680.
3. *Chr. Trad.* 1:1.

As they were enumerated here, the consequences of this *fides qua creditur* were fourfold: (1) "to open their eyes, that they may turn from darkness to light": illumination through the revelation that had come through the word of the gospel (→8:25); (2) "and [turn] from the power of Satan to God": rescue through the victory of Christ (→13:8–11) from the captivity and oppression of sin, death, and the devil (→10:38); (3) "that they may receive forgiveness of sins": conferred through "one baptism for the forgiving of sins" (→22:16); and (4) "and [receive] a place among those who are sanctified by faith in me": a sanctification that went beyond conventional morality to an authentic and transcendent holiness (→4:32). With variations and in different combinations, these gifts also attended other examples of *fides qua creditur* throughout the Acts of the Apostles and have gone on doing so in the lives of the saints.

Perhaps the outstanding episode of *fides qua creditur* in Acts, involving or at least implying all four of these consequences, is the account of the jailer at Philippi, who asked in his terror, "Men, what must I do to be saved?" The account continues: "And they said, 'Believe in the Lord Jesus [πίστευσον ἐπὶ τὸν κύριον Ἰησοῦν], and you will be saved, you and your household.' And they spoke the word of the Lord to him and to all that were in his house. And he took them the same hour of the night, and washed their wounds, and he was baptized at once, with all his family. Then he brought them up into his house, and set food before them; and he rejoiced with all his household that he had believed in God [πεπιστευκὼς τῷ θεῷ]" (16:30–34).

The same would apply to the description of Barnabas: "He was a good man, full of the Holy Spirit and of faith" (11:24), which certainly means the personal faith that was, together with the presence of the Holy Spirit, the defining force in the life of Barnabas as believer. An earlier episode of rescue through faith likewise uses the word "faith" in this personal, subjective sense, as Peter's words about the healing at the temple attest: "The Author of life, whom God raised from the dead. . . . And his name, by faith in his name, has made this man strong whom you see and know; and the faith which is through Jesus has given the man this perfect health in the presence of you all" (3:15–16). The victory over the oppression by the devil in his case included rescue from physical illness. And when the apostles are described as "testifying both to Jews and to Greeks of repentance to God and of faith in our Lord Jesus Christ" (20:21), this direct linkage of faith with repentance (→26:20), carrying unmistakable cross-references to the preaching of John the Forerunner (→19:2–3) and to that of Jesus himself (Mark 1:15), would argue for defining it, too, as *fides qua creditur*.

Less clear (→24:24–25a) are passages in Acts such as "and the word of God increased; and the number of the disciples multiplied greatly in Jerusalem, and a great many of the priests were *obedient to the faith*" (6:7) and "strengthening the souls of the disciples, exhorting them *to continue in the faith*" (14:22).

26:19 Because such visions and revelations were divine in origin and validation, they were entitled not simply to credence but to "obedience" (→16:9), as was "*the* faith" itself (Rom. 1:5; 16:26).

"The Forgiving of Sins": The Component "Parts of Penance"

26:20 TPR That they should [1] repent and [2] turn to the living God and [3] perform deeds worthy of their repentance.

The phrase "the forgiving of sins" (ἄφεσις ἁμαρτιῶν) appears in the text of the Niceno-Constantinopolitan Creed as part of the article about baptism: "We confess one baptism for the forgiving of sins" (ὁμολογοῦμεν ἓν βάπτισμα εἰς ἄφεσιν ἁμαρτιῶν).[4] Such a linking of baptism to the forgiveness of sins reflects the language of the New Testament, including Acts (→22:16). But as the experience and the pastoral practice of the church developed, and then as infant baptism gradually became customary, the question of how to cope with the sins that were committed after baptism demanded urgent attention, because there was only "one baptism," which was "for the forgiving of sins" that had been committed in the past but not of later sins. This struggle to cope with postbaptismal sins is documented with special poignancy in the writings of Saint Cyprian of Carthage, bishop, theologian, and martyr, particularly in the case of "the lapsed," those who had denied the faith or had otherwise struck a compromise with the Roman authorities during the persecutions under the emperor Decius.[5] The eventual outcome of the struggle was that penance came to be defined as a distinct sacrament, as this was systematically formulated for the Eastern church by Peter Mogila[6] and as it had been formulated almost a century earlier for the Western church by the Council of Trent on 25 November 1551, on the basis of existing practice and of earlier councils: "The form of the sacrament of penance, in which its effectiveness chiefly lies, is expressed in the words of the minister, 'I absolve you.' . . . The acts of the penitent, namely contrition, satisfaction, are as it were the matter of this sacrament. These are called parts of penance."[7] But these component "parts of penance"—contrition, confession, satisfaction, and absolution—which were now defined, following the medieval Scholastics, in the Aristotelian language of "form" and "matter,"[8] had been present in the teaching of the church since the New Testament, as can be seen with special clarity here in the Acts of the Apostles, including the present passage:[9]

4. Niceno-Constantinopolitan Creed 10 (*CCF* 1:162–63).
5. Cyprian, *The Lapsed* (ACW 25:13–42).
6. Orthodox Confession of the Catholic and Apostolic Eastern Church 1.112–14 (*CCF* 1:607–9).
7. Dogmatic Decrees of the Council of Trent 14.3 (*CCF* 2:850).
8. J. B. Lotz in *LTK* 4:203–5; M. Moser in *LTK* 7:164–65.
9. Nave 2002, 198–224.

1. *Contrition.* More fully it is called "contrition of the heart" (*contritio cordis*),[10] from *contrire* ("to wear down"), and could take a variety of forms. In some places, most notably in the three accounts of the conversion of Saul (→9:1–4), the details of such sorrowing over sin are left undescribed here in Acts. But the response to the penitential preaching of Saint Peter about "this Jesus whom *you* crucified" (2:36) was that "when they heard this they were cut to the heart [κατενύγησαν τὴν καρδίαν], and said to Peter and the rest of the apostles, 'Brethren, what shall we do?' And Peter said to them, 'Repent, and be baptized every one of you in the name of Jesus Christ for the forgiveness of your sins; and you shall receive the gift of the Holy Spirit'" (2:37–38). There is a parallel response in the description of the jailer at Philippi, who, "trembling with fear" and "about to kill himself," cried out, "What must I do to be saved?" (16:27–30). Therefore Peter could make the appeal: "Repent therefore, and turn again, that your sins may be blotted out, that times of refreshing may come from the presence of the Lord" (3:19).

2. *Confession.* The most complete and representative instances of the confession of sin in the body of Saint Luke's work do not appear here in Acts, but in two well-known parables unique to his Gospel: when the prodigal son in Jesus' parable said to his father, in words that became the standard formula of confession, "Father, I have sinned [Vulgate: *pater, peccavi*] against heaven and before you; I am no longer worthy to be called your son" (Luke 15:21); and when the publican, who could only entreat, "God, be merciful to me a sinner!" was the one who "went down to his house justified [δεδικαιωμένος] rather than the other" (Luke 18:13–14), with the verb "justify" apparently being used in the technical sense that is familiar from the language of the Pauline Epistles (→13:38–39). The theological and pastoral discussions of penance have traditionally drawn the sharpest possible contrast between the salutary contrition and confession of Peter, who "wept bitterly" after betraying his Lord (Luke 22:62), and the suicidal confession of Judas Iscariot, which is absent from Saint Luke's account of his end (1:18) but is recorded by Saint Matthew (and, as Saint Augustine notes,[11] "only by him"): "I have sinned [Vulgate: *peccavi*] in betraying innocent blood" (Matt. 27:4). Both said, "I have sinned" (*peccavi*)—but to diametrically opposite outcomes.

3. *Satisfaction.* To "perform deeds worthy of repentance [ἄξια τῆς μετανοίας ἔργα]" in this passage pertains to the entire life of the penitent. But it may be taken in a particular sense to refer to the restitution of any ill-gotten gains, as Saint Luke in his Gospel records that Zacchaeus promised after his repentance and conversion: "If I have defrauded any one of anything, I restore it fourfold" (Luke 19:8). Thus the definition of sin as "defrauding"

10. Blaise and Chirat 1954, 217–18.
11. Augustine, *Harmony of the Gospels* 3.28 (*NPNF*[1] 6:191).

God of the honor due him (→12:21–23) led, in the medieval Western penitential systems, to the developments of casuistic "penitential books" and other prescriptions of acts of "satisfaction through a deed" (*satisfactio operis*), which could be a prescribed penance such as reciting several Pater Nosters and Ave Marias or even "tak[ing] up [the] cross" (Matt. 16:24) by embarking on a crusade. This concept of "satisfaction"—rather than, as is sometimes suggested, the feudal system—was also to provide the vocabulary and conceptual framework for Saint Anselm of Canterbury in the doctrine of the atonement set forth in his *Why God Became Man* (*Cur deus homo*) to describe the crucifixion and death of Christ as the ultimate restitution and *satisfactio* rendered to the violated honor and *rectitudo* of God for all the sin of all humanity, making it possible for both the justice and the mercy of God to be sustained and upheld (→3:18).

4. *Absolution.* In the Aristotelian terminology of the Council of Trent, this is the "form" of the sacrament of penance, while the three component "parts of penance" are the "matter"; therefore it would in some respects be more precise to call it "the sacrament of absolution" rather than "the sacrament of confession." Like the formula of confession, the formula of absolution has taken a variety of forms in the history of penance: personal or individual absolution, pronounced by the priest upon the penitent; and general absolution, which came to be favored in the Reformation churches once personal confession had declined or even disappeared. The "comfortable words" of the forgiveness of sins prescribed by the Book of Common Prayer after the confession of sins, though lacking the declaratory form cited by the Council of Trent, "I absolve you," have been seen as sacramentally tantamount to the pronouncing of an absolution.

Public Evidence for a Mystery?

26:26 This was not done in a corner.

In addition to, and sometimes in tension with, the primary sources of truth—the Old Testament revelation as this was being authoritatively interpreted (and reinterpreted) in normative Christian teaching (→8:30–31), the special revelation that had been granted in Christ and in his gospel (→1:2–3; →8:25), and the continuing private revelations through dreams, trances, and visions (→16:9), including those that came through the activity of Christian prophets (→21:9–10)—a prominent feature of the apologetics of Luke is his emphasis on the gospel as a public event. All of this adds up to the oxymoron that we have entitled "public evidence for a mystery," which is in some respects the obverse side of interpreting the language of negation as the affirmation of metaphysical transcendence (→17:23). The term μυστήριον itself, which was to become the technical term for "sacrament" in Christian

Greek[12] although the only one of the eventual seven sacraments to which the New Testament attaches it is matrimony (Eph. 5:32), does not appear in Acts and occurs only once even in Luke's Gospel (Luke 8:10).

It may be useful to review the three principal events that "these things" in "I am persuaded that *none of these things* has escaped his notice, for this was not done in a corner" included here in the immediate context of Paul's address to King Agrippa: yet another iteration of his conversion story (26:9–19; →9:1–4); his missionary activity and its perils (26:20–21); and the death and the resurrection of Christ (26:22–23; →2:31). Not only about the second of these, which had clearly not been "done in a corner" at all, but by now had become a public nuisance to many, "turn[ing] the world upside down" and providing the occasion for controversy and even riots (17:6), but also about the third, which had provoked unbelieving ridicule from both Jews (4:2) and Gentiles (17:32), Paul seemed willing to lay claim to public verification of some kind or other. This claim was in keeping with the recitation of evidence from witnesses in Paul's dissertation on the resurrection of Christ: "He appeared to Cephas, then to the twelve. Then he appeared to more than five hundred brethren at one time, most of whom are still alive, though some have fallen asleep. Then he appeared to James, then to all the apostles. Last of all, as to one untimely born, he appeared also to me" (1 Cor. 15:5–8). It does seem artificial when some interpreters of 1 Corinthians, in their reaction against an excessively rationalistic apologetics, have tried to deny that Paul was appealing to any kind of evidentiary "proofs" at all in this catalog. Some such appeal would seem to be at work in the report of Matthew's Gospel (not included by Luke) that at the crucifixion of Christ "the tombs also were opened, and many bodies of the saints who had fallen asleep were raised, and coming out of the tombs after his resurrection they went into the *holy city and appeared to many*" (Matt. 27:52–53).

But Luke, too, has assembled a catalog of such "proofs" (τεκμήρια) here in the book of Acts; it was characteristic of a τεκμήριον, according to Aristotle, that it was a "necessary [ἀναγκαῖον] sign . . . from which a logical syllogism can be constructed."[13] In fact, "proof" is the very word that successive English translations have employed, from AV to RSV to NRSV, at the opening of the Acts account: "To them he presented himself alive after his passion by many proofs [τεκμηρίοις], appearing to them during forty days" (1:3). In his Pentecost sermon Peter spoke of Jesus as "a man attested to you by God" (ἄνδρα ἀποδεδειγμένον ἀπὸ τοῦ θεοῦ εἰς ὑμᾶς) and made a point of reminding his hearers that the "mighty works and wonders and signs which God did through him" (→6:8) had not been "done in a corner," but "in your midst" (εἰς ὑμᾶς) (2:22); the same was said of Stephen's "great wonders and signs *among the people* [ἐν τῷ λαῷ]" (6:8). When the members of the Jewish council are quoted as hav-

12. *PGL* 891–93.
13. Aristotle, *Rhetoric* 1.2.16–17 1357b (LCL 193:27).

ing said after the healing at the Beautiful Gate "that a notable sign has been performed through them is manifest to all the inhabitants of Jerusalem, *and we cannot deny it*" (4:16), they were being cited as nonbelievers who nevertheless found the evidence for this "notable sign" (γνωστὸν σημεῖον) (→6:8) too overwhelming to deny or refute.

Yet it would be a mistake—and one into which much of conventional Christian apologetics has fallen, particularly during and since the Enlightenment[14]—to ignore the other pole of the evidentiary dialectic. The key passage about this other pole within the Acts narrative is in the message of Peter to "Cornelius, a centurion, an upright and God-fearing man" (10:22), and his friends, where the kind of evidence that is provided by the "proofs" for the resurrection of Christ was specified in a very particular way: "God raised him on the third day and made him manifest; *not to all the people but to us who were chosen by God as witnesses*, who ate and drank with him after he rose from the dead" (10:40–41). "Witnesses" (μάρτυρες) here does not have the technical meaning of "martyrs," though it soon would for Peter and others; but it does have the dual meaning it still has in the courtroom: "eyewitnesses" (Luke 1:2) who have seen the event in question; and those who are called upon to bear witness and "*testify* that he is the one ordained by God to be judge of the living and the dead" (10:42). As Chrysostom observed, the treatment of miracles in Acts

> is just the same as in what Christ Himself did. Namely, in His miracles though He does not let men see them in the act of being wrought, He furnishes the means whereby they may be apprised of the things wrought: thus, in His Resurrection, He did not let them see how He rose: in the water made wine, the guests do not see it done, for they have been drinking much, and the discernment He leaves to others. Just so in the present case, they do not see them in the act of being brought forth, but the proofs from which they might gather what had been done [τεκμήρια, ἀφ' ὧν ἠδύναντο καταμαθεῖν τὰ γενόμενα], they do see.[15]

Therefore Paul could say of the risen Christ that "for many days he appeared [in the first sense of 'witness'] to those who came up with him from Galilee to Jerusalem, who are now his witnesses [in the second sense] to the people" (13:31). In many respects, therefore, the idea of "public evidence for a mystery" can be said to be not only an oxymoron, but an argument in a circle.

Paul's word to Agrippa, "this was not done in a corner," continued to be a part both of apologetics and of church history. In the greatest of early apologetic works, the *Contra Celsum* of Origen, the pagan critic Celsus was quoted as citing "the claims to great antiquity put forth by many nations" of pagan and classical antiquity, with which he contrasted the contemptible "Jews, being bowed down in some corner of Palestine" (as well as the Christians), who were not worthy

14. L. Maisonneuve in *DTC* 1:1511–80.
15. Chrysostom, *Homilies on Acts* 13 (*NPNF*[1] 11:81).

of claiming any serious attention from sophisticated philosophers.[16] Reacting to the same type of snobbery, Eusebius, to refute the impression that Christian "doctrine is new and strange," extolled the "new nation" that had arisen through Christ as "a nation confessedly not small, and *not dwelling in some corner of the earth*, but the most numerous and pious of all nations, indestructible and unconquerable," therefore both ancient and universal.[17]

26:28 This is the first (and last) passage of Acts in which the name "Christian," after having been invented as a nickname at Antioch, is employed for the followers of the Way (→11:26), the only other instance anywhere in the New Testament being the admonition: "If one suffers as a Christian, let him not be ashamed, but under that name let him glorify God" (1 Pet. 4:16).

16. Origen, *Contra Celsum* 4.36 (Chadwick 1953, 211).
17. Eusebius, *Church History* 1.4.1–2 (*NPNF*[2] 1:87).

ACTS 27

"The Predicament of the Christian Historian"

27:1 It was decided that we should sail for Italy.

The we-passages of Acts, which is the term used for the three sections of the book employing the second-person plural, are 16:10–17; 20:5–21:18; and 27:1–28:16.[1] Already in Irenaeus's refutation of Marcion's attempt to discredit the other apostles and to "allege that Paul alone knew the truth," these we-passages formed an important argument for the integrity of the apostolic witness as a totality.[2] This entire chapter together with most of the next is presented as a personal account, based perhaps on a travel journal of the writer that has been incorporated into the narrative.[3] As Kirsopp Lake and Henry J. Cadbury say, "This section is very obviously a single connected story which either was written by one of Paul's companions or by someone who wished to describe what one of the voyagers might naturally have felt and written. Much the most natural view is that it really represents the actual experiences of Paul and his friends."[4]

In the Acts of the Apostles (whatever its original title may have been) the writer, in his "desire to preserve Christian history for Christians,"[5] has been presenting his narrative of the church during the first generation following the resurrection and the ascension as a fitting continuation—even "extension" does not seem to be too strong a word, also because of the continuity between Christ's "giv[ing] commandment *through the Holy Spirit* to the apostles whom

---

1. On the history of their interpretation, see Dupont 1964, 118–26; Wehnert 1989, 47–124; and Hemer 1989, 308–64.
2. Irenaeus, *Against Heresies* 3.13–14 (*ANF* 1:436–39).
3. Stanley E. Porter in Winter and Clarke 1993–94, 2:545–74.
4. Kirsopp Lake and Henry J. Cadbury in Foakes Jackson and Lake 1979, 4:324.
5. Enslin 1938, 414.

he had chosen" (1:2) and his sending the Holy Spirit on them at Pentecost (→2:1)—of the history of the life and teachings of Jesus, as he had narrated it earlier to the same reader, an otherwise unknown Greek named Theophilus. Moreover, on the basis of the prefatory words it does seem justified, indeed necessary, to treat the composition of the Acts of the Apostles as a product of the same historiographical methodology that its author had spelled out earlier to Theophilus in his dedicatory preface for what we now call the Third Gospel (which is here given the title "the first book"), where he explained: "It seemed good to me also, having followed all things closely for some time past, to write an orderly account for you, most excellent Theophilus" (Luke 1:3). That explanation does not appear a second time here in Acts, perhaps because it would have seemed redundant in the second volume of a two-volume work.[6]

Whether the reference at the opening of Luke's Gospel to the "many" who had previously "undertaken to compile a narrative of the things which have been accomplished among us" (Luke 1:1) was intended as a criticism of those earlier efforts is not clear from the neutral tone of the language. Nor is it clear, on the other hand, whether this reference included one or more of what were to become the canonical Gospels (which may or may not have already been written by the time this Gospel was composed), or for that matter one or another of the noncanonical gospels that have surfaced only in modern times (if, of course, any of these had already been written). In any case it does seem to be a sound procedure, when citing parallels and precedents in the Gospels for passages in Acts, to look in the first instance at the Gospel according to Luke, which is what this commentary does. And on many theological issues and doctrines—for example the prominence of the Virgin Mary (→1:14), the doctrine of the Holy Spirit (→2:1), and the evidentiary public character of events in Christian history seen as part of Roman history (→26:26)—this second volume can be seen as having continued and deepened the insights and emphases of the first, although, as Nils Alstrup Dahl suggests, with "much greater freedom" because of the subject matter.[7]

The difference in this regard between the first book of Saint Luke and the second book of Saint Luke, the Gospel and the Acts—in addition to the absence of any reference here in Acts to any precedents (probably because there were none yet, at any rate in written form) corresponding to the "many [who] have undertaken to compile a narrative of the things which have been accomplished among us" (Luke 1:1) in the life and teachings of Jesus before Saint Luke wrote his own Gospel—is the we-passages in Acts. All of these pertain to the voyages and missionary journeys of Paul; and they do suggest that—whether or not the author is to be equated with "Luke the beloved physician" (Col. 4:14), as the traditional interpretation, perpetuated even by Adolf von Harnack, maintains,

---

6. On Luke the historian as the "confluence of two historiographies," see Marguerat 1999, 11–42.

7. Dahl 1976, 93.

but as modern interpretation, beginning with Henry J. Cadbury, questions[8]—he was an experienced sailor, whose grasp of the technical Greek vocabulary in this field (→27:24) was at a level at least as high as his medical vocabulary, on which in part this traditional attribution has been based. For his Gospel the author of Acts had been compelled to rely completely on "the traditions handed down to us by the original eyewitnesses[9] and servants of the Gospel" (Luke 1:2 NEB). It is sometimes urged that these "traditions" included interviews with Mary the mother of Jesus, especially for the first two chapters of the Gospel (→1:14).[10] But for the Acts he was in a position to draw in addition upon personal recollection. It is important not to overlook this difference between the two volumes of Luke-Acts, also because it helps to give the book of Acts a narrative immediacy and therefore a unique theological force as a witness. To at least those sections of this account, therefore, the characterization in the opening words of another book of the New Testament, which referred to the life and teaching of Jesus, was applicable as referring to the life and teaching of Paul: "That . . . which we have heard, which we have seen with our eyes, which we have looked upon and touched with our hands" (1 John 1:1).

But it is essential also not to exaggerate its importance. More important, especially to modern interpreters of Luke-Acts, most of whom have been scholars and professors, is that both the Gospel and Acts are the product of "investigating . . . carefully" (παρηκολουθηκότι . . . ἀκριβῶς) (Luke 1:3 NRSV), which seems to bear important similarities to the kind of research in which these scholars are themselves engaged.[11] Therefore this historical book needs to be read in the context of ancient Greek and Roman historiography.[12] None of the other Gospels, in fact none of the other books of the Bible in either the Old or the New Testament—in spite of the cross-references throughout the books of Kings to previous collections, particularly as "written in the Book of the Chronicles of the Kings of Israel" (1 Kgs. 14:19) and in the books of other rulers—can be said to be the self-conscious product of historical research in the same way or to the same extent; therefore "Luke's use of sources in Acts" is an issue of great importance,[13] for "uniquely in Antiquity, the Book of Acts describes the time of the beginning of a new religious movement."[14] This also implies that any interpretation of the book of Acts, even and especially one that concentrates primarily on theology rather than on philology, must have in view the method and the style of Greek and of Latin historiography in antiquity, as these are represented respectively by Thucydides[15] and by

8. See pp. 30–31 above.
9. C. S. Mann in Munck 1967, 268–70.
10. See pp. 31–32 above.
11. Trocmé 1957, 76–121; Barrett 1961; Hemer 1989; Marshall 1970.
12. Hengel 1979, 3–34; Plümacher 1972.
13. Witherington 1998, 165–73.
14. Eckey 2000, 1:21.
15. Luschnat 1942.

Livy,[16] including the use of classical and Hellenistic rhetoric and of stylized speeches to advance the narrative (→24:1–2). Any doctrine of biblical inspiration that describes the initiative of the Holy Spirit in such a way as not to incorporate an adequate appreciation of this dimension of authorial activity, as well as the variety in cultural-intellectual context and "literary genres,"[17] is by definition artificial and alien to the nature of Sacred Scripture.

As that issue illustrates, moreover, Luke may also be seen as the first to confront what Georges V. Florovsky calls "the predicament of the Christian historian."[18] As a historian among other historians, the historian of the church is bound by the same rules of the discipline as they are; yet if the historian is a believer, this creates unavoidable tensions. It is, someone has said, as if the Hippocratic Oath had required all young candidates in brain surgery to demonstrate their scientific objectivity and their professional ability "to do no harm" by performing a delicate operation on their own mothers. Ernest Renan claims to have found a way out of the predicament:

> To write the history of a religion, it is necessary, firstly, to have believed it (otherwise we should not be able to understand how it has charmed and satisfied the human conscience); in the second place, to believe it no longer in an absolute manner, for absolute faith is incompatible with sincere history. But love is possible without faith. To abstain from attaching one's self to any of the forms which captivate the adoration of men, is not to deprive ourselves of that which is good and beautiful in them.[19]

But this facile solution does not work, for Renan or Saint Luke or any other historian of the church. As Luke Timothy Johnson says, "Luke has no intention of writing a scientific disinterested history—if in fact there is such a thing. . . . As a whole, Luke-Acts should be read as an Apology in the form of a historical narrative. . . . Luke's Apology is . . . in the broadest sense a theodicy. His purpose is to defend God's activity in the world."[20] In confronting this "predicament of the Christian historian," Luke set a pattern that has continued to characterize (or to haunt) the discipline in one way or another to the present day. His immediate successor, Eusebius of Caesarea, "the father of church history," repeatedly drew upon the Acts of the Apostles for his own account of the early centuries.[21] And Eusebius's account, in turn, is an indispensable (if not always reliable) source of knowledge, without which it would be virtually

16. Burck 1964.
17. Dei verbum: Dogmatic Constitution on Divine Revelation of the Second Vatican Council 3.12 (CCF 3:656–57).
18. Florovsky 1972–89, 2:31–65; Morgenthaler 1949.
19. Renan 1927, 65.
20. Johnson 1992, 7.
21. Eusebius, Church History 3.4.7 (NPNF² 1:136–37).

impossible to construct anything even resembling a connected narrative of the ante-Nicene history of the church.

Having been inaugurated by Luke and then defined as a literary genre by Eusebius and his successors—Socrates Scholasticus, Sozomen, and Theodoret in the Greek East; Cassiodorus in the Latin West[22]—"ecclesiastical history" took its place as a way of doing Christian theology alongside the systematic exposition of Christian doctrine, as founded by the *De principiis* of Origen, and exegetical theology, also represented by Origen for the East and by Jerome for the West. It was not, however, part of what could be called, somewhat anachronistically, the "theological curriculum," and even the theological instruction in Constantinople or in the medieval Western university (most notably, the University of Paris) and even in the reorganized universities of the Reformation did not include it; there was an abundance of historical material in the curriculum, but it was seen as "tradition," not as historical narrative. Only with the Enlightenment did the discipline of church history find an established place within the formal study of theology.[23] For the study of the Acts of the Apostles, this meant that, being part of the New Testament canon as soon as there was a New Testament canon, it was studied with the same presuppositions and by the same methods (whatever these were) as the other books of Holy Scripture—and was at the same time also treated as the first in the succession of the histories of the church. That duality, canonical Scripture and yet historical narrative, is part of what we are calling, in Florovsky's formulation, "the predicament of the Christian historian," and it marks every commentary on Acts, including (obviously) this one.[24]

De amicitia: The Divine Gift of Friendship

27:3 TPR The centurion, being kindly disposed to Paul, permitted his friends to come to him and take care of him.

Two of the most influential of the philosophical treatises of Cicero were *De officiis* (*On Duties*) and *De amicitia* (*On Friendship*). But while Saint Ambrose composed a treatise entitled *De officiis ministrorum*, which adapted the categories and even the outline of Cicero's work while emphasizing the sharp contrast between Stoic and Christian morality,[25] he did not write one called *De amicitia christiana*, though he well could have, for the idea of the divine gift of Christian friendship plays a prominent enough role throughout the Bible, including Acts, to warrant such a special treatise unto itself.

22. Alanna Nobbs in Winter and Clarke 1993–94, 1:153–62.
23. G. N. Bonwetsch in *RE* 10:376–83.
24. Alter 1981, with important implications also for New Testament narrative.
25. Ambrose of Milan, *Three Books on the Duties of the Clergy* (*NPNF*[2] 10:1–89); Quasten et al. 1951–86, 4:166–67.

From the portrait of him in Acts as well as from his own epistles it is clear that as Saint Paul was prone to sudden and violent outbursts of anger (→21:13–14)—"God shall strike you, you whitewashed wall!" (23:3) he could shout at the high priest, and he could write to his congregation, "O foolish Galatians! Who has bewitched you?" (Gal. 3:1)—so he was capable both of expressing and of evoking deep and loyal friendship. This is nevertheless one of only two passages in Acts (the other being 19:31) where the actual word "friend" (φίλος) is used in connection with him. But because, to paraphrase the proverb, a friend is as a friend does, the theme of friendship, like the other "religious affections" (→21:13–14) that are portrayed here, comes through in the narratives of Acts primarily in concrete acts of friendship, from which it is possible to read off some of its characteristics:

1. Friendship is demonstrative, as Paul's friends at Tyre manifested it to him and to his traveling companions, who evidently, from the use of the pronoun "we" (→27:1), included the author of Acts: "And when our days there were ended, we departed and went on our journey; and they all, with wives and children, brought us on our way till we were outside the city; and kneeling down on the beach we prayed and bade one another farewell" (21:5). The contrast could not be greater between this effusive demonstration of friendship and a proper and formally correct expression of official civility, whether personal or governmental. A symbol of the demonstrative character of Christian friendship in the apostolic church was the "holy kiss" (φίλημα ἅγιον), to which Paul often refers at or near the conclusion of an epistle (Rom. 16:16; 1 Cor. 16:20; 2 Cor. 13:12; 1 Thess. 5:26); this has continued in the liturgy of many churches as "the kiss of peace,"[26] but in some cultures it is often the standard expression of Christian friendship also outside the liturgical context.

2. Friendship outlasts even sharp disagreement, as Paul and Barnabas showed in their contention over Mark: "And after some days Paul said to Barnabas, 'Come, let us return and visit the brethren in every city where we proclaimed the word of the Lord, and see how they are.' And Barnabas wanted to take with them John called Mark. But Paul thought best not to take with them one who had withdrawn from them in Pamphylia, and had not gone with them to the work. And there arose a sharp contention, so that they separated from each other; Barnabas took Mark with him and sailed away to Cyprus" (15:36–39). Because the language of Acts describing how "the company of those who believed were of one heart and soul" (4:32) can all too easily be sentimentalized into an idealistic caricature of a community where there were no strong differences of opinion, this account is an important reminder that Christian fellowship and Christian friendship can coexist with such differences. One way to formulate this

26. *ODCC* 932.

is to say that Christians can love one another even when they do not like one another very much. Instances from Christian history are numerous. One of the most fascinating, even as a purely human phenomenon, can be followed in Augustine's "long-drawn-out correspondence with Jerome . . . , a unique document in the Early Church. For it shows two highly-civilized men conducting with studied courtesy, a singularly rancorous correspondence."[27] Another becomes evident in the relation between Saint Basil the Great of Caesarea and Saint Gregory of Nazianzus the Theologian.[28]

3. Friendship grieves over parting, as becomes evident above all in the farewell of Paul to the elders of Ephesus: "And they all wept and embraced Paul and kissed him, sorrowing most of all because the word he had spoken, that they should see his face no more. And they brought him to the ship" (20:37–38). In this poignant scene, the relation of the missionary apostle to his converts, of the pastor to his people, blends into what even a cynical reader would probably have to recognize as an authentic friendship. And all the conventional reassurances that are heard so often at Christian funerals about being reunited in the presence of God had to yield, at least for the moment, to a grief that demanded to be expressed because it was an inseparable component of friendship.

4. Friendship cherishes the tangible mementos of the departed: "So Peter rose and went with them. And when he had come, they took him to the upper room. All the widows stood beside him weeping, and showing tunics and other garments which Dorcas made while she was with them" (9:39). No less touching in its own way than the scene of Paul with the elders of Ephesus, this description of Dorcas's friends in mourning adds the important touch that they brought "tunics and other garments which Dorcas made." This place of "material culture" in Christian friendship was elevated to a more sublime level with the cult of relics and of icons. Those who contemplate the relics of a martyr, Gregory of Nyssa explained, "embrace, as it were, the living body itself in full flower; they bring eye, mouth, ear, all their senses into play; and then, shedding tears of reverence and passion, they address to the martyr their prayer of intercession as though he were hale and present."[29] The same applies to the icons of the saints (→19:26).

5. Friendship between believers is grounded in Christ the friend: "No longer do I call you servants [δούλους]," Jesus said in his closing discourses (John 15:15), "for the servant does not know what his master is doing; but I have called you friends [φίλους], for all that I have heard from my Father I have made known to you." The title "Friend" did not make it into the catalog

27. Brown 2000, 271.
28. Malunowiczówna 1985; Pelikan 1993, 6–10.
29. Gregory of Nyssa, *Encomium of Saint Theodore* (PG 46:740) (trans. Ernst Kitzinger).

of official christological "titles of majesty" with "Lord," "Son of God," and "Logos."[30] But in the prayer life of millions of believers, especially within the evangelicalism of the nineteenth and twentieth centuries, it became a dominant image, as in the hymn of Joseph Scriven, "What a Friend We Have in Jesus": the inconstancy of human friends was overcome by the constancy of Jesus the heavenly friend.

6. Friendship between believers is an imitation (→7:59–60) of the God who "used to speak to Moses face to face, as one speaks to his very own friend [πρὸς τὸν ἑαυτοῦ φίλον]" (Exod. 33:11 LXX). This is the God who described Abraham as "my friend" (Isa. 41:8). Just as it is God as Father from whom every human father derives that title (Eph. 3:14–15), rather than the other way around, because, in the words of Saint Athanasius, "God does not make men His pattern; but rather we men, for that God is properly, and alone truly, Father of His Son, are also called fathers of our own children";[31] so, too, the "friendship with mankind" (φιλανθρωπία) (Titus 3:4) of God is the pattern for his gift of the friendship that becomes possible between his creatures.

27:9 The reference to a specified time as "the fast" (νηστεία) is a reminder both of the persistence of the Jewish liturgical calendar in this generation of the church (→7:47–48) and of the importance of such ascetic practices as fasting (→24:25b).

27:13–20 Luke includes a paragraph abundant with the technical terminology of ships and sailing (→27:24).

"Sail with Those Who Sail"

27:24 God has granted you all those who sail with you [πάντας τοὺς πλέοντας μετὰ σοῦ].

When the Liturgy of Saint John Chrysostom prays, "Sail with those who sail" (τοῖς πλέουσι σύμπλευσον),[32] this was not simply a way of speaking that was characteristic of a seafaring people,[33] like the quaintly British translation of Jesus' command to Peter after the resurrection, "Shoot the net to starboard!" (John 21:6 NEB); rather, it points to the place of sailing as a key element in Christian vocabulary. Political metaphors, above all "the kingdom of God" (→28:23), ap-

---

30. Hahn 1969.

31. Athanasius, *Discourses against the Arians* 1.23 (*NPNF*[2] 4:320).

32. Liturgy of Saint John Chrysostom II.G.3 (*CCF* 1:290).

33. Note, for example, the comments of Bede at this chapter on "our sea, that is, the British," referring to what is still called today the "English Channel"; *Exposition of the Acts of the Apostles* 27 (PL 92:992).

pear in the Gospels and elsewhere, and they have played a prominent part in the development of Christian thought. Related to these, as in the ideology of the medieval crusades and in the rhetoric of "Onward, Christian Soldiers," military metaphors are elaborated with great detail in Saint Paul's exhortation to "put on the whole armor of God" (Eph. 6:10–18). No reader of the New Testament could ignore its agricultural metaphors, most familiarly of all in the parable of the sower, which is one of the few parables to appear in all three of the Synoptic Gospels (Luke 8:4–15; Matt. 13:3–23; Mark 4:3–20) and is the only one of the parables to receive a detailed, point-by-point explanation from the mouth of Christ himself. Even athletic metaphors, so beloved in contemporary American culture (which speaks of "a ballpark estimate" in discussing the national budget and uses "the length of a football field" as a unit of measurement for a skyscraper or an aircraft carrier), have made a prominent contribution (1 Cor. 9:24–27), at least partly because of their familiarity to Greek and Roman readers.

But concentrating for the time being only on the Acts of the Apostles, the field of human activity that receives the most detailed attention, and in the most specifically technical vocabulary, is certainly sailing,[34] as Paul and his companions, having "escaped from the court of justice, . . . fall in with shipwreck and storm."[35] Descriptions of sailing are, moreover, concentrated in those portions of the book, such as chapter 27, in which the language shifts from the third-person singular or plural to the first-person plural—the we-passages (→27:1). In relation to the scholarly controversy over the question discussed earlier, whether the author of Luke-Acts is to be equated with the one identified by Paul as "Luke the beloved physician" (Col. 4:14), it is certainly the case that more impressive in some respects than the medical vocabulary of Acts is its nautical vocabulary. Instead of a book with the title *Luke the Physician*, therefore, it might have been preferable for Harnack (or, at any rate, for some latter-day epigone of his who was a passionate sailor) to have written *Luke the Mariner*.

It is impressive simply to recite the use of specialized sailors' jargon throughout the book, as for example: "Setting sail therefore from Troas, we made a direct voyage [εὐθυδρομήσαμεν] to Samothrace" (16:11); or "to port" (21:3 NEB). But because of the subject matter of the narrative, such jargon is concentrated here in chapter 27, in words and phrases going back in some cases to Homer's *Odyssey*, and in a literary form reminiscent in many ways of other classical descriptions of sailing and shipwreck:[36]

- "putting out to sea from there we sailed under the lee of Cyprus, because the winds were against us" (27:4), where ἀναχθέντες is "a nautical

34. Brian M. Rapske in Winter and Clarke 1993–94, 2:1–48.
35. Chrysostom, *Homilies on Acts* 53 (*NPNF*[1] 11:315).
36. Praeder 1980, 227–45.

t[echnical] t[erm] . . . , mid[dle] or pass[ive], ἀνάγεσθαι, to begin to go by boat, *put out to sea*"[37]

- ὑπεπλεύσαμεν ("sail under the lee of an island") (27:7)[38]
- ὑποπνεύσαντος δὲ νότου (27:13), a nautical term going back to Aristotle[39]
- τὴν σκευὴν τοῦ πλοίου (27:19), meaning "the tackle or rigging of a ship"[40]
- ἀγκύρας ("anchors") (27:29)[41]
- "the soldiers cut away [ἀπέκοψαν] the ropes of the boat" (27:32), ἐκπίπτω being used here in a specifically nautical sense[42]

Developing the nautical metaphor of Acts still further, Chrysostom could admonish his hearers in the maritime city of Constantinople: "Paul is sailing even now with us, only not bound as he was then. . . . Let us therefore abide where he bids us—in faith, in the safe haven: let us hearken unto him rather than to the pilot that is within us, that is, our own reason."[43]

How pervasive such nautical language could be in the vocabulary of the Bible and of early Christianity is evident, for example, in the way the Epistle to the Hebrews speaks about hope: "We have this as a sure and steadfast anchor of the soul [ὡς ἄγκυραν ἔχομεν τῆς ψυχῆς ἀσφαλῆ τε καὶ βεβαίαν]" (Heb. 6:19). Already in the Hebrew prophets ships and sailing were symbolic representations of the universal sway of the God of Israel:

> For the coastlands shall wait for me,
>   the ships of Tarshish first,
> to bring your sons from far,
>   their silver and gold with them,
> for the holy name of the Lord your God,
>   and for the Holy One of Israel. (Isa. 60:9 LXX/RSV)

And this continued in the Christian tradition. To select only two examples among many: Clement of Alexandria admonished believers to "look to the Lord with steady eye, as those who look for the nod of a good helmsman, what he wishes, what he orders, what he indicates, what signals he gives his mariners, where and whence he directs the ship's course";[44] and Gregory of Nyssa warned

---

37. BDAG 62.
38. BDAG 1040.
39. BDAG 1040.
40. BDAG 927, citing C. Voigt's *Die Romfahrt des Apostels Paulus.*
41. BDAG 12, citing A. B. Breusing's *Die Nautik der Alten* and L. Casson's *Ships and Seamanship in the Ancient World.*
42. BDAG 307–8.
43. Chrysostom, *Homilies on Acts* 53 (*NPNF*[1] 11:318).
44. Clement of Alexandria, *Who Is the Rich Man That Shall Be Saved?* 26 (*ANF* 2:598).

that "he who can steer a boat with its rudder into port can also steer it for the reef or the rock, if minded to destroy those on board."[45] Visible evidence of such nautical symbolism is provided in the ship models that still hang in churches, especially in Scandinavia, and in the designation of the auditorium of a church as *navis* ("ship")—although some scholars maintain that this term for a church comes not from that Latin word, but from the description in Greek of the church as ὁ ναὸς τοῦ θεοῦ ("the temple of God" [2 Thess. 2:4]).

27:35 In spite of the use of the term εὐχαριστεῖν here, there does not appear to be any convincing argument in favor of interpreting this breaking of bread as eucharistic and sacramental (→20:7).

45. Gregory of Nyssa, *Answer to Eunomius' Second Book* 2 (*NPNF*[2] 5:268).

ACTS 28

28:1–2 "Natives" is the RSV and NRSV translation for βάρβαροι, which AV renders as "barbarous people," a term that in modern English probably carries more pejorative connotations than it does in Greek, where it means, with relative neutrality, "non-Greek," as it does in its other appearances in the New Testament (Rom. 1:14; 1 Cor. 14:11 twice; Col. 3:11).

28:3–6 Luke includes here a dramatic illustration of the changeability of public opinion, from "murderer" to "god" in two verses—and not many more moments than that (→6:8; →19:28). It does not appear to be straining this text to see in this changeability an echo of the passion story and an imitation of Christ (→7:59–60), who, in Luke's account, was hailed with the cry (reminiscent of the Christmas angels in Luke 2:14), "Blessed is the King who comes in the name of the Lord! Peace in heaven and glory in the highest!" (Luke 19:38), and a few days later was denounced with the cry, "Crucify, crucify him!" (Luke 23:21).

Launched into World History

28:14 And so we came to Rome [καὶ οὕτως εἰς τὴν Ῥώμην ἤλθαμεν].

Six monosyllables in English (though not in Greek), this sentence is the signal that the Way (→11:26) was being transferred—or rather, already had been—to a world stage and was no longer hidden "in a corner" (→26:26). "Not to depart from Jerusalem" (1:4)—"and so we came to Rome" (28:16): these words from the first chapter and from the last chapter are the bookends of the Acts of the Apostles, marking the transition from Jerusalem to Rome and from the apostolic church to the catholic church. It is a tale of two cities.

To be sure, there are many other cities mentioned in Acts, more than in all the other New Testament books combined. The fame of Moses had spread "from early generations" to "every city" (15:21), and the message of Jesus was to do the same, and far more. In many respects the book of Acts is a book about the sea (→27:24), but about the sea as a highway between Greek-speaking cities, "as they went on their way through the cities" (16:4), first by land and then by ship. On these journeys, Paul explained, "the Holy Spirit testifies to me *in every city* that imprisonment and persecutions await me" (20:23). Paul linked the name of his own native city with his standing in the tradition of the covenant with Israel (→3:25) as part of his dual identity when he declared, with obvious pride in both, "I am a Jew, from Tarsus in Cilicia, a citizen of no mean city [οὐκ ἀσήμου πόλεως πολίτης]" (21:39). Every city or region (except Colossae) to which he eventually would address an epistle (→23:25) appears in these accounts of his travels. Wayne A. Meeks therefore properly devotes his pioneering study of the New Testament, and particularly of the Apostle Paul, to the cities of the Mediterranean world as the cradle of the early Christian movement, with all that this would imply for the social outlook and political position of the church.[1]

But the two cities of Jerusalem and Rome—the name "Rome" never appears in any of the Gospels, and "the Romans" only once (John 11:48), although elsewhere in the New Testament "Babylon" (1 Pet. 5:13), as "a name of mystery" (Rev. 17:5), is a code name for "Rome"—are in a class by themselves, as the pivots on which the entire narrative of the book of Acts turns. And the bipolar relation between them, which is dialectical, was clearly fundamental for the writer of Acts—and, according to the writer, also for Paul and for his Lord. Luke interprets the dialectic between Jerusalem and Rome as central to Paul's own definition of his divine mission after his conversion (→9:1–4): "Now after these events Paul resolved in the Spirit to pass through Macedonia and Achaia and go to *Jerusalem*, saying, 'After I have been there, I must also see *Rome*,'" not (though it might superficially sound that way) as a tourist but as a missionary and an apostle (19:21). Together with his strong sense that he might not receive a fair trial in Jerusalem, Paul's "resolution in the Spirit" to complete the circle by going from Jerusalem to Rome underlay the strategy of his appeal to Caesar as well (→25:11). Festus's report to King Felix gave an account of the theological dispute between Paul and other Jews (→18:15) and then it continued: "Being at a loss how to investigate these questions, I asked whether he wished to go to *Jerusalem* and be tried there regarding them. But when Paul had appealed to be kept in custody for the decision of the emperor, I commanded him to be held until I could send him to *Caesar*" (25:20–21). But the ultimate sources lay much deeper, for the divine odyssey from Jerusalem to Rome had its real origin in Christ's selection of him (→9:15) as a "chosen instrument of mine to carry my name before the Gentiles and kings and the sons of Israel": "The following night [after his appearance at the council] the Lord stood by him and said, 'Take courage, for as you have testified about me

1. Meeks 2003.

at *Jerusalem*, so you must bear witness also at *Rome*'" (23:11). And the writer of Acts had earlier described how Jesus, "when the days drew near from him to be received up, set his face to go to *Jerusalem*" (Luke 9:51).

While Jerusalem continued to receive the honor of being, in the language of Irenaeus, "the metropolis [i.e., capital city: μητρόπολις] of the citizens of the new covenant,"[2] although it was not accorded the rank of a patriarchate of the church until the Council of Chalcedon in 451 (after Rome, Constantinople, Alexandria, and Antioch),[3] the future belonged to Rome as, also in the language of Irenaeus, "the very great, the very ancient, and universally known Church founded and organized at Rome. . . . For it is a matter of necessity that every Church should agree with this Church, on account of its preeminent authority."[4]

And—to invoke a cliché that fits here if ever it fit anywhere—"the rest is history."

28:17, 20 To the very end of the narrative in Acts, Paul persisted in identifying the Christian eschatological gospel (→23:8), which, in the words of the Niceno-Constantinopolitan Creed, "awaits the resurrection of the dead and the life of the age to come,"[5] as not only the specifically Christian hope, but "the hope of Israel." This was in keeping with the theology of his epistles, above all of the Epistle to the Romans, in which, despite harsh language against Jews who "rely upon the law and boast of your relation to God" but who in fact "dishonor God by breaking the law" (Rom. 2:17–24), he voiced his personal heartbreak, "I could wish that I myself were accursed and cut off from Christ for the sake of my brethren, my kinsmen by race" (Rom. 9:3), together with his abiding hope and confidence that "all Israel will be saved" (Rom. 11:26) (→3:25).

"His Kingdom Will Have No End"

28:23 Testifying to the kingdom of God.

Among the theological topics or *loci communes* that span most of the text of the book of Acts from beginning to end, such as baptism (→22:16) or the angels (→12:7), instead of being concentrated in only one place, none comes as close to both ends of the book as does the doctrine of the kingdom of God, from the third verse of the first chapter to the final verse of the final chapter.[6] There are, in all, eight references to the "kingdom of God" in Acts; these may conveniently be grouped under five headings, each of which carries notable

2. Irenaeus, *Against Heresies* 3.12.5 (*ANF* 1:431).
3. W. de Vries in *LTK* 5:906–7.
4. Irenaeus, *Against Heresies* 3.3.2 (*ANF* 1:415).
5. Niceno-Constantinopolitan Creed 11–12 (*CCF* 1:163).
6. Darù 2001, 71–77.

theological significance for any attempt to comprehend this profound but
enigmatic doctrine that is confessed in the seventh article of the Niceno-Constantinopolitan Creed: "His kingdom will have no end" (οὐ τῆς βασιλείας οὐκ
ἔσται τέλος):[7]

1. "So when they had come together, they asked him, 'Lord, is it at this time
   that you will bring about the restoration, and when will the kingdom of
   Israel be?' He said to them, 'No one can know the time or season which
   the Father has fixed by his own authority. But you shall receive power
   when the Holy Spirit has come upon you'" (1:6–8 TPR). To place this
   incident into context, it is necessary to relate it to "the gospel of the forty
   days" (→1:2–3), in which Christ, meeting his disciples after his resurrection, "beginning with Moses and all the prophets, interpreted to them in
   all the scriptures the things concerning himself" (Luke 24:27). It seems
   obvious from the circumstances of that meeting, as reported by Saint
   Luke in the final chapter of his Gospel, that the primary component of
   the message from the risen Christ was the centrality of the crucifixion
   (→3:18) and of the resurrection (→2:31) in the saving plan of God: it was
   preeminently true of Jesus Christ as it was to be of his disciples in imitation of him (→7:59–60), "that through many tribulations we must enter
   the kingdom of God" (14:22). Attaching his narrative here in Acts to the
   narrative at the close of his Gospel, Saint Luke summarized that message:
   "appearing to them during forty days, and speaking of the kingdom of
   God" (1:3). And yet only a few verses after that summary, Luke attributed
   to the graduates of Christ's postresurrection seminar this shocking naïveté
   about the kingdom of God and attributed to Christ the kind of reproof
   that would have seemed more appropriate at a far earlier stage of their
   education.
2. "But when they believed Philip as he preached good news about the
   kingdom of God and the name of Jesus Christ, they were baptized, both
   men and women" (8:12). Coming as it does alongside not only the several homilies of Peter in the first chapters of Acts (2:14–36; 3:12–26;
   4:8–12), but the apologetic oration of Stephen on the history of Israel
   and the life of Moses (7:2–53), and coming before the concentration of
   the second part of Acts on the preaching of Paul to Jews and to Gentiles,
   this encapsulation of the preaching of the Apostle Philip might easily be
   overlooked. The two themes of that preaching that are explicitly identified here are "[1] the kingdom of God and [2] the name of Jesus Christ."
   The second of these, "the name," both because "there is no other *name*
   under heaven given among men by which we must be saved" (4:12) and
   because it had an unmistakable connection with baptism in the *name*
   of Christ (→22:16), stood alongside the designation of "the Way" as the

7. Niceno-Constantinopolitan Creed 7 (*CCF* 1:163).

party label of those who would eventually come to be called "Christians" (→11:26). But it does not seem to be forcing the text to conclude from this passage that the message of "the kingdom of God," now presumably purged of the naïveté of the question (attributed to all the disciples, therefore including Philip), "Lord, is it at this time that you will bring about the restoration, and when will the kingdom of Israel be?" (1:6 TPR), constituted a central theme of the apostolic message.

3. "Strengthening the souls of the disciples, [Paul and Barnabas were] exhorting them to continue in the faith, and saying that through many tribulations we must enter the kingdom of God" (14:22). Although there is no direct indication in the preceding reference, which dealt with the preaching of Philip, just how much of an eschatological or even apocalyptic content there was to his message about "the kingdom of God," this reference, dealing with the preaching of Paul and Barnabas, does seem to carry such a content, for to "enter the kingdom of God" or "to inherit the kingdom" was a term for the attainment of the eschatological hope of life eternal (Luke 18:18); it was used that way in the miniature apocalypse with which Jesus closed his teaching to the disciples before the Last Supper (Matt. 25:34).

4. Two of the references to the kingdom of God in the preaching of Paul here in Acts had as their context his special relation to the church at Ephesus (→21:13–14). At Ephesus, as described in the narrative, "he entered the synagogue and for three months spoke boldly, arguing and pleading about the kingdom of God" (19:8). Because of the particular emphasis (→3:25) that the apostolic message took in the setting of the synagogue or other Jewish "place[s] of prayer" (16:13, 16), this "arguing and pleading about the kingdom of God" at Ephesus seems to refer to stating the Christian case for the "spiritual sense" of Scripture (→8:30–31), which for the doctrine of the kingdom of God consisted in showing that the promises of God about an everlasting kingdom did not refer in the first instance to a place on the map (→7:47–48) or to a political government (→25:11), as though the messianic "King Jesus" had come as a replacement for Caesar (17:7). From Saint Paul's description of his ministry and message at Ephesus as "go[ing about] preaching the kingdom" (20:25), it seems fair to conclude that the kingdom of God was his theme not only to the Jewish community there, but also to the Christian community.

5. As with reference to Ephesus, so with reference to Rome in this concluding chapter of the Acts of the Apostles, there are two mentions of "the kingdom of God" in Saint Paul's message—which is twice as many as in his entire Epistle to the Romans (Rom. 14:17). Once again, it appeared as a central theme (or even *the* central theme) of his preaching, as in his communication to his fellow Israelites he was "from morning till evening, testifying to the kingdom of God" (28:23), but also "preaching the king-

dom of God and teaching about the Lord Jesus Christ" not to Jews alone but to "all who came to him," both Jews and Gentiles (28:30–31).

It is probably significant that the doctrine of "the kingdom of God" does not appear in the Niceno-Constantinopolitan Creed as a positive dogmatic affirmation, but as a polemic against the false teaching associated with the name Marcellus of Ancyra, that there would be an end of the kingdom of Christ.[8] Repeatedly, Christian confessions of faith have introduced the topic of the kingdom as a polemic, for example, against chiliasm[9] or, conversely, against an indifference to the social mission of the church.[10] Clearly it has been too central a biblical theme to be ignored, yet too comprehensive and diverse a concept in biblical usage to be amenable to precise dogmatic definition.

"Freedom from External Coercion"

28:31 Teaching about the Lord Jesus Christ quite openly and unhindered.

As Cassiodorus says about this verse in the final words of his commentary, "Although he was bound with chains of iron, he daily set believers free from the chains of their sins."[11] Somehow it seems particularly fitting, in the light of all that has gone before in the preceding twenty-eight chapters—as well as in the light of all that was to come for the next twenty centuries of the history of Christendom—that the very last word in the book of Acts should be ἀκωλύτως ("unhindered") (AV: "no man forbidding him"); and the reader will be forgiven for wanting to exclaim, "It's about time!" Just as beginning students of classical Greek who have taken up Homer in order to be able to read the poetry of the *Iliad* have often been appalled by all that gore, so it seems shocking to discover just how much fanatical violence and religious coercion there is in the book of Acts. In response to the consistency of this pattern throughout history, the Declaration on Religious Freedom of the Second Vatican Council declared "that the human person has a right to religious freedom," which it defined as "such immunity from coercion by individuals, or by groups, or by any human power, that no one should be forced to act against his conscience in religious matters, nor prevented from acting according to his conscience, whether in private or in public."[12]

The practice of such coercion runs like a bloody mark across the entire book of Acts. Chapter 9 is an especially blatant example: it opens with "Saul, still

8. *Chr. Trad.* 1:207–9.
9. Augsburg Confession 17.5 (*CCF* 2:68).
10. Confession of the United Presbyterian Church in the United States of America 9.54–55 (*CCF* 3:725).
11. Cassiodorus, *Commentary on the Acts of the Apostles* 72 (PL 70:1406).
12. Dignitatis humanae 1.2 (*CCF* 3:663).

breathing threats and murder against the disciples of the Lord" (9:1); a little later he himself, now a Christian believer, as his enemies "were watching the gates day and night, to kill him," escaped when "his disciples took him by night and let him down over the wall, lowering him in a basket" (9:23–25); and four verses later he was "disput[ing] against the Hellenists; but they were seeking to kill him," yet once more he escaped (9:29–30). But the topic is not confined to any one chapter or section of Acts. Chapter 17 is usually remembered, and properly so, for Saint Paul's encounter with Stoic and Epicurean philosophers (→17:18) and for his address about the unknown God on the Areopagus (→17:23); but it opens with a scene in which his enemies "recruited some low fellows from the dregs of the populace, roused the rabble [ὀχλοποιήσαντες], and had the city in an uproar" (17:5–9 NEB) to lynch him. The violence becomes a veritable refrain: "plotted to kill him" (9:23); "seeking to kill him" (9:29); "dragged him out of the city, supposing that he was dead" (14:19); "trying to kill him" (21:31); "shouting that he ought not to live any longer" (25:24)—in sum, "Away with such a fellow from the earth! For he ought not to live" (22:22).

Much of this coercion was "the violence of the crowd" (ἡ βία τοῦ ὄχλου) (21:35), but the relation of the powers that be (→25:11) to it was ambivalent. In Jerusalem near the beginning of the narrative, "the captain with the officers went and brought them, but without violence [οὐ μετὰ βίας], for they were afraid of being stoned by the people" (5:26); and near the end of the narrative Paul "was actually carried by the soldiers" to rescue him from mob violence (21:35). But sometimes it took place with the collusion of the authorities. King Herod had his guards put to death for negligence in dealing with the Christians, but then, by divine judgment, he died a violent death himself and was "eaten alive by worms" (12:19–24 TPR). The Roman tribune mistook Paul for "the Egyptian . . . who recently stirred up a revolt and led the four thousand men of the Assassins out into the wilderness" (21:38), but then protected his rights when he learned that this was not true. Likewise, in defense of the due process of law (→25:16), Claudius Lysias foiled an "ambush" against Paul (23:16–24). A special case of violence that was at once official and personal was the suicidal response of the jailer after Paul and Silas had escaped through a miracle (16:26–28).

The remembrance of such violence against the gospel did not disappear even when, under Emperors Constantine and Theodosius, Christianity moved from being the victim of religious coercion to becoming, all too often, its agent. Although they enforced it against each other, it became a Catholic, Orthodox, and Protestant consensus, expressed in the words of Henry VIII, "that unity and concord in opinion, namely in such things as doth concern our religion, may increase and go forthward, and all occasion of *dissent* and discord touching the same *be repressed and utterly extinguished*,"[13] by Christian rulers. As the Second Vatican Council went on to acknowledge, "at times in the life of

13. Ten Articles preface 1 (*CCF* 2:298).

the people of God, as it has pursued its pilgrimage through the twists and turns of human history, there have been ways of acting hardly in tune with the spirit of the gospel, indeed contrary to it"; but it insisted that "nevertheless the church's teaching that no one's faith should be coerced has held firm."[14] What the Second Vatican Council was forbidding was *external* coercion; the declaration of the apostles, "We cannot keep from speaking [οὐ δυνάμεθα . . . μὴ λαλεῖν] about what we have seen and heard" (4:20 NRSV), described a no less powerful compulsion, which may have sounded like the "irresistible grace" decreed by the Synod of Dort in 1619,[15] but which was actually an *internal* compulsion wrought by the Holy Spirit (→2:1).

14. Dignitatis humanae 1.12 (*CCF* 3:671).
15. Decrees of the Synod of Dort (*CCF* 2:590–91).

BIBLIOGRAPHY

Aland, Barbara. 1986. "Entstehung, Charakter und Herkunft des sog. westlichen Textes untersucht an der Apostelgeschichte." *Ephemerides Theologicae Lovanienses* 62:5–65.

Allen, O. Wesley, Jr. 1997. *The Death of Herod: The Narrative and Theological Function of Retribution in Luke-Acts*. Atlanta: Scholars Press.

Alter, Robert. 1981. *The Art of Biblical Narrative*. New York: Basic Books.

Apostolopoulos, Charalambos. 1986. *Phaedo Christianus: Studien zur Verbindung und Abwägung des Verhältnisses zwischen dem platonischen "Phaidon" und dem Dialog Gregors von Nyssa "Über die Seele und die Auferstehung."* Frankfurt: Lang.

Aulén, Gustaf. 1969. *Christus Victor: An Historical Study of the Three Main Types of the Idea of the Atonement*. Translated by A. G. Hebert. Foreword by Jaroslav Pelikan. London: SPCK.

Bachmann, Michael. 1980. *Jerusalem und der Tempel: Die geographisch-theologischen Elemente in der lukanischen Sicht des jüdischen Kultzentrums*. Stuttgart: Kohlhammer.

Barrett, Charles Kingsley. 1961. *Luke the Historian in Recent Study*. London: Epworth.

———. 1994–98. *A Critical and Exegetical Commentary on the Acts of the Apostles*. 2 vols. International Critical Commentary. Edinburgh: Clark.

Beardslee, William A. 1960–61. "The Casting of Lots at Qumran and in the Book of Acts." *Novum Testamentum* 4:245–52.

Beck, Hans-Georg. 1959. *Kirche und theologische Literatur im byzantinischen Reich*. Munich: Beck.

Bihler, Johannes. 1963. *Die Stephanusgeschichte im Zusammenhang der Apostelgeschichte*. Munich: Hueber.

Black, Matthew. 1981. "The Holy Spirit in the Western Text of Acts." Pages 159–70 in *New Testament Textual Criticism: Its Significance for New Testament Exegesis: Essays in Honour of Bruce M. Metzger*. Edited by Eldon Jay Epp and Gordon D. Fee. Oxford: Clarendon.

Blaise, Albert, and Henri Chirat. 1954. *Dictionnaire latin-français des auteurs chrétiens*. Strasbourg: Le Latin Chrétien.

Bogolepov, D. 1900. *Rukovodstvo k tolkovomu čteniu Četveroevangelija i knihi dejanij apostolškich* [Handbook for the interpretative reading of the Four Gospels and of the Acts of the Apostles]. 5th edition. Moscow: Stupina.

Boismard, Marie-Émile, ed. 2000. *Le texte occidental des Actes des Apôtres: Édition nouvelle entièrement refondue*. 2nd edition. Paris: Gabalda.

Brawley, Robert L. 1987. *Luke-Acts and the Jews: Conflict, Apology, and Conciliation*. Atlanta: Scholars Press.

Brown, Peter. 2000. *Augustine of Hippo: A Biography*. 2nd edition. Berkeley: University of California Press.

Bruce, Frederick Fyvie. 1990. *Acts of the Apostles: The Greek Text with Introduction and Commentary*. 3rd edition. Grand Rapids: Eerdmans.

Burck, Erich. 1964. *Die Erzählungskunst des T. Livius*. 2nd edition. Berlin/Zurich: Weidmann.

Cadbury, Henry J. 1920. *The Style and Literary Method of Luke*. Cambridge: Harvard University Press.

———. 1955. *The Book of Acts in History*. New York: Harper.

———. 1958. *The Making of Luke-Acts*. 2nd edition. New York: Macmillan.

Calvin, John. 1949. *Commentary on the Acts of the Apostles*. 2 vols. Translated by Henry Beveridge. Grand Rapids: Eerdmans. (Orig. 1585.)

Carrington, Philip. 1957. *The Early Christian Church*. 2 vols. Cambridge: Cambridge University Press.

Case, Shirley Jackson. 1946. *Origins of Christian Supernaturalism*. Chicago: University of Chicago Press.

Chadwick, Henry, trans. 1953. *Origen: Contra Celsum*. Cambridge: Cambridge University Press.

———, trans. 1992. *Saint Augustine: Confessions*. Oxford: Oxford University Press.

Cochrane, Charles Norris. 1944. *Christianity and Classical Culture: A Study of Thought and Action from Augustus to Augustine*. London: Oxford University Press.

Colish, Marcia L. 1985. *The Stoic Tradition from Antiquity to the Early Middle Ages*. 2 vols. Leiden: Brill.

Constantelos, Demetrios J. 1991. *Byzantine Philanthropy and Social Welfare*. 2nd edition. New Rochelle, NY: Caratzas.

Conzelmann, Hans. 1987. *Acts of the Apostles*. Translated by James Limburg, A. Thomas Kraabel, and Donald H. Juel. Philadelphia: Fortress.

Dahl, Nils Alstrup. 1974. *The Crucified Messiah, and Other Essays*. Minneapolis: Augsburg.

———. 1976. *Jesus in the Memory of the Early Church*. Minneapolis: Augsburg.

Daniélou, Jean. 1960. *From Shadows to Reality: Studies in the Biblical Typology of the Fathers*. Translated by Wulstan Hibberd. Westminster, Md.: Newman.

Darù, Jean. 2001. *Dio ha aperto anche ai pagani la porta delle fede (At 14,27): Una lettura degli Atti deli Apostoli*. Rome: ADP.

Davies, John Gordon. 1958. *He Ascended into Heaven: A Study in the History of Doctrine*. Bampton Lectures. London: Lutterworth.

Dibelius, Martin. 1949. *Die Reden der Apostelgeschichte und die antike Geschichtsschreibung*. Heidelberg: Winter.

Dobschütz, Ernst von. 1899. *Christusbilder: Untersuchungen zur christlichen Legende*. 2 vols. Leipzig: Hinrichs.

Donfried, Karl P. 1974. "False Presuppositions in the Study of *Romans*." *Catholic Biblical Quarterly* 36:332–55.

Dupont, Jacques. 1964. *The Sources of the Acts*. Translated by Kathleen Pond. New York: Herder & Herder.

Dvornik, Francis. 1958. *The Idea of Apostolicity and the Legend of the Apostle Andrew*. Cambridge: Harvard University Press.

Easton, Burton Scott. 1936. *The Purpose of Acts*. London: SPCK.

Eckey, Wilfried. 2000. *Die Apostelgeschichte*. 2 vols. Neukirchen-Vluyn: Neukirchener Verlag.

Enslin, Morton Scott. 1938. *Christian Beginnings*. New York: Harper.

Epp, Eldon Jay. 1966. *The Theological Tendency of Codex Bezae Cantabrigiensis in Acts*. Cambridge: Cambridge University Press.

Esler, Philip Francis. 1987. *Community and Gospel in Luke-Acts: The Social and Political Motivations of Lucan Theology*. Cambridge: Cambridge University Press.

Fennema, D. A. 1985. "John 1:18: God the Only Son." *New Testament Studies* 31:124–35.

Florovsky, Georges V. 1972–89. *Collected Works*. 14 vols. Belton, Mass.: Nordland.

Foakes Jackson, F. J., and Kirsopp Lake, eds. 1979. *The Beginnings of Christianity: The*

Acts of the Apostles. 5 vols. Reprint, Grand Rapids: Baker. (Orig. 1920–33.)

Gasque, W. Ward. 1974. "The Speeches of Acts: Dibelius Reconsidered." Pages 232–50 in *New Dimensions in New Testament Study.* Edited by Richard N. Longenecker and Merrill C. Tenney. Grand Rapids: Zondervan.

———. 1975. *A History of the Criticism of the Acts of the Apostles.* Grand Rapids: Eerdmans.

Gilson, Étienne. 1926. "Pourquoi saint Thomas a critiqué saint Augustin." *Archives d'Histoire Doctrinale et Littéraire du Moyen Age* 1:5–127.

Glawe, Walther Karl Erich. 1912. *Die Hellenisierung des Christentums in der Geschichte der Theologie von Luther bis auf die Gegenwart.* Berlin: Trowitzsch.

Grant, Robert M. 1952. *Miracle and Natural Law in Graeco-Roman and Early Christian Thought.* Amsterdam: Brill.

Grässer, Erich. 1957. *Das Problem der Parusienverzögerung in den synoptischen Evangelien und in der Apostelgeschichte.* Berlin: Töpelmann.

Grimaldi, William M. A. 1980. *Aristotle "Rhetoric" I: A Commentary.* New York: Fordham University Press.

Haenchen, Ernst. 1971. *The Acts of the Apostles: A Commentary.* Translated by B. Noble et al. Philadelphia: Westminster.

Hahn, Ferdinand. 1969. *Titles of Jesus in Christology: Their History in Early Christianity.* Translated by Harold Knight and George Ogg. New York: World.

Hall, Kermit L., ed. 1992. *The Oxford Companion to the Supreme Court of the United States.* New York: Oxford University Press.

Hanson, R. P. C. 1965–66. "The Provenance of the Interpolator in the 'Western' Text of Acts and of Acts Itself." *New Testament Studies* 12:211–30.

Harnack, Adolf von. 1907. *Luke the Physician, the Author of the Third Gospel and the Acts of the Apostles.* Translated by J. R. Wilkinson. New York: Putnam.

———. 1909. *New Testament Studies III: The Acts of the Apostles.* Translated by J. R. Wilkinson. New York: Putnam. (Orig. 1908.)

———. 1957. *Outlines of the History of Dogma.* Translated by Edwin Knox Mitchell. Introduction by Philip Rieff. Boston: Starr King. (Orig. 1893.)

———. 1961. *The Mission and Expansion of Christianity in the First Three Centuries.* Translated by James Moffatt. Introduction by Jaroslav Pelikan. New York: Harper. (Orig. 1905.)

Hatch, Edwin. 1957. *The Influence of Greek Ideas on Christianity.* Foreword by Frederick C. Grant. New York: Harper. (Orig. 1888.)

Hefner, Philip J. 1966. *Faith and the Vitalities of History: A Theological Study Based on the Work of Albrecht Ritschl.* Makers of Modern Theology. New York: Harper & Row.

Hemer, Colin J. 1989. *The Book of Acts in the Setting of Hellenistic History.* Tübingen: Mohr.

Hengel, Martin. 1979. *Acts and the History of Earliest Christianity.* Translated by J. Bowden. Philadelphia: Fortress.

Hodgson, Peter Crafts. 1966. *The Formation of Historical Theology: A Study of Ferdinand Christian Baur.* Makers of Modern Theology. New York: Harper & Row.

Holl, Karl. 1928. *Gesammelte Aufsätze zur Kirchengeschichte: Der Osten.* Tübingen: Mohr.

Jaeger, Werner. 1939–44. *Paideia: The Ideals of Greek Culture.* 3 vols. Translated by Gilbert Highet. New York: Oxford University Press.

———. 1961. *Early Christianity and Greek Paideia.* Cambridge: Harvard University Press.

James, William. 1990. *The Varieties of Religious Experience.* Gifford Lectures 1901–2. Introduction by Jaroslav Pelikan. Library of America. New York: Vintage. (Orig. 1902.)

Jervell, Jacob. 1972. *Luke and the People of God: A New Look at Acts.* Foreword by Nils Dahl. Minneapolis: Augsburg.

———. 1996. *The Theology of the Acts of the Apostles.* New Testament Theology. Cambridge: Cambridge University Press.

Johnson, Luke Timothy. 1977. *The Literary Function of Possessions in Luke-Acts.* Missoula, Mont.: Scholars Press.

———. 1981. *Sharing Possessions: Mandate and Symbol of Faith.* Philadelphia: Fortress.

———. 1983. *Decision-Making in the Church: A Biblical Model.* Philadelphia: Fortress.

———. 1992. *The Acts of the Apostles.* Sacra Pagina 5. Collegeville, Minn.: Liturgical Press.

Julian, John. 1957. *A Dictionary of Hymnology.* 2nd edition. Reprint, New York: Dover. (Orig. 1907.)

Kass, Leon R., et al. 2004. "Why Genesis? Why Now?" *Center Conversations* 27:1–14.

Keck, Leander E., and J. Louis Martyn, eds. 1966. *Studies in Luke-Acts.* Nashville: Abingdon.

Kennedy, George A. 1994. *A New History of Classical Rhetoric.* Princeton: Princeton University Press.

Klijn, A. F. J. 1949. *A Survey of the Researches into the Western Text of the Gospels and Acts.* Proefschrift Utrecht.

Kostof, Spiro K. 1965. *The Orthodox Baptistery of Ravenna.* New Haven: Yale University Press.

Kremer, Jacob, ed. 1979. *Les Actes des Apôtres: Traditions, rédaction, théologie.* Leuven: Leuven University Press.

Krodel, Gerhard A. 1986. *Acts.* Augsburg Commentary on the New Testament. Minneapolis: Augsburg.

Lacoste, Jean-Yves, ed. 1998. *Dictionnaire critique de théologie.* Paris: Presses Universitaires de France.

Levi, Virgilio, ed. 1982. *The Common Christian Roots of the Nations of Europe: An International Colloquium at the Vatican.* 2 vols. Rome: Pontifical Lateran University.

Lewy, Hans. 1929. *Sobria ebrietas: Untersuchungen zur Geschichte der antiken Mystik.* Brussels: Édition universelle.

Lintott, Andrew William. 1999. *The Constitution of the Roman Republic.* Oxford: Clarendon.

Lohfink, Gerhard. 1971. *Die Himmelfahrt Jesu: Untersuchungen zu den Himmelfahrts- und Erhöhungstexten bei Lukas.* Studien zum Alten und Neuen Testament 26. Munich: Kösel.

Loisy, Alfred Firmin. 1920. *Les Actes des Apôtres.* Paris: Nourry.

Löning, Karl. 1973. *Die Saulustradition in der Apostelgeschichte.* Münster: Aschendorff.

Lopuchin, A. P. 1895. *Biblejskaja istorija* [Biblical history]. Saint Petersburg: Tuzova.

Luschnat, Otto. 1942. *Die Feldherrreden im Geschichtswerke des Thukydides.* Inaugural dissertation, University of Leipzig.

Luther, Martin. 1955–. *Luther's Works: American Edition.* 55 vols. Edited by Jaroslav Pelikan and Helmut Lehmann. Saint Louis: Concordia/Philadelphia: Muhlenberg.

Macgregor, G. H. C. 1954. "The Acts of the Apostles: Introduction and Exegesis." Volume 9/pages 3–352 in *Interpreter's Bible*, edited by George Arthur Buttrick. New York/Nashville: Abingdon.

Maddox, Robert. 1985. *The Purpose of Luke-Acts.* Edited by John Riches. Edinburgh: Clark.

Malunowiczówna, Leokadia. 1985. "Le probleme de l'amité chez Basile, Grégoire de Nazianze et Jean Chrysostome." *Studia patristica* 16/2:412–27.

Manitius, Max. 1911–31. *Geschichte der lateinischen Literatur in Mittelalter.* 3 vols. Munich: Beck.

Marguerat, Daniel. 1999. *La première histoire du christianisme (Les Actes des apôtres).* Paris: Cerf.

Marshall, I. Howard. 1970. *Luke, Historian and Theologian.* Exeter: Paternoster.

McReynolds, Paul R. 1981. "John 1:18 in Textual Variation and Translation." Pages 105–18 in *New Testament Textual Criticism: Its Significance for New Testament Exegesis: Essays in Honour of Bruce M. Metzger.* Edited by Eldon Jay Epp and Gordon D. Fee. Oxford: Clarendon.

Meeks, Wayne A. 2003. *The First Urban Christians: The Social World of the Apostle Paul.* 2nd edition. New Haven: Yale University Press.

Méhat, A. 1956. "'Apocatastase,' Origène, Clément d'Alexandrie, *Act.* 3,21." *Vigiliae christianae* 10:196–214.

Meyendorff, John. 1989. *Imperial Unity and Christian Divisions.* Crestwood, N. Y.: Saint Vladimir's Seminary Press.

Morgenthaler, Robert. 1949. *Die lukanische Geschichtsschreibung als Zeugnis: Gestalt und Gehalt der Kunst des Lukas.* 2 vols. Zurich: Zwingli.

Munck, Johannes. 1967. *The Acts of the Apostles.* Anchor Bible 31. Garden City, N.Y.: Doubleday.

Murray, John Courtney. 1964. *The Problem of God Yesterday and Today.* New Haven: Yale University Press.

Nave, Guy D., Jr. 2002. *The Role and Function of Repentance in Luke-Acts.* Leiden: Brill.

Neusner, Jacob, Alan J. Avery-Peck, and William Scott Green, eds. 1999. *The Encyclopedia of Judaism.* 3 vols. New York: Continuum.

Newman, John Henry. 1962. *Callista: A Sketch of the Third Century.* Westminster, Md.: Newman. (Orig. 1855.)

———. 1985. *An Essay in Aid of a Grammar of Assent.* Edited by Ian T. Ker. Oxford: Clarendon. (Orig. 1889.)

———. 1989. *An Essay on the Development of Christian Doctrine.* Introduction by Ian T. Ker. Notre Dame, Ind.: University of Notre Dame Press. (Orig. 1878.)

Nickelsburg, George W. E. 2003. *Ancient Judaism and Christian Origins: Diversity, Continuity, and Transformation.* Minneapolis: Fortress.

Niesel, Wilhelm, ed. 1938. *Bekenntnisschriften und Kirchenordnungen der nach Gottes Wort reformierten Kirche.* Munich: Kaiser.

Nikanor (Brovkovič), Archbishop. 1905. *Tolkovij apostol* [The apostle interpreted]. 3 vols. Saint Petersburg: Synodical Press.

Nock, Arthur Darby. 1972. *Essays on Religion and the Ancient World.* 2 vols. Edited by Zeph Stewart. Oxford: Oxford University Press.

Norden, Eduard. 1913. *Agnostos Theos: Untersuchungen zur Formengeschichte religiöser Rede.* Leipzig: Teubner.

Nova vulgata bibliorum sacrorum editio. 1986. 2nd edition. Vatican City: Libreria Editrice Vaticana.

Onasch, Konrad, and Annemarie Schnieper. 1997. *Icons: The Fascination and the Reality.* Translated by Daniel C. Conklin. New York: Riverside.

O'Toole, Robert F. 1978. *The Christological Climax of Paul's Defense.* Rome: Biblical Institute Press.

Ouspensky, Leonid, and Vladimir Lossky. 1999. *The Meaning of Icons.* Translated by G. E. H. Palmer and E. Kadloubovsky. Crestwood, N. Y.: Saint Vladimir's Seminary Press.

Outler, Albert C., ed. 1964. *John Wesley.* Library of Protestant Thought. New York: Oxford University Press.

Pelikan, Jaroslav. 1968. *Spirit Versus Structure: Luther and the Institutions of the Church.* New York: Harper & Row.

———. 1987. "The Odyssey of Dionysian Spirituality." Pages 11–24 in *Pseudo-Dionysius: The Complete Works.* Edited by Paul Rorem. Classics of Western Spirituality. New York: Paulist Press.

———. 1988. *The Melody of Theology: A Philosophical Dictionary.* Cambridge: Harvard University Press.

———. 1990. *Imago Dei: The Byzantine Apologia for Icons.* Princeton: Princeton University Press.

———. 1993. *Christianity and Classical Culture: The Metamorphosis of Natural Theology in the Christian Encounter with Hellenism.* New Haven: Yale University Press.

———. 1997. *What Has Athens to Do with Jerusalem? "Timaeus" and "Genesis" in Counterpoint.* Jerome Lectures. Ann Arbor: University of Michigan Press.

———. 2000. *Divine Rhetoric: The Sermon on the Mount as Message and as Model in Augustine, Chrysostom, and Luther.* Crestwood, N. Y.: Saint Vladimir's Seminary Press.

———. 2003. *Credo: Historical and Theological Guide to Creeds and Confessions of Faith in the Christian Tradition.* New Haven: Yale University Press.

Pelikan, Jaroslav, with Valerie R. Hotchkiss and David Price. 1966. *The Reformation of the Bible/The Bible of the Reformation.* New Haven: Yale University Press.

Plümacher, Eckhard. 1972. *Lukas als hellenistischer Schriftsteller: Studien zur Apostelgeschichte*. Göttingen: Vandenhoeck & Ruprecht.

Praeder, Susan Marie. 1980. "The Narrative Voyage: An Analysis and Interpretation of Acts 27–28." Dissertation, Graduate Theological Union, Berkeley.

Prestige, George Leonard. 1956. *God in Patristic Thought*. London: SPCK.

Quasten, Johannes, et al. 1951–86. *Patrology*. 4 vols. Westminster, Md.: Newman/Christian Classics.

Raby, F. J. E., ed. 1959. *The Oxford Book of Medieval Latin Verse*. Oxford: Clarendon.

Rahlfs, Alfred, ed. 1979. *Septuaginta*. Athens: Hellenikē Biblikē Hetairia/Stuttgart: Deutsche Bibelgesellschaft.

Rahner, Karl, and Herbert Vorgrimler. 1965. *Theological Dictionary*. Edited by Cornelius Ernst. Translated by Richard Strachan. New York: Herder & Herder.

Rakocy, Waldemar. 2000. *Obraz i funkcja Faryseusy w dziele Łukaszowym (ŁK-DZ): Studium literacko-teologiczne* [The image and function of the Pharisees in the work of Luke (Luke-Acts): A literary-theological study]. Lublin: Catholic University of Lublin.

Renan, Joseph Ernst. 1927. *Life of Jesus*. Introduction by John Haynes Holmes. New York: Modern Library. (Orig. 1863.)

Sanders, James T. 1987. *The Jews in Luke-Acts*. Philadelphia: Fortress.

Schleiermacher, Friedrich Daniel Ernst. 1960. *Der christliche Glaube nach den Grundsätzen der evangelischen Kirche im Zusammenhange dargestellt*. 7th edition. 2 vols. Edited by Martin Redeker. Berlin: de Gruyter. (Orig. 1830.)

Seeberg, Reinhold. 1953. *Lehrbuch der Dogmengeschichte*. 4th edition. 4 vols. Basel: Schwabe.

Sherwin-White, A. N. 1963. *Roman Society and Roman Law in the New Testament*. Oxford: Oxford University Press.

Sophocles, Evangelinus Apostolides, ed. 1870. *Greek Lexicon of the Roman and Byzantine Periods (from B.C. 146 to A.D. 1100)*. Boston: Little, Brown.

Strange, W. A. 1992. *The Problem of the Text of Acts*. Cambridge: Cambridge University Press.

Talbert, Richard J. A., ed. 2000. *Barrington Atlas of the Greek and Roman World*. 3 vols. Princeton: Princeton University Press.

Tannehill, Robert C. 1990. *The Narrative Unity of Luke-Acts: A Literary Interpretation*. 2 vols. Minneapolis: Fortress.

Tarazi, Paul Nadim. 2001. *The New Testament: An Introduction*, vol. 2: *Luke and Acts*. Crestwood, N. Y.: Saint Vladimir's Seminary Press.

Tavardon, Paul. 1997. *Texte alexandrin et le texte occidental des Actes des Apôtres: Doublets et variantes de structure*. Foreword by Marie-Émile Boismard. Paris: Gabalda.

Trocmé, Etienne. 1957. *Le "Livre des Actes" et l'histoire*. Paris: Presses Universitaires de France.

Troeltsch, Ernst. 1960. *The Social Teachings of the Christian Churches*. Translated by Olive Wyon. Introduction by H. Richard Niebuhr. New York: Harper.

Verheyden, J., ed. 1999. *The Unity of Luke-Acts*. Leuven: Leuven University Press.

Vööbus, Arthur. 1951. *Celibacy: A Requirement for Admission to Baptism in the Early Syrian Church*. Stockholm: Estonian Theological Society in Exile.

Ware, Kallistos. 2002. *The Inner Kingdom*, vol. 1 of *Collected Works*. Crestwood, N.Y.: Saint Vladimir's Seminary Press.

Watson, Philip S. 1949. *Let God Be God! An Interpretation of the Theology of Martin Luther*. Philadelphia: Muhlenberg.

Wehnert, Jürgen. 1989. *Die Wir-Passagen der Apostelgeschichte: Ein lukanisches Stilmittel aus jüdischer Tradition*. Göttingen: Vandenhoeck & Ruprecht.

Wilckens, Ulrich. 1961. *Die Missionsreden der Apostelgeschichte: Form- und Traditionsgeschichtliche Untersuchungen*. Neukirchen-Vluyn: Neukirchener Verlag.

Wilson, Stephen G. 1973. *The Gentiles and the Gentile Mission in Luke-Acts*. Cambridge: Cambridge University Press.

Winter, Bruce W., and Andrew D. Clarke. 1993–94. *The Book of Acts in Its First*

Century Setting. 6 vols. Grand Rapids: Eerdmans.

Witherington, Ben. 1984. "The Anti-Feminist Tendencies of the 'Western' Text in Acts." *Journal of Biblical Literature* 103:82–84.

———. 1998. *Acts of the Apostles: A Socio-Rhetorical Commentary*. Grand Rapids: Eerdmans.

Wuellner, Wilhelm H. 1976. "Paul's Rhetoric of Argumentation in *Romans*." *Catholic Biblical Quarterly* 38:330–51.

Zahn-Harnack, Agnes von. 1951. *Adolf von Harnack*. 2nd edition. Berlin: de Gruyter.

Zimmerman, H. 1961. "Die Sammelberichte der Apostelgeschichte." *Biblische Zeitschrift* 5:71–82.

Zimmern, Alfred. 1931. *The Greek Commonwealth: Politics and Economics in Fifth-Century Athens*. 5th edition. Oxford: Oxford University Press.

SUBJECT INDEX

Abraham, 69, 100–101
absolution, 217, 275
Adam, 132
adultery, 180
Aeschylus, 255
Agabus, 226
agricultural metaphors, 287
Agrippa, 200, 201, 245, 249, 269
Aland, Barbara, 33n47
alcohol, 50
Alexander the Great, 150
Alexandria, 292
Allen, O. Wesley, Jr., 150n19
Alter, Robert, 283n24
Ambrose, 88, 191, 283
American constitution, 201, 264, 268
Anabaptists, 240
Ananias, 124, 127, 236, 238
Ananias and Sapphira, 67, 80, 81, 82, 134, 138, 143, 151
Andrew, 43
Andrew of Crete, 32
angels, 29, 85, 99, 104, 144–47, 186, 214
anger, 228–29
Annas, 72
Anselm, 65, 152, 154–55, 275
anti-Semitism, 86
Antioch, 292
apocatastasis, 66
Apollos, 65, 115, 202, 204, 208, 255
apologetics, 194, 277
apophatic theology, 165, 193–96, 246
apostasy, 73–74
apostles, 46, 58, 92–93, 225

Apostles' Creed, 63, 79, 196, 243n23, 249n8, 258, 266, 267
apostolic church, 28, 86–88, 203
apostolic council of Jerusalem, 130, 131, 170–72, 175–77, 179–81, 219, 252
Apostolopoulos, Charalambos, 192n19
Aquila, 115, 204, 208
Aramaic, 35, 231, 233, 234, 271
Aratus, 132
Areopagus, 249
Arianism, 41
Aristotelianism, 192
Aristotle, 56, 148, 149, 256
Arius, 230
armor of God, 287
Arnou, René, 193
Artemis, 214
asceticism, 131, 210, 250, 259–61
Asia Minor, 207
assent, 120
Athanasian Creed, 73
Athanasius, 73
Athens, 101, 165, 174, 194, 196–97, 207
athletic metaphors, 287
atonement, 65–66, 133, 152, 154–55, 275
Augsburg Confession, 89, 295n9
Augustine, 46, 47, 134, 138, 198, 206, 227, 239
Augustus, 106, 243, 265, 266
Aulén, Gustav, 155
authority, 89–90, 175–77
Ave Maria, 205

Babylon, 291
Bachmann, Michael, 75n8, 104n15

baptism, 40, 51, 57, 60, 83, 95, 116–17, 211,
    217, 236–41, 273
    of John, 210–11
barbarous people, 290
Barmen Declaration, 89
Barnabas, 164, 196, 212, 215, 225, 230, 272,
    284
Barrett, Charles Kingsley, 29, 165n15, 252n12,
    281n11
Basil, 198
Basil the Great, 138, 195
Batak Confession, 89
Baur, Ferdinand Christian, 28
Beardlsee, William A., l47n35
Beck, Hans-Georg, 27n21
Bede, Venerable, 27, 35
belief, 258
Bellamy, J., 25n9, 92n3, 119n31, 239n13
Beroea, 190
Beza, Theodore, 32
bickering, 200–202
Bihler, Johannes, 86n18, 104n14
bishop, 59, 91–93
Black, Matthew, 33n49, 240n20
Blaise, Albert, 206n16, 274n10
Blass, Friedrich, 32
blood, 130, 180, 181, 259
body of Christ, 123–24
Bogolepov, D., 58n34, 117, 165n14, 171n3
Boismard, Marie-Émile, 34, 47n36, 116n18,
    182n9, 186n17
Bonaventure, 227
Bonhoeffer, Dietrich, 169
Bonwetsch, G. N., 283n23
Book of Common Prayer, 275
Braund, David C., 270n1
breaking of bread, 59, 124, 203, 216–18
brethren, 230
Bride, A., 110n1, 266n7
Brown, Peter, 285n27
Broyde, Michael, 181n5
Bruce, F. F., 32n43, 129n3, 181n6
Brucker, J., 232n18
Bunyan, John, 137
burning bush, 103, 146, 228, 248

Cadbury, Henry J., 31, 116n19, 165n16,
    205n12, 231n15, 255n8, 260, 264n3,
    279, 281
Caesar, 188, 189, 265, 266–67
Caiaphas, 72
Calvin, John, 46, 125, 194, 226, 228n8
cannibalism, 266

canon law, 181–82
Cappadocians, 195, 235
Carrington, Philip, 32, 33n45, 148
Case, Shirley Jackson, 135
Caspari, Walter, 26n12
Cassiodorus, 27, 283
cataphatic theology, 196
catholicity, of church, 52, 61, 79, 243–44
celibacy, 261
Celsus, 277
ceremonial law, 130–31, 260
Chadwick, Henry, 114n14, 192n20
charismatic renewal movement, 52
charity, 143
cherubim, 147
chief priests, 96
chiliasm, 295
Chirat, Henri, 206n16, 274n10
Christian (term), 139–41, 278, 294
Christology, of Acts, 118
Christus Victor, 66, 133, 135, 152, 153–55
Chrysostom, John, 27, 50
church, 57–61
    as body of Christ, 123–24
    continuing apostolic witness, 116
    social mission, 295
church calendar, 261
church councils, 175–77, 226
church growth, 57, 244
Church of Armenia, 201
church order, 91
Cicero, 192, 256, 283
circumcision, 58, 129, 240
citizenship, 241–43, 266, 267
civil law, 181–82
civil rights, 267
Claudius, 106, 266, 270
Claudius Lysias, 201, 252, 267
Clement of Alexandria, 33, 35
Cochrane, Charles Norris, 254n1
Codez Bezae Cantabrigiensis, 32
coercion, 188, 250, 295–97
comma johanneum, 84
commentary, 25
communicatio idiomatum, 213, 221–22
communion of saints, 58
communism, 61, 80, 169
confession, 274
Confession of Dositheus, 89, 181n8
Confession of the United Presbyterian Church
    in the U.S.A., 295n10
confessional imperative, 73–75, 257
conscience, 245–47, 257

Constantelos, Demetrios J., 143n16
Constantia, 213
Constantine, 187, 265, 267, 296
Constantinople, 43, 283, 292
contrition, 274
controversy, 170–72, 200
conversion, 51–52, 66, 120–22
Conzelmann, Hans, 29
Coppens, J., 94n6
Cornelius, 128, 129, 137, 145, 215, 228
Council of Chalcedon (451), 38, 176, 183,
　　201, 222, 292
Council of Constantinople (381), 50, 59, 83,
　　176
Council of Ephesus (431), 45, 176, 205, 222
Council of Nicea (325), 45, 59, 172, 176, 267
Council of Trent, 122n10, 210, 236n5, 275
covenant, 68–70, 173, 180
Crawford, Michael H., 264
creation, 132, 165–67, 196–98
creed, 40, 75, 116–19
Cyprian, 33
Cyril of Alexandria, 222

Dahl, Nils Ahstrup, 280
Damascus road, 64, 185–86, 234–35, 238
Daniélou, Jean, 45n25, 146n3
Dante, 122, 167
Darè, Jean, 175n15, 292n6
David, 55, 227
Davies, John Gordon, 42n14
de Vries, W., 292n3
De Zwaan, J., 231n15
deacons, 59, 77, 91–93
death, 155
Decius, 242, 266, 273
decree, 182–84, 259
deification, 164
Delphic oracle, 185
demonic powers, 134–35, 188
denominations, 140
determinism, 160, 256
devil, 155
Diaspora, Martin, 105
Dibelius, 75n7, 255n8
diet, 58
Diocletian, 242
Dionysius the Areopagite, 147, 192
disagreement, 170, 178, 284
disciples, 46, 53, 92–93
discipleship, cost of, 90, 167–69
dispensations, 173
divinization, 185

Dobschütz, Ernst von, 32
Docetism, 163
doctrine, 59, 76, 193, 202–4, 217, 230
dogma, 182–84
Donatism, 168, 239
Donfried, Karl P., 30n29
Dorcas, 127, 229, 285
Dositheus, 89
Dostoevsky, F. M., 154
doxology, 60
drunkenness, 50
Dryden, John, 150
dualism, 262
due process, 85, 268–69
Dupont, Jacques, 26n11, 279n1

Easton, Burton Scott, 107n22
ecclesiastical history, 283
Eckey, Wilfried, 155n4, 281n14
economy, 51, 173–75
Edwards, Jonathan, 227
Edwards, Mark Julian, 192n20
elders, 92, 93, 169, 218, 230
election, 159–61, 236
Elijah, 88, 227
Elizabeth, 205, 221
Encratites, 261
Enlightenment, 277, 283
Enslin, Morton Scott, 279n5
Ephesus, 208
Ephraem of Syria, 33
Epicureans, 153, 160, 190, 191–93, 203, 249
epistles, 250–52
Epp, Elton Jay, 33nn46–47, 33n51, 220n7
eschatology, 100, 248–50, 262, 292
Esler, Philip Francis, 57n31
Essenes, 140–41
eternal life, 100
Ethiopian eunuch, 63–64, 112, 114–16, 117,
　　119, 146, 229, 238
Eucharist, 37, 60, 69, 114, 124, 216–17, 257
Eunomius, 195
Europe, 207
Eusebius, 168, 213, 282–83
Eutychus, 149
Eve, 45, 122
ex opere operato, 239
exodus, 111–12
extraordinary magisterium, 172
eyewitnesses, 41, 87, 99, 187, 277

Faber, Eva Maria, 122n10
faith, 56, 63, 73, 166, 218, 237, 241, 257–59,
　　271–72

faith and order, 60, 91–93
false doctrine, 140, 204
fasting, 169, 260–61
Fee, Gordon D., 220n7
Felix, 245, 249, 252, 267, 269
fellowship, 59, 203, 217
Fennema, D. A., 220n5
Festus, 54, 201, 204, 242, 245, 252, 263, 264, 269
fides quae creditur, 258–59, 271
Filioque, 82
Fishkin, Amy Lynne, 181n5
Fitzmyer, Joseph, 84
Florovsky, Georges V., 192–93, 282, 283
foreknowledge, 46, 53, 159–61
forerunner, 208, 209–10. *See also* John the Baptist
forgiveness of sins, 158–59, 217, 237, 239, 272, 273
free will, 46, 53, 159, 160, 170
friendship, 283–86
fulfillment, 46, 70
fullness, and Holy Spirit, 48–50

Gabriel, 209
Gallio, 106, 191, 203
Gamaliel, 90, 174
Gasque, W. Ward, 31n34, 255n8
Gaventa, Beverly Roberts, 114n13
generosity, 62
Gentiles, 62, 68, 125–26, 129–31, 177
Gilbert and Sullivan, 149
Gilson, Étienne, 193n24
Glawe, Walther Karl Erich, 254n2
Gloria Patri, 50
Gnostics, 39, 110
God
    as creator, 132, 197–98
    as friend, 286
    sovereignty, 79, 88–90, 97, 198
    transcendence, 196
Goethe, 135
golden calf, 104, 215
Golden Rule, 177, 180
Goodspeed, Edgar Johnson, 23–24
gospel, 111–12, 157, 218, 226
"gospel of forty days", 38–40
grace, 137–39, 170, 229
Grant, Robert M., 97n13
Grässer, Eric, 42n16, 49n5
Gratian, 181
graven images, 147
Gray, Thomas, 150n17

great awakenings, 121
great commission, 211
Greek jurisprudence, 264
Greek language, 35, 230–32
Greek philosophy, 101, 190–93, 194, 254
Gregory of Nazianzus, 195, 227, 261
Gregory of Nazianzus the Elder, 261
Gregory of Nyssa, 24, 66–67, 102, 192, 195, 198, 220, 261, 285
Gregory Palamas, 236
Grimaldi, William M. A., 56n28

Haenchen, Ernst, 31n33, 42n15, 79n28, 97n12, 121n4
Hahn, Ferdinand, 78n24, 90n31, 286n30
Handel, George Frideric, 78
Hanson, R. P. C., 33n48
Harnack, Adolf von, 17, 25n7, 29, 31, 163n7, 193n26, 229n14, 280, 287
Hatch, Edwin, 192
healing, 52, 94, 108
Hebrew language, 35, 232–33
Hedde, R., 169
Hefner, Philip J., 28n26
Heidelberg Catechism, 89, 237n6
Hellenistic Judaism, 190, 192
Hellenization of Christianity, 254
Hemer, Colin J., 252n13, 279n1, 281n11
Hengel, Martin, 31n35, 281n12
Henry VIII, 296
heresy, 140, 204
Hermes, 150, 196, 212, 214–15
Herod, 67, 215
Hippolytus, 33, 226
historiography, 279–83
Hodgson, Peter Crafts, 28n25
holiness, 79–80, 239–40, 272
Holl, Karl, 17, 261
holy kiss, 284
Holy Spirit
    deity of, 82–85, 138, 162–63
    and fullness, 48–50, 78, 210, 229
    procession of, 51, 82
    sovereign freedom, 136
    variety of manifestation, 51–52
Homer, 194, 287, 295
hope of Israel, 71, 145, 200, 211, 292
Hotchkiss, Valerie R., 33n52
Houbant, H., 210n6
household, 199, 240
humanity, unity and equality of, 131–33
humor, 24, 148–50, 162, 218
hypocrisy, 260

icons, iconography, 31–32, 44, 76, 213
idols, idolatry, 79, 130, 145, 163, 180, 181,
        190, 198, 212–13, 214–15, 259
illumination, 272
images, 213
imitation of Christ, 94, 96, 106–8, 127, 167
immortality, 192, 200
imprisonment, 85
incarnation, 163–64
infant baptism, 199, 239, 240, 273
instruments, 125
Irenaeus, 27–28, 33
irresistible grace, 297
Isaiah, 212, 228
Israel, 125

Jaeger, Werner, 190
jailer at Philippi, 241, 272, 274
James, 176–77, 180, 252, 255
James, William, 120, 122
Jeremiah, 228
Jerome, 206
Jerusalem, 101, 108, 179, 211, 243, 259,
        290–92
Jervell, Jacob, 25n9, 57, 129n1
Jesus Christ
    ascension, 42
    baptism, 237
    brothers of, 45–46
    exaltation, 90
    faith in, 258–59
    as friend, 286
    as image of invisible God, 213
    post-resurrection appearances, 38–40, 293
    poverty, 142–43
    resurrection, 42, 47, 54–57, 64, 65, 72,
        276–77
    second coming, 42–43
    suffering, 38, 64–65
    teaching, 38–39
    transfiguration, 235
    and universal restoration, 66–68
Jewish epistles, 251–52
Jews, 68–71
John Paul II, Pope, 53, 202n7
John the Baptist, 88, 156, 207–11, 226, 236
John (writer of the Apocalypse), 186, 187, 226
John XXIII, Pope, 175
Johnson, Luke Timothy, 29, 58, 80, 85n17,
        173, 175n12, 209, 217n1, 282
Joseph (patriarch), 101, 227
Josephus, 23, 24, 129, 190
Joshua, 95, 222

joy, 229
Judas Iscariot, 46, 47, 67, 78, 87, 151
Judas Maccabeus, 251
Julius Caesar, 227
justice, 85, 157, 263
justification, 100, 126, 157–59, 246, 259
Justin Martyr, 33
Justinian, 265

Karekin I, 202n7
Katz, Steven T., 100n1
Kennedy, George A., 83n6
Ker, Ian T., 120n1
King, Martin Luther, 88
kingdom of God, 42, 68, 209, 211, 218, 248,
        286, 292–93
Kirn, D., 258n14, 271n2
Klijn, A. F. J., 33n47
Knox, John, 252n14
Kostof, Spiro K., 237n9
Kremer, Jacob, 121n4
Krodel, Gerhard A., 23, 105, 214n13
Kunze, Johannes, 30n30

Lake, Kirsopp, 87n19, 116n19, 165n16,
        194n29, 279
language, 52, 230–32
lapsed, 273
law, 101, 226, 235, 263–69
laying on of hands, 94–95, 217, 239
legalism, 181
Lent, 261
Leo I, Pope, 11, 116, 177, 222
Leo X, Pope, 181
Levites, 95
Leviticus, 181
Lietzmann, Hans, 238
light, 234–35, 270
Lima Text: Baptism, Eucharist, Ministry, 93,
        218
Lintott, Andrew William, 264n4
liturgy, 26, 116
Liturgy of St. John Chrysostom, 155n6, 205
Livy, 75
locus communis, 29
locus theologici, 30
Lohfink, Gerhard, 42n14
Loisy, Alfred Firmin, 30n31, 229n9
Löning, Karl, 121n4, 125n18
Lopuchin, A. P., 193n27
Lord's Prayer, 60, 77, 135
Lord's Supper. See Eucharist
Lossky, Vladimir, 45n31, 48n2

lots, casting of, 47
Lotz, J. B., 273n8
Luke, 27, 30–31, 37, 54, 63, 106, 118, 125,
    235
  as historian, 279–83
  language, 230–31
Luschnat, Otto, 281n15
Luther, Martin, 32, 45, 88, 121, 134, 181, 227
Lydia, 122
Lystra, 163–64, 165–66, 168, 174, 196, 197,
    212, 231

Macedonian vision, 186
Macgregor G. H. C., 117n24
Macrina, 66, 195
Maddox, Robert, 267n9
magic, 134–35, 214
Magna Carta, 268
Magnificat, 205
Mahler, Gustav, 50
Maimonides, 25
Maisonneuve, L., 277n14
Malta, 215
Malunowiczówna, Leokadia, 285n28
Manichean determimism, 134
Manitius, Max, 27n21
Mann, C. S., 281n9
Marcellus of Ancyra, 295
Marcion, 33, 58, 110, 230, 279
Marcus Aurelius, 265
Marguerat, Daniel, 32n42, 54n23, 97n12,
    121n4, 280n6
Mark, 235
marriage, 181, 217, 236
Marshall, I. Howard. 281n11
Martin, J., 110n5
martyrdom, 56, 90, 107, 167–69, 228, 266
Martyrdom of Polycarp, 168
Mary, 31–32
  perpetual virginity, 45–46
  as mother of God, 44–45, 146, 213
Masia Creed, 55
Matthew, 235
Matthias, 46
McReynolds, Paul R., 220n5
medicine, 97
Meeks, Wayne A., 291
Melanchthon, Philip, 30
Menander, 110
Messiah, 64, 65, 248
Meyendorff, John, 189n1, 267
Michel, A., 151n23
Michelango, 167

Middle Platonism, 192
Mikado (Gilbert and Sullivan), 149
ministerial office, 91–92
miracles, 62, 73, 85, 96–98, 127, 229
Mogila, Peter, 273
Monophysites, 201–2
monotheism, 84, 88, 131, 181, 212, 214–15
Montanism, 187, 226
moral law, 130–31, 181, 260, 265
Morgenthaler, Robert, 195n39, 268n14,
    282n18
Mosaic law, 58, 62, 70, 115, 128–31, 175,
    180, 183, 230, 259
Moses, 23, 24, 88, 102–3, 115, 146, 190, 228,
    235, 248
"Mother of God". *See* Theotokos
Mount Sinai, 215, 235
Mount Tabor, 236
mutual support, 142–43
mystery, 275
mysticism, 50, 61

name, of Jesus Christ, 293
natives, 290
natural law, 264–65
natural world, 165–66
nautical metaphors, 286–89
Nave, Guy D., Jr., 273n9
Nazarenes, 140–41
Nazis, 89, 169
Neoplatonism, 192–93, 249
Nero, 266
Neusner, Jacob, 38n3
new creation, 133
New Testament, 112
Newman, John Henry, 59, 120, 205, 231
Nicene Creed, 48, 75, 107, 132, 138, 183,
    189, 220, 257, 266
Niceno-Constantinopolitan Creed, 38n2, 40,
    42, 48, 51n15, 52n19, 54n24, 58, 63,
    75, 79, 82, 88, 117, 119, 138, 154,
    163, 183, 196, 203, 222, 224, 239n18,
    248, 257, 267, 292, 293, 295
Nickelsburg, George W. E., 107n20, 248n5
Niesel, Wilhelm, 91
Nikanor, Brovkovič, 54n25, 77n22, 90n30,
    117n21, 163n1, 195n40
Noah, 180–81
Nobbs, Alanna, 283n22
Nock, Arthur Darby, 32n44, 254n1, 255n8
Norden, Eduard, 194n29

obedience, 181–82, 272–73
offense, 265
Old Testament, 45, 112, 116, 251
Onasch, Konrad, 31n39, 44n24, 46n34,
        209n4, 237n8
oral word of God, 112–13
oratory, 256
ordained ministry, 91–96, 217
ordinary magisterium, 171–72, 175
Oriental Orthodox Church, 202
Origen, 33, 45
Origenism, 66
original sin, 239
Orthodox Church, 209
orthodoxy, in worship and doctrine, 75–76
Otto, Rudolf, 228
Ouspensky, Leonid, 45n31, 48n2

paganism, 63, 212
partiality, 131–32, 196
Patmos, 186, 187
Paul
    addresses, 255
    affections, 223
    on anger, 228–29, 247
    apologias, 245–46
    apostolic claim, 46–47
    and Barnabas, 284
    before Sanhedrin, 88
    as chosen instrument, 124–25
    conversion, 251, 270
    epistles, 112, 252–53
    on friendship, 284–85
    imprisonment, 241
    martyrdom, 230
    as Pharisee, 145
    preaching, 149, 294–95
    Roman citizenship, 241–42
Paul of Samosata, 230
Pelagians, 138, 239
Pelikan, Jaroslav, 33n52, 74n4, 88n21,
        117n23, 126n21, 166n17, 175n14,
        175n15, 177n20, 181n7, 190n3,
        192n21, 195n34, 196n41, 209n4,
        220n4, 238n10, 254n1, 256n9,
        258n13, 285n28
penance, 66, 217, 273–75
Pentecost, 41, 48–52, 69, 106, 210, 231, 238
Pentecostalism, 52
Pericles, 227
persecution, 144, 169, 266
persuasion, 256

Peter, 44, 176, 255
    as married, 261
    primacy of, 46, 86–88
Peterson, David, 49n6
Pharisees, 129, 140–41, 145, 200, 248–49, 257
Philip, 63–64, 114–16, 229
Philo, 23, 24, 25, 129, 190, 192
philology, 29
Plato, 192, 194
Platonism, 192–93, 249
pleasure, 229
Plümacher, Eckhard, 255n5, 281n12
politics, 263, 266
Polycarp, 168, 243
polytheism, 163, 194, 198, 214–15
Pontius Pilate, 54, 63, 86, 266, 267, 269
Pontus, 58
Porter, Stanley E. 279n3
possessions, 80–81
poverty, 62, 142–43
powers, 267–68
Praeder, Susan Marie, 287n36
prayer, 60, 75–78, 105, 203, 217, 224
preaching, 162, 238, 293, 294–95
predestination, 159–61, 170
presbyter, 91–93
Prestige, George Leonard, 163n5, 194
Price, David, 33n52
priests, 96
Priscilla, 115, 204–6, 208, 225
proofs, of resurrection, 56, 276–77
prophecy, and fulfillment, 70
prophets, 92, 153, 156, 178, 224–25, 226
Psellus, Michael, 103
Pseudo-Dionysius. See Dionysius the Areop-
        agite

Quasten, Johannes, 27, 117n25, 198nn42–43,
        261n23

Rackman, Emmanuel, 181n5
Rahner, H., 261n26
Rahner, Karl, 151n22, 171n1, 239n15
Rakocy, Waldemar, 71n16, 248n6
Rapske, Brian M., 287n34
reason, 170, 256, 263–64
reconciliation, 154–55
Reformation, 89, 91, 126, 138, 157, 159, 171,
        210, 232, 240, 283
religious affections, 226–30
religious freedom, 285
Renaissance, 232
Renan, Ernest, 282

repentance, 66, 158, 210–11, 218, 237, 273–75
Requiem Mass, 236
resurrection, 155, 200, 248–50, 257
revelations, 128, 146, 184–87, 199, 225, 241
Revell, E. J., 33n53
rhetoric, 75, 250, 254–56
Rhoda, 148, 229
righteousness, 100, 157, 259
Ritschl, Albrecht, 28
Roman citizenship, 241–42, 250
Roman law, 264
Rome, 207, 211, 242–43, 290–92
Rowe, Christopher J., 249n7
rule of faith, 27, 116–19, 173, 226, 230, 257–58

Sabbath, 70, 105, 106, 115, 129
sacraments, 59–60, 203, 217, 236, 239, 275–76
sacred space, 104–6
sacred time, 104–6
Sadducees, 129, 140–41, 145, 200, 248–50, 257
sailing, 286–89
Samaritans, 110
sanctification, 159
Sanhedrin, 90, 245
Sargentich, Thomas O., 268n154
Satan, 134–35, 214
satisfaction, 65, 152, 154, 274–75
Satterthwaite, Philip E., 254n3
Saul, 109, 120, 121, 228. See also Paul
Schaff, Philip, 75
Schelkle, K. H., 27n15
schism, 140
Schleiermacher, Friedrich, 227
Schnieper, Annemarie, 31n39, 44n24, 46n34, 209n4, 237n8
Scripture, 112
Scriven, Joseph, 286
Second Commandment, 212, 213
Second Council of Constantinople (553), 66, 171, 176, 553
Second Council of Nicea (787), 176, 213
Second Helvetic Confession, 157n8
Seeberg, Reinhold, 40, 154n3
self-denial, 131, 259
self-examination, 247
Seneca, 106, 191
Septuagint, 34–35, 95, 232
Sergius Paulus, 203
Sermon on the Mount, 77, 260

Shema, 84
Sherwin-White, A. N., 268n12
shipwreck, 217, 287
Sholz, R., 151n22
signs, 73, 85, 96–98
Silas, 241
Simeon, 69, 98, 125
Simon Magus, 96, 109–10, 135, 152, 241
simony, 96, 110, 135
sin, 133–34, 150–52, 155, 265
slavery, 80
Smalcald Articles, 171n2
social mission, of church, 295
Socrates, 194, 256
Socrates Scholasticus, 283
sola scriptura, 116
Sophocles, 53n21, 194, 237n7, 255
sorcery, 134–35, 214
speeches, in Acts, 75
spiritual gifts, 84–85
Stephen, 47, 90, 93, 98–99, 104–5, 151–52, 255
    death, 106–8, 109, 123, 168, 215, 229
Stoics, 153, 160, 190, 191–93, 203, 249
Story, Joseph, 201
Stowers, Stanley K., 251n10
Strange, W. A., 32n43
strangled, 130, 180, 181, 259
suffering servant, 64
superstition, 214
synagogue, 105, 106, 156, 189
Synod of Constantinople (1341), 204, 236
Synod of Constantinople (1351), 236
Synod of Dort, 297
Synod of Ephesus, 177
Synod of Orange, 134

Tabitha, 127
Tannehill, Robert, 229n10
Tarazi, Paul Nadim, 32n42, 38, 54n23, 259n16
Tatian, 33
teachers, 225, 226
temple, 90, 204–6, 256
Ten Commandments, 104, 146, 180
Tertullian, 33
Tertullus, 269
Tetragrammaton, 103
textual variants, 32–34, 219–21
textus a parribus receptus, 33–34, 219
theodicy, 282
Theodore of Studios, 88
Theodoret, 283

Theodosius, 265, 296
theology, of Acts, 26, 197
Theophilus, 31, 118, 207, 254, 280
Theophylact of Bulgaria, 27
Theotokos, 45, 122, 205, 209, 221
Third Council of Constantinople (680–81),
    176, 236
Thomas à Kempis, 107
Thomas Aquinas, 30, 103, 138, 166, 193,
    197–98, 256
thorn in the flesh, 187
Thucydides, 75, 281
Tiberius, 106, 266
Timothy, 130
Titus, 130
Tolstoy, 159
tongues, 51, 52–53, 233
Torah, 115
totalitarianism, 89
Tower of Babel, 52, 231
tradition, 116, 182–84, 226
trances, 225, 241
translator, 24
Trinity, 84, 139, 201, 238–39
Trocmé, Etienne, 32n43, 281n11
Troeltsch, Ernst, 81
Tübingen school, 28
twelve, 47, 53, 92
typology, 45

Unam Sanctum, 89
unchastity, 130, 180, 181, 259–60
unhindered, 295
universal restoration, 66–68, 211
University of Paris, 283
unknown God, 65, 164, 165, 194–95, 246,
    296

Vatican II, 175, 282n17, 295, 296–97
Venard, L., 25n9, 27n22, 31n40, 44n23
violence, 86, 90, 188, 189, 228, 241, 250, 257,
    263, 295–96

viper, 215
Virgin Mary, 122–23, 205, 213
visions, 128, 184–87, 199, 225
Vööbus, Arthur, 261n22
Vorgrimler, Herbert, 171n1, 239n15
vow, 250
Vulgate, 232

Ware, Kallistos, 67
Watson, Philip S., 150n20
Way, The, 140–41, 211, 234, 246, 265, 278,
    290, 293
we-passages, 187, 216, 279, 280
Wehnert, Jürgen, 279n1
Wesley, John, 121
Western text, 33, 219
Westminster Confession of Faith, 220, 225n3,
    232n19
whole counsel of God, 55, 219
Wieseltier, Leon, 25
Wilckens, Ulrich, 165, 207n1
Williams, George Huntson, 267n11
Wilson, Stephen G., 129n2, 191
Winter, Bruce W., 245n1
wisdom, 101–3, 263
Witherington, Ben, 33n50, 204n11, 205n12,
    225n2, 254n4, 281n13
witness-bearing, 41
witnesses, 41, 47, 56, 277
women, in ministry, 204–6, 225
wonders and signs, 60, 96, 98, 127
word of the Lord, 113–14
worship, 60, 75–78, 111, 157, 203
Wuellner, Wilhelm H, 30n29

yoke, 175

Zahn, Theodor, 32
Zeus, 150, 196, 212, 214–15
Zimmern, Alfred, 255

SCRIPTURE INDEX

Acts

1:1 31, 111, 145, 207, 218
1:1-2 30
1:1-11 26, 54
1:2 87, 92, 206, 280
1:2-3 58, 64, 113, 124, 141, 144, 183, 207, 211, 223, 248, 275, 293
1:3 276
1:4 49, 87, 125, 144, 290
1:4-5 113
1:5 210
1:6 43, 68, 87, 248, 294
1:6-8 40, 293
1:7-8 87, 248
1:8 47, 56, 125
1:10 146, 214
1:10-11 87
1:11 57, 117-18, 218
1:13 87
1:14 76-77, 122, 146, 156, 176, 206, 213, 221, 244, 266, 280, 281
1:15 47, 87, 92, 203
1:16 112, 151
1:16-20 67, 115, 160
1:18 151, 274
1:21 206
1:21-22 209
1:23 88, 176, 206
1:23-24 86
1:24-25 78

1:25 53
1:26 53
2:1 41, 58, 69, 78, 84, 112, 116, 133, 136, 137, 139, 144, 203, 210, 229, 240, 280, 297
2:1-13 26
2:4 49, 53
2:5 52, 69, 243
2:8 53, 133
2:10 52, 69, 129, 253
2:13 50
2:14 88
2:14-36 54, 255, 293
2:14-46 224
2:15 50, 149
2:16 153
2:16-20 115
2:17 205, 206
2:17-21 185
2:18 186, 206
2:22 69, 97, 98, 124, 276
2:23 55, 160
2:24 55
2:24-32 198
2:27 55
2:28 49
2:29 69, 74
2:29-30 56
2:30 153
2:31 41, 42, 47, 55, 59, 64, 72, 73, 81, 87, 97, 101, 106, 109, 119, 133, 155, 160, 204, 250, 257, 276, 293
2:32 56

2:36 59, 69, 118, 274
2:37-38 274
2:38 158, 211, 237
2:38-39 210
2:39 161
2:41 203
2:42 28, 58, 76, 96, 124, 139, 170, 172, 193, 202, 203, 216, 217
2:43 98, 127
2:44 79
2:44-45 143
2:44-46 124
2:44-47 80
2:45 79
2:46 216, 217
3:1 77, 104
3:1-26 105
3:6 79, 124, 127
3:11 101
3:12-26 255, 293
3:13 70, 182, 269
3:13-15 70
3:14-17 68
3:15 55, 97, 119
3:15-16 272
3:16 258
3:17 70, 269
3:18 64, 115, 133, 152, 154, 155, 156, 160, 167, 189, 199, 248, 266, 275, 293
3:19 158, 274
3:21 41, 72, 174, 185, 192, 198, 200, 211
3:22 115
3:25 54, 61, 62, 77, 90, 99, 100, 101, 103, 104, 125, 129, 153, 156,

159, 160, 173, 188, 190, 197, 211, 215, 234, 246, 248, 250, 257, 260, 264, 265, 291, 292, 294
4:1 105
4:1-2 250, 257
4:2 56, 276
4:8 49, 52
4:8-12 293
4:10 55, 140
4:12 174, 200, 293
4:13 73, 74, 103, 108
4:16 98, 277
4:18 108
4:20 59, 236, 257, 258, 297
4:24 78
4:24-30 44, 48, 50, 60, 62, 78, 106, 111, 113, 131, 157, 165, 169, 188, 203, 224, 225, 241
4:29 74
4:30 78, 98
4:31 49, 74, 112, 113
4:32 58, 61, 62, 152, 188, 189, 214, 239, 259, 262, 272, 284
4:33 54, 56, 139
4:34-35 143
4:35 62
5:1-11 67, 143, 151
5:3 134, 138
5:3-4 49, 75, 119, 163, 266
5:4 80, 134, 138
5:12 98

5:15 97
5:17-20 23
5:19-20 146
5:20 105, 110
5:26 296
5:28 108, 199
5:29 44, 46, 47,
  53, 58, 78, 79,
  89, 92, 145, 176,
  182, 206, 264,
  265, 267
5:30 55
5:31 158
5:33 228
5:38-39 269
5:39 174
5:42 69, 105, 111
6:1 46, 80, 143,
  231
6:2 113
6:2-4 46, 59, 95,
  169, 171, 218,
  225, 226, 230
6:3 49
6:4 77
6:5 49, 129
6:6 51, 59, 86, 127,
  135, 152, 153,
  217, 239, 240,
  261
6:7 92, 113, 182,
  259, 272
6:8 49, 52, 53, 60,
  62, 73, 85, 94,
  108, 124, 127,
  163, 188, 207,
  211, 229, 276-77,
  290
6:8-11 107
6:8-14 26
6:11-13 108
6:12-7:53 107
6:13-14 69, 105,
  123
6:14 182
6:15 107, 146, 147,
  214
7:1-53 93
7:2 23, 197
7:2-53 156, 255,
  293
7:4 129
7:4-5 69, 104
7:7 76, 105
7:8 69
7:22 23, 25, 73,
  129, 131, 132,
  170, 190, 256,
  263
7:30 146, 214
7:30-35 151
7:31 185

7:31-32 228
7:32 70
7:33 104
7:34-36 70
7:36 98
7:37 115
7:38 265
7:39-41 215
7:41-42 152
7:42 76, 145
7:42-43 76
7:45 68, 222
7:47-48 62, 69, 70,
  77, 99, 100, 122,
  129, 131, 153,
  187, 188, 195,
  198, 217, 224,
  241, 256, 265,
  286, 294
7:49-50 105
7:53 146, 265
7:54 107, 228
7:54-59 26
7:55 49, 152
7:55-56 107
7:55-60 168
7:56 47, 123
7:58-8:3 90
7:59 50, 138, 215
7:59-60 54, 62, 63,
  69, 70, 72, 73,
  94, 96, 99, 124,
  127, 139, 142,
  154, 167, 207,
  228, 241, 247,
  263, 269, 286,
  290, 293
8:1 123, 152
8:2 229
8:4 111
8:8 229
8:9 134
8:9-24 135
8:10 152
8:11 134
8:12 111, 241, 293
8:15-16 51
8:15-17 94
8:16-17 238
8:18-19 152
8:19-20 96
8:23 152
8:25 52, 57, 76, 78,
  111, 153, 157,
  159, 162, 169,
  178, 190, 197,
  199, 218, 254,
  258, 272, 275
8:27 76
8:28 112
8:30-31 25, 35, 40,
  42, 43, 45, 46, 59,

  64, 65, 68, 70,
  77, 84, 93, 103,
  112, 128, 156,
  170, 185, 190,
  202, 226, 257,
  275, 294
8:34 55, 65
8:35 55, 64, 111,
  112
8:36 210, 238
8:37 25, 27, 34, 37,
  40, 42, 57, 59, 68,
  75, 81, 84, 90,
  112, 116, 139,
  146, 164, 171,
  173, 184, 196,
  200, 202, 215,
  217, 219, 222,
  226, 230, 238,
  257, 259
8:39 51, 146, 229
8:40 111
9:1 296
9:1-2 92
9:1-4 39, 42, 47,
  52, 57, 64, 93, 99,
  109, 128, 134,
  138, 139, 144,
  158, 160, 165,
  170, 188, 189,
  200, 211, 228,
  234, 251, 256,
  270, 271, 274,
  276, 291
9:1-19 185
9:1-22 26
9:2 141
9:4-5 58, 107
9:5 123
9:8 238
9:9 261
9:10-16 185
9:12 94
9:13 124
9:15 86, 93, 95,
  109, 125, 160,
  171, 261, 291
9:16 169
9:17 49, 124
9:17-18 94
9:18 238
9:19 261
9:20 105, 107, 117
9:21 140
9:22 95
9:23-25 296
9:26 93
9:29-30 296
9:36 92
9:39 127, 229, 285
10:1 145
10:1-8 228

10:2 122, 129, 215
10:2-7 146
10:3 105, 214
10:3-4 145
10:3-6 128
10:3-7 185
10:4 145
10:9 77, 105, 106
10:10-22 185
10:11-16 128
10:15 54, 58, 62,
  70, 102, 115, 130,
  175, 180, 181,
  230, 260, 262,
  263, 264, 268
10:16 133
10:17 128, 185
10:19 128, 185
10:22 129, 277
10:25 76
10:25-26 128, 215
10:28 133
10:30-33 185
10:34 196
10:34-35 197, 246
10:34-43 26, 255
10:36 111
10:36-38 209
10:38 65, 68, 76,
  82, 96, 134, 151,
  152, 154, 186,
  272
10:39-40 55
10:40-41 56, 277
10:42 277
10:44 51, 240
10:47 240
11:4-18 185
11:13 146
11:14 113
11:15 51
11:16 113, 210
11:17 131, 139
11:19 113
11:20 111
11:23 58, 138, 142,
  229
11:23-24 139
11:24 49, 272
11:26 58, 72, 90,
  92, 115, 130, 146,
  169, 180, 183,
  190, 200, 202,
  206, 211, 228,
  234, 249, 265,
  278, 290, 294
11:28 106, 226
11:29 61, 124, 203
11:30 92
11:38 266
12:1-2 168
12:1-11 85

12:5 78
12:6-11 23
12:7 29, 41, 85, 99,
    104, 122, 131,
    205, 214, 292
12:7-9 128
12:9 145, 185, 186
12:12 78
12:13-15 147n7
12:13-16 24, 30,
    50, 53, 135, 162,
    218, 229, 269
12:19-24 296
12:21-23 65, 68,
    76, 79, 82, 104,
    134, 145, 154,
    215, 256, 259,
    275
13:1 95, 225
13:2 225
13:2-3 95, 261
13:2-4 77
13:5 105, 113
13:6-12 135
13:8-11 55, 66, 82,
    133, 152, 188,
    203, 211, 214,
    241, 272
13:9-10 49
13:12 203
13:14 70, 105
13:15 114, 115
13:16-17 197
13:16-41 255
13:23 156
13:24 211
13:25 210
13:26-39 26
13:27 114, 115
13:28-30 55
13:31 277
13:32 111
13:38-39 100, 101,
    126, 246, 259,
    263, 274
13:42 156, 159
13:43 76, 139
13:44 70, 113
13:46 113, 125
13:48 46, 47, 54,
    122, 161, 170,
    174, 198, 219,
    229, 236, 240,
    256
13:50 76, 206
13:50-51 162
13:51 24, 230
13:52 49, 229
14:1 105
14:3 97, 98, 113
14:7 111
14:8-18 98, 215

14:11 214, 231
14:11-15 172, 190,
    198, 212, 215
14:11-18 150
14:12-13 214
14:14-18 255
14:15 111, 165,
    173
14:15-17 174, 196,
    197
14:16 68
14:19 168, 296
14:21 111
14:22 90, 107, 108,
    109, 123, 127,
    208, 228, 259,
    265, 266, 272,
    293, 294
14:23 77, 92, 94,
    261
14:25 113
14:26 138, 139
14:27 169
15:1 130
15:2 25, 59, 62, 92,
    93, 116, 172, 175,
    178, 200, 204
15:3 229
15:4 92, 93
15:5 140
15:6 92, 93, 177
15:6-7 88
15:6-21 70
15:7 111, 126, 171
15:7-11 176, 255
15:8 196
15:8-9 47, 51, 54,
    55, 57, 68, 73, 90,
    100, 198
15:10 115, 129,
    131
15:12 98
15:13 88, 177
15:13-21 43, 255
15:14 58
15:16-18 174-75
15:18 159
15:19 88, 177
15:19-20 252
15:20 130, 180,
    259
15:21 106, 114,
    115, 291
15:22 92, 93, 177
15:23 92, 93
15:23-29 130, 252
15:28 28, 58, 85,
    88, 90, 93, 170,
    183, 226, 252,
    257
15:29 34, 113, 130,
    180

15:32 226
15:35 111
15:35-36 113
15:36-39 284
15:37-39 204
15:39 172
15:40 138
16:1 253
16:1-3 70, 130
16:3 253, 294
16:4 28, 38, 62, 84,
    92, 93, 99, 113,
    116, 119, 131,
    170, 171, 172,
    176, 177, 182,
    184, 189, 219,
    226, 252, 262,
    291
16:5 129, 244
16:6 186, 207, 253
16:7 186
16:9 42, 47, 94,
    128, 139, 145,
    147, 153, 175,
    185, 186, 199,
    224, 225, 241,
    273, 275
16:10 111, 185,
    279
16:11 287
16:12 253
16:13 70, 105
16:14 76
16:14-15 122, 237
16:15 238, 240
16:16 77, 105, 186,
    294
16:16-18 135
16:16-19 80, 152,
    214
16:19-40 85
16:20-21 71, 267
16:21-22 241
16:23 241
16:25 77, 78
16:25-34 98
16:26 241
16:26-28 23, 296
16:27 241
16:27-30 274
16:30-31 241
16:30-34 272
16:33 238, 241
16:34 230
16:37 242, 267
16:38-39 242
16:40 206
17:1 253
17:1-3 122
17:2-4 65
17:4 52, 76, 256
17:5 189

17:5-6 79
17:5-9 296
17:6 139, 276
17:7 184, 189, 266,
    294
17:10 105
17:11 112, 253
17:13 253
17:14-15 253
17:16 193, 212,
    215
17:17 76, 153
17:18 25, 39, 41,
    101, 111, 153,
    160, 165, 194,
    203, 231, 248,
    249, 254, 296
17:19-20 203
17:21 97
17:22 165, 214
17:22-31 174, 255
17:22-34 255
17:23 65, 102, 155,
    164, 165, 170,
    173, 187, 214,
    222, 235, 246,
    275, 296
17:24 105
17:24-25 166
17:24-29 78, 97,
    173
17:26 132, 133,
    160
17:27 164
17:28-29 132
17:29 212, 213,
    214
17:30 68
17:31 56
17:31-32 249
17:32 97, 203, 204,
    276
17:32-33 192
17:32-34 72
17:34 147
18:1 253
18:2 169, 253, 266
18:4 70, 105
18:5 65, 253
18:7 76
18:8 238
18:9 185
18:9-10 186
18:11 113
18:12 106
18:12-17 191
18:13 76, 130, 256
18:15 140, 172,
    204, 268, 291
18:19 105, 253
18:21 70, 253
18:23 253

18:24 115, 253,
    255
18:24-25 65
18:24-26 33, 34,
    46, 58, 59, 75, 84,
    85, 87, 92, 93,
    115, 140, 144,
    170, 171, 185,
    193, 200, 204,
    205, 208, 209,
    219, 222, 230,
    235
18:26 105, 216,
    225
18:28 65
19:1 51, 253
19:1-7 46 240
19:2 84, 238
19:2-3 51, 140,
    156, 221, 226,
    236, 272
19:2-6 50
19:5 238
19:6 51, 84, 95
19:8 105, 256, 294
19:9 141
19:10 243
19:11 62, 85, 97
19:12 97
19:13-17 149
19:13-19 135
19:17 253
19:19 63
19:21 242, 253,
    291
19:22 253
19:23 141, 149
19:23-25 214
19:23-41 80
19:26 76, 96, 99,
    147, 176, 194,
    196, 198, 253,
    267, 285
19:27 76, 105
19:28 84, 96, 104,
    131, 145, 151,
    163, 173, 180,
    188, 190, 194,
    198, 212, 232,
    290
19:31 284
19:32 149, 269
19:33 254
19:34 71, 149
19:35 105, 253
19:38 268
19:40 269
20:1 216
20:2 216
20:4 253
20:5-21:18 279
20:6 253, 260

20:7 27, 40, 61, 77,
    106, 124, 131,
    203, 216, 236,
    266, 289
20:7-12 149
20:11 216, 217
20:16 106
20:16-17 253
20:17 92
20:18-35 255
20:23 291
20:24 92, 111
20:25 294
20:26 86, 247
20:27 55, 73, 117,
    160, 207
20:28 32, 60, 62,
    63, 67, 70, 84, 87,
    92, 113, 116, 159,
    174, 177, 179,
    213, 218, 238,
    252, 259, 260
20:30 204
20:32 139
20:33 247
20:33-35 80
20:35 37, 39, 108,
    113, 142, 247
20:36 78
20:37-38 229, 285
21:3 287
21:4 186
21:5 106, 241, 284
21:5-6 78
21:9-10 92, 112,
    153, 178, 186,
    205, 241, 275
21:11-13 108
21:13-14 30, 78,
    90, 92, 103, 109,
    127, 149, 160,
    188, 204, 223,
    247, 284, 294
21:14 77
21:18 92
21:19 92
21:20-22 130
21:22-26 105
21:25 130, 179,
    180, 250
21:31 296
21:33-34 150
21:35 296
21:37 52, 76, 133,
    141, 157, 163,
    234, 271
21:37-39 70
21:38 296
21:39 70, 291
21:40 35
22:1-16 121, 185,
    270

22:1-21 255
22:2 35, 233
22:3 70, 90, 269
22:3-21 245
22:4 141
22:6 94, 127, 134,
    147, 176, 271
22:14 160
22:15 74
22:16 40, 51, 57,
    60, 83, 95, 117,
    124, 136, 167,
    188, 199, 203,
    217, 238, 239,
    272, 273, 292,
    293
22:17 77, 105
22:17-18 185
22:18 108
22:20 99
22:22 296
22:25 267
22:25-28 188
22:25-29 241
22:27 52, 58, 211,
    250, 252, 266
23:1 132, 191, 234,
    250, 257, 265,
    270
23:1-6 245
23:3 260, 284
23:4 108
23:6 145
23:7 145
23:7-8 257
23:8 56, 57, 72,
    100, 109, 129,
    145, 147, 191,
    198, 200, 262,
    270, 292
23:9 146
23:11 242, 253,
    292
23:11-13 261
23:12-14 70
23:16-24 296
23:25 141, 171,
    180, 227, 268,
    291
23:26-30 252
23:27 267
23:28-29 201
24:1-2 52, 57, 75,
    93, 122, 132, 145,
    149, 162, 165,
    189, 200, 211,
    234, 245, 250,
    270, 282
24:2-8 245
24:5 140
24:6 105
24:8 269

24:10-21 255
24:11 76
24:14 70, 76, 140,
    141, 246
24:14-15 74, 249
24:15 57
24:16 246, 247
24:17 70
24:18 105
24:22 141
24:24-25 57, 63,
    73, 75, 117, 182,
    184, 188, 199,
    200, 202, 237,
    259, 271, 272
24:25 77, 80, 130,
    131, 153, 169,
    210, 225, 247,
    250, 286
25:3 108
25:8 54, 85, 88,
    101, 129, 130,
    131, 157, 254,
    259, 268
25:8-11 245
25:10 242
25:11 54, 79, 85,
    89, 131, 167, 182,
    183, 188, 189,
    199, 201, 203,
    242, 252, 265,
    269, 270, 291,
    294, 296
25:11-12 188
25:12 242
25:13-26:32 126
25:16 30, 85, 252,
    257, 269, 296
25:17-27 201
25:18-20 204
25:19-20 54
25:20-21 291
25:24 296
25:25 266
25:25-26 252
25:26 252
25:27 269
26:1 254
26:1-23 255
26:2 254
26:2-3 200
26:2-23 245
26:3 129
26:5 140
26:6-7 249
26:7 76
26:8 57, 249
26:9-19 121, 185,
    276
26:13 235
26:14 35, 154, 233
26:16 160

26:17-18 159
26:18 63, 100, 117,
  134, 154, 199,
  218, 237, 248,
  258
26:19 186
26:20 57, 65, 66,
  124, 188, 210,
  217, 237, 247,
  272
26:22 65
26:22-23 65, 276
26:24 254
26:26 42, 53, 55,
  56, 72, 73, 98,
  106, 136, 137,
  139, 145, 165,
  168, 242, 243,
  280, 290
26:28 140
27:1 28, 54, 74, 77,
  80, 99, 105, 135,
  159, 160, 187,
  216, 217, 284,
  287
27:1-28:16 279
27:2 253
27:3 178, 192, 223
27:4 287
27:7 288
27:9 261
27:13 288
27:19 288
27:23 76
27:23-24 186
27:23-26 97
27:24 23, 24, 30,
  94, 96, 197, 216,
  224, 266, 281,
  286, 291
27:29 78, 288
27:32 288
27:33 216
27:34 216
27:35 216
28:3-6 97
28:4 215
28:6 215
28:8 94
28:14 39, 41, 69,
  108, 121, 125,
  126, 187, 190,
  211, 216, 218,
  242, 253, 268
28:16 253, 290
28:17 70
28:17-20 255
28:17-29 153
28:20 71, 145, 211
28:21 251
28:22 141, 251

28:23 40, 97, 115,
  211, 218, 248,
  266, 286, 294
28:24-25 161
28:30 80
28:30-31 295
28:31 23, 73, 79,
  86, 90, 123, 144,
  160, 167, 188,
  189, 203, 228,
  230, 241, 250,
  257, 263, 268

Amos
9:11-12 174

2 Chronicles
14:2 104

Colossians
1:15 213
1:24 123
2:8 191, 193
2:9 213
2:14 184
2:15 155
2:18 145
2:19 123
3:11 290
3:16 77
4:10 172
4:14 31, 97, 280,
  287

1 Corinthians
1:10-17 79
1:12 205, 255
1:17 238
1:20 103
1:22-25 98
1:23 37
2:1 255
2:13 52
4:1 60
5:1 265
6:11 159
7:5 261
7:10-12 37
8:1 181
8:5 155
9:1 47
9:5 261
9:24-27 287
10:32 246
11:23-26 216
11:23-27 37
11:24-25 114
11:25 69, 112
11:27-28 247
11:27-34 217
12:1 52, 84

12:4 84
12:4-11 52
12:11 85
12:27 123
14 53
14:11 290
14:25 164
14:40 181
15 42, 250
15:4-8 56
15:5 87
15:5-8 39, 42, 276
15:7 87
15:8 56
15:8-9 93
15:13 57
15:21-22 45
15:24 155
15:24-28 67
15:26 155
15:28 66, 67
15:29 42
15:37-42 42
15:39 132
15:54-55 42
16:2 70
16:19 106, 217
16:20 284

2 Corinthians
3:7-8 235
4:7 125
5:16 47
5:19 155
6:2 174
6:4-5 245
8:1-5 142
8:4 59
8:9 142
8:18 31
10:5-6 202
10:9-10 252
10:13 79
11:23-28 242
11:24-25 242
11:25-27 263
11:26 23
12:2-4 187
12:4 125
12:7 187
12:19 254
13:5 247
13:12 284

Deuteronomy
6:4 84
6:5 180
18:15 103, 115
18:18 103
25:3 242
34:9 95

Ephesians
1:23 123
2:15 184
2:20 225
3:14-15 286
4:11 225
4:12 123
4:26 229
5:4 148
5:18-19 50
5:32 60, 217, 236,
  276
6:10-18 287

Exodus
2:2 101
3:2 146
3:5 104, 228
3:6 248
3:14 25, 102, 103
4:10 24
7:10-13 203
20:4 147
20:4-5 212
20:7 140
20:8 105
20:8-11 104, 129
20:14 180
24:1-2 24
25:20 147
32:6 151
33:11 286
34:29-35 235

Ezra
4:7 251
4:11-16 251
4:17-22 251
5:7-17 251

Galatians
1:1 93
1:8 230
2:3 130
2:11 126, 171
2:14 126, 171
3:1 227, 284
4:4 44, 49
5:1 129
6:14 37
6:15 133

Genesis
1:1 198
1:16 197
3:1-6 45
3:15 65
11:1-9 52
15:5 197
15:6 100, 258
50:20 55, 101

Hebrews
1:14 29, 144
2:14-15 55
4:8 222
4:15 163
6:20 209
9:5 147
10:31 173
11:1 194
11:3 166
11:8 100
11:36 23
12:1 26

Isaiah
6:5 228
40:3-5 34
41:8 64, 286
44:12-17 212
45:21 174
52:13 64
53 43, 65
53:4 64
53:7-8 55
60:9 288
65:25 43
66:1-2 105

James
2:19 271

Jeremiah
1:6 228
12:15 174
13:1-11 226
31:33 14

Joel
1:14 260
2:12 260
2:28 115, 185, 224

John
1:18 235
1:33 113
3:3 51, 121
3:5 236
3:8 51, 136
4:21 106
4:24 106
5:2 233
7:24 158
10:30 107
11:35 148
11:35-44 222
11:48 291
12:8 81
13:27 82
14:6 141
14:12 96

14:16 37
14:16-17 49
14:18 58
14:26 41, 51
15:15 285
15:16 78
15:26 41, 51
15:26-27 49
16:7 51
16:7-15 49
16:12-14 203
16:13-14 112
16:13-15 41
16:15 143
17:21 60
18:13-14 72
18:22 108
19:13 233
19:17 233
19:20 35, 233
19:26-27 44
20:21 40
20:23 40
20:28 40
20:30 39
21:15-19 86

1 John
1:1 75, 281
1:5 221
1:7 221
2:16 151, 259
3:17-18 143
5:7 84

Jude
3 73, 258, 271

Judges
9:24 86

1 Kings
14:19 281

2 Kings
19:35 146

Leviticus
18:7-8 265

Luke
1:1 37, 280
1:1-2 183
1:1-3 223
1:1-4 31
1:2 44, 56, 187, 202, 277, 281
1:2-3 99
1:3 32, 207, 280, 281

1:4 118
1:8-23 208
1:14 32
1:16-17 209
1:26-28 122
1:26-38 208
1:28 205
1:31 222
1:38 45, 122
1:39-56 208
1:42 44
1:42-43 205
1:43 221
1:47 230
1:47-55 205
1:54 64
1:63 208
1:68 43
2:1 183, 243, 266
2:1-2 106
2:8-14 145
2:14 290
2:19 44
2:31-32 69
2:32 125
2:34-35 98
2:49 105
2:51 44
3:1 266
3:4-6 34
3:7 210
3:14 211
3:15 156, 208, 210
3:16 113, 156, 210
3:19-20 208
3:21-22 124, 209, 210, 237
3:23 209
4:1-13 55
4:16-30 156
4:21 43
4:38-39 261
5:21 239
5:32 237
6:13 46
6:14-16 87
6:31 114, 177, 180
6:40 96
7:28 209
7:33-34 210
8:1 53
8:4-15 287
8:10 276
9:1 92
9:5 230
9:9 208
9:10 92
9:12 92
9:23 108
9:29 235
9:35 68
9:51 49, 292

9:51-53 108
9:58 62, 142
10:30-37 81
10:31 96
11:1-2 77
11:2-4 60
11:4 135
11:20 42
11:29-32 98
11:42-44 145
12:2 49
12:11 254
12:12 41
12:51-53 162
15:17 147
15:21 66, 274
16:16 209, 226
17:21 42
18:11 216
18:13-14 274
18:14 158
18:18 294
19:8 274
19:38 290
19:46 105
19:47 105
20:27 145
21:14 254
21:37 105
22:3 82
22:4 182
22:14-20 216
22:20 69
22:32 87
22:47-48 151
22:53 134, 151
22:62 274
23:2 69
23:5 228
23:21 290
23:34 63, 70, 124
23:46 107, 124, 138, 215
24 54
24:1 77, 106
24:4 41, 146
24:10 87, 206
24:25-27 64
24:27 39, 40, 115, 293
24:30 218
24:35 218
24:47 39
24:50-51 42
24:50-53 54

1 Maccabees
1:44-51 251
4:30 90
8:23-32 251

2 Maccabees
9:8-9 150
9:19-27 251

Malachi
2:10 132
3:2 43

Mark
1:8 113
1:15 124, 218, 237, 272
2:7 84
3:16-19 87
4:3-20 287
5:41 127
9:2-3 235
12:29 84
12:34 163
14:22-26 216
14:24 69
16:7 86
16:9 39
16:15 39, 113
16:16 40, 67, 236
16:18 94

Matthew
1:18-25 208
2:1 134
2:7 134
2:16 134
3:1 208
3:11 113
3:16 123
4:1-11 154
5-7 39
5:10 169
5:13 259
6:9-13 60, 77
6:13 135
6:16-18 260
7:12 114, 177, 180
9:18 94
9:22-25 127
10:2-4 87
10:4 182
11:27 182
11:29 108
11:29-30 131
11:30 175
13:3-23 287
14:1-13 208
15:2 183
15:3 183
16:15 210
16:16 39, 118
16:18 87, 176
16:18-19 40

16:24 275
17:2 235
17:9 185
18:8 67
18:10 147
18:18 40
19:24-25 81
22:21 267
22:29-32 249
22:38 180
23:15 129
24:1 105
24:14 39
25:34 294
25:40 142
26:13 39
26:26-29 216
26:28 69
26:59-61 108
26:60-61 123
27:3-10 151
27:4 274
27:24-25 86
27:25 199
27:40 104
27:52-53 276
28:19 39, 40, 83, 84, 236, 238, 239
28:19-20 124, 211

Numbers
8:10 95

1 Peter
2:9 96
4:16 140, 278
5:13 291

2 Peter
1:4 164
3:15-16 112, 252

Philippians
2:6-11 117
2:7 213
2:7-8 163
2:9 42
2:10-11 222
2:11 259
3:20 242, 266
4:1 227

Proverbs
8:22-31 101

Psalms
1:1 141
16:8-11 55

16:10 55
16:11 49
19:1-4 166
31:15 175
32:1-2 158, 247
51:3 246
51:4 265
59:10 122
69:25 115
90:8 47
109:8 206
115:3 198
115:4-5 212
119:46 126
139:1 47

Revelation
1:6 96
1:11 250
5:10 96
7:9 243
17:5 291

Romans
1:1 93
1:5 186, 273
1:14 232, 290
1:16 125
1:16-17 111
1:17 121, 158
1:20 166
2:1 247
2:4 68
2:11 131
2:14-15 247, 264
2:15 254
2:17-24 247, 292
3-5 157
3:19 247
3:22 258, 271
3:28 126, 159
4:3 258
4:5-8 158
4:7-8 247
5:12-15 45
5:15 132
6:3-11 237
6:5 167
6:12-14 155
6:17 184
8-11 71
8:3 163
8:29-30 161
8:32 100
9:3 292
10:9 258
10:9-10 74
10:17 75, 112
11:26 292

11:33 46, 196, 256
12:5 123
13 89
13:1-2 266
13:2 182
13:3 266
14:17 294
14:21 181
15:22 242
16:14 214n14
16:17 204
16:25 111
16:26 186, 273

1 Samuel
12:15 154

1 Thessalonians
4:13 228
4:15-5:4 43
5:26 284

2 Thessalonians
2:1-12 43
2:4 289
2:15 52

1 Timothy
1:1 59
2:3-4 67
3:1 59
4:1 204
4:14 59, 95
6:4 201n3
6:20 59, 201n3

2 Timothy
1:1 59
1:6 95
3:16 52, 112
4:1 31

Titus
1:1 59
2:11 139
3:4 286
3:4-8 237
3:5 239
3:6-8 240

Wisdom
13:3-5 167
13:5 195, 196
5:6 141
5:7 141